Ethical Maturity in the Helping Professions

by the same author

Integrative Approaches to Supervision
Edited by Michael Carroll and Margaret Tholstrup
ISBN 978 1 85302 966 0
eISBN 978 1 84642 197 6

of related interest

Mastering Social Work Values and Ethics
Farrukh Akhtar
ISBN 978 1 84905 274 0
eISBN 978 0 85700 594 6
Mastering Social Work Skills series

Working Ethics
How to Be Fair in a Culturally Complex World
Richard Rowson
ISBN 978 1 85302 750 5
eISBN 978 1 84642 481 6

What Makes a Good Nurse
Why the Virtues are Important for Nurses
Derek Sellman
Foreword by Alan Cribb
ISBN 978 1 84310 932 7
eISBN 978 0 85700 452 9

Humanizing Healthcare Reforms
Gerald A. Arbuckle, PhD
Foreword by Dr Maria Theresa Ho
ISBN 978 1 84905 318 1
eISBN 978 0 85700 658 5

Emerging Values in Health Care
The Challenge for Professionals
Edited by Stephen Pattison, Ben Hannigan, Roisin Pill and Huw Thomas
ISBN 978 1 84310 947 1
eISBN 978 0 85700 365 2

How We Treat the Sick
Neglect and Abuse in our Health Services
Michael Mandelstam
Foreword by Lord Justice Munby
ISBN 978 1 84905 160 6
eISBN 978 0 85700 355 3

Ethical Maturity in the Helping Professions

Making Difficult Life and Work Decisions

Michael Carroll and Elisabeth Shaw

Foreword by Tim Bond

Jessica Kingsley *Publishers*
London and Philidelphia

First published in 2013
by Jessica Kingsley Publishers
116 Pentonville Road
London N1 9JB, UK
and
400 Market Street, Suite 400
Philadelphia, PA 19106, USA

www.jkp.com

Library of Congress Cataloging in Publication Data
A CIP catalog record for this book is available from the Library of Congress

British Library Cataloguing in Publication Data
A CIP catalogue record for this book is available from the British Library

ISBN 978 1 84905 387 7
eISBN 978 0 85700 355 3

Printed and bound in Great Britain

I would like to dedicate this book to Sam and Louise (Loulou) who entered our lives six years ago and are now established firmly as members of our family. It has been challenging at times to stay connected and together. To Loulou, your interest and energy for ethical dilemmas is amazing. It is never dull when you are around.

Michael

Thanks to my husband Mark, who is a partner in the true sense of the word, always supportive of my projects despite the possibility of living with a distracted and obsessed person until they are complete. He now knows they take double the time and energy of my first description, but is still at my back at all times. Thanks to my children, Abby and Jake, who always inspire me with their rich ideas, imaginative wisdom and humorous distractions. Family life and being a working mother is a rich source of ethical quandaries and discomforts. However, children often have the best ethical antennae, if we just listen to them.

Elisabeth

When the book was being edited, the influence of Kenny Rogers slipped in. First as a quotation from his song, 'The Gambler', added to the text to see if we were all awake as we proofread. The iconic lines from the song evolved as a recurring theme quoted, and indeed often sung, when mischievous spirits overtook serious work. Kenny became a symbol of the book and the community from which it has sprung. It would be unfair not to acknowledge his influence for what has become our theme song:

> You got to know when to hold 'em, know when to fold 'em
> Know when to walk away and know when to run.
> You never count your money when you're sitting at the table
>
> There'll be time enough for countin' when the dealing's done.
> Every gambler knows that the secret to survivin'
> Is knowin' what to throw away and knowing what to keep.
> 'Cause every hand's a winner and every hand's a loser
> And the best that you can hope for is to die in your sleep.

Contents

Foreword

These are exciting times for professionals who want to commit themselves to being ethical. It is a time of unprecedented social and intellectual change that has profound implications for what it means to be human, and how we rise to the challenge of offering our professional services ethically.

I have known for a few months that I would be writing this foreword and have been waiting eagerly for the next version of draft chapters to drop into my inbox. I have not been disappointed. As I read them, I have noticed subtle changes and influences in how I approach being ethical in my work as head of a large and complex academic department, a teacher and a counsellor. I think it is reading the draft chapters that has had this effect, but cannot totally exclude a personal background of family life in which two teenagers bring their own joys and challenges as they move towards adulthood. This book is a good counterpoint to a full, and sometimes overcommitted life that many of us experience as professionals. It stimulates new insights and thoughts rather than provides definitive answers. As I read each of the chapters, I find myself prompted to reflect on aspects of my work and reconsider what it means to be ethical, and re-evaluating the extent to which being ethical guides my practice.

What makes this book so thought-provoking and enriching? Several aspects are distinctive.

The focus on 'ethical maturity' widens the scope of the book well beyond many manuals on ethical problem-solving, or the professional codes and frameworks that shape professional practice. 'Maturity' implies a journey from youthful exuberance to a more grounded state of being rooted in experience and reflection. It is open to the possibility that some insights may have been hard won, and that the journey may be of varying degrees of difficulty for different people. It is a state to which professionals at the beginning of their careers can aspire and is therefore highly relevant to students and trainees. On the other hand, there is a quizzical and unsettling dimension to notions of ethical maturity for those of us further down the line in professional experience. 'Maturity' is not just longevity but, in the context of ethics, suggests a quality of judgement akin to wisdom. However, maturity does not sound like a constant state which, once attained, can be secured totally forever. There is the possibility of partial or momentary states of maturity, or even movement from maturity to decline analogous to the physical life cycle. Maturity is not a static or abstract state of being to which we can aspire as an ideal steady state that lifts us above the risks and uncertainties of professional life. Instead, maturity suggests a quality of engagement in how we respond to the challenges of professional life.

Another aspect that has caught my attention is the way 'ethical' is presented throughout the chapters. In some texts, ethical is claimed firmly as the territory of philosophers and theologians. In others, it is a label adopted by virtuous practitioners as the basis for explaining what is important from a particular personal or professional perspective. This book has some of the best features of both approaches. However, it also introduces new potential points of reference from recent developments in biomedical and social sciences. There is a spirit of playfulness around what it means to be ethical that allows ideas from psychology and neurology to be introduced. These sources seem very appropriate to the way ethical maturity invites questions about the implications for relationships between people in professional and personal encounters. Novel sources are used to suggest ethical metaphors or provide new insights without trying to be too authoritative or definitive.

This brings me to the third characteristic that has engaged me — the voices of the authors. Sometimes books about ethics can create a rather arid landscape full of 'shoulds' and 'oughts' in which the warmth, diversity and curiosity of lived humanity is pushed firmly off the page. This book has a very different character. It may disappoint anyone wanting a wholly coherent and authoritative declaration of what it means to be ethically mature. Instead, this book offers something quite different. The authors question themselves and their ideas in ways that draw us, as readers, into questioning ourselves. The idea of six components to ethical maturity provides loose scaffolding in which many different ideas can find a place.

One of the hallmarks of a good book is whether I feel more engaged in its topic and am more actively observant of what is going on in my life around that topic. A really good book renews me with new insight and a sense of vitality. This book has delighted me with these qualities.

As preparation of the book drew to its conclusion, we noticed it omitted to include the topic of research ethics, an element of my current work as a research ethics officer for social sciences and law in a research-intensive university in the UK. Wisely or foolishly, we agreed I would write a chapter on this topic. I leave it to you to decide if I managed to contribute something compatible with the rest of this book. It is the first time in my career that writing a foreword has extended into the main body of the book. This tells you something about the free spirit and creativity that characterises this book.

Professor Tim Bond
Head of the Graduate School of Education
University of Bristol, UK

Acknowledgements

We would like to thank a number of people who have contributed to this book, some directly and some by default. Special thanks to our families who have been deprived of time and energy, but hopefully not love. We are indebted to Tim Bond for his interest and enthusiasm. More than contribute a foreword and a chapter, he read, gave feedback, but most of all believed in going that extra mile with enthusiasm (a sign, for us, of maturity). We also thank Dr Simon Longstaff, CEO of the St James Ethics Centre for his generous guidance and comment on the book. We want to acknowledge our working relationship. Working on a book while living on different sides of the world should have been difficult. It wasn't. We clicked, even though we had never worked together before. We are both fast writers, fast returners on material and avid readers. It helped that we are gripped equally by the theory, ideas and possibilities of ethical maturity, and seek to advance them in our personal and professional development, and our work with others. We agreed easily on the way forward and worked almost as if we were one mind on ethical maturity.

Preface

'*Many a one cannot loosen his own fetters, but is nevertheless his friend's emancipator.*'

(Nietzsche, 1974)

'*Much is revealed about people's moral characters by what does or doesn't appear as a moral question.*'

(Callahan, 1991, p. 121)

We spend much of life standing at ethical crossroads as life and work decisions confront us and demand answers. Sometimes we are aware when these crossroads confront us with moral issues, and sometimes we are not. Sometimes we don't realise there are crossroads.

Ethical decisions can feel very individual and, to emphasise this, most of this section is written in the first person. For example, when it comes to elections, how should I vote? How will I make up my mind about how I will vote? It is time to do my annual tax returns. Will I be scrupulously honest about the cash I was paid for a particular job? Or will I decide I pay an inordinate amount of tax anyway and a small amount of money will make little difference to the Exchequer's budget? My daughter, who is 17 years old, has invited her new boyfriend to spend the weekend at our home. I anticipate she will suggest they share her bedroom. I am torn. It is her bedroom and she has a right to make decisions about who shares it, but we have some say in what actions take place in our house. What should I do? How should I make a decision about this situation? My best friend is drinking too much—I know it, I see it. What is my responsibility as his friend? Do I say nothing in the hope he will manage to resolve this issue himself before it becomes a health and social problem, or do I share my concern with him knowing it could lead to a rupture in our relationship? My wife tells me she knows her friend's husband is having an affair. What is her responsibility to her friend? To say something, or to say nothing?

My post this morning has several letters pleading for money to support abused children, neglected animals, political prisoners who have been tortured and victims of the earthquakes in Haiti. What should I do with these requests? Do I bin them with the other letters selling me home, car and house insurance? Do I try to respond to each of them personally?

There are other moral crossroads where I stand scratching my head and wondering which path to take. Some are ongoing debates on abortion and euthanasia. Where do I stand on these even if neither affects me personally—at the moment? What about the environment and my lacklustre involvement in anything to do with sustainability and the future of the planet? I feel guilty I don't do more. There is the moral question of AIDS and the fallout that results. What do I think of the Catholic Church's position of not allowing the use of condoms, even though they might avert the spread of AIDS? They are holding to their opinion. I admire moral stances and courage. Is this one of those? Should I oppose their certainty and arrogance and what looks like putting principles before people? What should I do? And how should I make the decision?

And there are everyday, run-of-the-mill, small moral crossroads. Should I tell a white lie when my wife asks if she looks good in a particular dress and settle for contentment all round, or be honest and give my negative opinion and muddy the connubial waters of life? Will I donate some money to my local charity that looks after wounded animals? I could afford it easily. Or maybe there is a more deserving cause? Should I cut back on drinking wine, not only to be healthier, but to have more cash for good causes? I have been known to go over the speed limit in built-up areas. I know I shouldn't, but I still do. I know I am a hypocrite—there is a yawning gap between what I preach so loudly and what I practice so pathetically. I find so many good reasons for doing what I do, even when it falls short of what I ought or should do, and I so easily assess, evaluate and condemn others for what they do. There is no comparison between how I treat me and how I treat you. I treat me with such exquisite understanding, empathy and compassion, and I treat you with suspicion and automatic judgement for the worst. I am skilled in self-deception, a genius at rationalising my way out of difficult ethical dilemmas. '*Justify that for me*', my decision says to my rational brain *after* the unethical decision has been made. My rational brain, good servant as ever, obliges willingly like a capable and committed lawyer. I have sat with sex-offenders, some in prison, and listened to them do the impossible—justify how they sexually abused children by quoting the Bible. What amazing intellectual gymnastics! Why should I be surprised by their ability to deny what they did, to reconfigure their intentions, to convince themselves they are doing good when the evil they commit is obvious to all? I do the same all the time with my own sins and intentions.

I moved a long time ago from a 'wounded healer' to a 'fatally wounded healer'. With the best will in the world, and the strongest intentions imaginable, I still do what I do not want to and what I know is childish, immature and unacceptable. I still throw my toys out of my pram (even though I am well beyond the age of either toys or prams). With clear intent and tunnel vision I can be so unethical, so immoral that it not just surprises and shocks me, it makes me wonder if I have another, different person inside who does these things while my real persona watches on disapprovingly, but does little to change the course of immoral events. At times, I seem to have two sets of values. There are the values I think and say I believe in, and another invisible set that inform my decisions and actions. The two sets of values do not talk to each other often and seem to have no connecting links.

I can be morally apathetic and decide there is no moral issue at stake, knowing deep down this is not the case. I can deny what I know wilfully, proclaiming I have no knowledge. I can be ethically immature and keep the code or the law, but know I have fallen short of what I could be, and often want to be. I can be ethically juvenile, ethically indifferent and ethically deaf and dumb. I can be ethically blinded by thinking short-term and not allowing myself to think of future consequences or long-term implications of what I do in the present.

To my embarrassment, I notice how I make moral decisions often on premises such as:

- Can I get away with this?
- Will anyone notice?
- Compared to the significant ethical decisions other people seem to make, this decision is small or insignificant.
- Someday, when I have time, I will go in-depth into the issue and give it the deliberation I know it deserves.
- Maybe I don't have the full story. Maybe it is none of my business.
- I need to compromise.
- My contribution is truly little and a tiny drop in a vast ocean—it won't make a difference.
- No-one will get hurt.

Nothing to be proud of there. I am not beyond taking the moral high ground and looking down on those I think make poor ethical decisions for themselves and others. I am amused by the TV evangelists who preach so ardently and wholeheartedly, and yet, time after time, have been discovered to engage in the very behaviour they criticise publicly in others. I enjoy their comeuppance! But I wouldn't want my own life, actions and decisions to be scrutinised too closely in public—the TV evangelists would be able to get their own back. I hate fundamentalism, but is that itself a fundamentalist stance? I like to think I am liberal, but am not quite sure if that just reflects my white, middle-class values.

Then there is the death penalty, nuclear arms, melting ice-caps, terrorism, religious conflicts, the role of science in making decisions. I get confused and am not sure which way to turn. Should we allow stem cell research so that we all have a better life? Where do we start and end in any experimentation with human life? Should we use animals to test our products before using the products ourselves? I am aware of: the mammoth divide between the rich and the poor; the status of women in the world where so many are still commodities to be used by men; and, undernourished and uneducated children, who still die from malaria because they don't have a net to sleep under at night. There is corruption in high places with despots lining their own nests at the expense of their own people. There are organisations and companies who have little time for what is right or good or better, but bow deeply before the god of profit and commerce. Again, what is glaringly obvious and somewhat sensational in the public arena is written in small print all over my life and actions. Who am I to stand up and condemn when my own life is cluttered with poor, immature and often bad ethical decisions, or worse, no decisions at all? Finding in myself what I am so quick to condemn morally in others is a task I do not undertake readily.

I know something of the heroism of moral champions. I still see the young man, disappeared now, standing before the tanks in Tiananmen Square. What was in his mind? What led him to make such a momentous, deliberate choice? What price is he now paying for his moral heroism? Would he do it again? I read with awe the words of Natan Sharansky (1988), a prisoner of the KGB in modern Russia who could have been released if he had confessed his guilt falsely: 'When I was stripped and searched, I decided it best to treat my captors like the weather. A storm can cause you problems, and sometimes those problems can be humiliating. But the storm itself doesn't humiliate you. Once I understood this, I realised that nothing they did could humiliate me. I could humiliate myself—by doing something I might later be ashamed of... *nothing they did can humiliate me. I alone can humiliate myself*' (p. 8). His words echo the words of another hero, Victor Frankl, who stood tall in a concentration camp when all around him despaired. I think of the Mandelas of the world, the Gandhis, the Martin Luther Kings—none of them saints, but all with great moral courage as they stood up for what they believed in and suffered for as a consequence. Fools or moral martyrs? I know whistleblowers who have exposed bullies in organisations, only to be fired themselves and the bully to be promoted. I remember the uncovering of accountancy inaccuracies that were not welcomed with open arms—quite the opposite. I have seen collusion and colluded in saying nothing, yet knowing something wrong was taking place. I stood down, instead of standing up, and I know why.

Even as I stand at my moral crossroads, looking right and left, forwards and backwards, wondering, I know I am surrounded by the past, the present and the future. The past clings to me like a morning mist and refuses to be ignored. It is not just behind me, but is also inside me. Well-etched in stone are my moral templates, dictates and moral communities. Not only are they alive, but they all speak loudly and all vie for my attention. They would tell me so easily what I should do, and what I ought to do, and they often speak with the seductive voices of certainty and loyalty. I am never alone at the crossroads, as invisible individuals, pairs, groups and communities from my past hold onto me and will never let me journey alone. They insist on being part of my ethical decision making, and wail and moan when I don't give them enough time or attention. They want me to make decisions as I have always made decisions to such an extent that I wonder at times who is really making the decision. Is it me, my father, my church, my best friend? How much freedom do I really have when faced with my ethical dilemmas and ethical choices? What voices need to be silenced and which ones encouraged, which banished and which taught a new language? As I am faced with the decision of who else, what else and which voices need to be allowed into the ethical decision making room, I ask:

- What voices need to be heard?
- What words need to be spoken?
- What truth needs to be acknowledged?
- What connections need to be made?
- What assumptions need to be challenged?
- What beliefs need to be reviewed?
- What emotions need to be expressed?
- What actions need to be taken?
- What relationships need to be named?
- What secrets need to be uncovered?
- What strengths need to be seen?
- What limitations need to be articulated?
- What victories need to be celebrated?
- What losses need to be grieved?
- What mental maps need to surface?
- What is the shift that needs to be enabled?
- What fears am I not facing?
- What movements do I need to make?

I know I should be more active in moving:

- from the unexamined life to continual reflection
- from the same things over and over again (mindlessness), to new ways of thinking and doing (mindfulness)
- from individual to communal
- from isolation to connectedness
- from sameness to surprises
- from static to developmental
- from head to head and heart
- from competition to co-operation
- from greed to generosity
- from denial to facing monsters
- from authority to experience
- from teaching to learning
- from the 'what' of learning, to the 'how' of learning, to the process of learning
- from fear to courage.

Perhaps it is not so much a movement from one to another, but an integration of both. Maybe ethics is not so much 'either/or' as 'both/and'.

Not only am I accompanied by my past, but the future beckons me—many of the hopes I once had that are now in tatters, shattered dreams and aspirations of greatness that will never be, and the remaining visions of what is possible. What is possible now? What leaps from the future and grabs me, pulling me into its embrace, asking me to choose it—what emerging future directs me in the present? What fears of what will happen, or might happen, impact the decisions I make now—my fear of death, of growing old, of being alone, of not having enough money, of not being 'seen' any more. How do these 'memories of the future' influence my ethical decisions?

And, in the present, I wait. I gather myself, knowing the demands of the present can never be met by drawing on habitual ways of being only, or by allowing the demands of the context to dictate the outcome, or by trying to imagine the future possibilities. While I hope to harness the past and future as friends who will help, I know I am alone in the present, and must face with some honesty and openness what the present uniquely asks of me. To be true to myself and my values, and to be authentic in my attempts to be ethical, can enable me to make the best possible decisions, even in areas I have never encountered. It may be a decision I would have made in the past, or it may not. Or a decision I will make in the future, or not, as the case may be. I don't know. I just know that, for this moment, there is no past or future, but a challenging and forceful present that demands I treat it as a stranger — a place I have never been, with people I have never known and situations I have never experienced. Like all strangers, the present comes with mystery, awe and uncertainty.

I am reminded of the Native American story handed down from generation to generation when a young person asks an elder, 'What should I do if I am lost in the forest?' And the answer comes back from centuries of wisdom:

"Stand still. The trees ahead and the bushes beside you are not lost. Wherever you are is called Here, and you must treat it as a powerful stranger, must ask permission to know it and be known. The forest breathes. Listen. It answers, I have made this place around you. If what a tree or a bush does is lost on you, you are truly lost. Stand still. The forest knows where you are. You must let it find you' (Whyte, 1994, p. 221).

Perhaps, in the present, I need to allow my ethical decisions to find me. Maybe they have been made already and await discovery!

My mind is a moral maze where I end up continually facing yet another dead end. I long for the easy answer that removes any responsibility for having to go on an ethical journey where the destination is unclear. I would like it if there were answers to many moral questions in the way there are mathematical answers to mathematical questions, and yet I know, with Claxton and Lucas (2007) that my ethical problems 'are much more like tangled fishing nets than they are like mathematical equations' (p. 80). Would a belief in God or adoption of a religious stance make ethical decisions easier? Would it help or hinder if I leave God totally out of the ethical equation?

I stand at the crossroads between the amazing heroism of those who live what they preach and make a mammoth difference for the better, and those who do horrible and unbelievable things to their fellow human beings. I know of the worst and the best — these two intermingle in us all. The saints were probably the first to know they were sinners and that their shadow sides lurked close to the surface of their lives. I know that by not deciding, I have decided. I know that by not committing to a position, I have committed. Not making an ethical decision is, itself, an ethical decision. What should I march for, be outraged by, write letters of protest for or against? What should I tolerate, accept and endure? When should I wait in the hope that something might change for the better? When do I do something, and when do I do nothing? When will I be proactive, and when reactive? When am I colluding by doing nothing, and when am I just observing when it is best to do nothing? When am I right, wrong, negligent, culpable, foolish, gullible, naive, insightful, courageous, compassionate or brave? When do I anesthetise myself with the drug of money, or success, or comfortableness so that I no longer see, or hear, or speak. When do I stand at the ethical crossroads and scratch my head while I work out the best ethical decision I can make?

At least I know I am at a crossroads and that moral issues are at stake. And I am scratching my head! I think that is a start.

Questions that confront us, and are the focus of this book, include:

- How do we, as humans, arrive at what we call morally or ethically good or bad decisions?
- What processes are involved in making ethical decisions? Psychological, emotional, intuitive, cognitive, social?
- What processes are involved in making bad, poor or immature ethical decisions?
- What are the environmental and relationship impacts on making ethical decisions?
- Is there a developmental process involved in moving towards ethical maturity? Are there discernable steps on the way (an upward movement or change) to becoming a better, more moral person?
- Can training or coaching help individuals, groups and organisations to become more ethical?
- What is the connection between the ethical decisions I make and the practical implementation of those decisions?
- Is it possible to think of ethical decisions as a systemic process?
- What do insights from education, psychology, business studies, neuroscience, biology, primatology and other professions tell us about ethical processes?

Introduction

A medieval king visited the building site of a new cathedral he had commissioned. Making his rounds, he met three stonemasons, and he asked the first man, 'What are you doing?' He said, 'I'm cutting a stone. My boss told me to.' The king asked the second craftsman, 'What are you doing?' He replied, 'I'm cutting a stone. We're building a parapet together, and the money I earn allows me to feed my family.' The king asked the third man, 'What are you doing?' He answered, 'I'm cutting a stone. We're building a cathedral that will glorify God for centuries to come.'

So why are we writing this book? Why are you reading it? What is in your mind? Stones, families, cathedrals, practicalities, duty, ideals? Intention, motivation and values make a huge difference when we begin to think about ethics.

Hauser (2006), in *Moral Minds*, considers a single action (as did the medieval king) and tells us what makes it moral, ethical, or neither as the case may be:

'If my hand hits your face and you cry, your judgement about this action and its consequences depends on your reading of the cause of my action. If I intended to hit you and make you cry, then my act is morally reprehensible. If I intended to hit you to move you out of the way of a hurtling rock, then my act is morally praiseworthy—I saved you from greater injury. If I intended to reach for a glass but slipped and hit you in the face, I am clumsy but my action shouldn't evoke moral derision. What I did wasn't right or wrong, but the result of an accident. If I intend to reach for a glass on the shelf near your face, and was also aware of the slippery floor next to you, my hitting your face was an accident, but reckless or negligent given the circumstances...when do (we)...have access to this rich psychological machinery of intention?' (p. 206).

Five friends met every ten years to celebrate. They had grown up together, gone to school together and pledged to meet every decade to keep in touch. Coming up to their 50th birthdays the perennial question arose—where shall we go for our special meal this year? One suggested going to Chez Gerard in Dover Street in London. 'I hear,' he said, 'that the waitresses there are fabulous looking—we should check it out.' They go to Chez Gerard.

Coming up to their 60th birthday, the same question arises. Where should we meet for our meal this year? 'Let's go back to Chez Gerard,' one of them suggests, 'the food is magnificent there.' They do.

Arriving at their 70th birthday they again wonder where they will go this year to celebrate. 'Why not Chez Gerard,' asks one of them, 'the toilets are on the same level as the restaurant and we won't have to climb up and down stairs.' Again they go to Chez Gerard.

On their 80th birthdays, the usual question emerges, 'Where should we go this year to celebrate?' 'Why don't we go to Chez Gerard in Dover Street,' one of them says, 'I don't think we have been there before...'

Why are we writing this book at this stage in our lives? Why are you reading this book at this time in your life (and with the needs you have now)? Why now? Where you are does matter. You will see from where you are. Where are you?

An old Cherokee chief is teaching his grandson about life:

'A fight is going on inside me,' he said to the boy. 'It is a terrible fight and it is between two wolves. One is evil—he is anger, envy, sorrow, regret, greed, arrogance, self-pity, guilt, resentment, inferiority, lies, false pride, superiority, self-doubt and ego. The other is good—he is joy, peace, love, hope, serenity, humility, kindness, benevolence, empathy, generosity, truth, compassion, and faith. This same fight is going on inside you—and inside every other person, too.' The grandson thought about it for a minute and then asked his grandfather, 'Which wolf will win?'

The old Cherokee replied, 'The one I feed' (Anonymous).

Divisions, dilemmas and conflicts are part and parcel of life—especially internal ones. We sometimes help to create them by what we give attention to, and what we feed. There are times when I am the problem and not the solution—I imagine I will only know which of these I am when I go inside.

What about our own intentions in writing this book? We would love to have cathedrals in our heads...well, lofty ideals. We hope we have not forgotten who we are and where we are headed. We want to accept responsibility for our behaviours and how those behaviours fashion who we have become. We have already begun our ethical journey as we write this book on ethical maturity. It seems to us that the journey is as much about writing the internal book, as it is about the book you are now reading.

Overview of the book

Ethics evolved from traditions in moral philosophy now some thousands of years old. However, considerable changes have occurred in our current ethical landscape on the basis of what we have discovered in the past ten to twenty years. There has been a slow and pervasive influence on the ethical literature by new insights drawn from neuroscience, education, psychology and organisational development. This book is our attempt to update that realm to a small degree.

In Part One, we provide an overview of what we see as the most influential ideas in ethical thinking and theory across the ages. These span philosophy, psychology and science; we now have a rich palette from which to consider our ethical evolution and capacity. However, before we start our journey, it is important to consider why unethical behaviour occurs. It is tempting to think such behaviour occurs as a result of ignorance, omission or naivety. While moral immaturity will hamper decision making, we explore in Chapter 2 the reality that many good people have lapses in judgement. In fact, it is more often the highly skilled and experienced people who transgress most seriously. How can this happen? The focus of our attention here is not 'those other people', but rather the opportunity for us to examine ourselves through learning about the pathways to ethical disengagement. How could I fail myself and others? How could my own moral compass go awry?

In Chapters 3 and 4, we explore the rich traditions of moral philosophy. Chapter 4 deals with the influence of the ethical leaders, Socrates and Aristotle, who ask us to reflect on what it means to lead a good life, and what it is to be of good character and lead with our virtues rather than our vices. These questions are as relevant today as when they were asked in the streets of Athens over 2000 years ago. However, there are two significant areas of departure with the theories of our forefathers.

Much literature on ethics and morality sees us as having a singular duty to make good decisions, as if we are islands divorced from context: What is a good decision, regardless of my subjective experience? In Chapter 5 we consider the more recent traditions of relational ethics, and how context can help us make better, more congruent decisions, rather than derail us. Second, there has been the pervasive notion that reason and rationality are our best skills in ethical decision making. In contrast, Chapter 6 considers significant discoveries in brain function and development that help us to understand and appreciate the important role of emotion and intuition in reacting to and guiding effective ethical action. In Chapter 7 we outline our argument for, and the process of, the development of ethical maturity.

In Part Two we work through the six component model of ethical maturity:

Component 1:   Creating ethical sensitivity and mindfulness.

Component 2:   An introduction to ethical decision making (Chapters 9–12).

Component 3:   Implementing ethical decisions.

Component 4:   Ethical accountability and moral defence.

Component 5:   Ethical sustainability and peace.

Component 6:   Learning from experience.

In this process, we explore how we make decisions, both consciously and unconsciously, influenced not only by what we know in the present, but also how the foundational past shapes us in subtle and pervasive ways. We argue that only with the discipline of conscious reflection and dialogue can we know what we don't know, and be open to the possibilities of change. Even though this pursuit of ethical maturity can involve deep discomfort and challenge, we argue that it is worth the journey.

In Chapter 17 we conclude Part Two with a focus on training in ethical maturity, which provides some structure and ideas for teaching contexts and the enhancement of moral character and development. Clear and repeated discussions of ethical codes do not ensure moral behaviour. We argue that the best teaching methods to prepare students to make ethical decisions more effectively are experiential learning, challenging thinking and emotions, and extending the capacity of students to think flexibly and responsibly when they encounter new situations.

In Part Three we consider ethical challenges in the contexts of organisational and research sectors, and the particular challenges around gifts, bribery and other work seductions.

We do not claim to be experts in all the areas we bring together in this book — neuroscience, moral philosophy, psychology, education, business and organisational development studies. However, both of us are translators. In the service of exploring ethical maturity in practice, we read widely with a view to thinking outside established professional territories that can limit our thinking to particular discourses and mindsets. As practitioners, we look to theories of usefulness rather than theories for their own sake. We want to know what works and what is based on solid fact, on research and on creative thought. We end up with the simple questions that, once asked, make you realise there are few simple questions. Questions are like dominoes, set one off and you have an ongoing impact down the line. Incisive questions lead to other questions. Who knows where you will end up and what questions will emerge? This letter from Rilke comes to mind:

'I would like to beg you dear Sir, as well as I can, to have patience with everything unresolved in your heart and to try to love the questions themselves as if they were locked rooms or books written in a very foreign language. Don't search for the answers, which could not be given to you now, because you would not be able to live them. And the point is to live everything. Live the questions now. Perhaps then, someday far in the future, you will gradually, without even noticing it, live your way into the answer' (Letters to a Young Poet, 1993).

The future always brings up the issue of hope and faith. There is no way to begin a book without faith. Faith is what makes a difference. Faith is one of those words used so widely, but so often not 'believed in'. It is easy to say we have it, but our actions often show we do not:

A village in a remote land went through several years of severe drought. Eventually, having tried their usual methods of praying for rain, the chiefs decided that one final effort was needed. They decreed that everyone in the village and the surrounding areas would come together and collectively pray for help from their rain god. How could their god not listen to such a concerted effort? They met at noon. Three thousand people gathered from the immediate village and the surrounding hills. They came with hope, with optimism and deep faith. However, only one person brought an umbrella — a girl of ten!

We start with intention and awareness of our changing needs, knowledge of the conflicts and turmoil within, lots of questions, and hopefully with an ethical umbrella. What do you need to bring with you as you start to read this book? What do you need to attend to in order to read it well? Most of all, what do you need to consider in order to aspire to ethical maturity and ethical excellence? We offer the advice once given at the entrance to the Edinburgh Institute of Contemporary Art: 'As you come into this centre please bring your gallery bag with you. In your gallery bag you will find: a new pair of eyes; a mind's eye, because real eyes are not enough; a new brain; a special camera; lots of questions; a pair of lips (preferably smiling); and a tape measure.'

Part One
The foundations of ethical maturity
History, philosophy and science

....

Overview of Part One

In Part One we review the 'anchors' on which our theory of ethical maturity rest. These anchors represent what we see as the seven most significant philosophical and research traditions in ethical development. They provide the foundations that underpin the six components of ethical maturity—the central tenet of the book, which we outline in Part Two.

In Chapter 1 we present an overview where we hope to engage the many themes that arise when we begin to unravel the meaning of 'ethics'. We consider where ethical awareness comes from, and how we begin our journey as ethical beings. We lay out the underlying principles that will guide us on our ethical search, and the foundations on which we rest our understanding of ethical decision making.

A key question for exploration is why people behave unethically. Before exploring ethical maturity further, we want to identify and understand the factors that trip us up, tempt us and make us morally deaf and blind. There are many ways to transgress, whether by omission, ignorance, neglect or conscious planning. We have to understand our own capacity to transgress, and not assume this is always something *other people do*. In Chapter 3 we present seven traditions in ethical history and trace some of the eras in devising ethical codes of practice. These seven traditions weave their way throughout history, sometimes connecting, sometimes isolated. Each has a pedigree and illuminates some aspect of ethical maturity. All contribute to the bigger picture. You might note some traditions reflect your preferred ways of thinking, while others might offer you new areas to explore.

In Chapter 4 we undertake a detailed consideration of Socrates and Aristotle as ethical guides. Socrates has become our 'guiding light' on what it means to be ethically mature—the questioning and curious stance, the honest thinking and critical self analysis, the authenticity of practicing what he preached, the humble stance of 'not knowing' as the beginning of the journey to wisdom, and the ultimate in ethical maturity, being prepared to die for his beliefs. Socrates challenged us to think about what constitutes a 'good life'. Aristotle also explored the territory of 'the good life' in relation to what constitutes happiness and flourishing. He argued that to lead a good life we need to be of good character, and that moral character is the basis for moral action. Moral character develops when we are able to work from a virtuous place, rather than from our vices. When it is tempting to keep evaluating the circumstances outside of ourselves—other people, events and situations—Aristotle argues that looking at ourselves is crucial. He moved the moral question from What ought I do? to What ought I be? He also argued that having a teacher guide us in moral development will be crucial as we traverse a life full of invitations to moral temptation. The work of Socrates and Aristotle is thousands of years old, yet their questions are relevant at whatever point in history they are asked.

Over the long tradition of moral philosophy, the roles of subjectivity, emotion and intuition were minimised, if not dismissed. However, feminist researchers from the 1980s onwards have turned our attention to relationships and ethics, and how much of ethics is concerned with being with others and taking them into account. Chapter 5 on relationship ethics concentrates on how ethics often only make sense when we place them within the context of relationships with ourselves, other humans, animals and our world. Relationships and emotions can guide us to better, more effective ethical decisions.

In Chapter 6 we review the current literature on neuroscience and present thoughts that connect ethics and our brain (or brains, as the case may be). We explore attachment theory as the neural basis of morality and ethics, and attempt to connect the 'three brains' as the focus of ethical maturity.

We conclude this section in Chapter 7 with an overview of our understanding of ethical maturity and review what maturity means, especially in the areas of ethics and morality.

The chapters do not need to be read in sequence, as you may have more interest in one area than another. In Part Two we roll out the components that make up ethical maturity.

Chapter 1
Setting the scene
The moral landscape

....

'The best way to teach ethics is to live ethically: the best way to teach ethics is to teach ethically: the best way to write about ethics is to write ethically…I believe I am teaching ethics ethically when I enter into a faithful and trusting relationship with you.'

(adapted from Nash, 2002, p. 33)

There are numerous codes of ethics and ethical[1] frameworks throughout the helping professions and beyond. In fact, one of the signs of advancement and coming of age in relation to ethics is that professions, and more recently organisations, devise codes of ethics to support and guide their practitioners in doing what is good and avoiding what is harmful in their work. These codes and frameworks usually contain principles to support members to make ethical decisions and, at times, articulate clear, unambiguous directives on what should or should not be done in certain circumstances. However, being paid up members of a profession and subscribing to their code of ethics does not ensure automatic ethical behaviour—all of us are aware of how often we know what we should do without actually doing it. There are also times when we know what we shouldn't do, and still do it. Furthermore, there are times when we are confused morally and don't know what to do. Even when we behave ethically, there are times when we are not able to articulate why we did what we did, or provide a coherent explanation of the processes that went into our decision making that resulted in action. We cannot always justify, defend or explain our ethical actions. Even when we can explain what we did and connect it to the guidelines and principles, we may still not be sure we did the right thing—we are not always at peace with the moral decision/s we made. Hindsight, after-action reviews and occasional rumination keep our

---

1   While a distinction is often made between the terms 'moral' and 'ethical', we use these terms interchangeably throughout this book. We use the terms 'ethical' and 'unethical' to describe what is right or wrong, good or bad, and good or better.

previous ethical decisions alive for us—it is easy for us to replay them obsessively. From a positive perspective, recall enables retrospective insight that assists us to learn from ethical decisions already made.

In summary, six components are needed if we are to look beyond decision making in ethics to what we call ethical maturity:

1. To foster ethical sensitivity and watchfulness: the creation of ethical antennae that keep us alert to when ethical issues/dilemmas are present. This results in a moral compass/moral character.
2. The ability to make an ethical decision aligned to our ethical principles and our values.
3. To implement ethical decision/s made.
4. The ability to articulate and justify to stakeholders the reasons why ethical decisions were made and implemented.
5. To achieve closure on the event, even when other possible decisions or 'better' decisions could have been made. The ability to live peacefully with the consequences of ethical decision making is crucial to ongoing well-being.
6. To learn from what has happened and 'test' the decision through reflection. The integration of what we have learned into our lives develops our moral character and extends our ethical wisdom and capacity. Part of the process of developing ethical maturity is learning from experience.

In our view, these six components result in ethical maturity. The development of ethical maturity is the central focus of this book.

We define/describe ethical maturity as: 'the reflective, rational, emotional and intuitive capacity to decide actions are right and wrong, or good and better; the resilience and courage to implement those decisions; the willingness to be accountable for ethical decisions made (publicly or privately); and, the ability to learn from and live with the experience.'

This conscious learning is undertaken in the service of developing our moral character and capacity, and lays the foundations for future decision making and leadership in ethical action.

We will return to this definition/description later. However, we want to make the point early that ethical maturity is not a 'done-deal', a definitive endpoint in a journey, but is an ever-unfolding process. Ethical maturity is not a destination to be arrived at, but involves conscious attention to ethical reflection and the accumulation of ethical wisdom. It is a process of continual lifelong learning.

Drawing on these six components, we will present a model of ethical maturity. Our belief is that this model can be applied in professional fields such as counselling, life and executive coaching, organisational development and supervision. It may have wider uses in other areas where individuals, couples, teams and organisations face issues of right and wrong, good and bad, and good and better such as human resources, business ethics, and even life decisions. We have subtitled this book as—*Making Difficult Life and Work Decisions*—since discerning the right, the better, or the good action is a part of our everyday lives, and such decisions are based on our abilities to 'suss out' the best decision we can make in complex situations. Often we do not have compasses to help guide us in the right ethical direction. Not only do we live complicated lives, but we have to make difficult and complex decisions almost on a daily basis—decisions that require us to have some guidelines to ensure we are on the right moral track. Having said that 'a considerable body of evidence indicates that people have little, if any, insight into the processes underlying their judgements and decisions...people's reports on their own behaviour are essentially rationalisations' (Hardman, 2009, p. 186).

Ethics at arm's length

Ethics is one of those areas, a bit like research, where most of us know we should have an interest in it, feel guilty about not being more interested in it, and still keep it at arm's length. For many of us, the topic of ethics was taught as a one-off lecture at the end of a semester's work, despite the assumption ever after that ethics is crucial in almost every professional step we take. Ultimately, we are informed more implicitly about ethics than we are through explicit dialogue about it (Pope and Vasquez, 2007). Even when provided with opportunities to take the learning further, we do not feel the urgency or the attraction to do so in the face of pressing clinical needs and interests. Allan, Passmore and Mortimer (2011) recount experiences similar to our own: 'over the past few years one of us has presented several conference papers on the topic (of ethics), while at the same event running workshops on other topics including mindfulness... While the ethics event struggled to draw a dozen participants, the session on mindfulness was so popular it was difficult for the presenter to get in the room' (p. 161). Ethics and ethical thinking remain somewhat vague in our personal and professional backgrounds until something happens that forces us to reflect on them—and often that reflection comes a little too late. We have accompanied a number of individuals through ethical complaints and that journey has made us more ethically aware and alert to when ethical problems might lurk close to the surface. This can be a painful way to learn.

There is good reason for this arm's length approach to ethical training. First, most of us don't think of ourselves as being unethical or acting unethically. Why waste time delving into theory, research, literature and frameworks that may not be needed? There are other more pressing practical needs on our workfront agendas. It can be easier to question ourselves in areas of least certainty such as skills deficits, rather than in areas we feel more certain of, such as examining our ethics. It also can be easier to question the ethics of others than to question our own (Pope and Vasquez, 2007). When there is any hint, never mind the severity, of a formal complaint it often comes as a surprise to individuals to consider their behaviour might be unethical.

Second, ethics, ethical decision-making and ethical dilemmas are all areas of great uncertainty. There are rarely clear answers about what to do, or not to do, and we can come away from ethical training more confused than enlightened. Except for a few universals (do not have sex with your clients, have professional liability insurance, keep appropriate client notes), there are few 'hard and fast' behavioural rules that tell us dogmatically what the right course of action is, or how we should behave. Ethics falls within that area of life that King and Kitchener (1994) call 'ill-defined problems', and Kegan and Lahey (2009) see as the difference between 'technical' versus 'adaptive' challenges and problems. Unlike well-defined problems, ill-defined problems are ones that do not have a single or simple answer. Changing a light bulb involves knowing the one right way to complete the task. How to manage my money usually has a similar right answer. Ill-defined problems require capabilities other than knowledge or skills to resolve them. There are no givens. For example, how do I deal with my depression, i.e., what mindset do I need to change to tackle this issue? Or, when might I share information with a third party that breaks my confidentiality agreement with a client? For Kegan and Lahey (2009), technical problems are ones that are solved by developing a new skill set, e.g., flying a plane, performing brain surgery, managing your finances. *You* don't have to change *you* to resolve these problems, you don't require any specific self-awareness. Adaptive problems, however, need more than simply new skills to resolve them. They require the person changes to meet the challenge—they must adapt rather than simply learn new skills. The fact that I am not getting a job despite my many interviews may be an indication I need to change something about myself (the passive way I present at interview, my brusque manner, the bitterness from being made redundant in my last job that still leaks out and contaminates my current interviews).

Many see ethical dilemmas as the first of these approaches and utilise the technical method—there are answers out there if only I can find them, or I need to develop some rational or logical skills to resolve the ethical issue. To view ethical problems or the solving of ethical dilemmas from an adaptive approach demands other resources—how do I need to think about this differently? What new mindset do I need to develop to think ethically? Perhaps it is not an 'either/or' approach (certain or uncertain, technical or adaptive) but more of a 'both/and' position—sometimes there are clear answers, and sometimes we have to change and adapt to meet the situation. How do we know which situation might require a technical or an adaptive approach?

Most of our codes, guidelines and frameworks provide principles to support us, but the interpretation and application of those principles are left up to ourselves. For example, many codes include an ethical requirement that practitioners keep up to date, invest in ongoing training and continue their professional development. Some specify time to meet this requirement, e.g., 30 hours a year. Others leave it open to interpretation. Would reading one article a year suffice? Hardly! A one-day training course? If you interpret the ruling in a minimalist way you calculate what you can get away with to fulfil the requirement. On the other hand, if you take an excellence perspective then you will read journals, go to training programmes, ensure you attend supervision, and attempt to keep up with contemporary research. Sometimes the guidelines don't seem to fit your own special circumstances. Even trickier, you are not always dealing with a 'wrong' versus 'right' situation, but a 'right' versus 'right' dilemma, for example, when you have to choose between competing values such as truth (I promised confidentiality) versus justice (this person has harmed others and I should disclose). When the territory of ethics is not always clear, and can be influenced by context and circumstances, why look into it too deeply until there is a specific need? It would be understandable if you thought there was no way to ready yourself for such a plethora of possibilities!

We know there are no easy, 'fix-it' right answers to many ethical questions, dilemmas and problems. There are 'fundamentalist moralists' who believe every situation we encounter as humans has a right ethical response written in stone for all time. Some even claim to be able to access those right answers. While we believe there are universal principles to which we can all subscribe as humans (e.g., the golden rule first formulated by Confucius: 'Do unto others what you would want done unto you'), we note that many of these principles need to be applied in certain practical situations, and there can be a surprising lack of fit between them. We believe (with Nash, 2002) that there are two fundamental stances on ethics. The first stance is that there are objective, 'out-there' moral truths waiting to be found that will tell us what to do, and the second stance is that there are no givens, we create our own moral truths. If these are the extremes on the continuum of ethical stances, then there are a number of positions between them that combine the two positions in particular ways.

This book does not adopt the stance that there are clear and universal answers to all ethical questions, and if your belief is that some objective authority (person, group, religion or wisdom tradition) provides that thesaurus of moral answers this book will disappoint you. We do not want to be arrogant enough to ignore the wisdom of the ages, and the amazing insights and knowledge handed down to us from generations past. We really do stand on the shoulders of ethical giants. To pretend that the wisdom of Confucius, the insights of Buddha, the teachings of Jesus, the learnings of Siddhartha, or the writings of Aristotle (to mention but a few) have nothing to teach us today is to ignore that the same questions they faced face us today but are 'written differently'. The big questions of life resurface with each generation: how will I live my life? What values will I adopt? How can we learn to live together as humans? What is the difference between good and bad? And, why do evil and harm exist? However, there are some ethical issues we have never had to face before—the environment and our human relationship with it, the internet and its use, reproductive technologies, nuclear weapons and their morality. While circumstances and contexts change, and our knowledge and insights increase, we have much to learn from the attitudes and stances adopted by those who struggled with similar questions.

- What do we mean by 'ethics'?
- How can we build up ethical character?
- Why does unethical behaviour exist?
- How do we make ethical decisions?
- How can we move from a position of ethical minimalism to one of ethical excellence?
- Do we need to believe in God or religion in order to be ethical?

To question and reflect is part of the development of ethical maturity. Even though, throughout the ages, there have been these key questions to wrestle with that remain as challenging as ever, this does not mean we have made insignificant ethical advances. There are some accepted universal truths, e.g., around the care and treatment of children, and there is growing impetus on other issues, e.g., the environment and female genital mutilation. We have more critical awareness of positions of moral relativism (the 'When in Rome...' position) that can be respectful of other communities, but can also be used to take advantage of other communities. An example of this was exposed when Western companies moved to developing countries in order to capitalise on cheap labour and poor working conditions in the name of increased profit.

There are, after all, key principles and values to be upheld, personally and socially. These are being explored in philosophical, as well as scientific, circles. As Harris (2010) writes: 'If there are objective truths to be known about human well-being—if kindness, for instance, is generally more conducive to happiness than cruelty is—then science should one day be able to make very precise claims about which of our behaviours and uses of attention are morally good, which are neutral, and which are worth abandoning' (p. 9).

Harris talks about 'neuroethics' which 'encompasses our efforts to understand ethics itself as a biological phenomenon' (p. 206). His recent book argues for 'well-being' as the objective norm against which we can judge values and behaviours as objective facts. The possibility that science one day will unravel the mysteries of human behaviour and reveal why we think, feel and behave the way we do, is not a new stance. While science, and (in Harris's case) neuroscience, is opening up new vistas of knowledge and information, it is not our intention to put all our moral eggs in this one basket. We believe that while biological bases of behaviour inform us enormously, they do not give us the full picture, and every profession (psychology, philosophy and biology) suffers when it tries to 'go it alone'.

So where do we stand ethically as we begin this book? We believe in journey ethics rather than destinational ethics, i.e., that we have to make journeys to find most answers and they are not 'givens' like destinations that guide you. In other words, we think it is difficult to start with an answer before we have the problem, i.e., I know what to do if I am faced with this moral choice. This does not mean there are not ethical principles to guide us, and ethical attributes that distinguish us from other animals. We believe that many ethical decisions are made unconsciously and intuitively, and that we don't access often enough our inner fonts of knowing—tacit knowledge—which is there for the taking. We think that moral intuition can be a wonderful guide to help us do what is right and good. We believe the basis of all ethical decision making is moral character—whether an ethical decision comes in an instant flash, or whether that decision has to be worked on and worked through systematically, i.e., consciously. However, we are aware there are times when contexts and circumstances override moral character, and individuals and groups engage in actions they would not normally. We believe that sometimes we have to wait for the way forward to emerge and this waiting can itself be an ethical stance. We believe also that there are times when we make major ethical decisions that we don't implement immediately because of relationships and contexts. For example, we know of instances where parents decided not to separate at this moment because they felt their two children needed the security of their home for some time longer. They separated a few years later. Their courageous decision to find ways of being together for three years that were not destructive to them or their children was impressive. We also know an instance of a priest who had made the decision to leave his ministry, but he delayed the implementation of that decision for four years until his mother died. These too can be ethically mature decisions.

We have used 'ethical maturity' in the title of this book. The concept of ethical maturity is used here in an attempt to move from simple ethical decision making to a larger picture of ethical excellence of which ethical decision making is a part. For too long, codes and frameworks have been used as the sole criteria for competency in ethical decision making. As Pope and Vasquez (2007) point out, while awareness of ethical standards and codes are crucial to ethical competence, such documents 'do not take the place of an active, deliberate and creative approach to fulfilling our ethical responsibility' (p. 14). Rules tend to be helpful, but insufficient. It is frustrating that ethical problems often seem to sit in the spaces between the guidelines.

It is significant to note that simple adherence to our ethical codes or frameworks means we often work to minimum standards, rather than standards of excellence. Bond (2006) makes the point clearly: 'For all sorts of laudable reasons, our collective professional ethics have been driven by a concern to set minimum standards for the safety of clients' (p. 77). He writes about moving from 'an ethics of duty' (this is what I ought to do, should do, because my code tells me — the minimum) to 'an ethics of trust' where ethics is based on faithfulness to relationships and the welfare of clients is central to the decision making process.

In using the term 'ethical maturity', we are aware we are making a value judgment. In suggesting there is ethical maturity, by implication, we are saying that ethical immaturity exists — some ethical decisions are better (more mature) than others. Do we mean that? While we accept most people do the best they can in the circumstances in which they find themselves, we also believe that some ethical decisions are less mature than others. What is healthy and unhealthy for us can be documented. Most of us would agree that smoking is an unhealthy habit, as are certain foods and certainly a lack of exercise. Most of us would fail on some aspects of what is generally recognised as a healthy lifestyle. But there is some agreement on what is a healthy lifestyle. So, for us, there are recognisable signs of ethical maturity that are not around when ethical indifference or amoral stances or ethical insensitivity emerge. While we want to avoid dogmatic and prescriptive ethics that tells us what to do ('We know what is good for you ethically'), we want to recognise that ethical excellence, or ethical maturity, is the attempt to attain what is best in ethical decision making. So we have an ethical stance—that some ethical decisions and some ethical actions are more mature than others. What ethically mature actions and decisions look like is what this book sets out to investigate.

The most difficult jigsaw puzzle, we believe, comprises 1000 pieces, where all the pieces are the same colour and the design is a circle. This image came to mind when we decided to write a book on ethical maturity. The vast number of issues involved is itself off-putting. There are ethical theories, ethical principles, ethical rules, guidelines, frameworks and codes. There are departments of moral philosophy and moral theology, and ethical committees exist to monitor research in many departments of medicine, psychology, nursing, social services, etc., and most professional bodies have an ethics complaints procedure. Hardly a day passes when there is not a TV or radio discussion on what is the right thing to do in a particular situation. Rarely do the interviewees agree on a way forward. Getting the pieces into some sort of order provides its own difficulty—values, relationships, dilemmas and conflicts all connect and disconnect to create our modern ethical landscape. There is no one agreed approach. Some of the greatest minds of history have engaged with what constitutes ethics. There is business ethics, personal ethics, community ethics, feminist ethics and environmental ethics. Not to mention communications ethics, relationship ethics, ethics of care, ecological ethics and more. There are discussions on moral intelligence, moral minds, real world ethics and ethical organisations. There is moral psychology and moral character.

There is no way we can cover this labyrinth of ethics and morals. It is too vast and too confusing for one book. Our aim is simpler. We want to help you and ourselves to live ethically, make ethical decisions and be able to live peacefully with the decisions we have made. We are interested in applied ethics. We want to learn from experience, our own and others, how to think ethically and act ethically in a way that is consistent with our aspirations to do the best for ourselves and others. We would like to understand the processes that go into making ethical decisions, and how to set up and conclude a deliberate conscious ethical decision making procedure. We hope we can be excellent without being perfectionist, have the highest standards while recognising our humanity and vulnerabilities. We want to accept who and where we are, and we want to look beyond—as is the calling for us all. This must be our vocation as humans—to see beyond, to find paths beyond, to search for what can be better.

So what is the moral landscape we believe in and the principles on which we base this book?

There is no one agreed theory of how and why we make ethical decisions, or on what ethics/morals are and what makes actions right or wrong—there are a number of theories. There is much debate on whether free will exists, and if not, who or what is really in charge? There is controversy around whether or not we are born with moral intelligence, or whether our moral sense evolves through culture, or a combination of both. Theories of moral development and predictable stages of moral growth through which individuals move have been suggested. Some think these stages are somewhat different for men and for women. There are various stances on moral responsibility, blameworthiness and accountability for human behaviour, and whether or not we should designate human behaviour as voluntary. There are also various positions on the roles of religion and God in moral behaviour, with some claiming that without religion and God ethics does not make sense. Others see no reason to include concepts of religion and God in ethical discussions and claim ethical behaviour can stand on its own without reference to spirituality or religion.

This book will not provide a definitive answer to the questions raised by these multiple theories and stances—and it is unlikely that such answers will emerge in the foreseeable future. However, in order to provide some guidance across a subject with such variety, we have to take some stances (and make some [principled] assumptions) and these are ours.

Our ethical anchors/principles/ beliefs/assumptions

We believe we are born with some form of moral intelligence that does not exist in other animals. Children are not born blank slates. Just as we are born with the existing ability to speak (have language), so we are born with a rudimentary ability to know what is good and bad, right and wrong. At this early stage, before reason, language and culture influence human development, there is an existing facility for determining good and bad, right and wrong. There is, as it were, no content in this moral ability. It is like hardware waiting for software to get it up and running. There are exceptions to this when damage has been done to the prefrontal cortex and some individuals do not seem to have this in-built moral intelligence.

Culture, communities of practice, experiences and relationships all combine to make particular what is right and wrong, good and bad in our lives. Whether we are born in China or the USA, relate to different people, have membership of particular communities, along with our own relationships and experience, all contribute to form different moral templates through which we view the world. These moral views are inherited and formed in the contexts in which we live and we come to know them through socialisation. These form our moral characters and quickly become unconscious in our lives. We call this Phase 1. Our intuitive and fast ethical decisions emerge spontaneously from here to such an extent that we do not know or often cannot articulate this source.

There comes a time when we begin to question our inherited moral values formed in Phase 1. When asked to review them we can accept, reject, modify, or change them. This begins Phase 2, the development of moral character where we re-create or reconfigure what we have inherited and have a personal say in the values that will guide our lives. There are some individuals who never reach Phase 2, and never question the scripts and moral teaching given to them by others. Others make small or radical changes to their inherited moral characters.

We can make moral decisions in two ways: unconscious and intuitive, or conscious and deliberate. The first comes spontaneously from the moral character we have inherited or constructed. The second emerges when we have to deal with novel or creative situations where we have had little prior experience. Language enables us to put these thoughts, dilemmas, deliberations and reflections into words so we can share them with others, listen to the narratives of others, and create shared pools of ethical wisdom.

The human movement (and the way the brain works) is always towards the creation of unconscious moral templates that guide and direct our moral actions. The brain moves conscious learning into unconscious learning. This process has value through the continuous formation of moral habits that allow our moral decisions to emerge spontaneously and intuitively. However, these unconscious templates can be detrimental when they become mindless and unreflected stances that are no longer helpful or mature.

As we move towards ethical maturity, we use a combination of methods to come to ethical conclusions: intuition, emotion, reason, action analysis, risk assessment, evaluations and reflection are all used in different combinations depending on the context and the complexity of the issue or dilemma. There are various theories about the order in which these human facilities are used. Kant (1995) views 'reason' as primary, Hume (1996) views 'emotion' as primary, while Rawls (1971) views 'action analysis' as primary. We don't take a strong position on which comes first, or which is primary. But we do believe all are necessary for ethical maturity.

We move towards ethical maturity—we do not start there.

Levels of moral reasoning accompany this journey to ethical maturity. These levels seem to move into more morally abstract ways of thinking and towards principles that guide our lives. Development takes place at cognitive, emotional and psychological levels that change us from holding superficial views of good and bad to more sophisticated methods of thinking about and making moral decisions.

We believe the two qualities that best sustain ethical maturity are empathy and compassion. There are levels of empathy and degrees of compassion. Both can be taught to some degree, but not to everyone and not always. When we do not have empathy and compassion it is easy to objectify others. Being 'in relationship' with others is a strong basis for ethical understanding and action.

Ethical immaturity exists and expresses itself in the harm, cruelty and evil that results in immoral and unethical actions. Internal and external factors can impact individuals, groups and organisations, and result in inhuman and horrendous harm being done. We are aware there are times when contexts can override character in making moral decisions. Our need to belong, to be included in groups, as well as our adherence to authority often put demands on us that override our values.

Moral reasoning does not automatically result in moral action (but ethical maturity does).

We often do not know why we act the way we do. Our justifications or explanations for our moral actions are confabulations (after the fact rationalising of why we do what we do). This can be explained partially by seeing our 'self' as a series of mini-selves who sometimes work in harmony, and sometimes are in conflict. At times one 'self' dominates, at other times a different self dominates—I can be generous and I can be mean, I can love and I can hate, I can be open and diverse, I can be horribly prejudiced. There are times when I am out of touch with the 'mini-me' from which my actions emerge, and I find a way to explain it that may have little to do with what is actually happening. The ability to think about and reflect honestly on why we do what we do is an important stage in ethical maturity.

We believe there are degrees of freedom and free will in our moral decisions. However, free will is not a given. Many people do not have personal free will, but have given over their moral decision making to others (individuals, groups, institutions, God), or more tragically, have their free will taken from them by others. Some people have their free will diminished or eliminated by illness, biology or life experiences. Free will is connected to consciousness, which is our ability to know ourselves and our intentions. There is less free will around than we think, although most of us live with the illusion that we are the authors of our behaviours.

We are masses of contradictions, illuminated through the metaphor of the 'three brains' drawn from neuroscience—the reptilian, the limbic and the prefrontal cortex—all of which vie for supremacy and contribute something towards the process of our ethical decision making. This process helps us to reconcile and connect these contradictions so that we can make the best decisions possible. Our attempts to harness the best of each brain is part of ethical maturity.

Part of life and growing up is living with the less-than-mature ethical decisions we have made. We all make poor decisions we live to regret. Part of moral development is to recognise our limitations and live with and learn from the decisions we have made. We are 'wounded' healers for ourselves and others, and limited in what we know and how we know 'it'.

Our book aims to integrate the more recent scientific research on moral decision making with the rich traditions of philosophical thought and our own practice experience. We believe that spending time thinking about how we think ethically, how we come to act ethically, and how we grow ethically through evaluation and integration of that experience is a worthwhile pursuit. Many think they have their ethical positions 'sorted' and there is nothing else to consider. Yet, the fact that professions have to invest so heavily in regulatory frameworks and mechanisms says that many people are not 'sorted'. It is obvious to us in our professional practices, teaching, supervising and delivering human services that issues of ethics are on the agenda constantly and in a myriad of ways.

This book offers a framework for ethical decision making. More broadly, it offers a variety of ways to consider your own learning, and hopefully, to learn more about how you operate when faced with making ethical decisions. If we accept the premise that moral character can be developed (and we argue that is the case) then any time spent in critical reflection will be part of a useful journey towards ethical maturity.

Why is ethical maturity worth seeking? Ethical maturity provides a solid foundation from which to counter and manage the ethical vicissitudes of life, and to offer leadership to others with whom you live and work. It means, at its best, less time in the ethical struggle and more in the territory of moral certainty. This is not the certainty that comes with blindness, arrogance and self-referential decision making, but that which comes from knowing oneself well, having the confidence to seek consultation, holding a useful toolkit to help in most situations, and being prepared to make and learn from mistakes.

Bon voyage!

Chapter 2
Ethical maturity and unethical behaviour

'Time has dimmed my memory of the extent of creative evil in which many of the guards engaged, the extent of the suffering of many of the prisoners, and the extent of my passivity in allowing the abuses to continue for as long as I did—an evil of inaction.'

(Zimbardo, 2007, p. ix, reflecting on the Stanford Prison Experiment, 1971)

'The masterful hypocrisy of the immoral brain demands a certain grudging respect. It lazily applies nothing but the most superficial and disapproving analysis of others' misdemeanours, while bending over backwards to reassure that you can do no wrong.'

(Fine, 2007, p. 73)

'If we limited our examination of evil to acts that perpetrators themselves acknowledge as evil, there would hardly be any such acts to examine.'

(Baumeister, 1999, p. 6)

'Pilate took water and washed his hands before the multitude, saying, I am innocent of the blood of this just person: see you to it.'

(St Matthew, 27:24)

'The just man falls seven times.'

(Proverbs, 24:16).

'Nemo sua sponte peccat: No-one willingly does wrong.'

(Socrates, cited in Bruns, 1992, p. 24)

'I finished him off in a rush, not thinking anything of it, even though he was a neighbour, quite close on my hill. In truth it came to me only afterwards: I had taken the life of a neighbour. I mean, at the fatal instance I did not see in him what he had been before: I struck someone who was no longer either close or strange to me, who *wasn't ordinary anymore. I'm saying like the people you meet every day. His features were indeed similar to those of the person I knew, but nothing reminded me that I had lived beside him for a long time.'*

(Kassimeris, 2006, p. 8, Rwandan genocide
participant who killed a Tutsi neighbour)

'It is in the very nature of things human that every act that has once made its appearance and has been recorded in the history of mankind stays with mankind as a potentiality long after its actuality has become a thing of the past. No punishment has ever possessed enough power of deterrence to prevent the commission of crimes. On the contrary, whatever the punishment, once a specific crime has appeared for the first time, its reappearance is more likely than its initial emergence could ever have been.'

(Arendt, 1963, p. 98)

Exercise

- Think of an unethical decision you made recently or in the past. It does not matter whether in your view it was a minor unethical decision (I told a lie), or a major one (I took advantage of a vulnerable person). Put yourself in a position of curiosity rather than evaluation regarding your decision. You are wondering what happened, rather than evaluating what happened.
- What was unethical about the action you took?
- What happened that made you make that decision? Trace the process you went through.
- As you look back, with hindsight, what have you learned about ethical decision making?
- What have you learned about yourself? What would you do differently now?

Preamble

The questions we will consider in this chapter comprise the following: you might want to reflect on them in light of your own experiences in answering the questions above.

- Why are individuals, teams, groups and organisations unethical?
- What happens to make us do bad/wrong, or harm (or evil)?
- Is harm, hurt and cruelty intentional?
- What could I do to make someone act unethically?
- How can ordinary people do terrible things to others, and yet, during or after the event, find ways to deny the meaning (and even the reality) of what they have done?

Introduction

We know there is a gap between what we would like to be and do, and what we are and do. My best intentions to get up earlier and exercise are dashed on the rocks of laziness when the alarm goes off and I turn over for a few more minutes' sleep. I keep putting off that article I know I want to write and it is now near its deadline for submission. What is stopping me? I have had a great time and do not need any more wine, and yet, I cannot resist another glass. I am a hypocrite, preaching loudly what I never practise. The hurtful remark makes its own way out of my mouth unsolicited and unwanted; my cruel condemnation of a friend who was giving me some feedback I didn't like, and the gut-wrenching twists of envy and jealousy as I see a colleague get an award I would have loved to attain (though would never admit to wanting). I can find bad easily in the good around me, and discover continually the chasm between what I ought to be and what I am. Like St Paul, I find myself doing what I don't want to do, and not doing what I would love to do. The Roman poet, Ovid, captured it too: 'I am dragged along by a strange new force. Desire and reason are pulling in different directions. I see the right way and approved it, but follow the wrong' (cited in Haidt, 2006, p. 4). It is almost as if there were several people in one, several subpersonalities, all battling for what is good, and yet, somehow ending up doing what is bad. Why is that?

Our human history feels like a story of two extremes. While there is no other species that can equal humans for altruism, care and compassion, there is also no other species that matches us for harm, cruelty and sadism. We are amazed at what we can, and have, achieved as humans, from the extraordinary lengths we go to support and help those in need (e.g., Children in Need, Red Nose Day, Comic Relief), to wonderful leaders who set examples of unselfishness and dedication (Mother Theresa, Nelson Mandela, etc.). And organisations that have trailblazed altruism. However, you won't have to travel far, or read widely, or listen to radio or television much until you come across how unethical the human race can be.

Our world is filled with examples of the inhumanity of man to man. The inhumanity of women to women has also been documented (Chessler, 2001). There were almost 150 wars taking place in the world between the years 1950–1990. 106 million people died in war situations in the twentieth century, more in one century than all the previous centuries together. During this century we have also witnessed concentration camps, ethnic cleansing, displacement of millions of people, refugees fleeing horrendous situations.

Our newspapers remind us almost daily of:

- children who have been subjected to horrendous abuse

- examples of individuals and groups being tortured
- whole nations under attack from terrorism
- day-to-day examples of physical attack, racial abuse, robbery, etc.
- bullying and psychological terrorism
- organisations where unethical behaviour has had far-reaching consequences (Enron, NASA, BP Oil)
- leaders from whom we expect more (Catholic Bishops who covered up abuse issues, MPs who fiddled their expenses, leaders who killed their own people, journalists who hack into the private phones of others).

The pain we inflict can be:

- *physical harm*: torture, abuse, beating, starvation, causing trauma
- *emotional harm*: bullying, humiliating, shaming, emotional flooding
- *mental harm*: giving wrong information, falsifying, spin, lies, cover ups
- *spiritual harm*: destroying values; not respecting values, cultures, differences; and, taking away hope.

This chapter looks at why we as individuals, couples, groups and organisations engage in unethical behaviour, and reinforces the three psychological truths offered by Zimbardo (2007).

1. The world is filled with good and evil—was, is and always will be.
2. The barrier between good and evil is permeable and nebulous.
3. It is possible for angels to become devils and, perhaps more difficult to conceive, for devils to become angels.

Sustaining an ability to hurt others

Many think that unethical behaviour results from omission, thoughtlessness and/or naivety. While this is true some of the time, this view protects us from facing what is often the real truth: that certain forms of moral corruption take a great deal of thought, planning and sustained commitment. Take for example the need over a prolonged affair to deceive and justify to oneself, to develop and deliver the lies, and plan the deceptions involved. What about consistent tax evasion? Or planning a scam that will rob the elderly of their retirement savings? Or creating the mammoth infrastructure that results in a concentration camp. Often we can use justifications and disengagement strategies that will excuse us 'successfully' from examining a one-off event too closely. However, it takes a lot more (morally flawed) fortitude to hold a position that will harm others over a longer period. Seabright and Schminke (2002) suggest that such behaviour needs to be understood differently. While it is common to attribute malevolence and cruelty to a failure of moral reasoning or a lack of moral imagination, they suggest immorality could be viewed as 'an active, creative, or resourceful act' (p. 19). Instead of picturing the well-being of others at the end of one's decision making, 'immoral imagination' can include fantasies of revenge, or harm to others that could be considered an unavoidable collateral cost, if not a sought-after end in itself. The person can 'bracket off' feelings for others by dehumanising them, inflating their level of threat, attributing blame to them, thus enhancing the justification to act. 'My wife deserves my neglect after the way she neglects me. She is too busy with her career to notice anyway. Surely I deserve some happiness after all I have had to put up with?' Thieves will say, 'It's covered by insurance anyway'. Workers may say, 'If I was paid properly I wouldn't need to take (stolen) supplies home to my family.' These descriptions and justifications have to be worked at hard enough to cover any alternative information (e.g., a wife in tears, a [too small] pay rise) in order to work for the desired (if flawed) outcome. De Waal (2009) suggests the German word 'schadenfreude' captures this— it is the opposite of empathy and involves taking delight in the misfortune or hurt experienced by others.

The language of harm

A number of words are used when we describe unethical behaviour. The first and strongest is 'evil'.

Two of the quotes that introduce this chapter use the term. We have noticed when we talk about 'evil' that there is often a negative reaction to the term itself, and people move quickly toward more acceptable substitutes, e.g., 'harm', 'cruelty', 'immoral behaviours'. We hear little of 'evil' in the world and, as Baumeister (1999) points out, people hardly use the term in everyday life anymore. However, we want to preserve the word here not only because of its graphic qualities, but because it best captures what we have the capacity to do to one another as human beings. We are not using the term in a religious sense of 'evil' and 'sin', but to capture the time when we can cross the moral line and engage in thoughts and behaviours that can only be described as unethical or immoral and with the potential to cause immense harm.

Evil is the extreme of immoral or unethical behaviour. It is the nature and severity of the harms done that make evil different from other forms of wrongdoing. It is not only doing harm, but the intention to harm that creates evil.

Johnson (2012, p. 121ff) presents six types of evil.
1. Evil as *dreadful pleasure* (as a combination of dread and pleasure).
2. Evil as *deception*. Peck (1983) refers to evil people as 'the people of the lie'.

3. Evil as *bureaucracy*. This is a form of administrative evil where evil regimes and systems set out to destroy and inflict harm (e.g., the Nazi system).
4. Evil as *sanctioned destruction*, usually of particular people (we see this in attacks on gay people or people of colour).
5. Evil as *a choice*. How do we choose evil? Probably not immediately, but over a period of time as we become immune to the harm we do. Fromm (1964) puts it well: 'Between the extreme of when I can no longer do a wrong act and the other extreme when I have lost my freedom to right action, there are innumerable degrees of freedom of choice' (p. 136). Terrorism falls into this category, as might the decision to torture.
6. Evil as *ordinary*. This considers how ordinary people can do evil things. The Zimbardo experiment, described later in this chapter, provides a good example of why ordinary people do evil deeds to others. To some degree, with global media being so graphic and immediate we can become inoculated towards evil and the need to act. Arendt (1963) coined the phrase 'the banality of evil' to depict how ordinary evil can become.

Zimbardo (2007) defines evil as: 'intentionally behaving in ways that harm, abuse, demean, dehumanise, or destroy innocent others—or using one's authority and systemic power to encourage or permit others to do so on your behalf' (p. 5).

Evil is a term we reserve for human action and human beings. No matter what other animals do, we would hesitate to call them evil. Intention to harm or hurt is what makes the difference. While we see other animals behave in ways we would describe as cruel, hurtful or harmful, it is the intentional capacity of humans to do harm that we describe as evil. Even when our intentions are 'good' (idealists, getting the justice we deserve, seeking payback, teaching the person a lesson), we know our desire to cause hurt and harm is intentional. This is what we mean by evil.

The in-built desire not to harm others

Although we have a capacity to hurt, the truth is that our limbic brains carry strong in-built instincts to be decent with each other. De Waal (2009) contends that cooperation, being social and getting on together are in-built qualities of mammals, and presents examples of this process from his work with primates. While acknowledging the competitive and 'selfish gene' side, he insists this must be balanced with the 'social gene' with which we are born. Lehrer (2009) tells the story of Brigadier General S.L.A. Marshall who surveyed thousands of US troops during World War II.

The surveys took place soon after the troops had been in combat. His shocking conclusion was that less that 20 per cent of the solders (one in five) actually shot at the enemy, even when under attack. 'It is the fear of killing', wrote Marshall (2000), 'rather than the fear of being killed, that is the most common cause of battle failure in the individual' (p. 78). When faced with killing others, soldiers became incapacitated. After 1947, when these findings were published, the US army realised it had a problem. It immediately revamped its training programme to increase the ratio of fire. How did the programme achieve this? It taught soldiers to be automatic in what they do, not to think about what they were doing, and to become de-sensitised to the act of killing so that it became an automatic response. The US command realised that if they desensitised their troops, drew physical and psychological distances between them and the enemy (e.g., seeing the enemy as less than human, dropping bombs from great heights) then their soldiers did not think of themselves as killing another person. In the Korean War, the US Army had upped its ratio of fire of 55 per cent, and in the Vietnam War to 90 per cent. The US Army found a way to bypass our natural instinct to be decent in order to ensure its troops did their jobs. There are similar stories about individuals and groups having to go against their natural instincts to do deeds they know are wrong (e.g., there are photos of German policemen killing individuals in concentration camps with tears running down their faces).

Why do people do unethical things?

It is often thought that evil is perpetrated by monsters. This is how we can push evil away, and how we fool ourselves that it can be recognised easily. Instead, Hannah Arendt (1963), observed that it is often 'ordinary' people living in communities that can be swept into evil pursuits, as was the case in Nazi Germany. Her essays on Adolf Eichmann controversially suggested him to be a 'clown' more than a 'monster', yet he perpetrated monstrous crimes. For Arendt (1963), the most frightening thing from the Eichmann trial was 'the fearsome, word and thought-defying banality of evil'. Others have questioned this interpretation and suggested that had Arendt stayed for more of the trial, and not just the beginning, she would have seen a different Eichmann, one who developed new creative policies for extermination and who had an active pride in his achievements (Haslam and Reicher, 2008). How does such behaviour come about in 'ordinary' people? Two important pieces of research go a long way towards answering this question.

Milgram (1963) and Zimbardo (2007)

Two of the most important experiments in psychology are the well-known Milgram and Zimbardo research projects. Both have a lot to tell us about ethical and moral behaviour. In 1961, Stanley Milgram, a postdoctoral researcher still in his late twenties, designed his now famous 'obedience to authority' experiments at Yale University, and unwittingly discovered some answers to the question of how humans can be so cruel to each other. Milgram, of Jewish background, has acknowledged how the Holocaust inspired him to ask the question of how and why people can do such horrendous things to other human beings.

In brief, Milgram assiduously and carefully set up a situation where a volunteer, who was told he or she was involved in a memory experiment, was asked to administer electric shocks to a learner when told to do so by an authority. Milgram asked his volunteers to give the learner a mild 15-volt shock for the first mistake on a memory test, and as questions were asked and mistakes made, the volunteer was asked to increase the voltage in 15-volt increments. The final voltage was 450 and carried a sign which shouted: 'Danger: Severe Shock' and had three red Xs. The shocks were not real, and the person receiving them was not suffering or in pain. Although the person receiving the 'shocks' was placed in a different room to the volunteer, they could be heard by the volunteer when, as instructed, they expressed their 'pain' out loud after the 150-volt threshold.

Without going into more detail (see Milgram, 1974; Zimbardo, 2007, for more extensive coverage of these experiments), Milgram demonstrated the power of context in influencing human behaviour. Two out of every three (65%) volunteers went up to the maximum 450 volts. In further experiments, Milgram demonstrated how compliance rates could move to over 90 per cent of people continuing to the 450-volt maximum, or be reduced to less that 10 per cent (when models of rebellion were introduced). What is it about context that influences humans to do what they would not normally do? Burger (2011) reviewed the experiment in the light of modern insights focused on four situational factors:

1. *The use of small increments.* By slowly increasing the shocks (15 volts at a time), the experimenter worked on the principle that behaviour will begin to change if they can get someone to respond initially to a small request and then continue to ask for small increases. (Once individuals have started on a process they want to remain consistent).

2. *Diffused or missing responsibility.* In the Milgram experiment, the experimenter took responsibility for what was happening, and reassured the volunteer about continuing (despite the cries and

protestations from the other room). Volunteers saw themselves as 'just following orders'. When people are released from personal responsibility, can allow others to assume responsibility, see themselves in a 'one-down' power situation with an 'authority' (white coat and credentials), they are inclined to give up their own authority and accountability.

3. *Placing participants in a novel situation.* In new situations, individuals are unsure what to do and often rely on others to guide them. We can assume the Milgram experiments were new situations for the volunteers with no prior norms to guide them, and no previous personal experiences to help them. All they had was an 'expert' in the room and it was 'natural' that they would be guided by him/her. This is a situation of trusting another, rather than trusting what one's own experience revealed.

4. *Giving volunteers limited time to think, reflect and act.* Burger (2011) points out the difficult tasks of the volunteers: 'The teacher's role required him or her to find and read the correct test item, note the leader's responsibility, determine whether the response was correct and inform the learner, give the correct response for incorrect answer, find the next shock lever, announce the strength of the shock, administer the shock, and then repeat the process. Any pauses or delays were met immediately by the leader with prods to continue' (p. 657).

There was no time for volunteers to stop and think about what they were doing, no reflective pauses, no intervals to review what was happening to them, no time to argue the case one way or the other.

Zimbardo (2007) extracted ten methods from Milgram's experiments which could be used to get ordinary people to do harmful things to others:

1. Pre-arranging contracts to control the individual's behaviour (getting the volunteer to agree to the tasks and procedures beforehand).

2. Giving volunteers meaningful roles to play that have positive values and response scripts.

3. Presenting basic rules as reasonable, but then using them for compliance (or keeping the rules vague and then interpreting them to suit the leader).

4. Reframing unpleasant reality with desirable rhetoric (you are helping us find out data, these people are the enemy, not just women and children).

5. Diffusing or abdicating the responsibility (someone else will take responsibility).

6. Starting with small steps and then increasing the demands.
7. Introducing gradual steps that do not seem to make much difference.
8. Changing the nature of the authority figure from benign and kind to demanding and even irrational.
9. Making the exit costs high.
10. Offering an ideology or big lie to justify what is being asked (e.g. helping with research to improve memory).

What can this work tell us about ethics, ethical behaviour and ethical decision making?

Philip Zimbardo (2007) states his intention in writing 'The Lucifer Effect' was 'to understand the processes of transformation at work when good or ordinary people do bad things' (p. 5). He uses the term 'evil' unashamedly, and defines it as 'intentionally behaving in ways that harm, abuse, demean, dehumanise, or destroy innocent others—or using one's authority and systemic power to encourage or permit others to do so on your behalf' (p. 5).

Zimbardo was born in 1933, the same year as Milgram, and they were former high school friends. While Milgram's experiments at Yale took place in 1961, Zimbardo's Stanford Prison Study was conducted in 1971. With a grant from the US Office of Naval Research, Zimbardo randomly assigned 24 volunteers (college students) to be 'prisoners' or 'guards' in a mock prison in the basement of the Psychology Department at Stanford. The two-week study ended after six days due to the level of emotional trauma suffered by participants.

Details of the study can be found in Zimbardo (2007). However, what happened does not surprise us in light of Milgram's study. 'Prisoners' and 'guards', after an initial short period where it was all treated very lightly, soon got 'into role' to such an extent that one-third of the guards were judged to show sadistic tendencies.

While Zimbardo (2007) was not looking at anything specific (he had no hypothesis to test), he was 'assessing the extent to which the external features of an institutional setting could override the internal dispositions of the actors in that environment' (p. 195). The results were clear: 'the experiment has emerged as a powerful illustration of the potentially toxic impact of bad systems and bad situations in making good people behave in pathological ways that are alien to their nature' (p. 195). This has deep implications for ethical behaviour—that situations, contexts and circumstances can override moral character and given the right kind of circumstances (as with Milgram and Zimbardo) ordinary moral individuals will engage in highly unethical behaviour. But not all do. There were 'good' guards.

Zimbardo (2007) suggests that a set of dynamic psychological processes can induce good people to do evil.

- *De-individuation*: not seeing the person as an individual or a person.
- *Obedience to authority*: 'I just did what I was told.'
- *Self-justification and rationalisation*: finding or concocting reasons to justify what I did and wanted, e.g., 'He had it coming to him because of the way he treated me.'
- *To make the world a better place*: the 'gardeners' mentality' of removing the weeds from the garden—ethnic cleansing, killing those who perform abortions, terrorists committed to their cause. This is the stance of the idealist whose values allow him or her to hurt others in the pursuit of these ideals.
- *Did not intend evil or harm*: the harm came about as a consequence of other actions, rather than what was intended, e.g., the mugger who wanted money, but ended up killing his victim.
- *I couldn't help it*: factors beyond my control—a rationale often given in cases of domestic violence. 'I couldn't help myself, she provoked me.'
- *Fully justified action*: a legitimate reason—'I was administering justice that would not have been done: she needed to be taught a lesson.'
- *Blurring the line*: where there is ambiguity, uncertainty and misinformation sometimes the rules contradict each other. 'I wanted a good story for the newspaper. I thought that gave me permission to hack into someone's phone.'
- *Keep people ignorant for as long as possible*: do not give advance warning and so allow no luxury of reflection. Thrust them into the situation (tired, under stress, disoriented).
- *Self-control stops*: criminals show lack of control throughout their lives, including desensitisation to harm, hurt and evil. Living with wrongdoing and harm can result in becoming desensitised to what is happening (e.g., German soldiers in concentration camps were oblivious to the harm and hurt around them after they had been involved for some time).

These two well-known research experiments highlight why unethical behaviour takes place and how contexts, leadership and group participation can influence moral behaviour.

Personal factors that can influence unethical behaviour

A number of personal factors, singly or collectively, can influence unethical behaviour:

- *Lack of self-awareness*: not knowing myself and my character well enough to realise that at times I can be harmful and unethical.
- *Lack of awareness of others*: Being insensitive to the needs of others and lacking empathy and compassion.
- *Impulsive behaviour*: where time to think and reflect is not taken. Sometimes the influence of alcohol and drugs can result in behaviours that lower inhibitions and result in unreflected action.
- *Lack of attention to the strength of the shadow side within our lives*: How what we repress can often emerge to influence us.
- *Power and its misuse*: Especially 'power over', used to get others to do things through threat, punishment or manipulation.
- *Flying under the radar*: Zimbardo (2007) describes this as 'Conditions that make us feel anonymous, when we think that others do not know us or care to, can foster anti-social, self-interested behaviours' (p. 25).
- *Taking advantage of others or of a situation that arises*: e.g., a colleague is off sick and another takes the opportunity to take over his or her domain. De Waal (2011) illustrates how in his work with chimps he has to be careful when drugging a male chimp. When other males notice his weakness they can move in quickly to take advantage of him.
- *Early deprivations*: injuries that occur early in life can lead to corrupt acting-out within relationships, due to having developed less empathy in the face of the primary rage against others, and greater need to focus on one's own deprivations (Firestone and Catlett, 2009). This constant need to attend to the sense of being 'owed' has been called 'destructive entitlement', and can result in morally and relationally corrupt behaviour being repeated over the course of one's life, if not resolved (Boszormenyi-Nagy and Krasner, 1986).

Situational factors that impact ethical behaviour

Besides individual factors, there are contextual, environmental and situational factors that can influence unethical behaviour.

- When power is used inappropriately and there is a culture of 'power over' that uses people or takes advantage of them, then domination, incivility and tyranny can rule (see Kusy and Holloway, 2009).

- When individuals and groups feel pressure to take part. Referred to as 'group think'—our need to be accepted and be a part of groups can involve us in unethical behaviours that we would rarely perform on our own.
- Obedience to authority. Fine (2007) tells us, 'What Milgram famously (and repeatedly) found is that about two thirds of ordinary men (and women) will obediently electrocute a fellow human being all the way up to a highly dangerous 450 volts because a scientist in a lab-coat tells them to do it' (p. 68).
- Thinking that the special features of this behaviour excuse it from usual decision making—finding exceptions to the rules.
- Expediency and opportunism: balancing the behaviour with the fact you have to continue working with the people involved; the cost of whistle blowing; the hope that someone else will deal with the problem (Smith, McGuire, Abbott, and Blau, 1991).

Organisational factors that impact ethical behaviour

Particular institutional and organisational issues can be part of the context or situation and can influence unethical behaviour.

- Culture of an organisation: 'This is the way things are done around here' is often a reason why individuals conform, even when they know that conformity results in unethical behaviour.
- Systems thinking and the development of (collective) moral responsibility can impact individual behaviour for better or for worse (Werhane, 2002).
- Imitating others is a form of learning, often underestimated in its influence, that can result in harmful action (e.g., teenagers who may not want to be involved, but do so when the members of their group behave in a certain way—they imitate what they see).
- Collusion: organisations often ask members to collude with actions undertaken on behalf of the organisation (Harvey, 1996).

Idealism and 'group think'

Idealistic groups often ask members to engage in behaviours on behalf of the group that can be unethical using terms such as 'we are all in this together'. In demanding trust and loyalty, groups often suppress private doubts. At times the group will justify special circumstances in relation to others outside the group. For example, it was controversially argued in relation to the Nuremberg trials that war criminals were often not 'monsters'; the trouble being that 'there were so many (the same), and that the many were neither perverted nor sadistic, that they were, and are, frighteningly normal…this new type of criminal…makes it well nigh impossible for him to know or to feel that he is doing wrong' (Arendt, 1963, pp. 103–4).

Brain and biochemistry (psychopathy)

Some of the most cruel and immoral people are psychopaths. Hare (1993) outlines the typical profile: 'He will choose you, disarm you with his words, and control you with this presence. He will delight you with his wit and his plans. He will show you a good time, but you will always get the bill. He will smile and deceive you and he will scare you with his eyes. And when he is through with you, and he will be through with you, he will desert you and take with you your innocence and your pride' (p. 21). Hare sees psychopaths as social predators who lack conscience and have no ability to feel empathy or compassion. He claims that up to 1 per cent of people in the US are psychopaths, most of them not in jail. However, it appears that around 15 per cent of the prison population are psychopaths (Babiak and Hare, 2006). Neuroimaging experiments done on psychopaths confirm that they suffer from 'a failure of emotional learning due to genetic impairments of the amygdale and orbinofrontal cortex, regions vital to the process of emotions' (Harris, 2010, p. 99).

Hare (1993) points out the lack of clarity on the causes of psychopathy, however, there is a trend to see it as biologically based, with some environmental factors. His conclusions are daunting: 'The shortest chapter in any book on psychopathy could be the one on treatment. A one-sentence conclusion such as, "No effective treatment has been found" or "nothing works" is the common wrap-up to scholarly reviews of the literature' (p. 194). Injury to the brain or brain changes (e.g., tumours) have also been known to result in personality disorders, and thus behaviours not normal (even immoral) to the individuals preinjury.

Environment and upbringing

Our environment and upbringing play a major part in why ethical and unethical behaviours take place. For example, early experiences of neglect, abandonment and injustice will inform (but not necessarily determine) how we operate in relationships and communities: what we feel owed, what we owe others. Is there a place for empathy and care when someone has been so ripped off at the start of life? What Nash (2002) calls 'the second language of morality'—the communities in which we are born and bred—have immense influence over our moral decisions. We catch the culture we are born into and live in, and our desperate need to be part of groups which makes us do all sorts of things we would not otherwise do (Zimbardo, 2007).

Hedonic adaptation

We can become so used to a situation that it no long affects us as immoral. Becoming desensitised to a situation can result in unethical behaviour becoming acceptable and even becoming the norm. This has been called 'hedonic adaptation', where more of the same is needed to gratify, for example, increases in risk-taking behaviour, or taking drugs. The more often someone is involved in harmful or unethical behaviour, the more it becomes their norm and the more easily they live with the behaviour and its consequences.

The use of power

When power is used inappropriately, unethical behaviour can emerge. For example, when power has no limits or checks and balances, or where it relies not on respectful relationships, but on submission of others, then the opportunities for unethical practices increases. For individual and institutional examples of this, see surveys on the Catholic Church and institutional power: Cloyne Report (2010); Ferns Report (2005); Murphy Report (2009).

Relationship to authority

There are numerous examples of people engaging in immoral behaviours (e.g., shooting others) on direct orders from people in authority. Adolf Eichmann stated famously, 'I was only following orders' (Arendt, 1963). The Zimbardo and Milgram experiments are good examples. Permission from an authority figure or a higher authority often justifies why someone does something, as someone else is seen to have responsibility.

Nietzsche (cited in Butler, 2005) said that people will only be ethical when forced to, and that ethical behaviour occurs only in relation to systems of authority. This is the question, 'Why be good if no one is watching'? If there is no one to police the act, maybe the act does not really count?

Egotism and revenge

Aggressive people tend to be arrogant, superior and conceited and this can result in harm to others. Revenge can also be a motivating factor in unethical behaviour—with the intention of making the other suffer. Often people who have been humiliated go on to act in in harmful and hurtful ways.

True believers and idealists

Idealism is often attributed to good motives and noble (if at times unrealistic) pursuits. Adolf Eichmann believed that an idealist was a man who lived for his idea, and was prepared to sacrifice everything, and everybody, in pursuit of that idea (Arendt, 1963). There are many examples of 'good men' doing a great deal of harm; part of the fallout from their actions can be the disillusionment of others who followed them. Examples such as the cult leaders David Karesh and Charles Manson come to mind, who were seen by their followers to be moralistic, virtuous and idealistic, yet ultimately were very harmful. Noble ideals sometimes equal evil actions. Idealistic harm is nearly always perpetrated by groups who may have good intentions alongside bad actions. Idealism often provides a right to hate, as those in 'the fold' are taught to be superior, elite. There is a 'discontinuity effect', whereby the group tends to be more extreme than the sum of its individual members. 'Making the world a better place' is often the mantra of idealist groups which gives them a perceived right to deal unethically with others who are different, e.g. non-believers, and this is justified on the basis of their (ignorant) status as non-believers. Within the dominant group, principles can be considered more important than people, e.g. rules related to reproductive health; those who tithe more will have a 'better spot' in heaven.

Omission as an unethical stance

Omission is another way in which unethical behaviour enters the world. While we can see the obvious effects of our actions and behaviours, we often miss the role of omission in ethical decision making. What we have not done often leaves us as culpable and blameworthy as what we have done. Few of us would not blame the individual who watched as a child walked into a river and did nothing about it when they could. We can engage in unethical behaviour by *not* giving information we have that would help others, *not* giving medical help if needed, *not* allowing others to make decisions about their life, or not ending a helping relationship with another because it was advantageous to us to keep it going. *Not* doing can be as evil as doing.

Standing up or standing down: The bystander role

Petruska Clarkson (1997), in *The Bystander: An End to Innocence in Human Relationships*, argues that the 'bystander stance' is a chosen ethical position, and not one where it is possible to deny responsibility. A well-known proverb is, 'All that is needed for evil to prosper is for good men [or women presumably] to do nothing'. Doing nothing, or colluding with doing nothing, is morally immature and ethically unsustainable. Clarkson defines the bystander as 'a person who does not become actively involved in a situation where someone requires help' (p. 6). There are many public examples of this, such as the well-known murder of Kitty Genovese in New York in 1964. She was murdered over a period of about half an hour while several dozen people watched, heard her shouting and did nothing. Why not?

Most of us know the feeling. How many have watched others being bullied or harassed, and done nothing? How many injustices have we seen in the workplace, and done nothing? How often have we witnessed comments and racist jokes, and done nothing? For Clarkson (1997), the 'bystander stance' or 'bystander apathy' generally involves one or more of the following:

- 'It's none of my business' (Pontius Pilate).
- 'I want to remain neutral (I don't want to take sides).'
- 'The truth lies somewhere in the middle.'
- 'I don't want to rock the boat.'
- 'It's more complex than it seems.'
- 'I don't have all the information' (ignorance is bliss).
- 'I don't want to get burned again.'
- 'My contribution won't make any difference' (Who? Me?).
- 'I'm only telling the truth as I see it.'
- 'I am only following orders' (the Nuremburg defence).
- 'I am just keeping my own counsel.'
- 'They brought it on themselves really' (victim blaming).

Fundamental to the process of the bystander position is discounting: discounting the existence of what is happening, discounting the significance of the situation, discounting that it has something to do with me, and discounting my ability to resolve the issue (Clarkson, 1997).

It may be interesting to reflect back on the exercise you did at the beginning of this chapter, and see if you used any of these mechanisms!

While there are times when it is good not to get involved, and times to stand by and watch and wait (without being a bystander), faithfulness to who I am (my responsibility) and to who you are for me (my responsibility to you), means there are times when not to act is itself a moral decision and, at times, an ethically flawed or immature decision. Marcel (1952) describes it well:

> In fidelity, I am making a response: I am not merely being consistent with myself, but I am bearing witness to another-than-me. Fidelity is not a mere act of will, it is faith in the presence of another-than-me to which I respond and to which I shall continue to respond. It is this continuous response in the bond of fidelity which is my life and my permanence… Fidelity is response to a person. (Clarkson, 1997, p. 12)

The bystander position is one of collusion. From an ethical perspective can we do anything about it? Clarkson (1997) suggests five steps to help us move from bystander apathy:

1. *notice* something is happening
2. *interpret* the situation as one in which help is needed
3. *assume* personal responsibility
4. *choose* a form of assistance
5. *implement* the assistance.

Denial

One of the most significant ways evil, harm and unethical behaviour can enter our world is through denial. We can block out and repress what is happening. We change reality to suit ourselves by how we interpret that reality. The following are examples of ways we can move into denial.

- *Outright denial:* It didn't happen, I didn't do it. I wasn't there. Denial of facts.
- *Denial of the implications:* Sure I drink, but I can handle it.
- *Denial of feelings:* Doesn't bother me, am I bothered?
- *Denial of need to change:* I am human, so what?
- *Discredit:* You are biased, gullible. It is more complex than you realise.
- *Rename it:* I was challenging her (bullying). I was fact-finding (torture).
- *Justify it:* Good came out of it, so that meant it was good to do.
- *Denial of responsibility:* Can't remember a thing. My urges got the better of me. She asked for it.
- *Denial of injury:* I was only joking. It was an accident. It didn't hurt that much. She bruises easily.
- *Denial of victim:* He hit me first. She asked for it.

Cohen (2001) suggests another framework for the analysis of denial.

- *Passive 'not knowing':* I cannot be blamed. Not my fault.
- *Active 'not knowing':* Not trying to find out, and, 'Don't tell me'. As the Nazi Albert Speer said about the death camps, 'I didn't inquire because I didn't want to know' (Callaghan, 1991, p. 154).
- *Passive 'not doing':* Indifference.
- *Active 'not doing':* Silence or collusion. Collusion is mutually reinforcing denials.

Developing and sustaining strategies to save ourselves from being unethical

In the face of the multitude of ways of being unethical, how might we avoid the seductions to do wrong? Some ways that can help us include:

- do not think *I*, think *we*
- consider issues of power, domination, privilege and how they can move over easily into abuse and harm of others who are less privileged
- ask yourself if you would recommend what you are about to do to someone else
- try to look at the behaviour, not the intention—what am I actually doing? Too often we use our intention (which is almost always good) to evaluate our behaviour (which is often not that good)
- ask yourself how this might this be perceived from the other's point of view—use empathy to view actions from the recipient's point of view, which helps us to realise that to experience it from that other viewpoint can create a radical change in what we do
- look for the truth in the opposite position to the one you hold— this can expose the error in your point of view
- ask yourself: what are my ways and habits of denial?
- identify your Achilles heel
- beware of the extremity of your ideals (fundamentalism).

Conclusion

In this chapter we have described many seductions into, and justifications for, evil and unethical acts. Two things are important to note. First, none of us are exempt from the influences for unethical behaviour. The idea that it is all beneath us can be the beginning of turning down our moral sensitivity and turning away from ethical reflection. Instead, it is important to consider: how can I imagine myself being drawn into that behaviour/ mindset? What would it take for me to cross a line? Ethical behaviour is about *all* of us, all of the time, not just the corrupt few. Second, ethical maturity means we have to bring our vulnerabilities with regard to ethical behaviour into conscious awareness. For example, how are we taking care of ourselves? Self-care and the slippage into burnout provides a context for some ethical fading. What areas do we think we have covered, and how do we know that for a fact? What is it that we have never discussed or considered? We will explore these issues in a lot more detail in subsequent chapters.

Chapter 3

A very, very short history of ethics

The field of ethics and ethical decision making is theoretically complex. Traditions of ethics and moral theory have been developed within philosophy, theology and, more recently, psychology. Many of the most influential historical figures, starting with Aristotle and his famous Nicomachean Ethics, have tried to make sense of ethical and moral decisions. Thomas Aquinas, Kant, Descartes, Hume are but a few who have given us theories on how morals and ethics work. In our modern era, academics and philosophers such as Peter Singer, Lawrence Kohlberg and James Rest have spent their professional lives considering ethical issues, ethical development and moral reasoning. Modern approaches to ethics explore human rights theories, ethics of trust, ethics of care, relational ethics, feminist approaches to ethics, ecological ethics and communicative ethics, among others. While space does not allow a detailed summary of these theories, it is important to get a sense of the historical components that make up thinking on ethical and moral development.

Hugman (2005) describes four traditions that combine to make up the historical journey of moral understanding, and we have identified three more. These traditions are not discrete, are not always exclusive of each other, and interweave throughout history. Figure 3.1 illustrates these seven traditions.

Kant, the undoubted patron saint of the rational approach, would find it difficult to accept that genuine moral decisions could be made by anything other than rational means. For him, 'moral instruction is the product of pure practical reason, unsullied by the conditional or the practical' (Thiele, 2006, p. 31). Such a view could not allow emotion or intuition to be a valid basis for moral judgement. However, other traditions sit well together and, at times, create effective learning partnerships, e.g., developmental traditions merge easily with other traditions.

Figure 3.1: Seven Traditions in Ethical History (Adapted from Hugman, 2005)

Most of the traditions have had an era or time of ascendency, not necessarily in any historical order. The philosophical tradition was a beginner in moral history, but reappears at different times to reassert its claim that ethical decisions emerge from who we are. Clearly, the zeitgeist or time in which we live influences how popular one tradition will be, and how unpopular another might become. Today, we shy away from universal laws applicable to all circumstances, and are wary of rules and regulations that cover all events and instances. We are all aware of diversity in race, culture, sexual orientation, to mention but a few, and anxious that we do not tread on the toes of others simply because they are different.

From our point of view, like the Dodo's verdict in *Alice in Wonderland*, 'Everybody has won and all must have prizes'. Each tradition represents what we consider a partial truth in ethical deliberation and, at times, each comes to the fore as the best method to support making ethical decisions in particular contexts. We do not see one tradition as any more important than another. However, which tradition we call on to influence what we do when faced with a moral dilemma or problem, or what combination of traditions we employ in this instance, will depend on a number of factors, e.g., how quickly and intuitively we know what to do (philosophical tradition), when to call on reason to work towards a logical conclusion (rationalist approach), or when we stay with the relationship and make it the central tenet of how we make a decision. Perhaps the skill of moral decision making is a bit like an artist mixing colours: to know which colours to mix together, and in what amounts, to attain the desired result is not an easy task.

Tradition one: Philosophical traditions

Tradition one, perhaps the oldest of the traditions, can be called the 'philosophy' era. The Greek philosophers (Aristotle, Plato and Socrates) were all exponents of this approach. Socrates famously accosted people in the streets of Athens and challenged them: 'Do you take care of yourself?' This is to say, do you think about what is truly important in life, and do you live your life accordingly? This tradition in ethical history comprises the era of a personal sense of honour and the character of the person. Being of 'good character' meant at the time to display virtues such as, being trustworthy, having integrity, being honest, prudent, having fortitude and so on. There were no codes of ethics as such, but rather an individual ethics combined at times with adherence to a common agreement (e.g., the Hippocratic Oath).

This focus on individual ethics and ethics of character (virtues) was enforced by European medieval culture, which prized honour, chivalry, character, one's good name and reputation. Its strength was the placement of responsibility on the individual, and its weakness was the lack of emphasis on any external controls or guidelines for the individual. This era of 'virtues' had roots in the Old Testament and was communicated through story, proverb and role models such as Socrates, who lived a virtuous life. Aristotle argued that, while we may not be able to apply virtue ethics as a sole assessment of ethical action, possession of moral character and moral sensitivity is crucial if we are to implement any rules well. For example, a judge who is an interpreter of the law first needs to be able to read the situation ethically and legally in order to apply the relevant laws and sanctions (Hinman, 2008).

Ultimately, as Haidt (2006) points out, an emphasis based solely on virtues was challenged with the beginnings of scientific inquiry, which searched for the laws underpinning moral stances. While there was an emphasis on the individual nature of ethics, at the same time there was suspicion of individual subjectivity, intuition and emotions, and even dire warnings about their role in decision making. In his famous analogy of the mind as a chariot pulled by two horses, Plato described the soul as conflicted, torn between reason and emotion, intellect and the senses. The rational brain is the charioteer, holding the reigns. One horse is rough and ill-bred, representing negative and destructive emotions; the other is well-bred and well-behaved. The task of the charioteer is to keep the dark horse (negative emotions, temptations) in check, and to keep the chariot moving forward in a reasoned and reasonable way. If the driver and horses want different things, the driver must prevail (Lehrer, 2009).

In 2011, we witnessed a contemporary example of the ongoing importance of moral character as one measure of ethical practice through the case of Wikileaks and the role of Julian Assange. While debate around the actions of Julian Assange focused initially on his argument that it was his duty to expose wrongdoing and it was the right of the community to have (classified) information, ultimately the debate turned to the question of his character, and whether any of his actions could be seen to have been initiated from a moral place. Aristotle, who was somewhat hard-line on this, would say that an assessment of character is crucial in any judgement of moral action. Others have argued that even immoral people can at times do good.

Tradition two: Religious tradition—universality and divine command theories

This era was notable in its search for universal truths to guide people in making ethical decisions. It is called the 'religious era' of ethics in that it was espoused and led by religion, and Christianity in particular. Its aim was to promote universal truths and 'divine commands' to guide understandings of ethics, making ethics more of an objective rather than a subjective decision, and taking away any emphasis on individual decision making, context or circumstance. A leading figure in moral theory in Western religion has been Thomas Aquinas, who argued that truth is known through reason (natural revelation) and faith (supernatural revelation). When there is conflict between reason and religion it is argued that religion should take precedence, as ultimately God's commands will provide the right path (and even natural revelation will commonly lead people to realisations about God). Some would still argue that religion is central to ethics. In Australia throughout 2010–11 there was vigorous and, at times, vitriolic debate about whether the teaching of ethics in schools should be offered at the same time as religous instruction, presenting an alternative to church teachings for developing the ethical sensitivity and moral frameworks of children. The fundamentalist argument is that modern day ethics only offers a relativist position, often parodied as an 'it depends' framework, which leads to a lack of the moral clarity that God and the church have always provided. This has rekindled the debate about whether ethics requires authoritarian, and in particular, divine guidance. However, in contemporary society we are less likely to see a strongly religious framework in the expression of 'universal truths' such as the ten commandments, and more likely to see an emphasis on accepted community or professional values through ethical codes and frameworks (which many relate to as 'Thou shalt not...' type documents). For example, in the ethical codes of the British Association of Counselling and Psychotherapy (BACP, 2010) and the Psychotherapy and Counselling Federation of Australia (PACFA, 2010) the core values of the profession are listed up front and shape subsequent clauses: respecting human rights and dignity, ensuring integrity of relationships, increasing personal effectiveness, etc. The strength offered by an emphasis on universal truths is the provision of clear, objective guidelines to support the making of ethical decisions: its weakness is that it can take responsibility away from the individual who ultimately needs to explore the 'rule' in their own circumstances and may not have developed the independence of thought to know what to do.

Another contemporary framework that reflects the application of accepted 'truths' relates to human rights theories. This body of work focuses on the establishment of a moral floor, under which there would be common acceptance that we, as global community members, should never sink. We live in times where there is an emphasis on respecting the positions of others, cultural and religious differences, and the importance of autonomy and self-determination. Given these, the question becomes: are there values that bind us, across communities and cultures, or is everything relative to individual circumstances? Debates in relation to this question have centred on possible absolutes, such as the rights of children to safety, the right not to be tortured, the rights of living things (not just people, but also animals), and the right to certain freedoms (e.g., speech, non-interference). While some of the earliest formulations of strong doctrines of natural rights (e.g., constitutions of countries such as the USA) saw them founded in religious terms, other considerations about rights have included appeals to self evidence (prima facie cases where rights are considered 'obvious at first glance', e.g., in relation to children), natural law, and the inherent characteristics of groups themselves that rights should be conferred. For example, if it is assumed that one of the fundamental characteristics of humans is their ability to reason, then there may be rights in relation to their entitlement to autonomy of decision making, or non-interference in their pursuit of rational decision making. Further, while Thomas Aquinas argued that only humans have rights, modern debates are much more likely to extend to animals, the environment and to future generations (Hinman, 2008).

Tradition three: The dominance of rationality and reason

This tradition represents the role of reason and rationality in ethics. It locates reason as the method, and possibly the only method for making ethical decisions. Haidt (2006) views Kant as the patron saint of the solely rational approach to ethics: 'Ten thousand pounds sterling to the first philosopher who can come up with a single moral rule, to be applied through the power of reason that cleanly separates good from bad. Had there been such a prize, it would have gone to the German philosopher, Immanuel Kant' (p. 161). Kant founded deontological theory, which argues that an action has moral worth if it is done for the sake of duty, and if it can be expressed as a universal law (Hinman, 2008). He called this the 'categorical imperative': Is what you are about to do able to be recommended as action that anyone should take in similar circumstances? This test is a useful way to screen out the unique and emotive aspects of a situation, which often have undue weight in any given decision, and can skew the outcome in a range of ways. Consider the following possibilities:

Arthur had been married to Bea for thirty years when she was diagnosed with severe dementia. Gradually, the woman he had known disappeared, and he became a carer of a woman he no longer recognised. Arthur always spoke vehemently about people who had affairs as morally corrupt and said that it was never acceptable in a relationship. However, he fell in love with one of his wife's nurses. Suddenly, he wondered: 'Is the rule that affairs are never acceptable to apply in this very unusual situation? Do I now say "affairs are never acceptable unless…" or is this a way of me just getting what I want?'

Roger was a family law specialist who had been single for some years. He worked very long hours and was dedicated to his work above all other things. He took on a new case of a woman in the middle of a messy divorce. They began a relationship. Roger knew this was professionally frowned on. However, he wondered, with both of them single and grown up, was there any real harm done? After all, don't the statistics say that most people meet their partners through work? Even though generally he wouldn't recommend this as a course of action to others in his field, could he justify this exception given how dedicated he was to his work and how significant his contribution to his profession?

If you were to apply the categorical imperatives relevant to these situations, then the debate becomes: when might the making of an exception that relates to the individual desires of the people involved be legitimate? Kant would say that if an exception is legitimate, then it should be able to be expressed in another categorical imperative. In the first example, one might imagine something like: 'Affairs are generally unacceptable in most committed relationships, except in cases where one person is no longer able to participate in the relationship.' However, even this would need to be worked through further. How do you define participation? Who gets to decide who is participating or not? In the second scenario, if the professional imperative was applied, i.e. that relationships with clients are not acceptable, then it would be harder to argue this exception, which does seem to relate to individual need and desire, rather than forming a basis for a genuine and generalisable exception. For Roger, it would look like: 'Lawyers should not form relationships with their clients unless they really want to and have no other immediate social life.' That probably would not slip past Kant.

Within this ethical tradition, there was no room for intuition, gut feeling, sense experience, or feeling. Kant would argue that doing the right thing is doing the rational thing; immorality is the result of illogical thinking (Lehrer, 2009). There is great value in working out logically and rationally how and why we make ethical decisions. It moves ethics away from relying on situation and character, and towards moral reasoning based on logic. Its weakness is twofold. First, it relies solely on intellect, rather than any other factor (emotion, situations and relationships) which can mean crucial aspects for consideration are missed, and second, we may not practise what we have reasonably worked out, largely because of those factors that have been excluded. Implementation is not always as straightforward as the decision making itself. Over the last 20 years in particular, the assumption that the best decisions are the ones that rely on reason has been questioned as inadequate, or at least too restrictive (e.g., Gilligan, 1982; Butler, 2005; Lehrer, 2009; Fine, 2007). Haidt (2006) pithily notes that, 'Trying to make children behave ethically by teaching them to reason well is like trying to make a dog happy by wagging its tail. It gets causality backwards' (p. 165).

Tradition four: Diversity and integration

There is intense interest in issues of diversity today. As we have come to grips with the reality of globalisation, so we need to live and work well on a local and global level with issues of difference. Hinman (2008) suggests that any serious consideration of race, ethnicity and culture should involve three main issues. First, the 'identity' argument maintains that race, ethnicity or culture is central to the identity of the moral agent, and partially determines what is morally right for that individual. Second, there is a question that relates to minority rights, and whether minority groups possess any special rights that do not belong to the population as a whole. This is an important question when we think about issues of differing levels of power, access and disadvantage. Third, there is the question of what virtues are required to live well in a multicultural society.

In addition to issues of cultural diversity, there are issues related to gender, and inclusion of female voices in what has largely been a male-driven ethics enterprise. As Hinman (2008) writes 'it is difficult to appreciate the enormity of the exclusion of women from the history of ethics...if one looks at the history of moral thought, it is as if women hardly existed' (p. 296).

This component in ethical and moral maturity requires us to combine and integrate a number of approaches: situation ethics, relational ethics, ethics of care, emotional and communicative ethics, and ecological ethics. It considers the contextual issues involved in ethics (situation ethics) with the particular demands of specific relationships. This approach also posits a 'moral intelligence', i.e., that we are born with a moral faculty that is fine-tuned by our context. Just as we have an innate facility to speak, and learn to particularise this in the environment and relationships that support us to speak a particular language, so too we are born with an innate ability to know what is right and wrong, which, in turn, is activated by the contexts in which we grow up. From these perspectives, impartiality is seen as a sham, a fanciful illusion. Instead, we are always working with active discriminations between people, between the dominant and minority groups, those 'with' and those 'without'. People identify with certain groups in complex ways that may or may not reflect the categories which governing powers choose to acknowledge. For example, Aboriginals were not officially included in the national census in Australia until 1971. Prior to that, they were in effect 'non-people' for the purposes of community identification. Ethnicity can also be a cultural phenomenon as much as biological phenomenon, with cultural groups identifying their ethnicity according to living circumstances, shared social experiences and community ties. In so far as ethnicity and culture are central to identity, they must also be central to moral identity (Hinman, 2008).

The work of Carol Gilligan (1982) has been crucial in reflecting on the influence of gender on moral reasoning and decision making. She suggests that differences in socialisation and personality development create key differences in the evaluation of moral issues. For example, relationships and dependency are experienced differently for boys and girls. Boys are encouraged to individuate, reduce their dependency on parents (especially their mothers), and to value separateness above intimacy. Thus the rational, logical approaches to moral reflection fit a style of gendered socialisation. It is certainly the case that the majority of philosophical figures who prize autonomy, reason and disconnection from individual circumstances and relationships, are men. What this excludes, according to Gilligan, is the connection with the female experience, which instead privileges trust in emotion and intuition, as well as reason. Further, a test of a good decision from a female standpoint is a measurement of its effect on relationships and connectedness. In traditional paradigms, this can only muddy the waters.

These traditions of ethical development place the focus of ethical decision making in different areas.

- The individual makes the decision based on his or her moral character and (cultural and gendered) identity as a moral agent.
- We look to universal truths which guide, influence and sometimes dictate what we should do.
- We reason our way to what is right and good.
- We build our ethical decisions on relationships, fidelity, trust and our involvement in the world.

Tradition five: Developmental models of ethics

Until the last 20 years, much of the theory developed in the field of ethics focused on people being moral or not, rational or not. There was no exploration of how people developed ethically and, as a result, this important literature has emerged, making a significant contribution to our understanding of moral development. A number of key researchers and theorists such as Piaget, Kohlberg, Gilligan and Rest have now suggested that there are definite, chronological stages, each with its own way of describing how we develop the capacity to think, reason and make ethical decisions. Developmental models are generally unhelpful if they become a tool to measure shortfalls and inadequacies. However, they can be of great assistance in the design of educational and parenting opportunities that foster the ability of children to think ethically for themselves. It is also sobering to note that this research has underlined the need for adults to keep learning in this area; the notion that we may be 'formed and complete' as adults is debunked. There is plenty to suggest that moral character is evolving and developing throughout the lifespan. All the more reason for institutions and associations to look at their obligations to enhance development of members/staff/community rather than only focus on regulation and rule setting.

Lawrence Kohlberg (1982) observed through his wartime experiences that some people defied orders and laws for the sake of an identified higher good. There are many examples of this through the resistance movements. Often these actions were not for personal gain, but for the sake of a higher (ethical) good. Kohlberg would go on to spend his life trying to answer the question: how is it that some people obeyed this higher ethic or principle, whereas others refused to deviate from the written law of the day? (Hinman, 2008).

Kohlberg's model expanded on the work of Piaget, and involved six stages within three different levels. Unlike Piaget, he believed that moral development is a continual process that occurs across the lifespan. People pass through stages at different rates, with most never getting past the fourth of the six stages. Through his research, Kohlberg saw these stages as universal, sequential and irreversible. These stages are:

Preconventional morality (stages 1 and 2—early childhood) dominated by the need to avoid punishment and to ensure reciprocity: If I do the right thing by you, you'll do the right thing by me.

Conventional morality (stages 3 and 4—adolescence and adulthood). These stages involve the desire to be good in the eyes of self and others, and the development of a 'law and order' mentality, i.e., internalising rules of the day.

Postconventional morality (stage 5) involves an orientation to social contracts, in which 'reasoned rights are given reasoned acceptance and revised in the light of well-reasoned critical discussions'. Stage 6, which he argued would only be reached by people such as Ghandi, is 'characterised by an orientation toward universal ethical principles of justice, reciprocity, equality and respect. These principles are arrived at through reason and are freely accepted' (Hinman 2008, p. 300).

Carol Gilligan constructed a different theory of moral development, which she believed went some way to correcting the masculine bias in the work of Piaget and Kohlberg. Piaget emphasised gendered differences. He reported that males had the more developed moral sense, through their favouring of legalistic (rule-bound) frameworks and fair procedures for managing conflict; females were reported as being more pragmatic and tolerant towards rules, more willing to make exceptions. Piaget believed that legalistic skills were essential to moral development, and ultimately concluded that this ability was far less developed in girls (Gilligan, 1982).

Gilligan argued that in order to understand moral development and moral struggle, the relational context in which people live has to be considered. Rather than the image of the separate, autonomous man that dominates much of moral philosophy, she argued that the dilemma for most of us (and to which women are more drawn) is how to be/become a 'self' independent of the weighty influence of others. Her focus was on the significance of power, gender and relational influence in any analysis of ethical reflection. She argued that relationships, being core to who we are in the world, provide a crucial context for moral development and an essential feature of our ethical decision making. Gilligan's framework of moral development, reflecting the experience of women and centred on an ethic of care, involves three levels and two transitional stages between levels:

1. Individual survival. Transition from selfishness to responsibility.
2. Goodness comes to be equated with self-sacrifice. Transition to include the self as well as self-sacrifice.
3. Caring for both self and others.

Tradition six: Intuitive moral intelligence

This tradition contains a number of approaches. First, it suggests that humans are born with a moral sense, a moral intelligence (Hauser, 2006). We know intuitively what is right and wrong. Some of these principles seem to cross human boundaries and are common in all cultures. While born with the reptilian stance of 'me-first', we are also born with compassion, empathy and mirror neurons that move us towards moral concerns and moral stances. 'Nobody has to teach a child to demand fair treatment; nobody has to teach us to admire a person who sacrifices for a group. Nobody has to teach us to disdain someone who betrays a friend or is disloyal to a family or tribe. Nobody has to teach a child the differences between rules that are moral and rules that are not…there is a great deal of evidence to suggest that people are actually born with more structured moral foundations, a collection of moral senses that are activated by different situations' (Brooks, 2011, pp. 285–6).

Second, the intuitive tradition suggests there are times when ethical decisions just emerge from within—we know what to do without thinking or even bringing the ethical process into deliberation. Aristotle favoured this approach where moral action instinctively emerges from who we are. While strong on deliberation and reflection, and on intelligence as a key virtue in making moral decisions, Aristotle reserved the highest moral virtue for the person of habit, the individual who just knows what to do. He writes, 'Habit…is practice long pursued, that at last becomes man himself' (Thiele, 2006, p. 23). Practical judgement or practical wisdom (phronimos) guides the person of good habits to know what to do automatically. This is action informed by thought, and Aristotle was always keen to link any ethical decisions with reflective deliberation.

Haidt (2001), an advocate of this approach, calls on neuroscience to back up this method of ethical decision making. Automatic or intuitive decision making is one of the brain's methods for coming to moral conclusions. Daniel Kahneman (2012) calls this 'system 1' (in contrast to system 2, our deliberate and conscious way of making decisions). 'As we navigate our lives, we normally allow ourselves to be guided by impressions and feelings, and the confidence we have in our intuitive beliefs and preferences is usually justified' (p. 4). Both Haidt and Kahneman see emotion as playing a key role in our intuitive decision making processes. Haidt considers common in-built morals in life, and suggests five moral concerns:

1. harm/care
2. fairness/reciprocity
3. authority/respect
4. purity/disgust
5. in-group/loyalty.

Tradition seven: Relational approaches to ethics

This seventh tradition places relationships at the heart of ethics, and sees our ability to connect to one another as the basis of ethical decisions and ethical decision making (for a fuller consideration of this tradition see Chapter 5 on relational ethics). De Waal (2009) is in no doubt about the evolutional basis of ethics—it emerges from the ability of mammals to relate to one another. Cooperation, familiarity, communication, emotional connection and resonance all play a part in relationships, as does attachment and rapport.

However, in this seventh tradition we are also looking at the concept of complexity theory as applied to relationships. This is what Stacey (2010) calls 'complex responsive processes of relating' (p. xi). In this approach, the self can only be formed in interaction with others. Just as Winnicott said there was no such thing as a baby (there was a mother and baby), so there is no such thing as a person who has not been formed in the relationships of life. We are who we are in relationship. Stacey argues that this is not social determinism, since the person has the ability to have spontaneous responses. He puts it as 'each person in the interaction is acting in the present on the basis of expectations for the future that arise in accounts of the past, all in the action of the present' (p. 4). In relationships, we constrain others and are constrained by them, we enable others and are enabled by them. Because futures are unpredictable, we make choices based on values and norms that emerge from the interplay in relationships that are co-created as we live them.

In the relational ethics traditions, relationships are seen to be foundational anchors in two ways. The first requires an awareness of being in relationship, understanding the requirements of relationships to maintain fidelity and connection, and using empathy and compassion to form the basis of decisions. Keeping promises to my friend are all the more ethical because he or she is my friend; being faithful in my relationship with my husband/wife prohibits certain actions that could contravene the relationship.

The second way to understand how relationships are foundational anchors for ethics is to see relationships as co-creations where we forge and fashion the dance with other participants that ultimately brings about 'our relationship'. In the present co-creation, we do not enter the relationship with foregone conclusions. Of course, we will have norms and values, and past experiences, and prior relationships, and even this relationship will have a history. However, what makes the relationship ethical is my ability to respond in the immediacy of the co-created relationship. Complex systems and adaptation to complex relationship and conversational systems does not mean ethical relativism (everything depends on the moment and everything goes), but requires us to be alert and watchful in relation to the present demands of the relationship.

Ethical codes

Besides these seven traditions that overlap, interweave and change between being foreground and background on the historical moral stage, there is also a history of ethical codes. Bond (2005) traces the history of how ethical professional codes came into existence and names Thomas Percival (1740–1804) as a key person in this development. Asked by the Manchester Infirmary to ensure the hospital never again closed its doors on needy patients during an epidemic, he and a committee devised a code of medical ethics (his book, *Medical Ethics*, was published in 1803, the first of its kind). He was the first person to use the terms 'medical ethics' and 'professional ethics'. His code incorporated several ideas that were new:

- It took ethical responsibility away from the individual and located it firmly with the profession. A collective responsibility took over from individual responsibility.
- The new code was written in a very different tone and voice from previous codes. It was written in the second and third person rather than the first.
- The code tended to be constructed as rules, which in turn gave rise to the tenet 'what is not explicitly forbidden is permitted'. This again can result in the mentality of 'What is the minimum I need to do in order to fulfil my professional responsibilities?', and in Bond's words, can result in 'skilled and informed obedience'. Bond makes the point that examples abound (two of which are the Enron scandal and the Nuremberg trials) showing how obedience to the rules and 'externalising ethical responsibility onto a supervisor authority can extinguish any sense of personal ethical responsibility' (p. 13).

Now all professional associations are required to have a code of ethics as part of their community obligation. While codes may be used as a rule book, this is rarely sufficient for the complexities of practice. What is far more important to consider are the principles and values on which the code was founded. If the rules don't fit the circumstances, the principles and values can provide guidance and a way forward.

Modern ethics

Bond (2007) presents slightly different eras in the modern history of ethics within the helping professions.

Era One (in the 1970s) continues the era of paternalism within ethics. This era was characterised by the fact that clients would trust those who were qualified to use their skills and expertise for the well-being of others. Bond (2006) puts it well, 'Trust me, I am a doctor, places both patient and doctor within an ethic of paternalistic beneficence that retains professional autonomy for the doctor and, at its most extreme, demands the silent compliance of the patient' (p. 80). Trusting others simply because they had the power of authority, or expertise, or qualification disappeared rapidly in the 1980s, with a whole raft of scandals and abuse of power, especially amongst religions and, in particular, professional religious people, such as priests.

Era Two saw respect for client autonomy placed centre stage. The focus moved from 'power over' to 'power with' and then 'power within' (autonomy). How could the professional facilitate the client to make decisions on his/her own behalf, and trust that clients knew what was best for them, given the right relationship (power sharing) and right environment (to take responsibility for themselves)?

Client autonomy was one of a number of principles that became the bedrock of ethical behaviour (see BACP Ethical Framework, 2010; PACFA Code of Ethics, 2011).

Era Three moved to 'bilateral trust as a bridge that could span substantial human difference'. This is an ethic of relational trust. Bond (2007) defines trust as 'a relationship of sufficient quality and resilience to withstand the challenges arising from difference, inequality, risk and uncertainty' (p. 436). The trust is two-way, with helpers providing the 'emotional container' that allows clients to begin their journeys to healing.

Some questions that emerge from the history of ethics

Throughout the various eras and traditions of ethical consideration, a series of perennial questions keep raising their heads. We all have to face these questions and find some method to make sense of them for ourselves. It is difficult to begin the process of finding ethical compasses if we have not struggled with some ethical questions and come to some personal conclusions about how to answer them. You might like to stop at this stage and consider where you are in relation to these questions and how you would go about answering them for yourself:

- Is truth to be found 'out there' or truth to be found within? Is there objective ethics and/or subjective ethics?
- How do conscious and unconscious aspects of ethical decision making relate to one another?
- Do we use rational approaches alone or a rational/emotional/ intuitive combination when making ethical decisions?
- Moral character or moral objectives? Which becomes the basis for ethical decision making?
- Are there stages to our ethical development as we move through life?
- Can we trust people to make ethical decisions? How much can we leave to the individual and how much should we prescribe? What is the role of authority in ethical decisions?
- Ethics in the profession, or ethics for the individual, or both?
- Why does harm and evil (unethical/immoral behaviour) enter the world?
- What kinds of harm are there?
- How do individuals, groups and organisations make ethical decisions?
- How have ethics/morals changed over the years? What is the role of context and environment in ethics?
- How much are we receivers of our moral codes and how much do we determine them ourselves?
- What is the connection between ethics, God, religion and wisdom traditions?
- Is there a moral intelligence alongside other forms of intelligence?
- How free are we to make ethical choices? Is there really free will?
- How responsible are we as individuals, as groups and as organisations, for the decisions we make, and how far should we be accountable for these decisions?

Conclusion

This chapter has presented seven traditions in the history of ethics and three eras in the development of ethical codes and frameworks. The traditions are not chronological, although some are particular to historical eras. To present them makes us realise the complexity of the field of ethical understanding, how little agreement exists on how to define ethics, and on what basis we make ethical decisions.

Chapter 4

Socrates and Aristotle
Moral character and moral action

....

'If you don't stand for something, you'll fall for anything.'

(Nash 2002, p. 26)

'The unexamined life is not worth living.'

(Socrates)

'Tell me, Socrates, can virtue be learned or taught?'

(Meno's question to Socrates)

We have introduced the concept of ethical maturity and outlined some issues that face us when ethical dilemmas and issues raise their heads. There is no doubt about the complexity of the ethical domains of life, and that ethical decision making can be difficult, if not demanding. In this chapter, we make a leap and present two ancient Greek philosophers who set the scene and modelled the meaning of ethics over 2000 years ago: Socrates and Aristotle. We engage them as our guides as we begin this ethical odyssey. Socrates focuses on the question of what constitutes a good life, and what reflective (and challenging) dialogue can assist us best on this journey, while Aristotle introduces the importance of moral character in guiding ethical decisions. For us, moral character is crucial to the development of ethical maturity.

Socrates[1]

In 399 BC Socrates was condemned to death—a vote of 280 to 220 by the Athenian jury swung the verdict against him and in favour of the prosecution. Socrates was found guilty on two counts: disrespect towards

---

1   Facts about Socrates and his life are disputed. He wrote nothing himself and what we know about him comes from others, his student Plato in particular. We are not sure how much is fact and how much Plato interpreted the 'facts' to present the writings of his mentor.

the gods and corruption of the young. In a spirited defence, he argued that he had the utmost respect for the Greek deities, and that his aim in life was to help people, and young people in particular, to develop a humble curiosity that allowed them to pursue what was noble and best. Even as he uttered those words, Socrates knew that some parents were dismayed by questions their children brought home from their contact with him. These young people had started to imitate the questioning style of Socrates. You can imagine how that went down in many Greek homes!

Socrates could have informed the courtroom that he had the habit of wandering the streets of Athens, stopping individuals and questioning them on how they lived their lives. Those stopped would have remembered what he asked them, as it must have been an unusual moment in a normal day. 'How do you live your life? Are you happy? What are the principles that guide you? Have you thought about the values on which you base your behaviour? What is the ideal life you should be living?' Imagine being stopped by a stranger on your way to work, still not quite awake, your mind already engaged with the processes of the day, and being asked philosophical questions about what makes you tick? Most of us would not be amused. Some of us would have suggested that Socrates get a real job and join the real world!

One of us had a Socratic-like experience of being stopped in Trafalgar Square, London, by a young man with a Bible, wearing a T-shirt printed with the words 'Jesus Saves'. You can ascertain how Socratic-like the conversation was:

Stranger: 'Sir, do you know where you are going to spend eternity?'

Michael: (*taken aback by the question and the questioner, and who uses humour when in an embarrassing situation*): 'Yes, I think so. I hope to spend my eternity in Ireland.'

Stranger: 'No, Sir. Unless you repent you will spend your eternity in hell.'

Michael: (*wanting to end conversation, but not wanting to be too abrupt*): 'Are you telling me that Ireland is not an option?'

Stranger: 'You are not taking this conversation very seriously.'

Michael: 'No, I'm not. I'm waiting for someone, and I really don't want to have this conversation just now.'

Stranger: 'Very good. Thank you, Sir, and I hope you have a nice evening.'

Socrates would *not* have been proud of Michael. However, it is noteworthy that Michael has not forgotten the conversation and the sincere young man. Most of us, a bit like the Athens populace, do not want to be stopped by strangers, no matter how well-intentioned, and asked fundamental questions about our lives and the principles that guide them.

Socrates believed that all our energies should be focused on the good life and how to live it. Grayling (2007) notes that the vast majority of people accept conventional views about what life is for: working, family life and leisure time. In our choice of work, we have to accept the terms required of us. These terms become a measure of what is 'good', remain largely unquestioned and are accepted as sufficient. Teachers, for example, will have a 'local' sense of what is required of them and why, but may not ask a broader question such as, 'Why teach?' People aim to balance their work with family and leisure pursuits, and look forward to retirement as a conventional view of a satisfactory life. For many, this may equate to a 'good life', and all that could be reasonably expected. For Socrates this was insufficient. Instead, he would ask, 'Is there a goal, a purpose, a value in life that is worthwhile as an end in itself, and not merely as a means to other things?' While many might choose 'happiness' as a primary goal, how is this defined? In Socrates' day, it was common for happiness to be measured by strength and wealth. In contrast, Socrates argued, 'It is not wealth and success that make goodness, but goodness gives value to wealth and success.' For Socrates, 'virtue is knowledge', and the ultimate aim is 'perfection of the soul' (Grayling, 2007, p. 24).

Socrates argued that reflection on what life is about, and what a good life is, is connected to the self of a moral and reflective person. He challenged people to question their assumptions and values in their choice of actions. To understand the relationship between values and action in leading a good life, Socrates pushed for a departure from the pontification, monologue and point scoring so commonly displayed by leaders (then and now), and a move toward dialogue. In such dialogue, 'truth' as an objective reality is put to the side, and we enter conversations to learn with an open mind and heart. For Socrates, 'being open' means putting aside beliefs about knowing and acknowledging one's ignorance. Socrates made his position clear (recounted by Plato): 'I am wiser than this man: it is likely that neither of us knows anything worthwhile, but he thinks he knows something when he does not, whereas when I do not know, neither do I think that I know.'

The Socratic dialogue was a form of 'communal meditation' for Socrates, where, in a gentle and compassionate manner, questions were asked and assumptions unearthed. The rules of the game were clear: no one was to be pushed to believe or change what they did not believe. Have an open mind. Listen carefully to the other and be open to what emerges. Follow the truth, not your truth. Armstrong (2011) puts it well: 'The Socratic dialogue was a spiritual exercise designed to produce a profound psychological change in the participants—and because its purpose was that everybody should understand the depth of his ignorance, there was no way that anyone could win' (p. 122). As Socrates asked his questions and probed for truth, he was aware that if you want to help people think, do not start by stating your own position. If you do, people may be swayed by who you are, or what you said, or become defensive or argumentative. Socrates wanted to move from being an advocate of a position, to being a guide or animateur who helped others find out what they think and believe. He never shared his opinion first. Instead, he waited, questioned, lead, listened, drew out ideas and, for the moment, left his own opinions and theories at the discussion door.

Socrates could have enlightened the court that the stance of his Socratic dialogue was to question people compassionately and gently until they realised how little they knew and, from this uncertainty, were open to learning. He might have put it succinctly, 'You are condemning me to death because I promote uncertainty as a way of learning.' He would have been right. How many leaders are open to being uncertain? How many admit they don't know? How often will they credit the other with good points, and be open to whatever aspects of truth walk through the door?

Had Socrates pursued his defence with more depth, he might have declared that the point of his questions and compassionate conversations was to help individuals have a dialogue with themselves in order to know themselves. Much of his actions and life were based on the Delphic oracle's statement, 'Know thyself'. For Socrates, self-development began with holding one's opinions, values, attitudes and behaviour up to the light, and examining them in detail. Would it have changed anything for Socrates to remind the court of one of his most famous sayings, 'The unexamined or unreflected life is not worth living?' Probably not. Questioning oneself was the beginning of living life and working towards fundamental or transformational change. He often compared himself to his mother who was a midwife, the difference being that he delivered people to themselves. He was a deliverer of new life, new insights and growth. He was a midwife of the self or, as he put it, a midwife of the soul.

The remainder of the life of Socrates is well known. The prosecutor even suggested that he might want to choose his own punishment, having now been found guilty of the charges against him. Socrates suggested an annual stipend from the state and free meals for the rest of his life. Clearly, this was not what they had in mind, and the poison hemlock was chosen as his method of death.

After Socrates was sentenced, friends and colleagues advised him to escape from what was clearly a biased and unfair trial. One even suggested he had a duty to escape since he had three sons for whom he was responsible and abandoning them would be immoral. His friends also let him know they had the means to bribe the prison guards—it would not have been difficult to flee. They knew the authorities would turn a blind, friendly eye towards his escape, allowing them an outlet from killing one of their best-known and loved philosophers. However, Socrates replied that he had committed himself to uphold the laws of his city and his country and would accept the just or unjust judgement of the authorities. He talked of the social contract he had entered into with his community, and that running away would break that contract. He asked his followers not to take action or revenge after his death. For Socrates, fight and revenge were ignoble. Before his death, he told his followers that, for him, death was a liberation rather than a defeat. He stated that if there was an afterlife, he would continue his pursuit of truth and his Socratic questioning, and that he looked forward to meeting and having wonderful discussions with other philosophers like Homer and Hesiod—truly eternal bliss. In a light touch, he proposed that if there was no afterlife, then perpetual rest was something to look forward to after his rather hectic life. He added that his examination of the fundamental principles of life and living was his passion and that, in killing him, perhaps people were afraid to face up to these principles.

What was noticeable about Socrates was his ability to live his principles. He was who he talked about, Socrates was the action. He had moral sensitivity and moral character. We could not imagine this man of integrity, authenticity, dialogue and conversation needing much reflection and deliberation when faced with ethical decisions about whether or not he should accept the death sentence, or whether he should flee the city and the prison when he could have done so. We imagine he just knew what to do, and that his decision did not require conscious reflection. His was an unconscious, intuitive knowing that had come from a life of fine-tuning his ethical sensibilities. Hollis (2003) describes him as 'the sum of his choices' (p. 98). It is as if the decisions finally made him, rather than he made the decisions. He knew what he had to do because his principles were deep and personal, and had become part of who he was as a person. Socrates acknowledged a strange experience of a 'daimonion', or inner voice, that prohibited him from doing certain things, some trivial and some important. This inner voice instructed him in what not to do, but had no advice for him on what to do. Could this have been his intuitive sense, his inner guide, or perhaps his conscience? Who knows? It is interesting that he referred to ethical decisions that came from within and needed little reflection or deliberation.

Socrates was one of those spiritual leaders who viewed a place of 'unknowing' and questioning as most advantageous to begin the journey of learning. Plato captured it well for Socrates: 'It is only when all things, names and definitions, visual and other sensations are rubbed together and subjected to tests in which questions and answers are exchanged in good faith and without malice that finally, when human capacity is stretched to its limit, a spark of understanding and intelligence flashes out and illumines the subject at issue' (Armstrong, 2011, p. 110).

Aristotle

Aristotle, a pupil and successor of Plato, approached ethics from a different angle. His preoccupation centred on questions of human flourishing, with the promotion of human happiness central to leading a good life. As happiness could be defined by people in very different ways, depending on social position, Aristotle was particular in his choice of the Greek word for happiness, 'eudaimonia', which translates more closely to 'flourishing' and 'well-being' (Hinman, 2008).

Aristotle would have argued that happiness and human flourishing are related to 'practical wisdom'. This term puts two seemingly paradoxical elements together: action and contemplation. He was trying to convey the practical application of one's general moral view of a good life to specific situations through wisdom, which adds up to more than the mere mechanical application of rules (Hinman, 2008). Wisdom is informed by virtues that are neither natural, nor inborn, but are acquired through education, modelling and practice. These virtues become 'habits of the soul', inform decision making and action, and are always steered to good outcomes by reason.

For Aristotle, a focus on 'What ought I do?' was limited if it was not balanced with the question 'Who ought I be?'. This interesting question turns our focus to moral character, rather than action alone. The development of moral character is concerned with virtues and vices: those strengths and weaknesses of character that promote or impede human flourishing (Hinman, 2008). Aristotle argued that ethics requires both principles (codes, laws) and persons, as it is people who make decisions about what laws and principles apply. If principles are to be applied justly, then it will take people of good judgement and moral character. Aristotle's pursuit of 'What is virtue?' and 'What is moral character?' started a philosophical tradition known as 'virtue ethics', which is still influential today.

Every virtue causes its possessors to be in a good state and to perform their functions well. The virtue of the eyes, for instance, makes the eyes and their functioning excellent, because it makes us see well; and similarly, the virtue of a horse makes the horse excellent, and thereby good at galloping, at carrying its rider, and at standing steady in the face of the enemy. If this is true in every case, then the virtue of a human being will likewise be the state that makes a human being good and makes him perform his function well. (Book 2, *Nicomachean Ethics*, cited in Hinman, 2008, p. 263)

While Socrates might have argued that people do wrong out of ignorance of what is right, Aristotle considered how people can know what is right, but still do what is wrong for a variety of reasons, most notably a weakness of will. Thus the dieter who still eats chocolate cake is making a choice between rational and non-rational desire, described by Grayling (2003) as 'a contest in which the latter wins, making it happen that the person "sees the better but does the worse"' (p. 33). A knowledge of competing influences and desires is important to ethical awareness. We may not always choose what is 'good', as giving in to 'non-rational desire' can, at times, 'make sense' (and allow more access to chocolate cake).

Flourishing, for Aristotle, meant using the most unique property of human beings—our ability to reason and think. He argued that people of practical wisdom are people who can deliberate well about what is good for their life as a whole, not just for particular aspects. Aristotle emphasised two additional crucial aspects to the application of reasons and virtue. First, as human beings are social beings, happiness is seen in its social and political context. Any definition of flourishing would be impossible without attention to community. Second, he argued that we flourish when we use these capacities for the purposes of contemplation. Aristotle thought that withdrawal from life to think and reflect was crucial to effective reasoning. This, of course, can be at odds with other conceptions of happiness, which emphasise activity and achievement. As a result, Aristotle was criticised as elitist and self-indulgent in arguing for such a thing as time to reflect and contemplate (Hinman, 2008). We tend to privilege 'quick thinkers' and promote 'people of action'. However, to prize this aspect of decision making in matters of ethics can be highly erroneous. Compared to many philosophers of his day, who tended to be more abstract in their approach, Aristotle was seen to be more 'down to earth' and to have common sense. He saw that it was important to respect the opinions and beliefs of the ordinary person, not because they were necessarily right, but because their views might contain clues as to what was right, or might demand that we examine them in order to at least understand more about why people would believe in them.

Aristotle also argued that: 'discussions about the good life are not for the inexperienced, who will not be able to appreciate the point; rather they are for people who have seen something of the world, felt its sharp corners, tasted success and defeat in the concerns of humankind, and who will therefore be able to recognise what conduces to moral success in life's manifold business' (Grayling, 2003, p. 30).

It would seem that Aristotle would argue that ethical maturity is the willingness to consciously foster the disposition that enables us to apply the right virtues, such as compassion, to a particular situation, such as human suffering. He saw that development of one's disposition can mean establishing a middle path between opposing vices, for example, courage is the middle path between cowardice and rashness, proper self-love is the middle path between servility and arrogance. He believed there are rarely codes or rules to determine action. Instead, it is up to the moral agent to determine the right course of action from the facts of an individual case, based on practical wisdom or prudence. 'If one cannot be practically wise, says Aristotle, one should imitate those who are. Eventually this has a good chance of helping one learn how to be prudent, for in any case identifying the mean and acting in accordance with it in given situations is a matter of developing habits of practical wisdom and becoming skilled in ethical judgement' (Grayling, 2003, p. 33).

Becoming wise is a lifelong project. Socrates and Aristotle are arguably most influential in the foundations of ethical reflection. In leading a good life, questions of 'What ought I do', in balance with 'Who ought I be', provide a solid platform for any ethical decision making process. If we make decisions based on rules and reason alone, we may be inauthentic in our actions, and perhaps thoughtless in their delivery. If we make decisions based solely on our own sense of what is right, we may exclude information pertinent to the situation, and may be out of step with other standards and conventions. Human flourishing is about asking ourselves challenging questions about what it means to be 'good' and to do what is 'right'. It means growing through contemplation and acquisition of knowledge about what is useful and good in particular circumstances. We cannot 'just know' this, although some situations could be seen to 'be obvious'. It is in dialogue with others, and with ourselves, where we consider what is not yet known, and where discomfort is tolerated, that we might develop ethical maturity.

In summary

So how might the work of Socrates and Aristotle provide us with some principles to guide us in the development of ethical maturity? Perhaps their top ten tips might look like the following:

1. Know how little you know. No matter how much you know, or how many books you read, there is so much more you don't know. Be aware of your ignorance and don't get complacent. Uncertainty is the beginning of wisdom.

2. Be open minded. There are other models, frameworks and theories that will teach you a lot. Yours is a partial truth—move away from 'aggressive certainty' (Armstrong, 2011). Continue to be curious and inquisitive—even after you have made decisions.

3. Contemplation takes time; good decisions are not judged by the speed by which they are made.

4. Keep talking to others. In dialogue where you are gently truth-seeking together you will come more easily to what is right for you. Consider what is said or known in the dialogue, and what is not yet said or known in the conversation.

5. Ethical responsibility remains ultimately with you. While others will help, advise and share with you, you must take final responsibility for the decisions you make. Your decisions reflect your own moral character, so asking yourself what will be right for you, as well as right for others, is important in delivering authentic action and living with yourself later.

6. Use your power wisely—not to overwhelm, or force others to believe what you believe, but to help them question. Create an atmosphere of trust, where it is safe to be curious and challenging of each other.

7. Above all, don't be afraid. Fear is the enemy of ethical excellence.

8. Given particular relationships, contexts and timing, there will be times when you choose to obey rules and regulations, even when not of your making and even when you disagree with them. It is important you do this thoughtfully and in a reasoned way, being conscious of why you have chosen to do this as the best option in the circumstances.

9. Take the ethical initiative—don't wait for others to do things.

10. Live the ethical stances you believe in. Why make ethical statements if you don't practise them as best you can?

Conclusion

We have outlined the thoughts of two philosophers who lived thousands of years ago. They combine the two elements we see as essential to ethical maturity, the knowledge of 'Who I am' and 'What I do'. These two are connected in understanding ethical maturity and becoming ethically mature. What I do emerges from who I am, and who I am impacts and influences what I do. Too often we focus on quick and expedient action, rather than on what our action reflects about who we are, how we come to know who we are, and how we might move beyond immediate conscious knowledge to access our emotional, intuitive and unconscious knowledge. The ability to be ethically mature involves a conscious effort to develop moral character, as well as improving skills in a range of other areas. It is to these elements and skills that we now turn our attention.

Chapter 5

The brain and ethics

'Where intellect and emotion clash, the heart often has the greater wisdom.'

(Lewis, Amini and Lannon, 2001, p. viii)

'Of all the differences between man and the lower animals, the moral sense or conscience is by far the most important…'

(Charles Darwin)

'I do agree with Darwin who…saw human morality as derived from animal sociality. An interest in others is fundamental. Where would morality be without it? It's the bedrock upon which everything else is constructed.'

(De Waal, 2009, p. 8–9)

Humans seem to be the only group of animals with the ability to make moral decisions about what is right and wrong, good and bad, and good and better. Other animals make decisions that can look like moral decisions. Animals such as dogs, horses and lions have pack injunctions around acceptable and non-acceptable behaviour that are built in and instinctual to their group lives. These behaviours come from the reptilian and mammalian brains, in contrast to human behaviour that can be chosen and reflected upon (and comes from the prefrontal cortex). Examples of rules that characterise the working lives of pack animals are: 'It is good to defer to the leader'; 'Don't hurt or damage the offspring of animals from our group'; and, 'Working together is more advantageous than working alone'.

Occasionally, we sit up in wonder when the natural order seems not to apply, e.g., a recent instance where a lioness adopted a baby antelope. Unfortunately, the other lions in the pride did not view the adoption in the same compassionate way. However, the fact that one lioness broke the rules of nature made us wonder about animal behaviour in comparison to human behaviour. De Waal (2009) would not be surprised by the action of the lioness at all. He quotes an example of a Bengal tigress nursing piglets in a zoo and refuses to call it a 'mistake'. He offers the explanation:

'mammals have been endowed with powerful impulses to take care of vulnerable young, so that the tigress is only doing what comes naturally to her. Psychologically speaking, she isn't mistaken at all' (p. 42).

De Waal's 2009 book, *The Age of Empathy*, is a powerful argument for the role of empathy and emotion in evolution. He illustrates how other animals care for and look after each other, and even cross boundaries to care for other species. He is not blind to the violence, competition and cruelty in the animal kingdom, but concludes all mammals are hardwired to reach out to others. 'The fundamental yet rarely asked question is: why did natural selection design our brains so that we're in touch with our fellow human beings, feeling distress at their distress, and pleasure at their pleasure? If exploitation of others were all that mattered, evolution would never have gotten into the empathy business' (p. 43). De Waal takes issue with the metaphor of the 'selfish gene' as the sole determinant of animal behaviour, and suggests that we have both a social and a selfish gene, the former based on our ability as mammals to be empathic and emotionally connected. His book is full of examples of how non-human mammals react to injustice and lack of fairness. Trust, for them too, becomes a fundamental source of community. De Waal argues that these in-built and natural tendencies are the basis for ethics and morality in humans. While animals other than humans may not think in terms of what is good or bad, nor can they be held morally responsible for their actions, there is no doubt that many have the ability to see reality from the perspective of others and to act accordingly. De Waal gives examples of rats who will not push a lever that punishes another rat while providing food for itself, and monkeys who will deny themselves food with no benefit to themselves so others might have it. Human consciousness provides us with insights into why we do what we do, and gives us choices and vetoing power over our instincts—which adds the distinctly 'moral' tone to human actions.

Our hope is that insights into the human brain (or 'three brains', as we go on to explore) will help us to make the distinction between animal instinctual behaviour and human instinctual/chosen ethical behaviour.1 We have assumed that the ability to make ethical decisions comes from the prefrontal cortex of the brain, what we call the executive brain, which is particular to humans. The basis of morality was laid down well before the 'executive' or 'human' brain burst on the scene. As we explored in Chapter 2, the history of ethical investigation has been weighted towards rationality as crucial to human ethical decision making. From Plato on,

---

1 Neuroscience is the empirical study of the brain and connected nervous system (The Royal Society, Science Policy Centre, 2011). There is still much debate and disagreement around how insights into the workings of the brain affect decision making and learning. We recognise that what we present here is equally open to discussion.

through philosophy and science, theorists keep coming back to the role of rationality, and a view of humans as deliberate and logical creatures (Lehrer, 2009). But should rationality have such importance? Some would argue that a focus on rationality is a distortion, and does not pay attention to other key aspects of decision making related to emotion, intuition and relationship (Hinman, 2008). While there is no doubt that this part of the brain plays a large role in human ethical decision making, we argue that other brain systems may be equally important in how we make ethical decisions.

Many of our moral decisions involve the future—what will I do when faced with this situation? We access our future through the gift of imagination, bestowed to humans through the prefrontal cortex. Gilbert (2005) writes humorously: 'The human being is the only animal that thinks about the future... Until a chimp weeps at the thought of growing old alone, or smiles as it contemplates its summer vacation, or turns down a Fudgsicle because it already looks too fat in shorts, I will stand by my version...' (p. 4).

The triune brain

Contemporary neuroscience proposes the 'triune brain' theory, which suggests that the human brain is actually three brains in one—the reptilian [amygdala.] brain, the mammalian or limbic brain, and the prefrontal cortex or human brain. Much of what we know about these brains, their differences and connections, is drawn from research on the brain over the past ten to twenty years. Can these findings inform us how we make ethical decisions?

In the metaphor of the triune brain, each 'brain' has a particular set of functions, and each corresponds to an evolutionary period. At times, the three brains communicate well, resulting in a united front for ethical decision making. At other times, they are in conflict and cause havoc with ethical decision making when one brain overrules the others. Let's look in more detail at each brain.

The reptilian brain (the 'me-first' instinct)   F/F/F.

This is the 'first' or oldest brain, and one that all animals, humans included, share. It is estimated that this brain is about 500 million years old. It is called 'reptilian' because it was the motivating force of the first living animals on earth, which were reptiles such as lizards, frogs, sharks and crocodiles. This brain regulates the basic functions of existence and life—breathing, swallowing and heartbeat—and its main purpose is to keep us alive. For most animals this means access to food and protection from others, and in the long-term, survival of the species through mating and reproduction. Neuroscientists have seen this brain as based on the six Fs.

1. *Feeding*: maintaining the body's physiological needs (food, drink).
2. *Flocking*: coming together with others for support and protection.
3. *Freezing*: minimising detection, pretending to be dead.
4. *Fighting*: protecting territory, young and self.
5. *Fleeing*: avoiding harm and danger through flight (moving away from).
6. *F**king*: maintaining and providing new generations through reproduction.

Perhaps this brain could be compared to the 'id' outlined by Freud—a seething mass of desires, needs and instincts at the most basic level.

Based on these motivators, reptiles are only interested in staying alive and reproducing their species. They are hard-wired to do this and have devised all sorts of mechanisms for finding food and mates. They know when to fight for territory, when to run, and when to freeze as a way of survival.

In fact, the term survival characterises those animals that exist with only a reptilian brain. In Maslow's Hierarchy of Needs (see Table 5.1), reptilian motivation revolves around the bottom two needs: physiological needs (food, shelter, mating), security needs (being and feeling safe), and, occasionally belonging (see areas in bold).

Self Actualisation	
	Growth-oriented (competency mode)
Self-Esteem	
Belonging	
Security	
	Deficit-oriented (survival mode)
Physiological	

Table 5.1: Maslow's Hierarchy of Needs and the Reptilian Brain

The six Fs take up a strong residence in humans and still dictate many of our actions and behaviours. While the reptilian brain is 'old', it remains a powerful force in contemporary human existence. Armstrong (2011) put it well, 'our reptilian ancestors were, therefore, interested only in status, power, control, territory, sex, personal gain and survival' (p. 10). We share this brain with all other animals and its task is the same as it always has been—to keep us safe and ensure the continuance of the species. This brain cares little about how that is done—killing a rival, fighting for survival, capturing a mate, and raping. It is a world of little choice and much deterministic instinct. It is a world where right and wrong are translated as 'What is good for me and how can I get what I need irrespective of others?' Curran (2008) describes reptiles as 'islands of individuality, not functioning parts of a larger social group' (p.7). The reptilian brain is appetite-driven. It is also a world where deceit and lying are used as strategies to get needs met, as evolutionary psychologists remind us (Smith, 2004).

It is not too difficult to see how the uncontrolled and undisciplined reptilian side of us plays out in the moral field. The 'me-first' syndrome looms large. There is little or no moral code in the reptilian brain and when, at times, humans use this brain to make their decisions without reference to the other brains at their disposal, we become the reptiles we are. In this instance, ethical decision making is made on the basis of 'All that matters is me and my needs'. Right, might and my ability to get my needs met predominate, irrespective of the needs of others. The times when the reptilian brain takes over provides a simple answer to man's inhumanity to man, and how we can do such horrendous things to others, e.g., set up concentration camps, be involved in ethnic cleansing, murder and attack innocent people, or betray those closest to us, e.g., child sexual abuse and infidelity.

The reptilian brain exists to keep us safe and ensures the survival of the species, but has nothing to do with emotions, or relationships as emotional arenas. As Lewis et al. (2003) remind us, 'reptiles don't have an emotional life' (p. 23). Individuals, couples, teams and organisations can be plunged into survival mode through relationship and life experiences that provoke the reptilian brain to take over, control and set the ethical agenda.

We are born with the 'executive brain' (the functioning of the prefrontal cortex), which becomes fully formed toward the end of our teenage years. However, access to this brain is not automatic. Events in life, traumas in particular, can have such an impact on the brain that they limit, even deny, access to the prefrontal cortex. While working with staff in a unit for prisoners with severe personality disorders, one of us had the opportunity to ask the head of the unit, if she had noticed anything these prisoners had in common. She replied, 'Every single man in here has been severely abused as a child: sexually, physically, emotionally, and psychologically.'

The early relationships in the lives of these men had made a mammoth difference in how they made ethical decisions in their later lives. Abusive, 'power over' relationships had been instrumental in their learning and their ability to learn. These men live in survival mode with little access to their prefrontal cortex, which could help them to make long-term plans, reflect on their lives, have self-awareness and manage their emotions. Many live reptilian type lives in so far as they cannot access the learning that comes from the executive brain. We do need to make the point that not all children who have been abused, even severely, go on to develop severe personality disorders. Many factors influence what happens in later life as a result of earlier experiences. The following factors allow the reptilian brain to take over and impede operation of the executive function:

- *Power over, domination and control*: when asked by the ruler of the times to guide him how to stay in power, Machiavelli advised, 'Keep your subjects in survival mode. Dominate them, use your power to keep them frightened, afraid, and full of fear. You will then remain powerful and they will do what you want.' Machiavelli was not aware that he was describing the power of the reptilian brain.
- *Trauma*: traumatic experiences often put people into survival mode.
- *Upbringing*: relationships affect the brain, and if relationships have been abusive or domineering, where 'power over' is the predominant relationship, then individuals and groups remain in survival mode.
- *Injury to the brain*: this can limit access to certain areas of the brain such as the prefrontal cortex and keep individuals imprisoned in survival mode.

When information comes into the human brain system it is first assessed by the amygdala, the part of the brain whose job is to ascertain whether we are in danger—physical, emotional or psychological. When the amygdala decides there is danger, its job is to send the individual into 'survival mode' to ensure safety. Survival mode results in five strategies for dealing with danger.

1. *Fight*: we attack.
2. *Flight*: we run away.
3. *Flock*: we gang together or find a strong patron.
4. *Fragment*: we go to pieces.
5. *Freeze*: we immobilise.

When the amygdala is activated it closes down other parts of the brain to ensure all its energy is at the disposal of survival. High levels of steroid stress hormones, adrenalin and cortisone, are released. This cocktail of hormones can mask the cortex part of the brain—our thinking, planning, decision making—and cause problems in the way we see, what we see, and put us out of touch with our internal states. Activation of the amygdala can be mild, moderate or severe, and impacts relationships and learning. When the amygdala is activated, this survival mode 'severely limits access to the more recently developed systems' (Porges, 2004). Curran (2008) describes this process: 'One of the extraordinary abilities that your amygdala has is the ability to take over basic motor and emotional function in your brain, while shorting out your higher centres...it is this ability that keeps you alive and is central to your amygdala's functions. As it can short out all your higher centres and get you reacting before you can think, you can be out of (and I suppose into) trouble before you even know it's there' (p. 137).

When we are in survival mode, we cannot access perception, social engagement and longer-term planning capacities to the same degree as we would had we access to the executive brain. We think short-term because all we want is to be safe. At these times, we cannot attend to the needs of others. The rise of cortisol leads to disengagement from the present situation.

Our information channels become more acute as we watch and listen for danger. We can become hypervigilant and see danger where it does not exist. In survival mode, we close down other functions—physical, psychological and emotional—in order to self-preserve. As Sapolsky (1994) points out, there is little point in using up valuable energy to digest your own lunch when you are about to become the lunch of someone else.

The limbic or mammalian brain

The role of the second brain, referred to variously as the limbic, mammalian or emotional brain, is critical in the evolutionary journey of humans and we begin to see its role in the evolution of ethics. This second brain has been around for about 150 million years, but only discovered and named in 1878 by the French surgeon, Paul Broca. The limbic brain wraps itself around the reptilian brain and is beneath the executive or human brain. The limbic brain emerged with the advent of mammals, who differed from reptiles in that they carried their young. More importantly, mammals entered into relationship with their offspring in ways reptiles did not. While reptiles are indifferent to their offspring, mammals create an ongoing relationship. They have feelings of emotional connection with their offspring, and it is from the limbic system that feelings such as love, compassion, affection and empathy emanate. Reptiles have no feelings that we are aware of, but separate a mother from her child, a cat from her kittens, or a puppy from its mother and watch the emotional reaction. Relating between mammals is observed in how puppies and children want to play. Mammals communicate, play, touch, feed and feel.

Cozolino (2008) emphasises the importance of relationships: 'For humans, our brains are our most important survival tool, and relationships are our primary niche, making emotional nurturance, attachment, and specialized caretaking central to the evolution of the social brain' (p. 23).

It is the limbic brain that moves us toward nurturing and social behaviour. For Cozolino:

- the brain is a social organ linked to other brains
- the brain is an organ of adaptation and change
- relationships are our primary environment
- the brain can only be understood in relationship to other brains.

Emotions: crucial to good decisions?

It is now understood that emotions play a crucial role in decision making. From Plato to Freud, the emphasis has been on the need to control unruly emotions, which can only lead you astray. Emotions have been associated with irrationality, irresponsibility and subjectivity, none of which are associated with effective and reasoned decision making. It was said that emotions were only generated by the limbic system, the source of 'animal emotions' such as lust, greed and impulsivity. We now understand that the limbic system and the frontal cortex have a role in emotion. In fact, reactivity is the beginning of an important process of ethical decision making. Lehrer (2009) writes that our initial reactions, and even twinges of feeling, are the distillation of details that are not perceived consciously, and much of what we 'think' is driven by our emotions. 'In this sense, every feeling is really a summary of data, a visceral response to all of the information that can't be accessed directly…feelings are often an accurate shortcut, a concise expression of…experience' (p. 29). Within this context, the purpose of emotionality becomes clear. As Cordelia Fine (2007) points out, emotions give us our sense of self. 'It is our feelings, no matter how trivial, that let us know we are alive. We see the toilet seat left up again and, while we writhe in fury, the brain chuckles to itself "Yep, still here"' (p. 51). While we can be left merciless to the impact of a constant 'raw nerve' of too much emotion, too little access to emotion can mean we lose a sense of ourselves and what matters to us in living our lives.

Emotions are also messengers. Ekman (2003) points out that emotional expressiveness equips human beings with a sophisticated communication system that provides access to the internal states of other people, irrespective of race or place. Children scan the faces of their mothers to read their internal worlds without words. As adults we are skilled, mostly unconsciously, to do the same. We read the minds of others and access their inner worlds through our limbic brain. This process is called 'limbic resonance', and other animals do it too. One doesn't have the same relationship with a lizard, a frog, a shark or a goldfish as one has with their cat or dog. A gold fish doesn't do emotional summersaults when its owner enters the room. The limbic brain monitors and reads face, body and expressions to discover intentions. We walk down the street and immediately notice the person who is different, instinctively picking up when that difference could spell danger. There are no words in this brain, just emotional connections.

Lewis *et al.* (2003) describe this process of limbic resonance as 'emotional attunement', which depicts how we relate to each other. We don't just monitor the internal worlds of others, and they ours, but we can adjust our own internal world to match. This connects further to the literature on 'mirror neurons' and the neuroscientific discoveries that these neurons allow humans to 'mind read, to be empathetic, to imitate learning and even to understand the evolution of language' (Ramachandran, 2000, p. 2).

Mary Ainsworth (1965), one of the pioneers of attachment theory, asked adults to look into the eyes of babies who were just a few weeks old without showing any emotion. The initial curiosity of the babies turned very quickly to anxiety and, after 90 seconds, if the adult continued to withhold any reaction or communication, the babies became very distressed. The limbic or mammal brain requires a constant exchange of signals, an emotional 'give and take'.

Studies from orphanages, from rhesus monkeys, and from attachment theory show that children, as well as other animals, die if they don't have this emotional attunement (Lehrer, 2009). Attachment goes to the inner core of what love means. Cyrulnik (2005) captures this process: 'Parents' states of mind, and the history that made them cheerful or sad, can structure their children's self-image. The medium for transmission is attachment. When we talk about our relationship with our parents we are talking about how we learned to love' (p. 114). If we are 'known limbically', we are able to grow and change. Cozolino (2008) defines attachment as 'a general term used to describe the physical, emotional and conceptual connections that link us to one another' (p. 36). This is what Gerhardt (2004) calls the 'social brain' and Goleman (1996) calls 'emotional intelligence'. In the limbic brain, feelings come first, and the premise is that rationality builds on emotion and cannot exist without it.

While the limbic brain is a world of relationship and communication characterised by empathy and compassion, it is a world without words, long-term planning, creativity and reflection. As Lewis et al. (2003) put it, 'Words, good ideas, and logic mean nothing to at least two out of three brains' (p. 32).

Empathy allows us to enter the world of another and begin to see it from their perspective. 'Mirror neurons', or 'empathy neurons', allow us to access and perceive life and events from the perspective of others. We can feel what others feel—watching a spider crawl up someone's leg can release in ourselves a sensation similar to what we would feel if this were happening to us. Lewis et al. (2003) summarise this process: 'A mammal can detect the internal state of another mammal and adjust its own physiology to match the situation—a change in turn sensed by the other, who likewise adjusts. While the neural responsivity of a reptile is an early, tinny note of emotion, mammals have a full-throated duet, a reciprocal interchange between two fluid, sensing, shifting brains. Within the effulgence of their new brain (limbic) mammals developed a capacity we call limbic resonance—a symphony of mutual exchange and internal adaptation whereby two mammals become attuned to each other's inner states' (p. 63).

When the amygdala does its job and perceives threat, it sends us packing to survival mode and, at the same time, cuts off or restricts access to the prefrontal cortex. Goleman (1996) describes this as the 'amygdala hijack'. How much we can access other brains and their functions at these times depends on how strong the threat to our safety is (although the level of threat depends on how they are perceived by the person experiencing them).

Mild threat: An insult, illness, accident, or putdown need not send us into full-blown survival mode. We can still access reason, empathy and compassion, and use them to support us in long-term strategies rather than knee-jerk reactions.

Moderate threat: Loss of one's job, more severe illness, breakdown of an important relationship, the death of a loved one; these begin to compromise our functioning.

Severe threat: Serious physical attack, childhood abuse, trauma and post-traumatic stress disorder, and life-threatening natural situations can cut off full access to the other brains.

The limbic brain adds belonging and elements of self-esteem to our abilities.

Self Actualisation	
	Growth-oriented (competency mode)
Self-Esteem	
Belonging	
Security	
	Deficit-oriented (survival mode)
Physiological	

Table 5.2: Maslow's Hierarchy of Needs and the Limbic Brain

The executive brain

The largest and youngest of the three brains, variously known as the neo-cortex, the prefrontal cortex, the human brain, the executive brain, the new brain, is what makes humans human and is about 4 million years old. Curran (2008) points out that while the human brain is capable of thousands of complex behaviours, the reptilian brain has approximately 27 behaviours within it, and the limbic brain has probably about one hundred. Among those human abilities are the following:

- planning for the future
- imagination and prediction
- self development
- ability to reflect
- introspection
- ethical decisions
- managing emotions
- creativity and change
- speaking
- writing
- reasoning
- abstracting
- problem solving (the better the problem-solver, the bigger the cortex).

Our prefrontal cortex helps us to regulate our emotions by enabling us to think about them, and to be able to contemplate our own mind. Lehrer (2009) reminds us that, 'the process of thinking requires feeling, for our feelings are what let us understand all the information that we can't directly comprehend. Reason without emotion is impotent' (p. 31). Just as emotions are often the first sign that something is not right with a particular situation, they can equally be a means by which we can misread the (ethical) situation, e.g., when flooded by fear. Or we can make decisions based on bias or pigheadedness. 'Being blinded by rage does nothing for our ability to perceive the subtle nuances of moral dilemmas', writes Fine (2006, p. 59). Aristotle would argue that making good moral decisions involves rightly ordered fears, self-confidence and good value judgements about ends (Hinman, 2008). These all require the critical functions of our executive brain.

Self Actualisation	
	Growth-oriented (competency mode)
Self-Esteem	
Belonging	
Security	
	Deficit-oriented (survival mode)
Physiological	

Table 5.3: Maslow's Hierarchy of needs and the Executive Brain

Working together or at odds?

Where does this leave us? The summary by Curran (2008) captures the triune brain well: 'A three part brain evolved from our earliest ancestors... yet it all works together like a huge orchestra of 150 billion players all being directed and controlled by the emotional part of your brain, the limbic system' (p. 51). Curran highlights some principles worth noting.

- The limbic/emotional brain seems to control and direct what you learn and how you learn it. Your emotional self is centrally involved in the vast majority of the things you learn.
- If you make good emotional connections with people then you increase the chance of learning from them, and them learning from you.
- The amygdala is the oldest emotional structure: the more emotion is removed from learning, the less effectively your brain will learn.

There is no doubt that the reptilian, the limbic and the executive brains do not live together easily. The older reptilian brain is the master, and we often see it highjack the other brains and have its way. Armstrong (2011) shows how that takeover by the reptilian brain plays out in everyday life: 'We are still programmed to acquire more and more goods, to respond instantly to any threat and to fight mercilessly for the survival of number one. These instincts are overwhelming and automatic: they are meant to override our more rational considerations...it has been fatal when humans have employed their new brain capacities to enhance and promote old brain motivation: when, for example, we have created technology able to destroy the enemies that threaten us on an unprecedented scale' (pp. 10–11). When we look at some of the major ethical scandals of the recent past we can see how the reptilian brain took over. In 1993, British Airways apologised unreservedly for its 'dirty tricks campaign' to deal with competition. In 2001, Enron collapsed amid accusations of collusion between accountants, lawyers, managers and auditors. The British members of parliament expenses scandal hit the headlines in 2007. These and other more horrendous happenings of the twentieth century (concentration camps, ethnic cleansing, terrorism and genocides) show the reptilian brain in full flight with little or no connection to the restricting impact or influence of the other two brains.

Not only can the reptilian brain get its way, but it can bully the executive brain to go along with its imperatives and present a rational justification for its actions. Worst of all, the reptilian brain, interested in its own needs (e.g., its sexual needs), can partner with the limbic brain, and use relationship and empathy to groom vulnerable people so it can abuse them sexually, and then highjack the executive brain to justify its actions. The executive brain is equally inventive. It can rationalise what it wants, for example, to kill off the opposition, whether political, religious, or business competitor; or foster illegal business activity through gangs and cartels. At such times, the compassion and empathy of the limbic brain is cut off, and the reptilian brain is locked in to do its dirty work, supported by the executive brain with elaborate justifications and deflected responsibilities for pain and suffering caused. This can look like a form of logic and reason, but is an elaborate process of moral disengagement.

It was long thought that moral transgressions occurred more as a result of ignorance or omission. It has now been argued that moral transgression can involve elaborate and extensive planning, thought and consideration (Seabright and Schminke, 2002). The ethical task is difficult: how do we keep the three brains talking and working in partnership, and how do we ensure that the partnership does not become collusive and destructive? Sometimes the distinction between moral engagement and moral disengagement is surprisingly unclear. We can use emotion and logic to make the best of decisions, as well as to justify corrupt action and ego-driven outcomes. All too easily, we stand on the edge of both ethical maturity and ethical poverty. Perhaps most of us would not be drawn to open corruption of a high order, but all of us can be morally tempted to transgress. Understanding how reactions and thought processes come into play, and how we can better utilise them for good is crucial in developing ethical maturity.

What would it be like if we were to devise a separate ethical framework within each of the brains? The characteristics of each brain would mean that each ethical stance would contain the following features:

Ethics 1	Ethics 2	Ethics 3
Reptilian Brain	*Limbic Brain*	*Executive Brain*
Fear	Relationship	Fidelity across relationship
Survival	Connection	Respect for autonomy
Safety	Paternalistic	Relational trust
	Unilateral	Bilateral
	Sameness	Difference
Power over	Power over	Power with and within
Strong rules	Relational rules	Internal principles
No rights	Rights	Rights and responsibilities
Strength	Relationship	Dialogue
Orders	Monologue	Dialogue
External	External	Internal
Zero tolerance	Limited compassion	Rational consideration
No caring	Limited caring	Unselfish caring
Only me	Me and chosen you	I-thou (universal)
Instinct	Emotional connection	Emotion and reason

A code of ethics based solely on the reptilian brain would be a series of 'do's and don'ts', rewards and sanctions that keep us safe and curtail our tendency to work on the 'me-first' principle. It would regulate our reptilian tendencies so they did not infringe on the rights of others, and would leave humans without emotional attachment, imagination, logic or reason. You might say there is no code that was not imposed. Would the ten commandments be enough?

A code of ethics based solely on the limbic brain would have two foci: one for how to treat members of our group, and one on how to treat others. The executive brain code of ethics would be rational and logical, and ethical decisions would be cognitively based.

Ethical stances by which the three brains work together

When all three brains work together we have a chance of ethical maturity. The reptilian brain ensures we look after ourselves, and that we are safe and well. The limbic brain provides us with our emotional world of connection, where empathy and compassion give us access to the world of others. We work together, not just to survive, but to connect and belong. The executive brain provides our ethical awarenesses with a voice, an imagination, creativity and a reflectiveness that allows us to think through and imagine how we can be together. What does this mean for our theme of ethical maturity and ethical excellence?

Our contention is that the best ethical decisions are ones where all three brains work together to bring their special gifts and warning signs.

Brain	Gift	Warning Sign
Reptilian	Keeping safe	Me-only
Limbic	Relational	Collusive
	Communication	Identified with
	Experience	No systemic thinking
	Emotions	My-group only
Executive	Rational	No emotions
	Imaginative	The present
	Reflective	Mindless
	Language	Manipulation
	Long Term	
	Manages emotions	

Conclusion

We have explored recent insights into how the brain works to help us understand the neuroscience of ethical behaviour and ethical decision making, and how we can construct ethical maturity using all three brains in some form of harmony or integrated process. Unethical behaviour can enter the world when one brain is missing from the ethical discussion, or one highjacks the others and refuses to allow their voices to enter the ethical dialogue. We are at our best to set up ethical frameworks when our codes are directed by the executive brain in dialogue with the reptilian and limbic brains.

Chapter 6

Relational ethics

'The starting point of moral modern theory...is the isolated individual, separate from everyone else and seemingly independent. The central task of moral philosophy then becomes one of constructing an account of how they can be brought into some kind of harmonious existence. It is, essentially, an ethics of strangers—that is, a set of rules for governing the interactions of people who neither know or care about one another.'

(Hinman, 2008, p. 296)

'If my humanity matters, so does yours; if yours doesn't, neither does mine. We stand or fall together.'

(Appiah, 2008, p. 203)

'People don't develop first and create relationships. People are born into relationships—with parents, with ancestors—and those relationships create people.'

(Brooks, 2011, p. 43)

'"Relational" in this context means acknowledging the inherently mutual nature of all social process, and therefore prioritising the importance of the co-created, "here and now" relationship as the central vehicle for development and transformation.'

(Critchley, 2010, p. 1)

In Chapter 5 we considered how insights into the brain reveal it as a relational organ (Siegel, 2007). We are affected by and, in turn, affect the brains of each other (as someone said, we leave our footprints on the brains of others). Relationships for humans are established from the dependency needs of the newly born. As mammals, relationships are not optional, but are essential for survival. As the human brain evolved, relationships have been propelled into a whole new dimension. Imagination, long-term planning, thinking and creativity have become part of relationships, and are used for destructive as well as helpful purposes. In Chapter 2 we outlined some of the horrendous harm we can do to each other. Not being 'in relationship' gives licence to hurt, kill and destroy. Being 'in relationship' makes this much more difficult.

We have also explored how philosophical and psychological insights provide further weight to the importance of relationships. Heidegger (1978) uses the phrase 'being-in-the-world-with-others' as a key existential principle of life. Another existentialist, Sartre, reframed that principle somewhat differently as 'Hell is other people'. A paradigm shift in psychotherapy, known as the 'relational turn', views the relationship as the central tenet for understanding the person in his or her context (Mitchell, 2000). This shift is seen as a movement from a 'one person psychology' to a 'two person psychology'. Attachment theory (Bowlby, 1973) has become an established and accepted theory in developmental psychology. Bowlby's main contention is that humans have an in-built need for attachment and relationships, and without them, especially in the early years, they wither and even die (the horrific scenes from orphanages in Romania back up his assertion). Attachment theory gives credence to what the brain reveals: that we are not only not alone, but depend on each other for much more than merely the existence and the continuance of the human race. Winnicott's famous saying, 'There is no such thing as a baby, there is only a baby and a mother,' can be read as 'there is no such thing as a person, only a person-in-relationship.' Modern primatologists and zoologists such as de Waal (2009) trace the roots of modern human ethics to the co-operation and relationships between mammals. Relationship becomes the foundation of what we mean by ethics—how we construct our moral identity and how we treat each other are the bedrock of morality and ethics.

With such importance on human relationships for life, development, growth and happiness, is it any wonder that a relational ethics should find its way into the heart of ethical maturity?

'Out-there' or 'in-here'?

We love the 'problem pages' in our magazines and newspapers. Many of our 'agony aunts' are almost as famous as film stars. Even serious journals have problem sections where an issue or dilemma is presented and experienced practitioners respond. The history of ethics has become famous for what has been called 'trolleyology'[1] (the ethical dilemma of what to do if a trolley is out of control and about to kill five people), where 'stylised scenarios' of a prepared ethical problem are presented and discussed. The more formal name given to this approach is 'quandary ethics' (Appiah, 2008), which typifies how we try to resolve and make decisions about situations

---

1 The trolley scenario is a fictitious ethical issue where a bystander witnesses a train engine (the trolley) out of control and heading towards a tunnel where 20 men are at work. The bystander has one option—he/she can push a lever and divert the trolley from one rail to another. If she/he does so then the train will head for another tunnel in which two people are walking. What should the bystander do?

from the lives of others, or situations thought up beforehand. Lawrence Kohlberg used this approach in his research on moral development, giving individuals a number of ethical scenarios and asking what they think the person in the scenario should do.

While this approach helps to sensitise people to ethical issues and to play with possible resolutions, the concern is that we can begin to see ethics as simply resolving a problem. From this place, problems are 'out-there' issues about which we can be dispassionate and rational. We are 'outside the problem', like the agony aunts. The people involved are not known to us, do not have a relationship with us, and so we have to deal with what Appiah (2008) calls the 'umpire fantasy'—that we are searching for a judge with the right answer. 'To turn to them for guidance in the arena of ethics', writes Appiah, 'is like trying to find your way around at night with a laser pointer' (p. 194). Kant (1964) was even more scathing in moving from examples to principles: 'We cannot do morality a worse service than by seeking to derive it from examples' (p. 411). This is an 'ethics of strangers', as contained in the quote that begins this chapter. When one of us (Michael) discussed the trolley problem with his 12-year-old foster daughter, her immediate response was, 'Do I know any of these five people? Who are the other people in the other tunnel?'. She surmised rightly, and intuitively felt, that being in relationship with someone would make a lot of difference when it came to making an ethical decision about their lives.

Most of us make ethical decisions that take relationships into consideration. It is precisely because we are in relationship with individuals, groups and organisations that we think and act the way we do. A man is faithful to his wife, even when opportunities not to be present themselves and the chances of him being found out are low, because he knows her, sees her, realises the pain his actions would cause her, because he loves *her* and cherishes his relationship with her. Whether to be faithful to her is not a problem to be solved, but rather a relationship to be considered. 'Being unfaithful' is not considered a solitary action divorced from a relationship, but a mindset within a relationship. Relationships make all the difference when ethical issues raise their heads, but to the agony aunt, who knows neither the writer, the partner, or what the relationship is like, there is only one abstract approach—how you deal with the issue of infidelity amongst married partners is a problem that is the same for all married couples everywhere. In such an environment we end up with what Appiah (2008) calls 'a moral dispensary for the afflicted' (p. 198).

However, as Hinman (2008) notes, the traditions of moral philosophy have not respected consideration of relational contexts, or valued subjective circumstances and experiences. The thinking has been that if we are to be at our most rational ('the prize') we must screen out any personal connection to the dilemma, including our own reactions, sympathies and empathy. If we were to make a decision for others that we would not make for our own family members, it would not meet the test of universalisability (Kant's guide for an ethically mature decision), and would fail as a 'morally correct' decision. On the face of it, this line of argument can seem convincing. If I make decisions for me that were different to what I would recommend to you, then I would have to consider whether I am simply making decisions to turn out the way that suits me, rather than what attends to the ethical imperatives of the situation.

It was not until the 1980s that relationships and social context began to be explored as a resource in decision making, and not the enemy to be feared. Through research on the differences in ethical decision making between men and women, Carol Gilligan (1982) came to describe an 'ethic of care' which emphasises the importance of relationships, i.e., how people take into account the influences and requirements of relational responsibility, justice and connectedness. Relational ethics has developed considerably and has been explored within other theoretical traditions, for example, organisational systems theory and psychology. Many of these traditions contain the given that relationships shape moral development; what is described is the often unconscious or implicit effects of relationships.

In this chapter we situate ethical experience and decision making in its relational context, and argue that without attention to relational factors many important elements are lost, decision making may be flawed or inadequate, and implementation of good decisions may flounder.

An early construction of relational transactions: Social contract theory and its counter-arguments

In the individualistic tradition of moral philosophy, relational factors were understood through social contract theory. This theory proposed that we are all independent agents driven by self-interest, who voluntarily subject ourselves to rules that ensure we all derive benefits. For example, I would not push into a queue to get on a crowded bus, not because I cared about anyone in the queue, but because it suits me to ensure safety and order, as it inevitably suits everyone else. Social contract theory has been argued to apply even in intimate relationships, where we do things to ensure outcomes for ourselves and to keep the relational 'show on the road'. This theory does not emphasise feelings between people, as it argues that we do things for reasons that are more rational and objective, i.e., because it suits us and attends to our duties and obligations. On this basis, social contract theory fitted nicely as an explanation for how relationships influence decision making in the tradition of 'rational man' without getting into all those messy feelings. This is not without relevance in application.

Carol is a devoted wife and mother. She hates housework, and especially cooking. However, she believes it is her duty and the right thing to do to provide for her family in these ways. She refuses to share the load, although others suggest it, even her husband who offers to help. She says that it is 'what mothers do', i.e., her duty. To share the load would disturb her view of exchanges made in the relationship. She believes her husband does certain things and she does others, and if that is compromised the 'deal' they have struck would no longer work. Her work is attached to values about 'good mothering' and 'fairness in relationships' through which she benefits, as well as contributes.

Even though it is a challenge for Roger to find the extra time for volunteer work, he makes sure he is available for the school working bee. He believes being present ensures good things for his children, such as getting the attention of teachers (Roger has done a lot for the school, so we will take special care of his children) and ensuring a good environment for his children. He is aware that most other dads are there for the same reason. Everyone does their bit to add to the community, but the voluntary work would not occur without the fundamental premise that his children (and other children through their dads) would benefit.

Social contract theory emphasises individuals stripped of emotionality and wedded to reason, while feminist philosophers argue that this perspective strips us of those elements that constitute our very humanity. While there is something fundamental about social contract theory that can make sense, it seems insufficient to explain our lived experience of relationships. We need to deepen our reflection further.

In her groundbreaking work, In a Different Voice, Gilligan (1982) began her exploration of moral philosophy through the study of psychological and moral development. In contrast to the individualistic tradition of moral philosophy, psychology starts with the premise that people live within influential relationships, and that some of the most fundamental dilemmas for individuals are concerned with how one becomes a self separate to the weighty influence of others. In this way, Gilligan exposes the significance of power, gender and relational influence in any analysis of ethical reflection.

Commencing with many ideas of Sigmund Freud, Gilligan argued that to consider our thinking as separate from other people, events and contexts is as illusory as saying we have choices about connectedness. In fact, separateness and connectedness are embedded features of the experience of interdependence, a series of emotional processes and skills to master on the way to effective and moral operating in the world. According to Freud (cited in Gilligan, 1982), being conected to others is part of our strength and our frailty, 'We are never so defenceless against suffering as when we love' (p. 82). We spend our lives trying to achieve the separateness which provides us with autonomy in life, while not compromising the relationships on which we depend. Gilligan argues that because relationships are core to who we are in the world, they provide a crucial context for moral development and an essential feature of our ethical decision making.

Richard wants to do an MBA in order to advance his career and provide more for his family. He can argue the long-term benefits to the family. He can draw on the support of his company, who validate his decision, and on community pressure that says men should achieve, to say that he is on a legitimate track. An obvious option is to go ahead and enrol. However, he is not a free agent, and to maintain relationships he needs to discuss it with the family. They raise the dilemma of the short versus long-term. They will miss out on his time for some years while he studies, all for the sake of long-term gain. They were not convinced this was a good thing, nor did they believe it would result in maximum gain for them all. Perhaps some would benefit more than others. His wife wants to do post-graduate study too, so there is also the dilemma of self versus other interests. How can Richard make a decision as if he is a sole agent, when he depends on these relationships for support, tolerance and resources while he completes his degree? After all, he wants them all there when he finishes.

James Rest (1984) outlines the first process in the production of moral behaviour: 'The person must interpret the particular situation in terms of recognising who is involved, what lines of action are possible for the actor, and how each of those lines of action would affect the welfare of each party involved' (p. 19).

Thus Rest places an assessment of context and relationship at the centre of moral decision making, and not just in analysing the problem, but all possible courses of action. This could be a good place for Richard and his family to start their discussion.

An ethic of care challenges the tenet of social contract theory that we can be stripped of personal identity, acting as an 'impersonal calculator' in our interactions with the world (Hinman, 2008). Instead, we begin to flesh out ideas more allied to the reality of our social context. This inevitably raises a whole raft of new questions. For example, how do we balance what we owe ourselves with what we owe others? How do we attend to the development of the self while staying connected?

Moral development and the relational construction of ethics

Lawrence Kohlberg (cited in Gilligan, 1982), in his pioneering work on moral development, argued that we move through stages that start with an individual focus and move to community focus as we grow and mature.

> Preconventional judgement is egocentric and derives moral constructs from individual needs; conventional judgement is based on the shared norms and values that sustain relationships, groups, communities and societies; and postconventional judgement adopts a reflective perspective on societal values and constructs moral principles that are universal in application. (p. 73)

In her research on women and moral development, Gilligan (1982) describes a staged-model building on, but also departing from, the work of Kohlberg. She traces the development of women from an initial concern for individual survival, followed by transitions from selfishness to responsibility, an awareness of goodness as self-sacrifice, permission to take care of self, and finally, a more integrated position in which moral goodness is seen as caring for both self and others (in Hinman, 2008). She explains this as 'a progressively more adequate understanding of the psychology of human relationships—an increasing differentiation of self and other and a growing comprehension of the dynamics of social interaction... This ethic, which reflects around a cumulative knowledge of human relationships, revolves around a central insight, that self and other are interdependent.' Belenky, Clinchy, Goldberger and Tarule (1986) confirm Gilligan's argument. They researched the stages women go through in their learning journeys. Using the theme of 'voice', they describe the process for women coming back into education as moving from silence, through received voice, to constructed voice based on dialogue in relationship with others.

The theories of Kohlberg and Gilligan depart with Gilligan's proposal that in an ethic of care, involvement in relationships through mutual interdependence and emotional responsiveness will play an important part in moral lives. The difference can be seen in terms of an ethic of relationship versus an ethic of justice, which has, at times, been depicted as the separate ways in which women and men view ethics. Few are as extreme as to put men and women exclusively in those camps. However, from her example of women's comparatively vulnerable position in relationships with men, Gilligan (cited in Dudley, 1994) extrapolates to other relationships that involve power and vulnerability, e.g., teacher/student, doctor/patient. In such relationships, she describes action determined by attunement to need, rather than a more detached assessment of rights and obligations. 'Thus the emotions seem to have a 'cognitive role', allowing us to grasp a situation that may not be immediately available to one solely arguing from a justice perspective... Sensitivity and emotional response to particular situations provide important guides to morally acceptable actions' (pp. 1–2). Beyond an emphasis on their cognitive function, emotion creates connection, which, in turn, influences how relationships are perceived. For example, research on the difference between doctors/surgeons in USA who have or have not been sued show that the relationship between doctor and patient is often the crucial factor. Gladwell (2005) highlights the finding that doctors who are liked or loved are sued rarely, even when they get things wrong. Of course, this can be read a number of ways, but it does suggest that emotion plays a role in ethical perception in relationships.

The work of Gilligan is crucial in reflecting on ethical development and maturity. She put emotion back into the moral equation, and argued that on the basis of emotional attunement we are better placed to make ethical decisions that also preserve relationships and connections. In this way, she was ahead of her time. As demonstrated in Chapter 5, research into the brain, and more specifically the limbic system, now provides more information about the role of emotion in ethical decision making.

Paul Bloom (2010), in his recent contribution to this discussion, states that 'emotional and non-rational processes are plainly relevant to moral change. Indeed, one of the main drivers of moral change is human contact. When we associate with other people and share common goals, we extend to them our affection. Increases in travel and access to information, as well as political and economic interdependence, mean that we associate with many more people than our grandparents and even our parents. As our social circle widens, so does our 'moral circle' (p. 490). However, he cautions that these processes alone do not explain significant changes in social and community opinion over time. He believes that our consideration of regular, everyday dilemmas, and our ability to generate and share stories, ultimately result in powerful influences on thinking about relationships, both locally and globally.

Tim Bond (2007) argues for an emphasis on relational trust in the establishment of ethical relationships, which requires getting involved *with*, not seeking emotional distance *from*, the people with whom we are related in family and community. 'Trust is a relationship of sufficient quality and resilience to withstand the challenges arising from difference, inequality, risk and uncertainty' (p. 436). Where there is trust, relationships will be of greater quality, more resilient, sustainable and robust in the face of the ordinary challenges we face in life, and the differences we encounter between us. In his experience of working cross-culturally, Bond found that it was the establishment of a trusting relationship that made differences and mistakes, sometimes on a significant scale, able to be worked through to preserve the relationship. Trust builds bridges—without it relationships never quite get established in a meaningful way, or are likely to flounder. In comparison to a more individually based ethical framework, 'the distinctive strength of an ethic of relational trust is the way it directs attention to the embodied and reciprocal relationship between two people' (p. 441).

If we consider that the ethical landscape of an individual is linked inextricably to the relationships in which s/he exists, it is important to understand how this works in more detail. We might also wonder about how it might play out within the wider groups in which we relate: workplaces, local communities and on a broader scale of other communities and global networks. Beyond the significant influences of power, gender and class, what influences ethical development and reason in the exchanges and behaviours between people?

The boundaries of a moral community

BEING RESPONSIBLE AND ACCOUNTABLE

Painter-Morland (2006) suggests that 'considering the way in which moral knowledge comes about and moral decisions are made, we may need to re-envisage a moral agent as someone who is accountable towards others or in terms of some shared sense of normative propriety' (p. 93). She argues that being in relationships, and needing to maintain these through conversation about ourselves and others, is central to how people come to account for themselves. Not only do we only account for ourselves because someone asks us to (i.e., because we are in relationship), but our account is only meaningful because of the significance of the other who is listening. Values are defined and demonstrated through an 'emergent order' within functional relationships. 'This order is unique in that it is not formulated in reference to some abstract and supposedly independent point of moral orientation... instead it spontaneously emerges over time and through the interaction of individuals who participate in the system' (p. 94). Accountability becomes a form of relational responsiveness, something we would want to achieve because we are in relationship and it is worth 'getting it right'.

Linda and Dave had a significant problem. They reported a shared belief that their relationship comes first, and they had been able to live this out most of the time. However, Dave managed to get a new and exciting job which involved travel and, as a consequence, unhinged a lot of their arrangements. He missed birthdays, anniversaries, school holidays and, finally, he missed the birth of their most recent child. This was the last straw for Linda. If he couldn't demonstrate these values, how could he say he still had them? Dave felt caught between a rock and a hard place: how could he enact his values and still perform at work? However, neither of these were the place to start. Linda needed Dave to acknowledge the hurt to the family and the significance of their loss. He had to be able to acknowledge this as a betrayal of core values, even though much of the time he felt he had little choice (which could be the subject of many future discussions). This was hard. It meant being able to put aside the understandable defensiveness he might feel and, instead, be able to say 'I wasn't there for you'. In attending to relational responsibility, the couple could get to work on their practical problems.

Shoemaker (2007) argues that whenever we hold someone morally responsible for their actions, we assume they belong to a moral community where such assessments and judgments have some validity. Such a community includes the 'interplay between at least two agents, one who addresses a moral demand to the other via praise or blame, and the other who ostensibly hears, understands or either accepts or rejects the demand, and such an exchange is only possible for those who have the capacity to enter into a certain kind of relationship with one another. Call those who share this capacity, then, moral agents, and call the collection of moral agents the moral community' (pp. 70–71). Moral membership involves the ability to enter into interpersonal human relationships, which includes the experience of a wide range of feelings and attitudes. It also includes the ability to respond to reasonable requests from people with whom we are in relationship. This choice of words within the definition is important. If the person is unwilling or unable to respond (such as a psychopath), or cannot engage with reasonable requests (such as someone with autism or psychosis), this can exclude them from membership of this moral community. We cannot expect the same things from the relationship.

Shoemaker (2007) suggests that the required capacities for engagement in the moral community are about self-management, but are also about skilled relationship behaviour. In order to attend effectively to one's moral responsibility within the community, we need to be able to reason, which involves the capacity for self-regulation, the ability to reflect on one's desires and impulses on the basis of a moral code, make decisions on the basis of critical deliberations, and perform actions based on these decisions. We also require relationship skills, such as attending to one's own capacity for harm, the ability to control our behaviour in relation to situations, care about those who demand things from us, attend to the emotional distress of the situation, care about the argument of the other person because we care about them. For Shoemaker, interpersonal engagement is a process in which 'one shares the cares of the object of empathy (at least with respect to the events giving rise to the empathy) that is, one is emotional, vulnerable with respect of the fortunes of the items the person with whom one empathises cares about and is vulnerable in a roughly similar way to the person with whom one empathises' (p. 98).

The drive to be ethical in relationships

If relationships are so important to us, why do so many destructive things occur within them? Why do we hurt the ones we love? Why is it that an ethic of care doesn't ensure that we work harder to preserve relationships and do good within them, rather than being able to justify unethical actions as often linked to the desired relationship? For example, 'I had to resort to gambling to pay for the private school fees for the children', or 'I was driven to have an affair as a result of my poor relationship', or 'I had to steal from the stationary cupboard as my boss pays me so badly'. People often construct poor moral choices within a relational context, and rather than simply reject this as faulty thinking, we need to engage with the meaning of the context and how it shapes possible outcomes.

These are big questions, and we will not get to cover all the possibilities here. However, it is important to touch on some of the literature that attempts to explain why even good relationships, and investments to preserve them, do not protect people from unethical conduct. Such literature tends to have been developed within the psychological sphere, and emphasises a struggle between unconscious drives and conscious motivations.

Intergenerational legacies and betrayals

Ivan Boszoremyi-Nagy was a Hungarian psychiatrist who departed from traditional understandings of psychological and relational difficulties within the field of family therapy, to focus on relational ethics and its influence on interpersonal dynamics. He argued that issues of ethics pervade families and are often the basis for relational trouble, in the current day and also across generations. Within his theory, trust and loyalty are considered crucial dimensions in relationships. Families must have 'balanced ledgers' in order to maintain effective relationships. These ledgers of loyalties, obligations and sacrifices accumulate simply as a result of being born into a family and being part of an interconnected web of relationships. He argues that many of these ethical obligations are both unconscious and inescapable. For example, he would argue that:

- young couples establishing their own families owe redefined loyalty to their family of origin for their national, cultural, religious backgrounds and values
- parents owe loyalty to their children
- siblings owe loyalty to each other

- people owe affectionate loyalty to their family that is non-sexual
- support is owed to nuclear families while also paying for or being available to elderly parents
- family members owe solidarity to each other, as well as good citizenship
- family members owe loyalty to maintaining the whole family system, as well as being able to accommodate new relationships and system changes.

(Boszoremyi-Nagy and Spark, 1984; Boszoremyi-Nagy and Krasner, 1986)

In this frame, relational ethics is based on the premise of maintaining fairness in relationships, and is focused on the reality of daily life. This involves a balance of ethical consideration for the interests of others, as well as one's own. No one should be exploited or scapegoated; no one can balance a ledger with negative behaviour. People often believe that if they were treated unfairly in their growing-up years, they are owed or entitled to better treatment from a spouse or employer, for example. This 'claiming' of payback outside the context of injury is said to always be doomed. People do not 'get over' injustices, nor can someone else make up for the past. Rather, exoneration is required through exonerating and/or being exonerated in the relationship within which the injury occurred. Within this frame, relationships become trustworthy to the degree that issues of entitlement and indebtedness are faced and dealt with effectively. If this occurs, relationships are said to be trustworthy, and this is fundamental to their viability and longevity (Boszoremyi-Nagy and Spark, 1984; Boszoremyi-Nagy and Krasner, 1986). Of course, this is not always possible. Relational accountability can be an advanced skill. Self-awareness can be the important link.

Sarah knew she could be hard on female bosses. Her mother let her down badly, and she knew that when in relationship with a woman of authority, she could unconsciously start to expect more and, at the same time, counter the longing for a reparative experience with a provocative stance of 'I don't need you'. In the past, this meant avoiding line management meetings, saying 'everything is fine' and, at the same time, being bitterly disappointed when she was not acknowledged sufficiently for her hard work. Over time and repeating patterns, Sarah realised that she needed to be more present in working relationships, own up to appropriate work needs, and seek feedback accordingly. To keep blaming 'bad bosses' was too easy and was not working for her. By holding herself to account in present relationships, she was able to manage her past in a more conscious way. In fact, through building a relationship with her boss, she did find a positive female role model to work with.

Defences and self preservation

Firestone and Catlett (2009) suggest that the immorality of people in relation to others occurs as a result of the defensive manner in which we deal with interpersonal and existential pain. When faced with overwhelming pain, we can develop intrapsychic defences that help us shut down emotionally and defend against the perceived threats in relationships. Once cut off from our feelings, we are desensitised to the feelings of others and our effect on others. Friends, family and co-workers become expendable in the face of the greater need to be self-protective.

> Damage to our psyche during our developmental years bends us out of shape and leaves us demoralised. It not only fosters aggressive responses, but also leads to toxic character traits that injure other people's self esteem. Character traits such as dishonesty, intrusive-ness, superiority, narcissism...and outright hostility are destructive manifestations that take a toll on other people. These could well be described as human rights violations in the interpersonal sphere. (Firestone and Catlett, 2009, p. xvii)

The dilemma of insight and change, and the ability to live ethically within relationships, is that when self-protective behaviours are relinquished, people can be more susceptible to real suffering. Being attuned in relationships increases the capacity for empathy and pain, for example, instead of maintaining distance through blame of the other, dropping this defence could mean getting feedback that is pretty challenging.

Tony was criticised constantly as a child. As an adult, he knows this criticism was not justified. However, the child in him can wonder if everything truly is his fault. In order to feel safe in any new relationship, he takes stock of what is wrong with the other person and the situation. He feels a lot more comfortable when he is sure any problem will not be about him, or as a second best, they will have equal dirt on each other. If he were to drop this defensive manoeuvre, he risks attracting criticism and awakening the dark voice that says, 'I knew it! You've been the problem all along!' However, by standing still and being accountable for reasonable concerns, he could deal with the criticisms that come his way.

Firestone and Catlett (2009) note that to be a person of integrity requires self-knowledge, self-differentiation, courage, honesty, lack of duplicity, an ability to be consistent and reliable, direct and willing to self-disclose, non-defensive, loving and compassionate, empathic, independent, tolerant, inclusive and interested in growth and a search for meaning. At best, these qualities are a 'work in progress' for most of us, and the ability to articulate and achieve them requires an exceptional level of conscious awareness. This may be hard to reach because pain can blind us, and people we relate to can collude with our defences and not challenge us. If we do not wrestle with what it means to be relationally ethical, it is easy to apply a self-interested focus to the groups in which we exist. If I argue for my work group, my school, parking in my street, my efforts can appear as if they have a relational focus when they are simply an application of individual interests to a group interest with a possible aim of personal gain. These can be grey areas, and the ability to think systemically about interests, stakeholders, values and needs will help us tell the difference. We may still proceed with the action or decision, but it is worth understanding one's motivations so they do not undermine any good work achieved.

Needing relationships for our own purposes

Kenneth Gergen (2009) suggests that if we accept the premise that individuals are the 'natural' unit of being, then it follows that relationships are 'artificial'. This means that we seek out relationships when they are required for our personal use or satisfaction. This may feel too uncomfortable to consider, as it sounds antithetical to what most of us would like to think we pursue in relationships. However, this position is worth considering. Relationships are about others, but they are always about ourselves in relation to others. Some relationships make us look good, feel loveable, reinforce qualities we value, e.g., great friend, wonderful talent. Gergen argues that while relationships bolster us, they can also imply, and perhaps inadvertently feed, a sense of insufficiency and inadequacy. As a chosen relationship partner ourselves, we are also under the constant threat of expendability. If relationships are a reflection of need, then that can lead to a double bind: 'I need you to be special enough to make me look good, but I don't want you to be so special that you make me look bad.' Such a view can result in us evaluating others constantly for their shortcomings and failures, and comparing and boosting ourselves to improve or borrow some self-esteem. Martin Buber (cited in Inger and Inger, 1994) described this in his distinction of the primary relationship modes of I thou and I it. I thou is a product of the *between* that is mutually created among beings in relation to one another. I tt involves the experience of the other for one's pleasure. 'Some people, through their previous relational experience, tend to lean towards a more relational or self-referential experience of their current partner. For example, in a conversation with one couple, the woman said that she wanted to pursue the relationship because she loved her partner. Her partner said he wanted the relationship because without it he would be lonely' (Shaw, 2011, p. 5).

It may not feel comfortable to admit to self-interested desires and pursuits, as this is frowned upon in many communities. However, being able to admit to our needs and be accountable for them is crucial in relational ethics. This involves the high-level skill of self-assessment and reflection, of making sense of one's needs in relation to others. 'If I need this in abundance, what will that mean for you? Or for others who know us? Even if your needs are so strong that they seem to hold central place in the arrangement, does that mean everything else has to get rubbed out?' For example, to seek work with someone because it will improve connections and career advancement is not an unfair pursuit, but if one did so without being mindful of the exchange, then the terms of it could be unethical. Consider the contrasting examples below:

Example One: 'I am going to enjoy working with Cheryl because she is famous and it will advance my status, but I am aware also that I can do the job, am a loyal employee and will respect what the arrangement might offer us both.'

Example Two: 'I am going to enjoy working with Cheryl because she is famous and I will be famous too. I'll stay as long as I need to build my launching pad for the next project. Cheryl is so privileged by her position that I don't owe her anything. She is used to people passing through and will easily replace me.'

Issues of identity and difficulties in saying 'no'

It can be difficult, even impossible, to deliver on sound ethical decisions because of the situation, context, or implications for relationships. For example, the repercussions for whistleblowers in organisations who disclose ethical misconduct can become ethical issues in themselves.

Peter was married for many years and had two adult children. He worked as a teacher in a Catholic school. When he left his family to commence a same-sex relationship with Steve, his family were supportive, but wanted to keep it hidden from the broader community. Steve felt increasingly that as a show of loyalty to their relationship, Peter should 'come out' at school. Peter also felt this was right, and would be a statement of solidarity to the gay community, but he was torn. If he disclosed his sexual preference he knew he would lose his job, and his family would be judged within their local parish. His friends were supportive, but would his family's friends be? He would lose his ability to meet his financial obligations to all those who depended on him, and he would have difficulty breaking into the state school system.

In such examples, the ethical dilemma resides in its local relational context, and, as Gilligan (1982) has suggested, to reach resolution means that the ethical tests do not just include the traditions around duties and outcomes, but also the preservation of connectedness.

Beyond the complexity of these situational examples, with all the competing external stakeholders, there can be the more personal difficulties of standing up for oneself in relationships. The ability to say 'no' is a key skill in managing relationship challenges, and can be difficult to do. We explored this in Chapter 2 when we considered the Milgram experiments, where subjects seemed to lose the ability to say 'no' to injustice and unfairness when there were agreed rules and an authority figure directing the task. Brandt (1981) notes the considerable popularity of the book *When I say no I feel guilty* by Manual J. Smith, and reflects on why it has struck a chord with so many people. He argues that the ability to say 'no' is a key part of our identity formation. When babies learn to shake their heads, even before they can verbalise 'no', it begins a process by which one is defined in relation to the other: 'I can reject what you offer if it doesn't suit me.' Freud suggested that negating is a function of our conscious mind and our ego, and allows us some independence from the emotions, drives and unmediated desire of our unconscious. Negation is said to be the origin of intellectual judgement, whereby one can choose between oneself and others (Freud cited in Brandt, 1981). Nucci (1997) argues that there can be no meaningful moral action in the absence of moral judgment, as morality by definition requires choice and intent. If we struggle to have a contrary opinion from others, it means our identity is fused with others rather than separate, and this will have a significant impact on being able to work with, and stand up to, relational factors in any ethical dilemma.

Sarah had been brought up to obey her elders. Independent thought was not prized, as the Bible, the minister or her parents had all the information she required. She was home-schooled and when she went to university she was marked down regularly for being unable to critique theory or to assert her own opinion. She had difficulty making friends as people found her 'wishy washy'. In her first romantic relationship, she found herself doing things she didn't want to do because she was uncertain how to negotiate saying 'no'. After working for five years without a promotion or any other workplace acknowledgement, she asked a coach to help her 'get noticed'. However, she asked if she could do this without standing out too much or making others feel bad.

It is important to note that to be a separate self in relationships, and have the ability to act ethically, one needs to be able to speak up when something is wrong. This requires self-development and courage, and can still be difficult to do. Even the most secure people can fear the disapproval of their partner, or the censure of their boss, or even the surprise of their friend when disclosing a non-conforming preference. In the case of whistleblowers, the stakes can seem far too high.

Relationships as moral framework and the case for partiality in ethical decision making

We have argued that relationships provide an influential context for ethics and moral decision making. We have also described some theories that highlight the ways in which we are bound by relational systems—by power, gender, history and trauma. Given the considerable impact of these systems in shaping who we are and how we operate, it is important to consider where this leaves us in relation to effective moral decision making. Are we so bound by relationships that we are not free to make effective ethical decisions for ourselves? Will any connection and subjective personal experience erode ethical decision making?

LaFollette (1995) states that good, loving personal relationships are fundamental to our developing morality, and to learning how to care and be motivated to care. Without them, our ability to become part of the moral community is impaired. However, it is possible to have impartial moral principles about intimate relationships that override one's situation and retain universal principles for this special class of relationships:

- intimacy itself has moral relevance in that it promotes significant values such as honesty, fidelity, loyalty, patience
- preferential treatment can teach us to extend good values towards others, for example, good parenting can provide the context for us to feel good about extending generosity to strangers.

This latter point is important. Much of the theory on relational ethics brings the point of reference in from the extremity of disconnected strangers to the intimacy of our own family groups. Our relational networks in life move from the most personal of partner, children and parents, to wider systems of work colleagues, school communities, interest groups, to the broader community of local politics and neighbourhood, and to national and global levels. Our relational considerations vary depending on our values and past influences. Some will think only in terms of their personal obligation networks; others will think of their global obligation networks such as contributing to women's causes, social disadvantage and giving aid in natural disasters. Security in oneself and one's past moral relational history will foster greater attunement to relational issues in the bigger picture. We argue that ethical maturity will enhance, and even compel, your moral sensitivity to the wider human condition, without the need for logical imperatives or personal connections.

Sound ethical decisions that take into account connectedness, care and trust require particular skills. While self-knowledge is important, the use or development of empathy as a moral capacity is essential (Baron-Cohen, 2011; De Waal, 2009; Johnson, 1993). Empathy is the ability to imagine ourselves in the other's shoes, in other situations and conditions, in past and future times. We might do this through the following relationally based skills and techniques:

1. Empathic imagination as a form of direct responsiveness, taking time to sort through other's experiences, interests and worries. To be morally sensitive we must be able to put ourselves in the path of others, and to use this information to tune in to the right response, not to turn away (Shaw, 2011). This can involve a nuanced and layered reflection on the 'self-as-the-same-as', as well as 'self-that-is-different' (Flaskas, 2009).

2. Envisage options by creatively tapping the possibilities of a situation, and overcoming our habitual responses in order to create imaginative moral responses (Fesmire, 2003; Johnson, 1993).

3. Dramatic rehearsal involves 'crystallising possibilities and transforming them into directive hypotheses'. Suspending action to reflect in this way provides opportunities to consider the possibilities. During this time, we can be preoccupied with others: what effect will my behaviour have? What will people think of me? We may examine our emotional state, and how we are influenced by and influence others. We may explore the multiple meanings and outcomes available, and grapple with uncertain outcomes and factors outside of our control (Caspary, 2006).

There will be times when the demands of personal relationships conflict with impartial moral standards. How this is resolved is crucial. In the common 'ethical tests' featured in the philosophical literature, the dilemma of struggling with partiality versus attending to the greater good becomes more obvious, e.g., the choice between rushing home to save your wife from a nuclear threat, or staying at work and having a role in saving hundreds of people from the nuclear threat. Williams (cited in LaFollette, 1995) argues that partiality is not only acceptable in many cases, it is expected as the 'morally right' choice. Take for example, the case of a parent with a child on the waiting list for a transplant. The parent will feel duty bound to argue most strongly for the case of their own child, even if others are sicker, as loyalty to one's own family is expected and valued by our community. To not argue for one's child abrogates one's duty to care for more vulnerable family members. The test of impartiality would require parents to think about the transplant list as a whole, and make room for other decision-making criteria. While this might reduce fights with medical staff, it is an unrealistic expectation. Instead, to have each child represented by a parent engaged in their particular slice of the ethical fight, and to work with the community of ethical voices and arguments, is the only thing that makes sense in this kind of situation.

There is something to be said for 'the ethical right of way', when relationships are seen as ethical arenas. When do certain relationships preclude others because, by their very nature, they might be viewed as incompatible, e.g,. a husband involved in a sexual relationship with a person other than his wife? When would certain relationships, legitimate in themselves and not necessarily incompatible with other relationships, be given up because one person finds it unacceptable, e.g., a man having a close and intimate, but non-sexual relationship with a woman that his wife or partner finds difficult to accept? Organisational settings often raise 'rights of way' where prior relationships may ethically influence and impact on future ones, e.g., a manager who feels he/she can coach a member of his team when coaching means looking in some detail at developmental issues that affect present behaviour. What does fidelity to an existing relationship mean, and what limitations does it put on other relationships? These are not easy questions to answer and often don't fall within the realms of 'rational' problem solving. At times, attention may need to be focused on 'this particular relationship' and what it means for both of us, or many of us, in terms of faithfulness, loyalty and love. Ethical rules, codes and frameworks may not be broken in relational ethics, yet ethical maturity can be missing.

It is important to note that while there can be a number of people in relationship, not all carry the same assessment of the ethical problem. Recently, Elisabeth's daughter developed chicken pox in the week prior to her participation in her first dramatic production. On the day of the performance, her doctor said that under no circumstances should she participate as it would be a public health risk. Her drama teacher said she should participate, as it would be terrible for her to miss out after all her hard work, and that other parents just had to deal with it. Although on the face of it there were 'right' and 'wrong' options, which made it look like there was no dilemma, the situation created much internal discomfort to say she could not go. The moral temptation to 'get away' with her going, acknowledge her hard work, avoid her disappointment, and get value from the audience tickets, costumes, video, let alone all the lesson fees, was sharp. In the web of relationships, everyone was clear and unconflicted about their opinion. The fact that a group can carry divergent opinions often sharpens the intensity of the dilemma, and makes the importance of an ethically mature framework all the more important.

So where does that leave us?

In exploring the influence of relationships, one could focus on the difficulty of ever achieving impartiality. In this chapter, we have considered whether impartiality is the wrong benchmark, or at least not the only benchmark, by which to measure ethical decision making. Instead, it seems important to note that relationships provide important foundations for moral development. At their best, they teach and reinforce values and norms that promote ethical behaviour. They may determine particular boundaries around choices, but this need not mean that decisions are poorer as a result. In daily life, one often needs to take only limited circumstances into account—the dilemma in the family can be a local one, not a global one.

Philosophical tradition has suggested that one must strive for detachment and impartial calculations. When taking a wider view of systems and psychological influences, the core task is to enhance self-knowledge and a capacity to attend to all elements at play in the ethical struggle. It is through self-knowledge that greater detachment is achieved, not through attempts to separate oneself from one's circumstances (as if this was ever possible). Asking people to think not like themselves is, in itself, a challenge impossible to achieve, and what is the point anyway? Instead, relational ethics seems to offer the possibility of bringing 'our baggage' with us, challenges us to know more about what drives us and then, 'given who we are', offers a more viable and richer place to start a moral debate.

Chapter 7
What is ethical maturity?

'Despite our bad behaviour, our moral progress seems to me unmistakable. Our powers of empathy are clearly growing. Today, we are surely more likely to act for the benefit of humanity as a whole than at any point in the past.'

(Harris, 2010, p. 177)

'Development is seen as a combination of changes in the organism manifested in a sustained, increased capacity to engage with and to influence the environment and to look after internal needs and aspirations.'

(Bachkirova, 2011, p. 77)

'North: Learning from our own mistakes.
West: Learning from the mistakes of others.
South: Learning from the mistakes of our teachers.
East: Being willing to make as many mistakes as it takes.
Centre: Learning there is no such thing as a mistake.'

(Quoted in Bachkirova, 2011, p. 166)

'The more advanced one's moral development, the better chance there is for good moral decision making. By understanding this development process, we can better understand ourselves and others, and may be able to help engender moral competence.'

(Callaghan, 1991, p. 171)

'Taking all this together…one must come to the conclusion that the evidence for a general developmental trend in moral judgment (as measured in the Kohlberg tradition) is overwhelming.'

(Rest, 1986, p. 29)

Since we have entitled this book *Ethical Maturity*, we must give some explanation of what we think that means. 'Maturity', as the term implies, involves elements of progress, development and growth. As we look back to where we were, and measure that against where we are, we look for signs of movement. We see this as an evolving towards maturity. We also see that there are times when we regress, and we move from a position of maturity towards immaturity. Movement is possible in both directions.

The ability of the human race to hurt, harm, kill and destroy is more sophisticated than it has ever been. New technology has brought new ways in which we can hurt each other, individually and globally. We can destroy individuals, groups and countries, and we do.

However, we have advanced too. Our increased ability for tolerance and acceptance of 'other ways' has been considerable. For example on a societal level we have achieved progress with issues such as racism, alternative sexual life styles, different religions and cultures. There is new thinking in Catholic circles about the use of condoms to combat AIDs, more awareness that we can live together not only tolerating difference, but enjoying the enrichment it can provide. However, there remain many signs of ethical and moral immaturity—e.g., the treatment of women in societies where they have no power and are traded as commodities, and female genital mutilation.

Evolutionary growth

In his book, *The Age of Empathy*, de Waal (2009) traces what he believes are the roots of ethics to the early days of mammals. The arrival of mammals signalled the arrival of the limbic brain which made parenting obligatory and propelled relationships, attachment and emotions on to the centre stage of development. The connections and cooperation that formed among animals eventually became human ethics. Our engagement with each other evolved two genes—a selfish gene and a social gene. The selfish gene, characterised by survival of the fittest, has been well-documented by Richard Dawkins (1976), the social gene less so. De Waal (2009) has many examples of how this social gene works out in the lives of other animals:

- If you give two monkeys different rewards for the same task, the one who gets the short end of the stick, will eventually stop performing. Even monkeys have a sense of justice. They will divvy up the spoils of a hunt so those who did the most work get the biggest portions, and those who did not take part do not share in the results. They have a sense of fairness.
- Monkeys will mediate when there are disputes. The Chinese Golden monkey (male) will stand between two disputing females and calm them by rubbing their backs until peace is restored.
- Empathy (and mirror neurons) are a fundamental part of animal life—experiments with rats and monkeys have shown that if pushing a button gets the recipient a food reward, it will refrain from doing so if that same reward means another rat or monkey

experiences pain. De Waal gives numerous examples of chimps offering consolation to others that have been hurt or injured in a way that indicates their ability to have empathy and compassion. He sees empathy as in-built.

- How can we destroy co-operation and working together among animals? De Waal suggests three ways: 1) put them with a stranger, 2) put the other out of sight, and 3) give their partner a superior reward. Competition then kicks in and interferes with generosity. On reflection, this is not a lot different to what happens to humans.

De Waal (2009) makes the point that there is a difference between what drives nature and what drives behaviour. Sex has evolved so natural selection breeds the strongest possible offspring and the species can continue. Yet procreation rarely drives human sexuality—ask humans why they have sex and there will be many responses, with only one being the procreation of offspring. De Waal demonstrates that what has emerged from evolution can be changed by humans to mean something else, so co-operation can evolve into empathy, and empathy can evolve into ethics.

What is maturity?

We want to introduce the six component model of ethical maturity by focusing on what is meant by maturity, and then offering a definition or description of maturity. While not wanting to get involved in an intellectual debate about what maturity means, it is important to have some sense of the term and the activity involved if we are to use it as a central tenet of ethical decision making. First of all, we are talking about human maturity. Many pack animals have clear codes of conduct and behaviour. These codes have been documented in animals such as horses (Roberts, 1996), wolves, dogs and more. However these codes of behaviour have not been chosen consciously, but are instinctual depending on the demands of the situation, i.e., they are not mature decisions. As outlined in Chapter 5, neuroscience proposes that we have 'three brains', the reptilian brain, the limbic brain and the executive brain. Each brain contributes to our moral sense and adds to our human ethical decision making.

The term maturity itself involves a movement, from immaturity to maturity. We all grow up physically. Infants make decisions in a different way to adolescents, who in turn make decisions in a different way to adults. There is a process involved in moving to mature stances.

Paul Bloom

Paul Bloom, psychologist and academic at the University of Yale, has concentrated his research on infant/child morality. By studying young children, his research aims to explore how biological evolution and cultural experience together shape human nature. The idea of baby morality may seem strange to explore, given the long tradition in psychology from Freud, Piaget and Kohlberg that we begin life as amoral creatures, and our ignorance is then assumed to extend well into childhood. Parents and educators are seen to have the key task of turning children into principled, empathic and socially responsible beings. However, since the 1980s studies have been exploring babies' 'naïve psychology'. What do the conclusions of this research tell us about ethics at a human age where language is not yet developed and reason has not clicked in? Before capacities such as rationality, critical reasoning, reflection, conscious deliberation and consideration enter the arena of moral decision making, the moral gestures that children make are emotional. As Bloom (2010) puts it, they respond on a gut level. At the age of one year, babies demonstrate compassion and empathy when they respond to the distress of other babies' cries, and stroke or offer toys in gestures of comfort. While this may not be moral conduct, Bloom suggests that 'to have a genuine moral system…some things have to matter, and what we see in babies is the development of mattering' (p. 5). He points out how this is in keeping with modern insights from neuroscience: 'In fact, one discovery of contemporary research in social psychology and social neuroscience is the powerful emotional underpinning of what we once thought of as cool, untroubled, mature moral deliberation' (p. 9).

In more detailed experiments into baby morality, researchers used puppets and simple stories with three-month-old babies and observed that the babies could tell the difference between helpful and hindering adults. Six-month-old babies demonstrated a capacity to evaluate others on the basis of their social behaviours, and were attracted to pro-social individuals and avoided antisocial individuals. At the age of 18 months, babies could distinguish more detailed characteristics, signalling that the helpful person was nice and good, and the hindering person was bad or mean. They were also drawn to puppets who distributed justice by punishing another bad puppet (Bloom 2010; Hamlin, Wynne, and Bloom, 2010). Other studies demonstrated that babies as young as three months, in line with studies of older children and adults, privilege negative information across a range of social assessments from a young age. This means that we take greater note of negative information than positive information in any given situation, using it to shape our decisions and reactions. This aversion to antisocial people and behaviours suggests 'that the capacity to evaluate others on the basis of their behaviour is a fundamental aspect of social cognition' (Hamlin, Wynn and Bloom, 2010, p. 6). It is a strong argument for the biological underpinnings of moral development.

From this body of research, Bloom concludes that morality and ethics arrive though cultural channels, and are the result of accumulated wisdom, rational insight and thinking. However, the beginnings of moral development are biological and emotional, and culture then moves us towards ethical maturity through reason and emotion. Dawkins (1976) emphasises how we need to look beyond the limits of biology, 'Be warned that if you wish, as I do, to build a society in which individuals cooperate generously and unselfishly toward a common good, you can expect little help from biological nature' (p. 3).

Bloom (2010) summarises: 'Morality, then, is a synthesis of the biological and the cultural, of the unlearned, the discovered and the invented. Babies possess certain moral foundations—the capacity and willingness to judge the actions of others, some sense of justice, gut responses to altruism and nastiness. Regardless of how smart we are, if we didn't start with this basic apparatus, we would be nothing more than amoral agents, ruthlessly driven to pursue our self-interest. But our capacities as babies are sharply limited. It is the insights of rational individuals that make a truly universal and unselfish morality something that our species can aspire to' (p. 11).

Developmental theories in general

Many theorists and researchers have outlined developmental theories that trace the stages individuals and groups go through on their journey towards different types of development and maturity. While there are too many to mention here, never mind critique, some of the better known ones are:

Erikson	(1950)	Life development stages.
Kohlberg	(1969)	Stages of moral development.
Gilligan	(1982)	Gender and stages of moral development.
Rest	(1986)	Stages of moral development.
King and Kitchener	(1994)	Stages of epistemological development.
Belenky, Clinchy, Golberg and Tarule	(1986)	Stages women go through on their journeys towards learning.
Fowler	(1981)	Stages of faith development.
Kegan	(1984)	Stages of consciousness.

What all developmental theories have in common is the belief that individuals evolve, move, change and develop over time. Some view these stages as sequential and linear. None of these theorists propose that this happens automatically, but that the change is dependent on a number of factors: the relationships in the life of a person; their experiences and early experiences in particular; and, the environments in which they live and relate. There is also connection to health, nutrition, and use of substances that impact on individuals. No easy formula gathers these together. Drawing from Bachkirova (2011), we have summarised some agreed principles about development below:

- human development is not automatic, but the result of complex interaction between the individual organism and the world (relationships, culture, environment) that can be intensified under certain circumstances
- development is manifested in an increased capacity to respond to external changes and to influence the environment in line with the unique internal needs and aspirations of the individual
- development happens with or without specific interventions to facilitate it, however, appropriate support, for example, through coaching, may contribute to the acceleration of development
- development is not equal, and individuals may be at different stages or levels of development in different areas of life, e.g., a highly intellectual person may be emotionally immature and make juvenile ethical decisions
- development happens at a different pace for different individuals, but may become static and even regress in some circumstances depending on the situation; e.g., holding and making high moral decisions may be affected if we are put in a situation that disorients us and makes us unsafe (as demonstrated in the experiments of Zimbardo (2007) and Milgram (1963) outlined in Chapter 2)
- internal predispositions and external conditions can help a person to become more conducive to development, e.g., a capacity for reflexivity
- there is a cumulative momentum in that we carry what we have developed as we come to the next area of development (p. 8).

The movements that take place in developmental theories include the following:

1. *Physical*: growth.
2. *Emotional*: includes relationships, managing one's feelings, making decisions, moving from 'socialised self' to 'self transferring self', and from dependence on others to interdependence (Goleman, 1995).
3. *Psychological*: cognitive development, dealing with complexity and depth, 'making sense of' in new ways, moving from subject to object, living with ambiguity, abstracting and reasoning.

Bachkirova (2011) outlines the stages, and characteristics of stages, that individuals go though in their journey towards adult development. These stages are also fundamental on the journey towards ethical maturity. Table 7.1 provides a summary of these stages.

STAGES	UNFORMED EGO	FORMED EGO	REFORMED EGO
COGNITIVE STYLE (based mostly on Kegan)	**SOCIALISED MIND Ability for abstract thinking and self-reflection**	**SELF-AUTHORING MIND Can see multiplicity and patterns; critical and analytical**	SELF-TRANSFORMING MIND Systems view; tolerance of ambiguity; change from linear logic to holistic understanding
INTERPERSONAL STYLE (Loevinger & Cook-Greuter)	**DEPENDENT CONFORMIST/ SELF-CONSCIOUS Need for belonging; socially expected behaviour in relationships; peacemakers/ keepers**	INDEPENDENT CONSCIENTIOUS/ INDIVIDUALIST Separate but responsible for their own choices; communication and individual differences are valued	INTER-DEPENDENT AUTONOMOUS/ INTEGRATED Take responsibility for relationship; respect autonomy of others; tolerance of conflicts; non-hostile humour
CONSCIOUS PRE-OCCUPATIONS (Graves)	**MULTIPLISTIC Social acceptance reputation, moral 'shoulds and oughts'**	**RELATIVISTIC/ INDIVIDUALISTIC Achievement of personal goals according to inner standards**	SYSTEMIC/ INTEGRATED Individuality; self-fulfilment; immediate present; understanding conflicting needs
CHARACTER DEVELOPMENT (Loevinger, Cook-Greuter & Kolhberg)	**RULE-BOUND 'Inappropriate feelings' are denied or repressed. Rules of important others are internalised and obeyed**	CONSCIENTIOUS Self-reliant, conscientious; follow self-evaluated rules; judge themselves and critical of others	SELF-REGULATED Behaviour is an expression of own moral principles. Concerned with conflicting roles, duties, value systems

Table 7.1. A Cumulative Description of the Three Stages in Adult Development (Bachkirova, 2011, p. 49)

While there has been criticism about applying these theories in an overly rigid and linear fashion, they help us to make sense of development, growth, learning and maturity. Maturity is the end result of a process of development and can entail such terms as wisdom, reflection, thoughtfulness and consideration. There is movement from 'surface' to 'depth' learning (Moon, 2004; Jarvis, 2006). There is more in these theories than simply the physical progression from one stage to another. Children become teenagers who become adults who face old age—all physical changes. Psychological, emotional and cognitive developments accompany these physical stages. We can become mature in some areas of life (e.g., physical and/or rational), and remain arrested or immature in other areas of life and living, e.g., highly rational leaders who are emotionally illiterate.

When is ethical maturity not ethical maturity?

Maturity, as mentioned above, is not seen here as a fixed point in a developmental process by which we can now be seen to have reached a maturity destination. Some equate maturity with seniority and/or experience. However, seniority, education on ethics and professional experience can sometimes involve people developing more complex language that they can use in a deceptive manner to obfuscate their ethical immaturity. This was a common experience in providing educational services to violent men by one of us (Elisabeth) and, in fact, one of the key public criticisms of such services is that some violent men come to sound a lot more respectful, while their abuse continues undetected. In the following example PP stands for programme participant and E for Elisabeth:

PP: I was worried about my partner going out with her friends. I felt worried that she wouldn't be safe. I talked to her about my fears and asked her if she would stay home with me. I didn't use any bad language and I really kept my cool while we talked, but it was very challenging when she said she really wanted to go. I really had to calmly persist in communicating with her about this, because I was really worried. In the end I convinced her.

E: Where were you while you were talking? Was she sitting or standing, was it a mutual conversation?

PP: I sat her down and stood next to her. I had to tell her not to move to get her attention.

E: How did you convince her to stay home in the end?

PP: I had to say the relationship is over if she goes out. But I also said I loved her and she understood that.

E: How long did this conversation go on for? What time of day was it?

PP: About four hours, between 12a.m. and 4a.m. It was really on my mind in the night, and you know how we have talked about talking issues through before they get heated? Well I was really worried so I woke her up to talk. I think it really cleared the air.

Another example concerns Peter, who was a psychotherapist in private practice. A qualified social worker from the United Kingdom, he had trained in existential approaches with some of the leading training institutes across the world. He held a senior position in a London training institute for some years, and lectured on clinical practice and ethics. His wife, a university lecturer in philosophy, shared his radical views on 'mainstream' society. Peter saw himself as a risk taker and an innovator, and would encourage students to not become 'institutionalised' by joining a professional association. He argued against the 'orthodoxy' of therapeutic practice, and claimed there was no greater respect you could show a client than to befriend them, as this reduced the power imbalance in the therapist/client relationship. He questioned the need for professional indemnity insurance, and refused to submit to the control of such 'oppressive authority'. He argued that professional indemnity insurance should be a choice. Peter was a convincing, skilled orator, who through the use of ethical language and the values of his profession, convinced people to follow his (unconventional) path, persuading them they were groundbreakers and the only ones *really* standing for critically evolved practice. In later years, the level of boundary violations he engaged in were exposed, but he continued to argue for the right to be an 'independent practitioner'.

Ethical maturity in some areas of ethical decision making can exist alongside ethical immaturity (being ethically juvenile) in other areas. It seems a large percentage of ethical complaints are initiated against accredited individuals. Khele, Symons and Wheeler (2008) reviewed complains within the *British Association for Counselling and Psychotherapy* from 1996 to 2006. Of the 142 complaints reviewed, a disproportionate number were brought against men and accredited members (p. 127). A recent example involved a very senior practitioner who had written eloquently about boundaries and parameters in counselling. In crossing an ethical boundary with a female client he attempted to justify what seemed to be a clear 'blind spot' in his ethical development. Ethical maturity is truly a never-ending task, with practitioners in all fields of the helping professions continuing to develop ethical sensitivity.

In another example, a client consulted her therapist about finishing an affair. In a complex and layered discussion about values, priorities, duties to others, the best outcomes for the wider group involved and her own needs for fulfilment, it seemed a decision was made to end the affair. As the client was leaving the room, she suddenly lost her moral courage. She asked the therapist, 'I know this sounds pathetic after all we have talked about, but could I tell him that you told me to end it? It sounds better if it comes from you, and then I won't look so bad.'

Baxter Magolda (1992) has gathered a number of other learning approaches into four domains of 'knowing' based on a continuum of beliefs that lead towards mature learning:

Domain 1: Absolute knowing: where knowledge is seen as certain. What I need to know is out there somewhere and I need to find the expert, book, code that tells me the 'truth'. This stage corresponds somewhat to the 'unformed ego stage' outlined by Bachkirova (2011) in Table 7.1. The features of individuals at this stage of development are that they:

- Look to others for guidance and support. They search for information outside themselves. Not only do they ask for guidance, they are likely to be influenced by others (e.g., my parents believed that and I do too).
- Have a somewhat uncritical view of life.
- Can be very selective in what information is allowed into their systems, especially what information they will allow to impact and influence them in their actual behaviour.
- Are conscious of self and of oneself 'acting'. This can result in deficiency in how they behave due to being overly self-conscious.
- Can be driven to make decisions solely on emotions or can make decisions solely on reason. Not an integrated approach.
- Have a need for social inclusion, which means they often accept the norms and culture of others without question and will even do things to belong as a member of a gang, group, cult, etc.
- Can be defensive and self-protective at times.
- Can experience shame and guilt strongly.
- Can be cautious, even overcautious.

While this stage of development is not age-related, we see that children and teenagers move through this stage as a natural process. However, many adults remain in this way of thinking and deciding.

What would an ethical stance from this perspective look like?

Justin was brought up in a strict Christian family where he was expected to be obedient to the rules of his family and his church. He was a 'good boy' in that he never rebelled seriously against the dictates of his family, and if he did he felt guilty and ashamed. He is uncritical in the views he holds and has not questioned them in any serious way. Now 28 years old, married with one child, in a settled job as an accountant, he sees himself living a normal life. If you asked him if he has chosen his values and his ethics he would say he had. However, he has never really considered or reviewed them. He tends to make ethical decisions about what is right and wrong using the guidelines he was taught and, in particular, the teachings of his church.

Domain 2: Transitional knowing: doubt begins to emerge that there can be such certainty about everything. The learner reaches the stage where there is certainty, but some uncertainty develops.

For many, their journey through life provides challenges that force them to review their values, cultures and beliefs inherited from family and community. They hold these up to the light to examine them. This may come about when they experience alternative ways of living through TV or in their contact with others. Alternative values and life styles open up their views to reflection and revision. They begin to see that there are other 'truths' in the world, and this begins to loosen what they have accepted as sometimes the only way to think about and see the world. Through a series of mini traumas and disturbances they allow themselves to look at other ways. They move from an external stance (the truth out there) to a more internal stance (I am responsible for what I believe in). Their lives are a series of small research projects where they put their values and beliefs under an investigative microscope, and compare and contrast them with those of others. They now move towards a more personal acceptance of values that have been fine-tuned on the anvil of experience, thinking, reflection and wondering. They accept values and decisions more in keeping with who they are, and see their stances as chosen personally rather than inherited. This would move naturally to:

Domain 3: Independent knowing: an awareness that knowledge is uncertain. Learners now take a position that everyone has a right to his or her opinion.

What would an ethical stance from this perspective look like?

Marian was raised in a strict Catholic family where, until her teens, she accepted and agreed with what she was taught. However, she lived in a mixed cultural area and her best friend came from a family where the children had no religious upbringing. She and her friend talked a lot about their different views and values. This made Marian question some of the beliefs handed on to her. At university, as her friendships widened, she made a decision not to follow in the religious or political persuasions of her parents. Now 28 years old, she is lawyer in a large city, living with her boyfriend and would describe herself as non-religious, but interested in spirituality. She practices meditation each day and sees herself seeking to live a healthy and fulfiled life. She makes her decisions based on values she has adopted, rather than ones she has inherited.

Domain 4: Contextual knowing: knowledge has to be worked towards while taking contexts, people and relationships into consideration. In this stage, people know what they can and cannot control. There is some realism about who they are, and how inconsistencies are a fundamental part of growing up. They have a good sense of identity and have keen self-awareness (their strengths and limitations, their abilities to fool themselves, their character structure and how it impacts on their lives). They are good at seeing 'the bigger picture' and can make decisions that not only have consequences in their lives, but have wider implications for others and for the planet. They can be highly critical of others, and indeed themselves, and combine emotional, rational and intuitive responses to the life situations they face.

What would an ethical stance from this perspective look like?

Bernard had to work hard to develop his values. He came from a deprived background where there were few moral values or guidelines, and no limits, boundaries or concerns for others. It was a 'me-first' environment. Through his bright attitude and an interested teacher at school, he developed his painting and is now an artist and graphic designer. He spent several years in psychotherapy 'trying to find himself', and now sees himself as responsible for who he is and what he does. He and his partner decided to formalise their relationship with a wedding because they believed in the ritual of commitment, and they try to involve their two children in what they consider major world issues. They are particular about the environment and ecology, as well as endangered species. Bernard would say he doesn't follow any ethical codes, but that he has worked out a set of ethical principles that guide his life. He would see his life as built on two bases: compassion and authenticity, and he uses both of these anchors when difficult decisions have to be made. He points out that he has spent time thinking about the policies of the government and he is not in agreement with them. He cannot sit by and watch injustice take place without doing something about it.

Towards maturity

Researchers like Piaget, Kohlberg and Rest trace theme movements (stages) that individuals go though as they move from ethical immaturity to ethical maturity. Their models have been criticised at times for being overly cognitive and too sequential. It is obvious that a child when faced with an ethical problem answers it differently to most adults. Children often miss the role of intention in ethical behaviour, while adults will be keenly aware that what is intended plays a major role in how ethical our decisions are, but know also that there is more to ethical decision making than intention alone. What kind of moves come into play in the evolution of ethical decision making? Drawing on Moon (2008), we have summarised ones we can subscribe to:

- from an absolutist ('we are certain') to a relativist stance ('it is not a given')
- from authority as the final arbiter to individual responsibility
- from single to multiple perspectives
- from static to moving truth
- from total objectivity to considering environment, motivation
- from rational alone to rational and emotional (thinking feelingly)
- from description of facts to widening narratives
- from zero reflection to in-depth critical reflection
- from simplicity to complexity
- from no questions to asking questions
- from subjective only (being stuck in our own view) to the ability to stand back from and be somewhat objective
- from a blank sheet to awareness of the impact of prior experience
- from reflection to critical self-reflection, i.e., reviewing one's own reflective processes (pp. 116–17).

These movements do not exclude each other. There may be some areas where I believe in absolute knowing and others where I have a contextual awareness of differences. However, it seems almost impossible to have ethical maturity if there is no awareness of ethical relativity—of how knowing is constructed and co-constructed. This does not mean that individuals more influenced by absolutist stances are not moral or ethical. In fact, it can be quite mature to have values that are absolute and non-negotiable. However, to have ethical maturity we argue that you need to be able to adopt a relativist stance when needed—fundamentalists, in our book, are not ethically mature. Ethical maturity is the ability to make ethical judgements that involve a growing ability to take the perspective of others into consideration (Gibbs, 2003).

Can we help individuals and groups move towards more ethically mature stances? Some ways that can help are:

- create a safe environment that supports questioning, inquisitiveness and openness
- support and be with people at the in-between times, which often feel uncomfortable and disorienting as they move from a dependent stance (of deciding on the direction of others) to an independent stance (making up own minds)
- help others listen to the information that is coming from the environment, and help them begin to trust their own experience
- support others to use their emotions, intuitions and reason

- trace their values and work on what values they want to infuse into their lives
- foster independence and responsibility for their own actions
- build up reflective capacity and reflective opportunities
- think in ways that are more connected and systemic
- challenge values, beliefs and attitudes, in a safe, non-shaming relationship
- foster awareness about how we fool ourselves and how our brains so often delude us and collude with us
- be vulnerable
- allow experimentation
- live with inconsistency and paradox.

James Rest (1986) concluded from his research that:

1. Moral judgement changes with time and with formal education.
2. Becoming more socially aware increases ethical maturity.
3. Moral education experiences and training can help move individuals towards more mature ethical decision making.
4. Similarities across cultures are more striking than dissimilarities.
5. Sex differences don't seem to make a difference in ethical decision making.
6. The stages of moral judgement (Kohlberg's six) are primarily about social co-operation and how it is organised (favour for favour, close relationships, society-wide networks based on laws and roles or ideal principles for constructing societies).
7. Experiences can change how people make meaning, and experience can change the structures of how we make meaning.

Conclusion

In this chapter we have outlined what we mean by ethical maturity and view it as a developmental process by which we move from dependency to an inter-dependent state involving cognitive, social, intuitive and emotional aspects of decision making.

Part Two

The six components of ethical maturity

....

Overview of Part Two

This section will outline what we call the six components of ethical maturity. Our intention is to give an overview of the model and then spend time looking in detail at each of the six components. This is not a sequential model in that we move from component one through to component six, and begin the process all over again when faced with the next moral issue. The components intertwine and interweave. When we started we called the components 'steps', but steps give the impression and image of sequences which we want to avoid. The use of the term '*stages*' gives the same impression. *'Elements'* is a better term as it gives a more random relationship to the components. However, there is more chronology and connection between the components than is suggested by the term elements. The implementation of a decision clearly comes after a decision has been made, and coming to terms with the decision occurs after having made and implemented the decision. Other than this, there is interconnection and influence throughout. In making decisions we become morally sensitive, and even our peacefulness with our past behaviours influences our moral stances. Thus we will follow Rest (1986) and use the term 'components'.

It is important to note that the components are not equal in terms of the tasks and time involved. Situations and stakeholders will demand more from some components than others on any given occasion. Our own struggles and interests will shape what draws our attention. It may be that as we develop sensitivity and discernment over time that decisions and implementation come quickly. We then move to the next process of integration and learning that slows us down again. This is not a process measured by such markers or measures. Some decisions may be years in the making, others may be made in minutes or hours. Some decisions are made and never implemented. At times, we are not quite sure why we made the decision we made. The decision maker can make decisions with which they are not 'at peace', and it is possible for us to *not* learn from the ethical experiences and decisions we have gone through.

There have been a number of background influences on the development of this model. Foremost is the work of Rest (1986), who asks the question, 'When a person is behaving morally, what must we suppose has happened psychologically to produce that behaviour?' (p.3). He devised the four components model to answer that question:

Component 1:   Initial awareness and interpretation that the issue is one of ethics or morality.

Component 2:   Moral judgement or moral reason. It is here that a decision is made about what to do.

Component 3:   Intention to do what is right.

Component 4:   Being able to implement the decision. Having the strength, perseverance and implementation skills needed to bring the decision to fruition.

Rest (1986) points out that his four-component model is based on certain assumptions:

- an ethical decision is not a single unitary process
- each component has distinctive functions and needs particular skills
- facility in one component does not necessarily mean facility in others
- this is not just a cognitive process, but involves emotion as well (there are cognitive-affective interactions particular to each of the four components)
- the processes are not about personality alone
- they are not necessarily linear—there is complicated interaction between the four components.

We could apply these assumptions equally to our six-component model.

Marquardt (2010) connects Rest's work (1986) with that of Reynolds (2006) to present a staged model of ethical decision making:

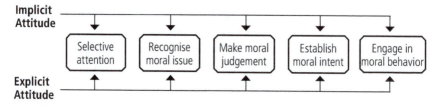

Figure 8. 1: Six-staged Model of Ethical Decision Making

Reynolds (2006) contributes to the stages of ethical decision making through his proposal of moral templates that become the filters through which we focus our initial attention. 'It is therefore not conscious. Accordingly, when a decision-maker is confronted with ethical issues, his cognitive system automatically searches for ethical prototypes that match the stimuli. Ethical prototypes are similar to implicit moral attitudes or moral schemes' (Marquardt, 2010, p. 130). We have extended Reynolds' work to include further components: the ability to justify ethical decisions rationally, being at peace with decisions made, and integrating learning from the decision-making process into our existing moral structure.

Six components of ethical maturity

From the above can we begin to describe what ethical maturity means? For us ethical maturity is:

> Having the reflective, rational, emotional and intuitive capacity to decide actions are right and wrong or good and better, having the resilience and courage to implement those decisions, being accountable for ethical decisions made (publically or privately), being able to live with the decisions made and integrating the learning into our moral character and future actions.

This needs a bit of unpacking. The first four features of the person making ethical decisions of a mature nature are being able:

1. *To reflect*: the ability to examine and look in some depth at various aspects of the ethical issue (see Carroll, 2009, 2010). Zero reflection is a slippery slope to possible unethical stances. We include reflection because we believe it is the mature, the adult and the holder of the thoughtful position for those who adopt ethical mature stances. We see later (in the chapter on Component 6) how it becomes an essential feature of mature ethical decision making in learning from experience. Reflection brings mindfulness, attention and deliberation to the process of ethical decision making.

2. *To rationalise or reason*: the ability to work logically and thoughtfully towards conclusions and decisions. The capacity to think critically and examine in detail using rational approaches is a key feature of being human and one of our best gifts. It is this feature that makes us different from other animals who act according to more instinctual, hard-wired, biologically driven codes of conduct. Rationality is our ability to reason, to reflect, to imagine, and to consider in depth why we should choose one course of action over another.

3. *To be in touch with our feelings and emotions about what is happening:* While the history of ethical and moral understanding often gives little sway to emotions in making ethical decisions, our awareness of the role of emotions in decision making in general has increased over the years and insights from neuroscience have helped us to give emotion a more central place in the making of ethical decisions, e.g., 'The madman (as Chesterton remarked) is not the man who has lost his reason. The madman is the man who has lost everything except his reason. After the emotions have made their decision the rational circuits in the cortex are activated. People come up with persuasive reasons to justify their moral intuition' (Lehrer, 2009, p. 165ff).

4. *To note the difference between intention and action:* Fine (2007) captures this in her work on the brain. 'Our appraisals of others also fail to take the same generous account of good intentions that we allow ourselves…we give others less credit for their good intentions than we give ourselves for ours. The masterful hypocrisy of the immoral brain demands a certain grudging respect. It lazily applies nothing but the most superficial and disapproving analysis of others' misdemeanours, while bending over backwards to reassure that you can do no wrong' (p. 65).

It seems to us that all areas (the ability to reflect, the capacity to involve our logical and rational capability, and being in touch with what our emotions and feelings are telling us) combine in the realm of ethics to create some form of ethical maturity. All three play central roles in ethical evaluation. It may not be necessary to use all three in all decisions we make, but access to all is essential if we are to show ethical maturity. Focusing on one to the detriment of the others can result in missing key ethical points.

Concentrate on reason alone: you can end up out of relationship and unreflective.

Concentrate on emotion alone: you can be driven by subjectivity and perhaps impulsivity.

Concentrate on reflection alone: you can end up navel gazing and inactive.

These three play major parts in mature ethical decision making but often come to the fore at different times in the ethical decision-making process. Hauser (2006) considers the historical development of these elements in moral decision making and presents a variety of 'computational mechanisms' that result in five modes of moral psychology:

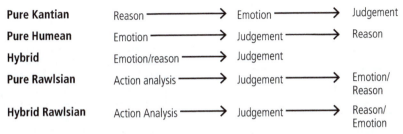

Figure 8.2: Five modes of moral psychology (From Hauser, 2006, p. 45)

Each mode has a somewhat different sequential order to how ethical decisions are made. Our 'take' is that all modes have 'won and all must have prizes': ethical decisions are made in different ways at different times, and in different contexts.

The chapters in Part Two take each of the six components in ethical maturity and considers them in turn. Chapter 8 reviews what we mean by ethical sensitivity, and asks how we build moral character as the ongoing basis from which ethical decisions emerge.

The next four chapters in Part Two (Chapters 9, 10, 11 and 12) all focus on ethical decision making and consider the processes involved in making ethical decisions. This first chapter will introduce an overall model of ethical decision making, the second chapter will look at unconscious ethical decision making, and the third chapter will review deliberate and conscious decision making. Chapter 13 will outline strategies for implementing ethical decisions followed by two chapters (Chapters 14 and 15) on ethical accountability. Here we will engage briefly with the concept of free will as a basis of human responsibility and the foundation stone of accountability. Chapter 16 reviews how we live with the ethical decisions we make, and Chapter 17 rounds off this section by suggesting ways in which we can learn from our ethical experiences and integrate that learning into ongoing moral development and ethical character. Figure 8.3 visually captures the six components and illustrates some of their inter-relatedness.

Components in Ethical Maturity

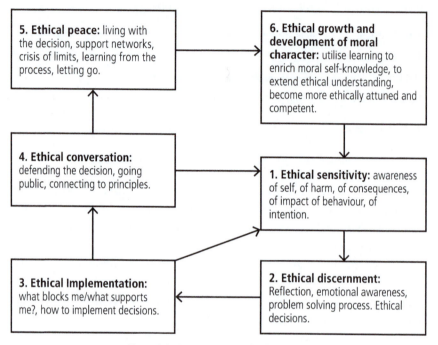

Figure 8.3: Components in Ethical Maturity

Chapter 8

Component 1
Creating ethical sensitivity and mindfulness

'Every resolution to an ethical dilemma, I maintain, must consider the act, the intention, the circumstances, the principles, the beliefs, the outcomes, the virtues, the narrative, the community, and the political structure.'

(Nash, 2002, p. 20)

'Your values are seen in the choices you make.'

(Sartre)

'Our emotions can be our best allies. The emotions faithfully respond to what our value system is — not what we would like it to be.'

(Keating, 1997, 19–20)

'A great many moral failures stem from ethical insensitivity.'

(Johnston, 2012, p. 236)

'Some people never become engaged in moral decision making because they seem morally tone-deaf: a certain awareness and perception of a challenging moral problem must occur before anything else can happen.'

(Callahan, 1991, p. 121)

Robert Cialdine (2001) tells the apparently true story of two brothers, Sid and Harry, who owned a men's tailor shop in New York in the 1930s. Whenever Sid had a customer trying on a suit he would admit to a hearing problem and ask the man to speak a bit louder. When the customer found a suit to his liking and asked the price, Sid would call to Harry: 'Harry, how much is this suit?', and he would describe the suit. 'Forty-two dollars' came back the reply. Pretending not to hear, Sid would ask again and get the same answer, 'Forty-two dollars'. At this stage, Sid would say to the customer, 'There you have it, twenty-two dollars'. Most customers would hurry to buy the suit before the 'mistake' was noticed and scamper quickly out of the shop with their 'bargain'.

If you were asked to evaluate the various behaviours outlined above from an ethical perceptive, what would you say? About Sid and Harry, who creatively and intentionally fooled the customer? About the customer who thought he had fooled the brothers? Is this manipulation? Good business? Greed at work—suits you, sir? Or are these all ethically neutral stances, and just the way business and life works? You might view it differently from outside the tailor's shop than from inside it—whether you are the owners, or the customers, or observers like ourselves.

Issues become ethical problems or dilemmas for us when we are aware that there is an ethical dimension to our behaviour. Awareness is the first step in ethical maturity, and the beginning stage in ethical decision making. For many people, certain actions have no ethical content—they have no moral awareness, no ethical problem or dilemma, and therefore no ethical issue to be resolved. Avoiding tax, claiming welfare benefits to which they are not entitled, embezzling money from a bank, trafficking in drugs, or children, or women or body parts, stealing from those who are rich, acts of terrorism—for some people these actions do not enter the ethical arena. Sometimes they are not allowed to become ethical questions, which of itself can be morally negligent—to stop myself intentionally from being aware can itself be a moral issue. There are many reasons for such stances and we considered some of those in detail in Chapter 2 on unethical behaviour and why it occurs. The first step in ethical maturity is the ability to create a moral character, or ethical compass, that has the sensitivity to identify an ethical issue when it presents itself.

The roots of ethical sensitivity

Nash (2002) talks about *three moral languages* that guide us and influence how we make ethical decisions: background beliefs, the influence of community, and the development of 'moral grammar'. We add to this a discussion about the role of values, which we see as equally influential in ethical decision making. Knowledge of each aspect can, in our view, help us build moral mindfulness and establish a moral character.

1. BACKGROUND BELIEFS

For Nash (2002), the first language is that of background beliefs: 'the most fundamental assumptions that guide our perceptions about the nature of reality and what we experience as good or bad, right or wrong, important or unimportant'. In explaining how the brain works, Curran (2008) uses the term 'templates', which is similar conceptually to what

Nash means by 'fundamental assumptions'. Templates are 'wired together nerve cells that form patterns… everything in your brain is stored in the form of templates…all your painful memories, your remembered slights, your damaged perceptions of the world, your happiest moments are all experienced through the activation of templates' (p. 48). These templates are filters through which we see reality, and through which we begin to make meaning of our experiences. They become our 'meaning-making perspectives'. Most are subconscious and many unconscious.

When one of us (Michael) grew up in Belfast in Northern Ireland he inherited a set of strong templates or meaning-making filters. Some of these templates revolved around: religion (Catholicism was the one true religion); politics (Catholics were discriminated against by the political system and had their rights denied); and, sexuality (being gay or lesbian or any other sexual orientation other than heterosexual was wrong, sinful and unnatural). There were many more templates laid down besides these three (sometimes it feels like they were laid down in concrete) through which reality continues to be filtered and its meaning distilled—though in these cases more determined than distilled.

We are not disputing the rightness or wrongness of these moral templates, just considering the process by which they are established. Nash (2002) calls this our 'primary moral subtext', and we see how important this becomes when we face ethical issues. The first moral battle is fought within us—what are we going to do about the templates we have inherited, and do we need to rewrite our 'primary moral subtext'? With templates, or 'brain maps' as they have been called, we learn our first moral language, and that becomes the medium through which we see, and eventually make, ethical decisions. If templates are so important in how and why we make ethical decisions, then it becomes crucial for us to trace them, articulate them and change them when they are not helpful so that we can 'see' and 'decide' differently. Our fundamental beliefs start here with what Luxmoore (2011) calls 'organising principles'. These are 'summaries of our lives condensed into a single phrase or sentence…and that's our autobiography in a nutshell, that's how we see the world' (p. 107). We can see them as the vocabulary, the words that capture our fundamental beliefs in a succinct manner. Examples of such statements could be: 'I wasn't wanted. I never get it right. You won't like me. It never works out for me. All my relationships fail. I never trust anyone. I am no good. Attack first before you are attacked. Reject before you are rejected. I am special. I am privileged.' Templates, fundamental assumptions, organising principles and statements, whatever term we give them, become 'the truth' and become embedded as tightly-held moulds through which we read our world and make decisions in respect of that world. If we are to become morally and ethically sensitive and mindful then we need to be aware of the existing templates that already influence our moral decisions. Nash (2002) highlights the power of our background beliefs: 'Sometimes we are able to bring these background beliefs into the foreground through a conscious act of retrieval. Sometimes these background beliefs remain inaccessible to us. So powerful are these beliefs, however, that even when we all look at the same ethical dilemmas, we do not always see the same dilemmas. To some extent, we each remain trapped in our own metaphysical life-space, our own tacit dimension' (p. 37). Wilson (2002) uses the term 'core narratives' to describe these sets of beliefs and offers the image of 'story-telling' as the method by which these beliefs are translated into our lives through behaviour and our explanation of why we do what we do. He emphasises their centrality in our lives and how embedded they become: 'Narratives are often like an oil painting to which we add a little daub every day. Revising that narrative would mean scraping away layers of paint and starting over again with a fresh canvas—a daunting task to say the least' (p. 11).

2. MORAL CHARACTER AS DEVELOPED FROM COMMUNITY

The second moral language of ethics goes beyond the inner world of the first, to what Nash (2002) refers to as 'the concrete moral communities that provide us with a framework for thinking about right and wrong' (p. 59). Our network of relationships, contexts and small communities create moral webs of which we are intrinsically a part—they create our moral character. You will recall from Chapter 4 that Aristotle wrote of this 2000 years ago when he said that any account of human flourishing was linked intrinsically to our community. This can be explained neurologically by Donald (2008):

> Individual decisions are made in the brain. Human brains are, however, closely interconnected with, and embedded in, the distributed networks of culture from infancy. These networks may not only define the decision-space, but also create, install, and constrain many of the cognitive processes that mediate decisions. Humans are collective thinkers, who rarely solve problems without input from the distributed cognitive systems of cultures. (Donald, 2008, p. 192)

Of course, this explains why what is seen as moral in one community (leaving old people on an ice floe to drift away and die, having several wives or husbands, slavery) would be seen as unethical, and even illegal, in another. Much of our ethical sensitivity comes from the small communities that influence us and where our initial moral character is forged. We know from the study of the brain that early environment and early relationships play a large part in fashioning our first moral stances. Nash (2002) put it like this: 'Who I am is the embodiment of my entire life lived in a variety of the small communities, shaped by pivotal experiences in a number of institutions and touched by influential others' (pp. 60–1). Our little plastic (as in plasticity) brains are moulded in those early years to form an initial moral inclination that guides us until we are able to make personal ethical decisions (Bloom, 2010). The time comes when we review our inherited moral stances, or choose not to review them, as the case may be.

Billy grew up in Belfast, where he inherited a deep mistrust and hatred for Catholics. Brought up in a totally Protestant area of the city, he attended an all-Protestant school. When he left school, jobless and without qualifications, he quickly drifted into one of the militant sectarian organisations, the Ulster Volunteer Force. There he learned what it was like to be part of an army. One night with two other members of his organisation, he planted a bomb in a restaurant in a mainly Catholic area. Ten people were killed. Billy was proud of what he had done for the cause to which he was committed—keeping Northern Ireland safe from a united Ireland.

This example shows how Billy's background beliefs influence his behaviour. Never having held them up to the light to examine them, Billy's ethical decisions are in line with his values and what he believes. His identity is tied up with his actions and he is 'trapped in his own metaphysical life space'.

We move to Eamonn, who shares a similar type of religious and political template. In his case, he joined the IRA and planted a bomb in a café in a Protestant area of Belfast. Eamonn, like Billy, was a product of his local community—their moral outlook and ethical sensitivity was fine-tuned to pick up the local dictates and they both lived out what the community believed.

3. THE THIRD MORAL LANGUAGE: MORAL PRINCIPLE/S

The third moral language is one where we attempt to create a 'moral grammar'—a set of principles that might be abstract enough to cover most situations, but practical enough to be translatable and applicable to real-life situations (Hauser, 2006). If the first language is one of the inner world and how I perceive reality, and the second language is the one of the relationships and contexts that have formed me ethically, then the third language is one of objectivity and principle. Being principled means having sets of norms or guidelines on which I base my behaviour. We find these principles in codes—written guidelines—such as those of the British Association of Counselling and Psychotherapy (2010) or the Psychotherapy and Counselling Federation of Australia (2010). BACP (2010) outlines a number of such principles to guide counsellors and psychotherapists:

- autonomy
- beneficence
- non-maleficence
- justice
- fidelity
- self-care.

Most professionals in the helping professions would claim these principles or virtues as ones they can subscribe to as 'guiding lights' in their search for ethical excellence. However, principles do not tell us what to do. They are 'general hypotheses for moral action, not dictates or imperatives' (Nash, 2002, p. 111). Beneficence is a wonderful principle to adhere to and a marvellous virtue to have—*do what is for the good of your client.* But what does that mean in a particular instance? Jill begins to sob during her session with you as she recalls her childhood and her sense of abandonment. Should you: offer a heartfelt gesture of caring; put your arms around her and allow her to grieve for her inner child; become the good mother she never had and set up a new reparative relationship with her; help her find a community that cares for her and provides a new family where she can discover what she never had as a child; or, listen to her and be present as she grieves. Would any of these responses transgress a boundary or intrude on her autonomy? Translating an excellent virtue into appropriate ethical behaviour is not always easy.

We have moral theories, moral principles, moral values, personal qualities, codes and rules—these are in descending order of how prescriptive they are. The BACP (2010) *Ethical Framework* illustrates this:

Ethical Theories	Principles
Deontological (the law) Teleological (the consequences) Situational (the circumstances) Responsibility (the other)	Trustworthiness Autonomy Beneficence Non-maleficence Justice Self-respect

Values

Respecting human rights and dignity
Protecting the safety of clients
Ensuring integrity of relationships
Enhancing professional knowledge and its application
Alleviating personal distress/suffering
Fostering a self that is meaningful to others
Increasing personal effectiveness
Enhancing the quality of relationships between people
Appreciating the variety of human experience and culture
Striving for fair and just provision

Personal Qualities

Empathy
Sincerity
Integrity
Resilience
Respect
Humility
Competence
Fairness
Wisdom
Courage

Figure 8.4: BACP (2010) *Ethical Framework*

Moral character is:

1. an aggregate of moral characteristics that distinguish one person from another
2. the adherence to and practice of certain virtues and avoidance of certain vices
3. a complex make-up of intention, thought, action, disposition, intuition and feeling
4. defined and fashioned in community
5. nourished and transformed by narrative stories (Nash, 2002, p. 61).

4. VALUES AND ETHICAL MATURITY

WHAT ARE VALUES?

A value is an assessment and belief about what is good. It is an evaluation in that we assess some principle, perspective or stance as a good one, or to use the same term, a valuable one. What we see as 'of value' is considered worthy. It is important or precious for us, something we can admire and respect both in ourselves and others. We can have different types of values:

Non-negotiable values: values we consider applicable to all situations and ones we would not compromise, e.g., fidelity in marriage, looking after my children.

Negotiable values: values around which I have some ambivalence (e.g., my belief in the death penalty may not be strong, but there are particular instances where I could see it as a credible response to certain crimes).

Temporary values: ones I choose for a while (e.g., in a different culture I may choose to dress a particular way even through it is not a value I hold, or observe a religious custom even though it is not one I have chosen). I can accommodate these within my other values.

Opposing values: ones I find it difficult to accommodate, e.g., in a culture where woman were stoned for having sex, or where children are sold.

Espoused values (values I say I believe in) and values in action (values that come through my actions): these values may be aligned (e.g., a person believes in helping those worse off than herself and contributes to Children in Need) or they can be 'out-of-sync' (I say one of my values is helping those in need, but I never contribute time or money to charities dedicated to those in need).

Conscious values and unconscious values: values I am aware of and other values not in my consciousness.

Values are the lenses through which we see and evaluate what we and others do. Values motivate us to act—when we look behind our behaviours we come across values. What motivates me to go to work in the morning will tell me my values, e.g., I want to earn money and travel the world. I want to earn money and feed my family. I love the contribution my work allows me to make to humanity. I go to work to find a life partner. Each of these motivators uncovers a different value. Peter Singer (1993) notes that many everyday life choices we make are, in fact, restricted choices made within a specific framework or set of values. For example, if I want to contribute to improving the environment there are specific ways I could pursue this, and I can select the elements that will mark my contribution and best fit my established values. Singer notes that in such restricted choices, the values are already assumed and the choice is more about the best ways to attend to them. He contrasts this with 'ultimate choices' in which we choose between different sets of values: 'Should I live such that self-interest or community values are paramount? When war breaks out, will my peace-loving values be called into question? If I fall pregnant accidentally, as distinct from intentionally, will abortion look more like an option?' Ultimate choices take courage because they call into question the foundational values on which we might have, consciously or not, based our lives up to that point.

While our actions and behaviours come from our values, where do our values come from? Quite a number are inherited, as described by the second language of morality, through the small communities to which we belong. These work their way into our lives and 'pop up' into our consciousness to have an impact on our behaviour. Over time, they slip from our conscious view and become unconscious. We also arrive at values through conscious acceptance, when we deliberately choose and accept a value as part of our lives. New or changed circumstances present us with new information, where we need to develop or change values to proceed. Sometimes that newly adapted or created value will supersede an inherited value of long standing. For example, consider a person brought up to believe in the value of not aborting a pregnancy who, through their own experience or changed social influences, now accepts the value of abortion as one acceptable moral choice among others.

Moral sensitivity

Moral integrity comes with moral character which, in turn, is fashioned on the anvil of making moral choices. These moral choices shape our moral characters. A good example is the life of Ivan Ilyich as outlined in Tolstoy's, The Death of Ivan Ilyich. Mahon (2002) traces his moral journey to how insensitive he becomes to moral issues: 'What is most telling about Ilyich's paintings after social approbation is how quickly he jettisons his former moral code. Ilyich had always regarded his own heavy drinking and occasional philandering as vile behaviour. But when he saw 'people of high standing' doing such things, though he did not immediately dismiss his own misgivings, he felt considerably less perturbed. Soon he was not bothered at all…inordinately worldly ambition leads to moral insensitivity' (pp. 69–70). Mahon uses the image of a 'bell ringing' to illustrate what happens when we know what we are doing is ethically wrong. We hear it loud and clear at the beginning as a warning: as time goes on the tones of the bell get fainter and fainter until no bell rings. Our sensitivities are dulled to what is good. Mahon captures it well: 'A ringing bell calls attention to the tendency to turn a deaf ear to the experiences that warn us of our moral evasiveness' (p. 76). John Dean (1976), President Nixon's lawyer during the Watergate scandal, is another example. He traces his journey in how he failed to live up to his own ethical expectations. 'Slowly, steadily, I would climb towards the moral abyss of the President's inner circle until I finally fell into it, thinking I had made it to the top just as I began to realise I actually touched the bottom' (p. 31). Johnson (2012) calls this 'ethical fading', where the ethical aspects fade into the background 'if we use euphemisms to disguise unethical behaviour, numb our consciousness through repeated misbehaviour, blame others, and claim that only we know the truth' (p. 237).

Mahon (2002) offers some pointers and questions to help us hear the bell ring.

- Review the emerging signals, the bells, to which you turn a deaf ear.
- What are your favoured avoidance techniques?
- Hold your own press conference and interview yourself—ask the questions you would hate others to ask you in an open and honest interview.
- Can you get in touch with the 'dark conversations of your heart?'
- Can you unmask the secrets of your own unadmitted attachments?
- Where are your 'evasive concealments' and your 'tranquilized everydayness'?

(pp.92–9)

Our moral sensitivities are fine-tuned in the moral decisions we make. As we make decisions we strengthen the neurons that create the moral templates, which affect our next decisions.

Fostering ethical sensitivity

To build a moral compass and to foster ethical sensitivity it helps if we have:

1. *Awareness of our own current values:* religious, role models, from family, work and home. This is not just awareness of espoused values (the values I say I believe in) but my values-in-action—the real values to which I subscribe (as Sartre said, in a beginning quote to this chapter, you know your values by your actions). Knowing there is often a gap between what I say I value (e.g., the autonomy of individuals to make their own decisions) and what I actually do (e.g., that I often influence them to follow what I think is best for them) helps me at least question why I am doing what I am doing.

2. *Awareness of why we do what we do:* our motivation. Why do I do what I do? What motivates me to do it? Knowing my own hidden agendas can help me notice when I am tempted to be less than ethically mature (e.g., I love the power this gives me. I am flattered that I am needed.). Scharmer (2007) talks about the 'blind spot' as being our not knowing where these motivations come from. We can be so blind to the hidden reasons of why we do what we do.

3. *Knowing how I tend to use power* ('power over', 'power with'): this can give insights into when I might feel the need to rescue, or give answers, or be authoritative when needed. Power over others can result in domination and abuse (the Catholic Church is learning that so much abuse happened within its confines because of the way power is used within it organisationally).

4. *Taking care of self:* physically, emotionally, mentally and spiritually means I have the energy to think and feel clearly, and am in a stronger place to notice ethical problems and dilemmas when they arise.

5. *Embracing my own fear and my hypocrisies:* this allows me to recognise and accept some of my limitations.

6. *Being able to reflect deeply and honestly:* this can support me when my own needs predominate. An ability to be humble in the face of my own limitations and realising there are times when I will get it wrong, will help me be more accepting of who I am.

7. *Staying 'in relationship with' others, rather than just 'relating to':* this means I see them as individuals with differences, rather than as objects or commodities, and helps me realise when I might be ethically naive or juvenile. An ability to be attuned to when I am not in relationship with others, and where I have lost touch or become isolated.

8. *Developing and utilising moral imagination:* empathy is the greatest of all skills to keep us ethically sensitive and allow us to see things from other perspectives. Allowing spaces for speculation about others' experience, imagining their views and perspectives and how our actions might impact on them, is incredibly fruitful in both staying connected and determining action that is respectful of relationships.

9. *Active listening to oneself and to others:* what am I not hearing? What am I not allowing myself to hear? Use thoughtful discussion, dialogue and debate to fine-tune thoughts and possible decisions.

10. *Staying with our emotions and feelings:* allowing them space and time to speak to us.

11. *Becoming aware of the difference between intention and action:* wow easy it is to judge the behaviour of others differently from our own. We tend to judge ourselves by what we want to do (our intentions), rather than what we actually do (our actions and behaviours).

12. *Developing compassion:* the language of relationships (see Pizarro, 2000; Gilbert, 2010).

13. *Reflecting on actions in order to learn from them:* see Chapter 16 on learning from experience (Component Six).

14. *Identifying the ethical responsibility and accountability:* this comes from being ethically sensitive.

Sensitising our ethical antennae will make us aware of ethical issues, problems, boundaries, and when our actions are ethically immature. We need ways to regularly stop and review. What are the signs that we are being ethically unaware? What checks and balances have we developed to prevent this happening as much as possible?

The role of empathy in moral mindfulness

'Because moral situations usually centre on the presence of some form of victimisation, and empathy sensitises us to the distress of the other, its presence acts as an efficient moral marker...empathetic arousal is thus a "first alert" signalling moral relevance' (Pizarro, 2000, p. 360). Developing empathy (the ability to experience the feelings of others as if they were our own) is crucial to being ethically alert. Many unethical behaviours take place because perpetrators of harm or cruelty are unable to put themselves in the place of their victims and experience what happens to them. Empathy can be cognitive (I understand what it is like from your perspective), or affective (I can feel with you). These two are not as separate as we state them here, and cognitive empathy is often a prelude to affective empathy. Moral empathy is influenced by existing beliefs and stances—I feel your pain in being let down by a close friend because I value loyalty and reliability in friendship. Even more so if I have been let down myself and can recall my reactions.

Scharmer (2007) defines empathy as the ability 'to forget about our own agenda and begin to see how the world unfolds through someone else's eyes...it is a skill that requires us to activate the intelligence of the heart' (p. 12). Greenson (1960) calls this a form of 'emotional knowing'.

Where there are differences (race, culture, gender, age, sexual orientation) it can be more difficult to elicit empathy, especially if that difference is one that causes us problems. 'Dehumanizing others' by building on their differences is one way to overcome any empathic reactions we might have. It has been documented that getting people to do things they would not normally do (kill women and children in war situations; kill individuals in concentration camps) works when they are convinced the 'other' is a danger, is not human, or deserves to die.

'Mirror neurons' have been identified within the limbic system as a method of connecting to self and others. Siegel (2007) explains, 'the mirror neuron system...shifts the limbic and bodily states so that the prefrontal region can reflect on those changes and create compassionate (feeling with another) and empathic (understanding another) responses...we feel the state of relational resonance' (p. 169).

Some factors influence when we are more or less likely to experience empathy:

- We are less likely to feel empathy when we attribute blame to a person rather than see what has happened to them as outside their control (you were sick and missed our appointment versus you missed our appointment because you overslept and did not set your alarm).

- Helping individuals put themselves in the shoes of others and asking them to imagine what it would be like to experience what the other has experienced, tends to increase empathy—this strategy is sometimes used by police services who bring victims and perpetrators together in the hope that perpetrators might learn what it is like to have been a victim in this instance.

- Creating 'sameness' can help empathy. Emphasising difference (you are Jewish, gay, a man, person of colour) can distance empathy, while building bridges to sameness (we are human, we want the same things, we are trying to live our best lives) augments empathy. Research has shown that we can elicit empathy when we can create common factors (e.g., a piece of research showed a more benign reaction to Hitler when it was disclosed that he had the same birthday as the participant in the research project). Making connections helps create empathy. That is why it is always easier to be empathetic with people 'in our own group' and to be less so with people in others.

- Being aware of the mental maps and beliefs we bring to situations, and the resulting moral prejudices and attitudes that affect our capacity for empathy. Vegetarians will react differently to the image of a butcher shop than will meat eaters. Where one cringes, the other salivates.

- Knowing when we use empathetic repression, i.e., we feel empathy, but repress it intentionally (a parent whose daughter is pregnant may feel for her, but suppresses it in anticipation of the shame this will bring on the family). In suppressing empathy, horrible behaviours can take place (e.g., there is a picture of Polish policemen in concentration camps shooting prisoners with tears running down their cheeks).

Empathy erosion

Baron-Cohen (2011) offers a new theory of human cruelty that moves away from the term 'evil' and suggests the phrase 'empathy erosion'. For Baron-Cohen, lack of empathy is the reason why cruelty enters our world. Empathy erosion can be a temporary state (being drunk, resentful, hateful), or a more permanent state (as with psychopaths, borderline or narcissistic personalities). He defines empathy as: 'our ability to identify what someone else is thinking or feeling and to respond to their thoughts and feelings with an appropriate emotion' (p. 11).

From this standpoint, Baron-Cohen suggests we can measure how much empathy individuals have and places these measurements on a six point scale:

Zero empathy: There is no empathy at all. He divides this section into two groups: a) zero-negative empathy, which he illustrates through three well-defined positions of the psychopath, narcissist and borderline personality; b) zero-positive empathy, those who are autistic or have Asperger's syndrome. The latter can and often do develop a moral code, not through empathy, but by systematising and finding patterns of behaviour that work to get a good outcome, and comply with others' expectations, in many instances.

Level 1 empathy: This includes individuals who have little empathy, but have the ability to reflect on what they have done to some extent and to show regret. However, they seem incapable of stopping themselves from hurting or being cruel to others.

Level 2 empathy: This is enough to stop people being physically aggressive. Individuals at this level have some insights into how others would feel and this inhibits some behaviours. They usually need feedback from others to realise they have overstepped the mark.

Level 3 empathy: This is someone who knows they have difficulty with empathy and avoids jobs and situations that involve a lot of interpersonal contact.

Level 4 empathy: This is low-average empathy with individuals who have some discomfort identifying with others and dealing with feelings and emotions. However, this does not stop them relating to or working alongside others.

Level 5 empathy: These people are above average in empathy and involve themselves in emotional intimacy, sharing confidences, and mutual support.

Level 6 empathy: These are individuals with remarkable empathy, who continually focus on the feelings of others and internal worlds.

Baron-Cohen makes the point that levels of empathy depend on a mixture of factors, genes and environment. He also enters the free-will debate: 'If zero degrees of empathy is really a form of neurological disability, to what extent can such an individual who commits a crime be held responsible for what they have done?' (p. 109). Baron-Cohen believes empathy can be learned and suggests that it is such an important element in life it should have a higher ranking in education. He ends his argument with:

> One of my motivations for writing this book was to persuade you that empathy is one of the most valuable resources in our world...without empathy we risk the breakdown of relationships, we become capable

of hurting others, and we can cause conflict. With empathy, we have the resource to resolve conflict, increase community cohesion, and dissolve another person's pain. (p. 125)

The role of compassion in ethical mindfulness

The Dalai Lama (2002), recounts a story about a Tibetan monk who had been imprisoned by the Chinese: 'He told me that while he was in a Chinese Communist gulag for almost eighteen years, he faced danger on a few occasions. I thought he was referring to a threat to his own life. But when I asked, 'What danger'? he answered, 'Losing compassion towards the Chinese.' He considered this to be danger! Most of us would feel proud to tell others about how angry we got, as if we were some kind of hero' (p. 62).

The second skill that helps us to create a moral compass is that of compassion. Compassion, like empathy and sympathy are other-suffering emotions—elicited when we are in touch with the pain or suffering of others. Frost (1999) connects the two: 'Compassion engages empathy to act where pain and suffering are involved' (p. 131). Armstrong (2011) describes compassion as the ability 'to endure (something) with another person' (p. 6). This is summed up in the most ancient of guidelines, 'the Golden Rule', 'Do unto others what you would have them do unto you.' Armstrong traces its evolutionary development in mammals and humans through parental attachment, where humans feel compassion towards their needy offspring and deny themselves in order that their children might develop. The process by which this happens is compassion—altruism is born—we care for others. Compassion is a partnership of empathy and altruism, and is 'rooted in desires to alleviate suffering, prosocial behaviour and loving-kindness' (Gilbert, 2005, p. 9). Thich Nhat Hanh (1993) describes it poetically: 'Please call me by my true names, so I can wake up, and so the door of my heart can be left open, the door of compassion.'

Conclusion

To create a moral compass and extend our capacities to be sensitive and mindful about ethics over time, the crucial skills needed include empathy and compassion. While there are times when we can be drawn to feel empathy and compassion instantaneously, there are other times when we are more conflicted and different processes may be involved. John Dewey (in Fesmire, 2003) described this well in his exploration of 'moral imagination', which involves the creation of dialogical space where speculation about the self in relation to other, attunement to the other's experience, identification of personal risks and threats, and development and testing of options and outcomes can occur.

Chapter 9
Component 2
The process of ethical decision making

'Every choice is seen as a creation of values.'

(Sloan, 1986, p. 59)

'When making a decision of minor importance, I have always found it advantageous to consider all the pros and cons. In vital matters, however, such as the choice of a mate or a profession, the decision should come from the unconscious, from somewhere within ourselves. In the important decisions of our personal life, we should be governed, I think, by the deep inner needs of our nature.'

(Freud talking to Theodor Reik, quoted in Sloan, 1986, p. 62)

'The central evolutionary truth is that the unconscious mind matters most.'

(Brooks, 2011, p. xii)

'Decision is an inherently emotional business.'

(Brooks, 2011, p. 17)

'The human brain is built to take conscious knowledge and turn it into unconscious knowledge…Learning consists of taking things that are strange and unnatural and absorbing them so steadily that they become automatic. That frees up the conscious mind to work on new things…automaticity is achieved through repetition.'

(Brooks, 2011, pp. 86–7)

Making decisions

Ethical decision making falls within the wider sphere of decision making in general. Decision making is fundamental to everyday life. People make decisions not just on a daily basis, but minute to minute: 'What will I eat? Will I get up now or stay in bed for another hour? What will I wear today? How will I deal with my next door neighbour who is causing me anxiety with the noise he is creating? Is it time to change my car?' Many day to day decisions are made automatically without much thought: I touch the brake on the car as I come to a red light; I brush my teeth in the morning as part of my routine of facing the new day. Others are made with a great deal of thought and deliberation: 'With all the family and financial responsibilities I have will I change my career from being a dentist to an interior decorator? Will I undergo chemotherapy for this malignant growth or try to treat my illness with less invasive procedures? Will I report poor professional conduct from a colleague? Will I break confidentiality because I think this client is in danger?' Some are simple decisions about what I might wear today (although my partner might disagree with this as an example of a simple decision). Other decisions are complex: 'How should I respond to environmental needs? Ignore them, stop travelling by aeroplane, give money and/or join an ecology group?'

Human decisions

Platt et al. (2008) define a decision as 'a commitment to a choice or course of action selected from more than one option' (p. 126). As we will see in Chapter 13, commitment does not always result in action. We can make decisions without implementing them. For the moment we will stay with decisions as commitments made, and will consider the processes that go into discerning what is the best moral course of action for us when faced with a number of options.

> A 'decision maker' is, by definition, someone faced with the task of choosing between alternatives or possibilities about something that needs to be done. Each possible action will result in the realisation of various, and probably different, objective and subjective values (Horan cited in Sloan, 1986).

Joan is 18 years old and wondering what career she would like to pursue. Mick is caught between saying nothing and telling his boss that one of his colleagues is accessing pornography on his work computer. Eleanor is pregnant at a very inconvenient time in her life, and an abortion would make life a lot easier for her—she is thinking through what she should do. All three are faced with choosing between future possible actions and of making practical decisions about their futures.

A decision is a projected action. I project what I will do into the future. At this point, because the decision is still in its embryonic stages, it is just a possibility. In deliberate decision making we involve ourselves in the possibilities of future scenarios or projects. A possibility is what the future permits, or more precisely, what *my* future permits. If my decision making is about possibilities in the future, then they will be dependent on what possibilities I allow myself to entertain. Clearly, possibilities are limited by a number of factors. Already, as I position myself to make a decision, I may have cut off certain possibilities that would conflict with my values (I cannot hurt this person. I cannot steal. I cannot take advantage of this vulnerability. I could never work for a company that makes nuclear weapons. I cannot allow myself to think of having an abortion. I would never be disloyal to my friends). These limiting possibilities can be a result of my past (I cannot love someone from another religion or race) or could be values I have come to believe in and subscribe to myself (being gay is another equally valid way to express sexuality). Possibilities, dealing with the future, are influenced strongly by the past, about what I can and cannot do, what I can and cannot allow myself to perceive, what I can and cannot hear, see, speak or imagine. My choices are also limited by biology (I am a man or woman), by age (Winning a tennis grand slam is physically beyond me); by location (I cannot choose to be President of the USA) and by time (I cannot go back and undo what I have done in the past).

Alisha has lived in Australia all her life. Her parents moved to Sydney 25 years ago from Pakistan. They are in the process of arranging her marriage. Alisha is highly ambivalent about this. On the one hand, she has been raised as a Hindu, to which she is committed, even if she does not see herself as a strong practicing Hindu. She is also aware that honour in her family means that she should trust her parents to organise an arranged marriage. On the other hand, she has been brought up in a wider multi-cultural environment where the ability to choose one's partner is valued. She wants to fall in love and decide who to marry. She struggles between two pathways: either agreeing to the arranged marriage, or telling her parents she has decided she will choose her own partner. She knows the latter will be extremely difficult for her parents to accept, her father, in particular. In making a decision about what to do, Alisha has to reconcile a number of values (religion versus autonomy, respect for tradition versus new ways of doing things, her own wishes versus the wishes of the community). She stands at the crossroads between the past and the future where whatever decision she makes may result in loss. Even as she hesitates before deciding, her imagination has propelled her into the future and she has envisaged a number of possible future scenarios. She has weighed these up automatically and sees the pros and cons in each decision: what risks does she take if she makes one decision, or another? What price will she pay for choosing? Underpinning her emerging decision are two factors: what values will she allow to impact her decision? What possibilities will she allow herself to entertain before making her decision? We will look in more detail at the second of these.

The rut of life and automatic decisions

Many authors speak about the human tendency to get into 'ruts'—routines that not only characterise our lives, but become the mould from which we make decisions. Our brains like habits. If we see a rut as a 'habitual pattern of response that is culturally learned and sanctioned, and which prevents us from acknowledging a wider range of possibilities in ourselves and in our relationships' (Gutknecht and Meints cited in Sloan, 1986, p. 87) then we have already connected our life stance to the decisions we will make. Being entangled and trapped in our routines means that decisions are almost made before we make them. We fall into our choices rather than become proactive deciders. Commitment to a way of life, an ideology, a religion or wisdom tradition becomes the backcloth from which decisions emerge rather than are considered, e.g., a traditional Catholic with a strong commitment to their beliefs would find it difficult to allow themselves to consider the possibility of an abortion. Even to engage with the possibility might be difficult. The decision emerges on its own. Having fallen into the jaws of routine, it becomes impossible at times, and difficult at others, to extricate ourselves (Sloan, 1986). Our routines, our mental maps, our meaning-making templates, our organising signatures (how we see ourselves and how we visualise our identities), our life sphere, our mental schema of the world (all phrases given to mean the same thing) can become powerful filters that weave our decisions for us rather than decisions made on blank pages. We are not saying this is bad or immature when applied to ethical decision making. Not allowing the possibility of certain actions into my moral decisions e.g., murdering others, being unfaithful to my partner, or conning the elderly out of their money, indicates strong moral values that are to be applauded. On the other hand, we can be caught in unhelpful and immature habits of mind that result in harmful behaviours, e.g., a belief that certain races are inferior to others. If this is the case for Alisha, then the decision to agree to her arranged marriage will not be one she brings into deliberate and reflective consciousness. She will assess the communal routine, the tradition and be part of the decision already made. She may do this willingly and with tolerance.

Kafka (1914) writes about how this happened in his life: 'I am almost thirty-one years old…The uniformity, regularity, comfort and dependence of my way of life keep me unresistingly fixed wherever I happen to be. Moreover, I have more than ordinary inclination towards a comfortable and dependable life, and so even strengthen everything that is pernicious to me. Finally, I am getting older; any change becomes more and more difficult' (p. 105). All this at the tender age of 31. When given an ethical dilemma, most of us have a characteristic response that emerges from our life space, the place within us that is our formed character based on the past.

We all too readily give our stock answer. It is only when we are disoriented, confused, experience cognitive dissonance that we are forced to do one of two things: retreat rapidly to the safety of our former life space and make decisions congruent with it or allow ourselves to be disoriented and begin the journey of a new engagement with a decision. The latter has built-in dangers that we are all too aware of—What will this mean for my settled and secure life? What small 'murders' will I have to commit if I hold this value up for review? What will this mean in light of my current situation and responsibilities, my community relationships and their beliefs, changes I might have to make, and living with uncertainty?

Decisions come from moral character

Ethical decisions are not made on a blank page where there is no past. Who we are is determined initially by who we relate to and the contexts, environments and communities in which we are born and raised. We tend, in the first instance, to inherit our ethical decisions as well. We start off as the products of our social and cultural environments and, over time, the decisions that emerge from these backgrounds become unconscious and are made outside our awareness. We come to our ethical decisions with an already formed ethical approach—what we call an ethical or moral character. This character has been built on the past, on previous decisions made, and all those elements that go into making us who we are in the here and now. We already have what Pizarro (2000) calls 'antecedent belief systems that are at work in the mental set of the individual' (p. 365). Moral templates and ethical schemata are already laid down in our brains. These existing belief systems or mental mindsets moderate and mediate emotions when faced with real-life situations. These emotions, in turn, influence the moral decisions we make, for example, having a mindset that a certain group of people are enemies and ought to be destroyed can result easily in a moral decision to kill someone. This decision may not be rational (although thought-deliberately), but based on the emotional reaction of being faced with an enemy. Sometimes we think we make these decisions consciously, when in reality they are made for us by the in-built moral templates fashioned by our upbringing and all this entails: our environments, relationships and experiences. 'Out of awareness' doesn't mean unconscious in the sense that we do not have access to what is happening, but means out of our immediate awareness in so far as we are dealing with habits.

Recently I (Elisabeth) was having a new air-conditioner installed in the office. I was told that if the previous one had failed due to a storm then I could claim it on insurance. If it was ordinary wear and tear I could not. I asked the technician what he thought had happened. He said he couldn't say one way or another, then he asked if I would like him to lie for me. The answer to that, especially in the middle of working on this book, was to say 'no'. Fortunately, I had no moral temptation in this regard, so it was an easy response. However, it was an interesting moment to experience: I was being asked whether I would make a conscious choice to be unethical, and it forced me to respond with a deliberate and definite position. Of course, moral temptation is often more subtle and covert.

In helping relationships (whether counselling, psychotherapy, coaching, consulting, supervision or management), a key issue is how individuals are viewed and how relationships become arenas for power, engagement and emotional attunement. Any decision I make, ethical or otherwise, rests on my view of people and how I relate to them. This, in turn, has been carved from my past. In Chapter 2 we noted that the research on evil and harm shows how difficult it is to hurt or harm those we see as people like ourselves. When we depersonalise other people, see them as commodities, paint others as threats, we can do all sorts of horrendous things to them (see Baumeister, 1997). Being 'in relationship with', having emotional connections to and attunement with, being able to empathise—these build in moral compasses that include us in a relational ethics of trust. Bond (2007) also uses the term 'trust', even calling it 'the missing ethics', and eventually describes the tenets of 'relational trust': 'Trust is a relationship of sufficient quality and resilience to withstand the challenges arising from difference, inequality, risk and uncertainty' (p. 436) (see Chapter 20). Our attitudes, values, ability to relate to and engage with others, and our sensitivity to differences, all define and colour the ethical decisions we make. Pruyne and Bond (2011) explain this in the context of narrative theory: 'There are two kinds of stories we need to learn to tell. The 'big story' is the story of who we are across time—a story of identity and purpose. The 'little story' is the narrative arc in the moment as we encounter the moment to moment challenges of our lives and make moral choices of consequence' (p. 10). The 'big story' to which they refer is what we call moral character, the little story is how we implement that character in the ethical choices we make on a daily basis.

The crossroads of life are the moments we stop to look at why we make the decisions we do. Why do I raise my children in this way? Why do I hold the values I do? By beginning to reflect on the underpinnings of my decision making I can start to see the templates that influence them, the backgrounds from which they come, and the influence they have over me. In that moment, I make another choice: I can continue to allow my habits and templates to have the influence they have, or I can begin the journey of reviewing, choosing or changing the templates.

Contexts play a large role in how we make decisions. Being part of a group can overwhelm our private values and make us do things we would not normally do consciously or unconsciously. Change the context, and values can change with them—often very unconsciously. Wanting to be accepted as part of the group can influence or determine our decisions, and even involve us in making decisions we would not normally endorse. Söderberg (1905), the Swedish author, explains this well in Doctor Glas:

> 'We want to be loved; failing that, admired; failing that, feared; failing that, hated and despised. At all costs we want to stir up some sort of feeling in others. Our soul abhors a vacuum. At all costs it longs for contact'.

Sometimes the price of our need to be noticed, to be accepted by others, and to be visible is that we allow others to make decisions for us. Or we make decisions that we might not make, were our need to be accepted and please others not so great.

Geraldine was raised as a strict Catholic and inherited her values and influences from her parents, teachers and church. If you asked her as an 18-year-old about her values she would tell you she had inherited them, and now chooses them as her own. She was anti-abortion, did not agree with sex before marriage, was a bit doubtful about the church's teaching on condoms and AIDS, but this did not impact on her life much, and felt strongly that being gay or lesbian was an unnatural mode of expressing sexuality. She made her life, relationships and particular sexual decisions based on these values. At university she was plunged into cognitive dissonance when new friends with different values and opinions surrounded her. Her polished arguments on abortion, pre-marital sex, gay lifestyles, were met with equally polished arguments for alternative stances. Not only that, but she realised that some new friends did not live up to the images she had formed of gay and lesbian people. Her first sexual experience with a young man she admired was fraught with guilt. However, towards the end of her university life she was still with John and sex was a regular part of her relationship with him, now without the guilt. Three things can explain this:

1. Geraldine changed one set of values for another due to the new context in which she lived. She went along with the values of the new context, rather than consciously challenging her inherited values and changing her own mind.
2. Second, she went through a transformational process of reviewing her inherited values and working systematically, rationally and

emotionally (or perhaps unconsciously) towards another set of values different from the ones she was born with.

3. A third, more difficult, option is that she still believes her old values, but has conveniently 'parked them' or repressed them to allow herself to practise a new set of values.

Over time, whatever led her to this new behaviour, it will become unconscious and she will automatically choose further actions aligned to the new tacit knowing. The human brain is built to take conscious knowledge and turn it into unconscious knowledge. Geraldine has new unconscious knowledge (through repetitive behaviour), which has become the background from which her decisions emerge. She sees the world, not as it is, but as her perceptions of it direct her and her perceptions include her values. Had you asked her about the change that took place within her she might not be able to give you an explanation. She was however, a different person to the 18-year-old Geraldine. Brooks (2011) puts it well in talking about a different person—it could have been Geraldine: 'It was the culmination of a long unconscious shift. She had never consciously rejected her old values. She would have fiercely denied if you'd asked. But those old ways of being had gained less prominence in the unconscious jockeying for supremacy inside' (p. 293).

Whenever a decision is to be made, information will be sifted by the brain with new information automatically sent into the collective pool to see if there are comparisons, other experiences, or learnings from the past already in place. When it connects to them (all done unconsciously) it will suggest a decision based on past experience congruent with values. If it does not connect with old patterns and ways of doing things, the brain will send the decision into consciousness to be thought through and worked through in order to make a decision. There could be a related past experience, but the new experience is different or somewhat contradictory or disorienting. Again, the brain suggests consciousness and deliberation is required to resolve the decision.

Decisions come from values

Lewis (2000) suggests there are six ways in which we make ethical decisions, each of them based on different values. For Lewis, we cannot separate the way we arrive at values from the values themselves. If I believe that values are based on an authority that directs them (e.g., the Bible, or the Koran, God or a church) then I will look to that authority to tell me what values I ought to adopt. Not only will I accept and make these values my own, but I will have a template value that authority is itself a value. The six ways proposed by Lewis are modes of knowing (how we come to know something—the mental mode by which we arrive at knowing) and contain sets of values:

1. VALUING SENSE EXPERIENCE

We would call this 'learning from experience' or experiential learning. Knowledge, in this mode, comes through our five senses and our experiences. It is a form of personal learning. For example, one of us (Michael) grew up in an environment where being gay or lesbian was seen as 'unnatural' and an unacceptable way to express sexuality. It was viewed as sinful and harmful. As a child, this was a value he accepted on the authority of teachers, parents, church and community. Over time, his experience of meeting and working with gay and lesbian people helped him change his perspective, and he now believes and accepts that being gay or lesbian is another way to express sexuality—no better or worse than heterosexual stances. The new value has been integrated into his life, and his way of being with and seeing gay and lesbian people has changed quite radically. His mode of learning this has been from sense experience.

Leonardo da Vinci would be the 'patron saint' of this kind of learning. The values are in the experience—sifting, reflecting, observing and coming to one's own conclusion. The value inherent in this form of learning is whether 'the alleged truth corresponds to their own entirely personal sense experience of the world—and if it does not, the alleged truth is quietly and decisively put aside' (Lewis, 2000, p. 23). A 'felt sense' of what is good and bad pervades this approach, and experience becomes the norm against which evaluations take place. Just as taste can tell us what we like and don't like, and even what is good for us, so experience becomes the yardstick against which actions are judged to be good or bad, or better.

In my (Elisabeth's) undergraduate degree, I undertook a subject tactlessly entitled 'deviant fieldwork'. I was assigned prison visiting tasks, going to visit prisoners who had no other visitors as a result of their community or family disenfranchisement or their appalling crimes. While I saw it as a grand (and if the truth be told) gratuitous adventure, I learned so much more. I was treated badly as a 'do-gooder', and seen as a naïve fool (perhaps not so far from the truth). I noticed also that the behaviour of the guards was such that the uniform seemed to be the main defining feature that distinguished them from inmates. The visceral assault of the environment, and the interactions, rules and procedures told me a lot about the values, norms and culture of the setting. In the end, the inmate I finally visited turned out to be the least daunting, and of least gratuitous value, in the whole event. There sat a person, someone to know and connect with. Perhaps I was still a do-gooder with thoughts that lacked political complexity, but I settled into more conscious reflection about the person, the visit, and what I might usefully offer.

2. VALUING LOGIC AND REASON

The second modality of learning involves reason, rationalising and working through the dilemma logically: looking at the pros and cons for each possible decision and weighing up the best thing to do when there are a number of viable options. The value is one of deductive logic where we can show how our conclusion follows from our premise and we can justify how we reached the conclusion we did. 'We will feel a range of emotions when confronted with an ethical dilemma: anger, fear, frustration, stress, concern, guilt and anguish. Any such emotion should be articulated, acknowledged and then set to one side as we begin our deliberation. Ethicability recognises the power of emotions, but also reminds us that deciding what's right is a rational and reasonable process between two emotional stages. At the outset we acknowledge our perhaps negative emotions and set them aside' (Steare, 2006, p. 91). Reason, logic, clear thinking and problem solving all help us come to a decision using our intelligence. We can even use this when there is no obvious conclusion for our logical reasoning, e.g., how do I accept that I have been diagnosed with cancer? I may conclude there is no answer to this in the way I would normally solve a problem, but can still come to accept it and live with it as part of my life. Problems may present themselves in different forms, yet we can approach them in a logical and rational manner:

1. *Puzzles:* a puzzle has one right answer. Sorting out the key elements and finding the right answer is the task. In ethical decision making, Jade is faced with such a situation: she works in a prison setting as a psychologist. During an assessment with an inmate he happens to let slip knowledge that shows there has been a security risk, i.e., how drugs are being smuggled into the prison. For Jade there is one right answer to this ethical question—she needs to let the appropriate authorities know. If Jade is unsure what to do, then her employment contract with the prison will soon enlighten her or her immediate supervisor will give her the information she needs. On the whole, puzzles are non-negotiable in that once I have the information I need, I have no ethical leeway to choose other options.

2. *A problem:* is a puzzle that has a number of solutions, but the solution will change from person to person, and situation to situation. Jacob is faced with whether or not he should break confidentiality when confronted with a client who is depressed and talks about suicide. A number of ethical options are available to Jacob: to ask his client's doctor to arrange medical/psychiatric or psychological

help for his client; provide his client with further sessions to help him through a difficult time; or help his client build in further strategies to ensure his/her safety.

3. *A dilemma:* is a situation where I am faced with a number of options that tend to conflict with one another, often in ethical circumstances around values. A dilemma arises because more than one option exists and the options compete as equally good or bad. For example, how do I choose between loyalty to my employer versus loyalty to my family? Ethical dilemmas also arise because we experience clashes in values. For example, I want to accumulate wealth for my children to have more options later in life, but that might involve them having less of me now. I value confidentiality and don't want to reveal what you tell me, yet I have a duty of care, value your safety, and am worried you will harm yourself. In a counselling situation I may be faced with these two values, both good in themselves, knowing I have to choose one over the other.

   We are a mass of clashing values. There are deep survival values that come from our reptilian pasts—to look after ourselves, to be fed, to mate, and to maintain territory and possessions. There are relationship values that connect us in loyal ways to our groups, and can put us in opposition and competition to other religious, political, racial, gender, and cultural groups. Then there are the sets of values that come with our executive brain—to be creative and imaginative, to plan for the future, to manage emotions. These value sets are often in conflict and we have to work towards resolving them. There are no clear-cut answers about which values have ascendancy or right of way.

4. *A paradox:* something that cannot be solved, but with which I have to learn to live, e.g., 'I am going to be made redundant and would prefer not to be.' 'My father has died and I am not sure how I can live without him.' Ethical paradox may involve living with a situation where justice will never be given. For example, in the case of a woman who has been abused as a child, but will never get justice or see the abuser brought to justice. How can she live with this? Or in a situation where you have a job with an employer who seems to offer good services, but not always with integrity. Should you stay and be part of the change, given that means you also become implicated in the behaviour short-term?

5. *A psychological problem:* a problem that keeps recurring or involves redundant, self-defeating or personally mystifying behaviours. People often feel stuck in their lack of conscious understanding of what is happening or how to change. Ethical issues arise when the

transgression implicates others. For example, all my relationships with male bosses end up in fights. This recurring and repetitive pattern leads to disrespect on both sides. In another example, a gambler has convinced himself he will double his children's private school trust fund if he takes it all to bet on his blackjack game. Once he lost it, the Christmas and holiday funds, and mortgaged the house, he realised he had a problem he couldn't solve alone. In general, such complex and multifaceted problems will require specialised help.

6. *A mystery:* events that happen in life that are difficult or impossible to make sense of, evocatively expressed in the title of Rabbi Harold Kushner's 1981 book, *Why Do Bad Things Happen to Good People?* For example, why do children get cancer? How did some people survive the death camps and others not? If there is a god, how does he allow suffering? How can I live a normal life when my daughter is missing? Ethical mysteries often involve questions about existential matters: how we can make sense of evil and suffering, what constitutes a worthy life, how to live in the absence of forgiveness and so on.

Each of the above needs a different intervention to resolve it: hence, the importance of knowing what you are dealing with.

In the modern Western world, reason has become the most important method we have for dealing with life and the best tool we have for decision making. Despite an awareness of its weaknesses when used alone we still rely on reason as the prime and, it is often argued, the only valid source for human decision making. And yet, time after time, the rational approach to resolving problems and making effective decisions has been shown to be deficient. The AIDS epidemic in Africa is continually cited as an example. There is a keen awareness of the dangers of AIDS, knowledge of how it is spread, and even access to condoms. And yet, despite knowing the problem and the solution, children who had nursed their parents as they died of AIDS 'were replicating the exact same behaviours that had led to their parents' deaths' (Brooks, 2011, p. 325). The issue is not technical, nor rational, but involves emotional and cultural behaviours that defy solely rational solutions. Reason may well be necessary, but it is certainly not sufficient.

3. VALUING EMOTION

Staying with emotions, listening to them carefully, sifting through them and deciding to trust them as a vital form of communication, can be a value that underpins our learning. Fine makes this point (2007): 'Our emotions play an important, if furtive, role in our moral condemnations and approbations'

(p. 54). Jonah Lehrer (2009) spells it out, 'When you are confronted with an ethical dilemma, the unconscious automatically generates an emotional reaction. (This is what psychopaths cannot do.)Within a few milliseconds, the brain has made up its mind; you know what is right and what is wrong. These moral instincts aren't rational—they've never heard of Kant…It's only at this point—after the emotions have already made up the moral decision—that those rational circuits in the prefrontal cortex are activated' (p. 167). In recent years, there has been a strong movement towards recognising and accepting the role of feelings and emotions in decision making, and in ethical decision making in particular. They are our oldest guides to what is good for us. For example, the feeling of fear is an in-built alarm system that keeps us safe through the fight or flight response. Feelings and emotions are also what connect us to others and bring about limbic connection and resonance (Lewis *et al.*, 2003). As mammals, our emotions help us to communicate, read the internal world of others and provide us with empathy and compassion that support our abilities to make ethical decisions.

Emotions are the currency of values. Values trigger our emotions and let us know what is right and wrong. 'Emotions assign values to things, and reason can only make choices on the basis of those valuations' (Brooks, 2011, p. 21). Accepting emotions as valuable sources of information allows us to include them in making decisions.

4. Valuing intuition

According to Haidt (2001), ethical decisions are made largely based on intuitions. He notes that logic, thinking, and rationality move in to justify the decisions intuition has made. The use of intuitive knowledge as the basis for making decisions has had a mixed press. Some see it as the highest form of decision making, while others are more suspicious of it as a way of knowing and as a basis for effective decision making. What is intuition? Lewis (2000) defines it as 'a highly developed and powerful mode of purely abstract mental processing, one that synthesises masses of facts and theories with extraordinary speed' (p. 84).

How does gathering up the wisdom of the years and monitoring intuitive thoughts and feelings shape the hunches and seemingly automatic decisions and 'gut responses' that emerge? Gigerenzer (2007) offers a reason, 'Stop thinking when you are skilled…reason can conflict with what we call intuition…good intuitions go beyond the information given' (p.103). Lehrer (2009), Fine (2007), Gigerenzer (2007) and Haidt (2001) all espouse the value of intuitive knowing and intuitive decision making as a key element in learning and in ethics. Sports psychology and sports coaching shows how thinking and deliberate reflection can affect performance negatively (Lehrer, 2009; Gladwell, 2005). They point out that reflection-in-action can result in what they call 'choking', where thinking impedes effective action. Imagine a soccer goal-keeper or a fire-fighter thinking too much before acting? Think before and after, they suggest, but not during.

Carl Jung defined intuition as a way of 'seeing around corners'—the fast, effortless and automatic process of *knowing*. The mind is not viewed as a blank slate at birth—we are born with knowledge and moral faculties waiting to be activated (Hauser 2006; Bloom 2010). Lewis (2000) presents six well-known scientists (Banting, Alger, Russell, Newton, Keynes and Kapor) who 'all readily admit their most fundamental creative ways of tackling a problem is intuitive' (p. 84). They offer hints on how to increase intuitive ways of knowing: settle the emotions to help the still, quiet stirrings of intuition to be heard; and, allow body and mind to rest together in an alert, relaxed fashion, and even practise techniques that help this, such as yoga, meditation and mindfulness.

5. VALUING AUTHORITY

There are two ways authority might influence us. At one extreme, Nietzsche offered a controversial account of how we become reflective about our actions and decisions. He argued that we only give an account of ourselves because someone from an established system of justice asks us to, and when there is threat of punishment. 'For Nietzsche, accountability follows only upon an accusation or, minimally, an allegation, one made by someone in a position to deal out punishment if causality can be established. And we become reflective upon ourselves, accordingly, through fear and terror. Indeed we become morally accountable as a consequence of fear and terror' (Butler, 2005, p. 11).

We are arguing for ethical reflection as a self-driven, and inherently valuable enterprise, if one is to be ethically mature. Nietzsche offered a frame for someone who is at the other end of the ethical spectrum, driven by authority, and perhaps immaturity, alone. However, it is true that many will not consider their actions until forced to, and that some of our best learning occurs at the pointy end of experience, when the action has taken place and exposure to others has occurred.

This mode of learning makes 'someone else' the authority. We accept what they say as of great value and as holding the greatest weight in any ethical reflection. Often this is useful and appropriate, and is not experienced as a burden, but a pleasurable way to 'fit in' and measure one's own opinion against a valuable yardstick. For example, we might rely heavily, even solely, on our ethical code, what our profession guides us to do, what a supervisor or senior colleague advises, what a key older figure said, i.e., a teacher, tutor, or what the Bible/Koran/other faith tradition decrees. According to Harris (2010), 78 per cent of Americans believe the Bible is the word of God, either literal or inspired. For many, the authority of the Bible is a value that influences how they make decisions, and what decisions they make. This mode of knowing places trust and faith in an authority outside ourselves and trusts that this authority will give us answers. Authority is often based on power and power comes from a variety of sources:

Legitimate power: power that comes from those we see as having recognised power that is accepted as legal or endowed. It comes more with a position rather than a person, e.g., a policeman or policewoman, a manager or boss, parents. We give such people power because of the position they hold.

Expert power: is power that comes from having an area of expertise e.g., doctor, lawyer, professor. Knowledge, skills and experience all build up this kind of power and it is often endowed regardless of the person.

Referent power: comes from our admiration for a person through which we give them a lot of influential or persuasive power. Our admiration for our parents or grandparents will give them extra power or influence in what they do or say.

Reward power and *coercive power:* these come from the ability of a person to be able to reward or punish us. Those who can promote or demote us, can influence our salaries and can give us grades, all wield this kind of power.

When we defer to authority as a value, we acquiesce to the demands or expectations of another (be that God, political party or parents) and allow them to influence our decisions. We can see the extremes of authority as a value system in 'cults', where the individual gives up autonomy and allows themselves to be directed and guided by the 'cult', or leaders of the cult. The individual does not make decisions that do not conform with, or are not aligned to the values and directives of the group. Less influential are other groups that we allow to influence us, depending on how much 'authority' we feel they deserve in determining our values and our decisions.

A common 'ethical test' by which one might measure a decision is called the 'wise person' test. This suggests you think of the wisest person you know and imagine them giving you advice or guidance on the decision you are about to make. This is an example of the use of authority to inform good decision making.

6. VALUING A SCIENTIFIC APPROACH

The scientific approach to knowing is founded on the value that the best information comes from careful, empirical observation that can be tested (and retested over time), and from which there are clear, factual inferences that can be drawn. The scientific approach sets up the ethical dilemma as an experiment, an action-inquiry that gathers evidence for and against possible outcomes. Close to the rational and reasonable approach, the scientific method treats an ethical dilemma as if it were a research project. How do we go about working towards a decision or conclusion using the best in research methods?

The stages of the scientific approaches to decision making can include:

- gathering the facts
- testing them
- immersing yourself in the findings and looking at the logical implications
- drawing your conclusions from the facts
- showing how your experiment is repeatable (replicable).

Mixing and matching

It is clear that each of the six value bases on which ethical decisions are made has strengths and weaknesses (see Table 9.1 below). For example, the authority approach accesses the wisdom of the ages, the experiences of others, and takes responsibility away from the individual for whom it is easy to get lost in the complexities and details of the ethical dilemma. On the other hand this method can keep individuals dependent on authority, can be an unreflective stance, and often doesn't take contextual or situational elements into consideration. Most of us would try not to make our final ethical decision using just one of the above approaches; it is in the interests of thorough decision making that all approaches are taken into consideration before finalising what to do with particular ethical dilemmas. In summary, we might ask the following: What do my feelings tell me? Is my intuition pointing me in a direction I can trust? How can I reasonably work it through? What have others (authorities, codes, guidelines, my values) to contribute to my final choice of action?

	Positive	*Negative*
Sense Experience	Keeps it personal	Becomes narcissistic
	Grounded in experience	Ignores others and wisdom
	Responsible me	Me-only
Logic and reason	Rational	Classifies (categories that imprison us)
	Objective	
	Fosters problem solving	Disconnected from others
Emotion	Connects and attaches us	In-group thinking
	Brings empathy/compassion	Collusion
	Helps us communicate	Illogical and irrational
	Drives us to act	Impulsive

cont.

	Positive	Negative
Intuition	Unconscious knowing	Unreflected knowing
	Comes naturally	Inherited nonsense
	Fast	Impulsive
Authority	Wisdom from others	Abusive power
	Direct/accessible	No personal responsibility
	Past experience	Unreflective acceptance
Science	Testable	Remote from
	Logical deductions	People as commodities
	Valid conclusions	Head knowledge only

Table 9.1: The Strengths and Weaknesses of the Six Value
Bases on which Ethical Decisions are Made

MODEL OF DECISION MAKING

Table 9.2 provides an overview of how we see the bigger picture of decision making, which we apply to ethical decision making:

Internal	Information Perception Awareness	External
Hunger		Senses
Sex	To respond or not?	Experiences
Threat		Threat
No choice		No choice
Pre-determined action		Pre-determined action
Choice	What to do? (Options)	Choice
	How to decide?	
Unconscious choice	**Preconscious choice**	**Conscious choice**
Decides for you outside awareness	Decides for you but you can override	You choose

Table 9.2: Overview of Ethical Decision Making

Examples

We will take two examples to run through this model (as presented in Table 9.2). One is an animal—a gazelle grazing on the Serengeti savannah. Alert as ever to danger, its antennae are monitoring internal and external sources of information. Its feeling of hunger and a decision to move toward grass come automatically. The gazelle has no choice, just as it has no choice when the mating season arrives. It moves to find a mate—automatically. Its action is predetermined. While there is some evidence that animals (rats and monkeys) can restrict their eating if by doing so pain is caused to another rat or monkey, they cannot choose to starve themselves. Instincts take over and make choices for all animals. Similarly, if external information hits their brains through their senses (a movement in the grass, the sight of a lion) they poise for a decision that will result in action. There may well be a hesitation while the senses sort out the information from the outside and give it some meaning. Is it really a movement or the wind in the grass? Is it a lion, and if it is, is it in hunting mode? Having determined it is a stalking lion, then choice disappears and the gazelle moves. Having decided there is no danger, the gazelle continues to graze. The process is simple:

- sensory receptors pick up information (or information comes from inside)
- the information is processed
- a trigger is sent to the nervous system which activates a command neuron
- decision cells come into play activated by the command neuron;
- movement takes place (behaviour/action results).

Wilson (2002) summarises that this 'ability to size up our environments, disambiguate them, interpret them, and initiate behaviour quickly and unconsciously confers a survival advantage' (p. 23).

Something different happens with humans, although the same process (above) can also apply. Again, information comes in from internal or external sources. For the moment we grant our humans an element of choice. A young man finds his female companion highly attractive and he is aware that he would like to make love to her. Unlike other animals, he has a choice. He can decide not to pursue his interest and urge, or he can decide to do so. Unlike other animals, he can choose to be celibate, despite the fact that he finds her attractive and feels the sexual urge to make love to her. He can also share with her his intentions in the hope that her intentions might be similar. He has instincts and urges, but has the ability to control these. He has a number of options open to him and he can, if he knows enough, look at the sources he will use to make his decision.

First, he could allow his reptilian nature to take over and force the young woman to have sex with him. In this instance, he would be allowing his instincts and urges to predominate and override any rational or long-term impact this decision might have on him or the young woman. He might argue in a court of law that he was not responsible and was unable to control his passions. Unless there were other mitigating circumstances, the chances are he will be held responsible for these actions—even though they come from his reptilian nature.

Second, his unconscious (or what Wilson (2002) calls his adaptive unconscious) can make the decision for him. Since he has no method of accessing or knowing his adaptive unconscious, he will just know a decision has been made. We look at the features of the adaptive unconscious in more detail in Chapter 11. In this instance, his adaptive unconscious can decide to refrain from making love to her because he is afraid of intimacy, while his conscious mind confabulates and tells him he should only have sex inside a marriage commitment.

Third, his preconscious, or habits of mind, can make the decision for him. Let us say he was raised in a strict, religious family where sex was only permitted within marriage. This template has been well established in his life and mind, and without any deliberation he can be guided by it. He does not allow himself to imagine that he might have sex with this female companion. It is behaviour that is not on his to-do list. On the other hand, he can override this template and make a decision on his own (those are values for my parents, but I am old enough to make up my own mind now).

Fourth, he can go into a conscious mode, and deliberate and reflect on what he should do. He could weigh up the pros and cons, consider his feelings and the risks involved, and make a decision in light of those considerations. He can access his intuitive responses and again decide in light of their communication to him. He can discuss with others, ask his peer group, read a book—there are many other sources of information he might use to help him make his decision. What process takes over if we move into a more conscious way of making ethical decisions? Clearly, a more considered method of ethical decision making takes time and focus and may not always pertain, especially if there is an urgency in the situation (which there may well be with our young man).

Wilson (2002) used the work of LeDoux to suggest there are two roads to decision making, the high road and the low road: 'The low road operates as an early warning system that quickly alerts people to signs of danger, whereas the high road analyses information more slowly and thoroughly, allowing people to make more informed judgements about the environment' (p. 126).

Deliberate decision making

In the fourth mode, the brain has now put us into deliberate, reflective mode because we are faced with making a decision that does not come automatically from our unconscious. In a contemporary example, at the time of writing it is a crucial week in the rugby league season in Australia. Darren Lockyer, the hero of the Brisbane Broncos, is faced with an important ethical decision which it is said could change the season's outcome for his team. The previous weekend he suffered a broken cheekbone on the field and has had surgery to insert metal plates in his cheek. His doctors suggest some weeks off, because another knock could result in blindness. However, commentators are speculating he will play regardless. His team management has come out saying they expect Darren to do the right thing by his team. Is his duty to himself and his long-term future, or to his club and his fans? Is he a hero for playing, or a fanatic? If he loses his sight, will everyone revere him or will they turn on him for his foolishness? His first stock answer, straight from the gut, is 'of course I will play if at all possible'. After all, in his context, playing rugby with some order of injury would be common and unquestioned. However, he has given himself the week to think about it. He is faced with conscious wrestling with whether this level of injury should change whether a decision to not play is an accepted response.

While there is little to suggest a common format by which we work towards a decision, a number of factors play a part in this process. Deliberate decision making arises when we face: a) a dilemma, or b) a conflict of motives, when there is risk I have to consider, and when time is needed because the action is unclear. Second, there are our motives in pushing for a decision (Sloan, 1987, p. 55), which are based on values. What are my values, and how much will my decisions be based on existing values, and how much will they change who I am, my identity? For Alisha to refuse the arranged marriage could mean mammoth changes for her, not just in her external world of family, friends and community, but internally in fashioning her identity as an Australian woman from Pakistani parents. She may define herself differently after she has made her decision.

Paul Ricoeur (cited in Sloan, 1987, p. 52) presents three stages in the process of decision making: *hesitation, attention* and *choice*.

Hesitation: We pause to consider the decision. For the moment the pause button is pressed on what action will take place. I am undecided and not quite sure what I will do. In deliberate decision making we hesitate. Hesitation, by definition, precedes the moment of decision. It is the pause, the waiting, the giving ourselves time to think and reflect before the decision is made. It can be a time of suspension where we allow ourselves to think more deeply about where we will go (Scharmer, 2007). It can be a time of indifference when we are not invested in any particular outcome, and where we consider how open we are to the possibilities that exist. Or has the decision already been made—do I already know what I am going to do? It might be time to hesitate for a last review.

Hesitation can result in a few things. The moment of hesitation centres the mind, and in hesitation we begin to realise what we can and cannot do. We can also give ourselves freedom. In hesitation we can know the 'I' who is deciding and begin to sift the mental maps and assumptions that underpin possible decisions. In hesitation we can talk to others. In hesitation, in waiting, sometimes something else happens that influences us in our decision—someone else makes a decision, the world moves on. 'Hesitation is the period of improvisation. It may be the locus of creative deciding, or of endless testing of unfeasible possibilities' (Sloan, 1987, p. 57).

Of course, there need not be a pause. Some act or react and never hesitate. Action can come automatically from the unconscious, and also from the conscious. The pause is not allowed. Cognitive dissonance, disjunctures and disorientations are not permitted to happen. Many people find it difficult to live with the uncertainty of not making a decision when one is required, and bypass any pauses, hesitations or deliberations and move directly to an often impulsive decision. They send their decision back to the unconscious for resolution. Darren Lockyear may stick to his gut response to play rugby against all odds. He said this immediately in response to being questioned, his club supports him doing so, the media is already saying he is a hero, so what would be the point of further questioning? Announcing he is not playing will have all sorts of uncomfortable ramifications, so he could decide that it is better not to go there.

The *first awareness* for all conscious decision makers is that they are watching themselves, giving *attention* to who is making the decision and the implications of possible decisions: each is aware that she or he is the one deciding. While it may not be at the forefront of consciousness, there is an awareness about *who is the person about to make the decision?* I see me in the process of deciding. Even at this early stage, I imagine myself in the decision made. Joan imagines her career ahead as a child psychotherapist working with the children she loves; Mick pictures telling his boss about his porn-loving colleague and already imagines that his colleague will feel let down and betrayed by someone he thought of as a friend; Eleanor projects herself into the future and sees her life with her unborn child as it might be or/and her life freed from the current burden of pregnancy, which is how it feels to her now. Alisha sees herself in an arranged marriage or sees herself in a marriage with a partner she has chosen herself. Darren sees himself carried on the shoulders of fellow players as he takes the Broncos into the finals, and he also imagines a life without sight. In the hesitation of decisions waiting to be born, we are already using our future barometer, our imaginations, to consider possible futures. We may even 'scenario plan' as we stop and pause. What if I did that, or that? Eleanor, struggling with whether or not she should have an abortion, has a number of possible scenarios in her mind: she has the abortion and envisages herself years down the line, childless and alone, beating herself up for not keeping the baby. Or she sees herself with her husband and family, happy and content and pleased that having the abortion allowed her to move into her career and set up the kind of life situation she wanted.

Responsibility accompanies awareness. Each of the individuals above considers themselves as taking responsibility for the decision they make. While Mick may feel angry at his colleague for putting him in this position, and Eleanor may rail against her husband who wants another child, both of them know they have to make and take responsibility for a decision. They are the authors of the future or at least co-authors of decisions made.

A third part of the process is the projection into the future, or *choice*. The me-in-the-decision aspect—there is a commitment to act, and this commitment involves *me*, and becomes more than an objective fact, so that even when the decision is made it may come back to trouble or haunt me. 'Me' is central to the future action and central to who will I become having made that decision.

There are two methods by which decisions are made. One is accommodative, where we make the decision in light of past experience, there is little reflection and the decision has almost been made for us. The other is more assimilated learning, where we go through a process of decision making based on openness and reflection. We work toward a decision that could be different from decisions in the past.

Conclusion

In this chapter we have reviewed the psychological processes that underpin decision making and have begun to apply them to ethical decision making. In the next chapter we will consider how many decisions are made unconsciously and how the brain works towards making all decisions unconscious.

Chapter 10
Component 2
Maximising choices
Free will, accountability and responsibility

'Despite appearances, the constraints on adult decision making are as intense as they have always been. Limitations due to character, social class, gender, ethnicity, location, the body, scarcity, finances, and the like black out the glowing accounts we often hear regarding life chances in a free society.'

(Sloan, 1986, p. 5)

'All our lives long, every day and every hour, we are engaged in the process of accommodating our changed and unchanged selves to changed and unchanged surroundings: living, in fact, is nothing else than this accommodation.'

(Butler, 2008, p. 300)

'Between stimulus and response there is a space. In that space is our power to choose our response. In our response lies our growth and our freedom.'

(Viktor Frankl)

'Human freedom is not an illusion: it is an objective phenomenon, distinct from all other biological conditions and found in only one species, us.'

(Dennett, 2003, p. 305)

'Don't worry that responsibility will vanish when humans understand that free will is an illusion...the proximate responsibility/ultimate responsibility distinction enables us to understand how we can be both responsible and not responsible.'

(Evatt, 2010, p. 57)

As a young boy I (Michael) played a dangerous game. I would hold my sister's hair and, when she pulled away eventually, and ran crying to my parents with her accusations, I would marshall my defences by claiming I had done nothing wrong and that she had hurt herself. After all, had she not pulled away, no harm would have been done. *She* was to blame for the hurt, not me. I was simply holding her hair. Ergo, I rest my case and my plea for acquittal. Needless to say, my parents, who knew little about the intricacies of the law, culpability or mental reservations, were skilled at reading intentions and were not the least impressed by my notional distinctions. With a keen mind for engaging in such mental gymnastics from an early age, you would have thought this was the beginning of a budding and lucrative career as a lawyer! Alas, no. However, it was one of my first experiments in understanding human behaviour, and perhaps one of my first excursions into ethical behaviour, although not a very ethical project.

Of course, I was guilty. I had engineered a situation where my sister was hurt indirectly by my actions. I was responsible despite claiming otherwise and, in my heart, I knew that even if I could argue a logical (if somewhat implausible) exoneration of my actions, my parents and sister all knew I was blameworthy. Even if they could not put into words the reasons why I should be held responsible, they knew intuitively and naturally. Had they been able, they would have articulated the situation in the following way: Your intention was to cause pain and upset to your sister, and you put her in an impossible situation where she would inevitably pull away, thus hurting herself. You are doubly guilty because you not only caused her pain, but pretended that it was her fault. You knew what you were doing. You are thus culpable and will be punished accordingly.

In the example above, we would accept that Michael had choices about how to act towards his sister. He had free will, which allowed him to be drawn to a choice and decide how to act. Thus, as the free determiner of his decision, he could be held accountable for his actions.

Michael was held to account because his family held values that this kind of treatment of a family member was not to be tolerated. These values clashed in some ways with what Michael wanted for himself (and his sister) at that time. In that clash of values, he and his family had to work out something about better choices, balancing needs for self and the need for family connectedness, the notion of 'doing the right thing', and the need to attend to authority. There was a lot happening in those few moments.

This chapter explores the nature and limitations of free will. We look at the development of choices and how choice is always associated with accountability and responsibility for decisions and actions. Assessing the associated responsibilities is an important part of considering our best moral choices.

What is free will?

Accountability and responsibility rest on acceptance of the presence of free will, and so it is essential that we start here.

Free will can be defined as the unique ability humans have to exercise control over their conduct in the fullest manner necessary for moral responsibility. A morally responsible person is not just able to do the right thing, but can be accountable for their behaviour. Free will is understood to be an essential condition when considering responsibility or accountability, as it would hardly be fair to attribute praise or blame if a person was not free to act any other way than the way they did. While we might accept that we have free will in many circumstances (i.e., we can act based on choices, unencumbered by external forces) this chapter explores the influence of predeterminants such as history and biology, and how they might detract from our 'freedom'. Based on factors outside our control, we will consider whether it is more accurate to say that we have 'freedom to act' rather than 'free will'. In any case, any notion of choice and freedom comes with accountability. How we understand, accept and live with ethical accountability is central to ethical maturity.

Responsibility and accountability

The terms 'responsibility' and 'accountability' are often used synonymously. However, they are quite different in some ways. Some distinctions suggest that responsibility involves more of the duties involved in the lead-up to delivering on individual tasks or projects, while accountability is more related to the duty in managing ultimate outcomes, or the overall end result. Thus, a CEO might resign over the way a company has performed because of overall accountability, even though different individuals were responsible for particular aspects of performance. Responsibility is often used in relation to individual action and linked to praise or blame, i.e., if you have been responsible for an action then you receive the appropriate acknowledgement for it. It is an important concept in law, as it relates to whether someone can be considered responsible for their actions, i.e., that they were of an age and mental ability to have known right from wrong. We note they are related terms: if one is responsible for the action, then accountability for the action flows. In ethical terms, if one is considered a moral agent with free will, then one must be accountable for decisions.

Responsibility and the law

Glimcher (2008) provides two examples that clarify how the law decides whether or not someone is guilty of an offence.

Example 1: Four different men with four different rationales for swearing in a public place:

1. The first suffers from Tourette's Syndrome (a syndrome where individuals cannot control what they say).
2. A second is approached by another person with a gun who commands him or her to swear loudly.
3. A third steps on a nail that pierces his foot and also swears loudly.
4. A fourth enters the environment and, seeing someone he or she dislikes, swears loudly.

Example 2: Two men return home to find their wives having sex with other men:

1. The first sees a loaded gun on the table and in an act of rage shoots his wife.
2. The second leaves the home, deliberates for a week, buys a gun and kills his wife.

All six of the actions above are judged blameworthy or not depending on whether the actor was considered to be rational and acting with intent to commit a crime. To quote Glimcher (2008), 'If it can be demonstrated that a specific criminal act engaged an emotional, automatic or involuntary process that limits or eliminates the agent's ability to act "rationally", then the process becomes exculpatory' (p. 346). The task of lawyers, judges, juries, psychologists, psychiatrists, doctors and others is to determine those factors, and there are many instances in which there are 'fine lines' in concluding whether an action is rational or voluntary. In the above examples, it is highly likely that 1, 2, 3 and 5 will all be acquitted, while 4 and 6 will probably be found guilty. When it comes to ethical evaluation we apply similar rules:

- Was the act deliberate (what was the intention)?
- Was it voluntary (did the person choose to do it)?
- Were there any extenuating circumstances that might mean the conduct should be viewed according to different standards, where the usual rules may not apply?

We have made the point several times that ethics is for humans. We do not ascribe ethical behaviour to other animals, even though they engage at times in cruel and harmful behaviour: male lions who take over a pride will often kill the cubs belonging to the preceding male; chimps will go on a rampage and kill and sometimes eat other chimps; and, males of many species will fight, maim and kill each other as they compete for mating rights. Furthermore, animals will also kill and hurt humans. Despite this, we do not ascribe moral or ethical blame to them, or call their positive or helpful actions 'good', e.g., when they care for and sacrifice themselves for their young, or even when they give up something for another animal.

Other animals, social animals like us, seem to share some of our human social emotions as well as demonstrate many community-based attributes such as sharing of food, warning of danger and looking after those who are injured, and live their lives with acceptance of pack rules (Singer, 1993). It is clear that biology and survival are not all that drive social animals.

However, the reason these actions do not fall within an ethical sphere is that they are not voluntary actions, i.e. they have not been chosen by the animal. In human terms, we do not see those actions as responsible, deliberate or culpable. This is what makes the ethical difference. We understand equally that children cannot be held responsible for their actions, for example, a boy of five who lifts his father's gun and shoots his brother would not be morally accountable for his action. This is because the intention to do something is not available to the animal or the child. Neither is conscious or aware of what they are doing, or why they are doing it, and that makes all the difference. When people plan consciously (I am going to buy a gun and shoot this person) with intention (my intent is to kill him) because he abused my daughter (which connects to my beliefs, sense of harm, justice being done), then we assume responsibility and free choice.

Responsible or not?

'The men and women on death's row have some combination of bad genes, bad parents, bad ideas, and bad luck—which of these quantities, exactly, were they responsible for?' (Harris, 2010, p. 109).

'Voluntary choosing' is not a universally accepted concept. There is a debate, ongoing for centuries, on what free will is and whether or not it really exists. In fact, Evatt (2010) suggests that free will is the most discussed philosophical problem ever. Are we free to choose what we do? To what degree can we be held responsible for our actions? Are there times when our responsibilities are so diminished that it can be said we did not choose to do what we did? We know, both from Freud and recent studies on the brain (Engel and Singer, 2008) that much motivation is unconscious, and much of our behaviour is involuntary (e.g., digestion, breathing, acting to stop a child walking into traffic). Perhaps this applies more widely than we have imagined. Singer (1993) writes: 'The evidence above contradicts our intuition that we can always freely decide what we are going to do next and which factors we are going to consider when we plan future acts' (p. 43). Harris (2010) puts it starkly, 'Many scientists and philosophers realised long ago that free will could not be squared with our growing understanding of the physical world... From the perspective of your conscious mind, you are no more responsible for the next things you think (and therefore do) than you are for the fact that you were born into this world' (pp. 103–104). The word 'responsible' is used in this sentence. If I am not responsible, then how can my action be termed 'ethical' or 'moral'?

'Diminished responsibility' is a term often used in courtrooms to argue that someone should not be punished for a crime committed because they cannot be held fully or partially responsible for what they did. If it were shown that, like other animals, we are driven totally by our instincts, then it would be difficult to see us as responsible for what we do.

Choice means accountability because we are responsible for our choices. When choice is eroded or weakened, diminished or disappears, we make allowance. Age, maturity, ability, mental and physical illnesses, and circumstances are all taken into consideration when deciding how 'free' a person is to make the decisions they have made.

Ethical maturity involves achieving as much choice as possible, from which we can consider our options before voluntarily proceeding with our (good) decision. In so doing, we operate inevitably within an environment of responsibility with us at the centre of our decision. Accepting that we have (and desire) free will, that we choose our courses of actions voluntarily, will mean also accepting the responsibility and culpability that comes with free will. This can be difficult at times, especially when we might believe that our choices were restricted or our hand was a little forced. Sometimes we might even be angry with our own ethics, which compel us into action that 'disadvantages us', such as handing back incorrect change.

Most law is based on the fact that we make rational choices or not, as the case may be. The legal term 'mens rea' is the standard used to assess culpability when someone has broken the law. Greene and Cohen (2011) inform us that this term means 'guilty mind'. 'Narrowly interpreted, 'mens rea' refers to the intention to commit a criminal act, but the term has a looser interpretation by which it refers to all mental states consistent with moral and/or legal blame. A killing motivated by insane delusional beliefs may meet the requirements for mens rea in the first sense, but not the second. Thus, for centuries, many legal issues have turned on the question: 'what was he thinking?' (p. 655). Holding someone responsible for an action is based on the assumption they could have acted otherwise. In other words, that they have free will. It is difficult to blame someone for an action when they could *not* have acted otherwise.

Fundamental to our choices are the values in which we believe and on which we base our decisions. Human values impact on human behaviour and become strong motivators for our actions. Sartre once said (as quoted at the beginning of Chapter 8) that we know our values from our actions. Look at what you do and you can mine out the values behind your actions. We would be somewhat suspicious of someone who said they loved reading books, but never read them. It would be difficult to believe this was a real value for that person. Values that do not result in actions, for most of us, are 'head' values or perhaps aspirational values, but are not lived as our real values. Espoused values (values we say we believe in) are not always the same as our values in action (the values we practise). We can fool ourselves easily in this regard and preach values we do not practise (as many tele-evangelists have shown us). But real values will 'out'—they tend to emerge eventually in who we are and what we do.

As mentioned, sometimes our choices feel restricted, imposed or determined by others. A classic example is reflected in the 1982 film *Sophie's Choice*. In this film, set in Germany in the Second World War, Sophie had to choose which of her two children would die in a gas chamber, and which would be sent to live in a concentration camp. In order to save one of her children, she had to sacrifice the other.

In common practice though, the law assumes that people assessed as being 'legally responsible' have a general capacity for rational choice, and thus rational behaviour. It is also assumed that more than one choice was available, and that the actor freely chose the final decision. In this way, the legally responsible person can be held accountable for their actions.

We know that our capacity to manage our freedom can be and, at times, is compromised, which in turn diminishes how responsible we are. David Eagleman (2011) recounts the story of Alex, who at the age of 41 years began to display very uncharacteristic behaviour. His wife noticed that he became intensely involved with child pornography, something that had not interested him in the 20 years she had known him. A visit to his doctor and a scan revealed a massive brain tumour on Alex's orbitofrontal cortex. With the removal of the tumour came the return of the old Alex and a discarding of interest in child pornography. However, six months later his interest in child pornography returned and, would you believe it, so had the tumour. Again, as before, removal of the tumour resulted in removal of his child pornography interests. Eagleman makes his point: 'Slight change in the balance of brain chemistry can cause large changes in behaviour...when your biology changes so can your decision making, your appetites, and your desires' (p. 157). Alex's human brain, we must presume, was affected by this tumour to such a degree that it did away with his ability to choose.

The example above, one of many that seem to compromise free will and choice, raises a number of key questions when thinking about ethics.

- How free are we to make the choices we do?
- How many of our decisions are made for us in a physiologically or psychologically predetermined way, as illustrated by the example of Alex?

- Did Alex's brain tumour simply bring to the fore what was there all along (his interest in child pornography) but held at bay by inhibitions, socialisation, etc.?
- How can we hold someone responsible for their actions (like Alex)?
- How free was Alex to resist his urges towards accessing child pornography? Was he free before to make his choices and now his freedom had disappeared?
- And how much is biology, upbringing and relationships connected to choice and decision making?

'If you think genes don't matter for how people behave, consider this amazing fact: if you are a carrier of a particular set of genes, your probability of committing a violent crime goes up eight hundred and eighty-two percent.' (Eagleman, 2011, p. 158)

'Probability' seems to indicate increased influence rather than determination. There is no doubt for those who study the brain that ethical choices are always influenced, even determined, by a combination of biology and life experiences. They see biology as the 'propensity towards' rather than an absolute outcome. Perhaps free will is on a continuum between: a) determined and no choice, and, b) freedom and choice. There are many possible positions in between that designate degrees of freedom ranging from total lack of freedom to the possibility of full freedom to choose what I want (with the usual limits of what is impossible for me).

We know already some of the factors that reduce our freedoms. Put individuals in situations where they are expected to conform to group behaviour, let them think that someone, an expert, is taking responsibility for what they do, and they will often do horrendous things. Of interest, there are always those who refuse to conform to group behaviour, even when authorities direct them to this behaviour. These exceptions make the point—free choice is possible. The factors that impinge on our decisions can influence, but do not take away, full freedom.

Our law is based on the assumption of the freedom to make choices, if not naming explicitly the concept of free will. And this is a subtle distinction—choosing does not equal free will. We are responsible for our actions until we have evidence that we are not free or have diminished responsibility. 'As long as there is nothing hindering mind in its control of the body, it is assumed that the actor is fully responsible for his actions' (Incognito, 2001, p. 162).

Free will or free won't

Aristotle kicked off the controversy about free will by suggesting that humans had souls (located in the heart) which were responsible for their actions. Other animals did not have such souls and therefore could not be held responsible for their behaviours. This discussion/debate continued throughout the Middle Ages (especially within the Catholic Church) where eventually it was decided that humans were free actors: choices were made by the soul and God was the final arbiter of what were good and bad actions. Descartes made a simple distinction between behaviours he called reflexes (deterministic actions of the person over which they had no control) and voluntary actions, which he again attributed to the human soul and for which the person was responsible. For reflexes, there could be no moral culpability: for voluntary actions the person was responsible. Thus began the voluntary–rational versus involuntary–irrational divide that was to be central, for centuries, in determining ethical responsibility.

The rise of materialism with its consequent emphasis on physics and the laws of science brought with it the notion that everything material was governed and directed by predictable laws, doing away with any role for free will. Put at its most simple, this means that human behaviour is caused by biological and environmental determinants, and if we knew enough about it we would be able to find and articulate all the background reasons why a person acts the way he or she does. Eagleman (2011) mentions other examples that show how free will is often not present in human behaviour, such as the case with Tourette's sufferers, where there is an obvious case of freedom being impeded by physical determinants. Individuals with Tourette's syndrome find themselves engaging in behaviours they do not want to have happen, but are powerless to stop. From a position of determinism: 'We...believe...that our environment and our heredity entirely shape our characters. But we aren't responsible for our environment, and we aren't responsible for our heredity. So we aren't responsible for our character. But then how can we be responsible for acts that arise from our characters?' (Evatt, 2010, p. 62). As a result of this argument, debates about the role of the law and culpability abound (Eagleman, 2011; Singer, 2011; Greene and Cohen, 2011).

Brain Waves Module 2 details the fears of those who see neuroscienceas taking a reductionist view on free will, and are anxious that it 'represents a deterministic view that our neurological inheritance sets us on a path that is unchangeable' (The Royal Society, 2011b, p. 17). Greene and Cohen (2011) take this further, arguing that: 'The problem of free will and determinism will never find an intuitively satisfying solution because it arises out of a conflict between two distinct cognitive subsystems that speak different cognitive 'languages' and that may ultimately be incapable of negotiation' (p. 670).

However, Singer (2011) introduces the possibility of a middle ground. He recognises that we think we are free, but 'the neurobiological evidence… is incompatible with the view that a person, at the moment of having reached a decision, could have decided otherwise' (p. 45). However, he also writes: 'The view that a person is responsible for what he does (meaning that they are the causal agents) is not invalidated by neurobiological evidence, because all authorship remains with the deciding and acting person'. On one hand is determinism (I could not act other than what I do), and on the other hand is responsibility (I am the author of my actions). This is, in essence, the argument for compatibilism.

Compatibilism suggests that while there may be forces outside our control that lead us to certain points in decision making, we still have the ability to determine our thinking about, response to and ultimately decision making in action. In light of this, the compatibilist approach is that it may be more accurate to refer to our 'freedom to act', rather than our 'free will'. This assumes that the moral agent mediates between determinants and other factors in order to generate action. Where the individual is seen to be the genuine source of the action, accountability can still be assumed. Where does all this leave us?

What is important to note is that our concept of free will is changing. That we 'feel free' is not in any doubt. Most people, when asked, would claim that their choices come from free will, and that they are the authors of their actions. They feel free and sense intuitively that they are the ones making choices about how they behave. Experience tells us the same: I have a choice at this very moment of whether or not to keep typing, to go and get something to eat or to simply gaze out the window. Isn't it free will if I have options about what I do, and I can choose from alternatives and possibilities of which behaviour I will engage in? There is no doubt that humans, like other animals, have options in their lives. Unlike other animals, humans can bring rationality to bear on their behaviours and look at the 'self' who is making the decision. While a hungry lion may have little option in killing a gazelle that wanders into its path, humans can bring deliberation, reflection and consideration to what they decide to do, even when strong instincts and urges counsel them otherwise. Does this make a difference when it comes to choices that are free or not? While the debate about determinism versus free will continues, our position is that freedom of will and freedom of action do exist. However, we are hampered at times by a lack of conscious awareness of the freedom we have, and by not taking enough time to deliberate consciously about our available choices. Thus, we will make a decision at times that seems reactive, intuitive, spontaneous, almost as if the decision has 'made itself'. This can feel akin to a deterministic position—the decision is made as if there is no active agent who is me. This is instead an unreflected-upon version of our free will at play: a quick decision is not always a well-thought-through decision, nor is it a mature decision. It is unlikely to have maximised our choices, and by not consciously embracing the role of active agent, it can later feel unfair to be held to account. Part of ethical maturity is working on how we can attain as much freedom of choice as possible in order to make mature ethical decisions, and even when we feel our choices are restricted, how we can still see the potential for ethics in action. It also involves slowing down the decision making moment, feeling the weight of the options, and the empowerment of being the 'I' who takes action.

An interesting by-product of the research on free will suggests that a belief in free will promotes pro-social behaviour, while those who do not believe in free will (or believe in determinism) are more likely to cheat and be aggressive (Baumeister and Tierney, 2011).

In summary, we believe in the choosing process. Evatt (2010) summarises this:

- options arise and we imagine outcomes
- we select one, or more, options
- we action our choice
- we judge (and others do too) the results of our choices and resulting actions (p. 18).

For humans, this choosing or decision making process is controlled by the prefrontal cortex. As different options appear, and begin to struggle for supremacy the prefrontal cortex mediates to come to the best possible conclusion (Should I break confidence and report what I have just heard to the police? Should I stay silent and hope to work with this person to calm him down and not kill the individual he has said he wants to?). The prefrontal cortex will take into account our values, many of which will be unconscious and part of our existing moral character. The brain helps us with intentional action.

Conclusion

In this chapter we have looked at two anchors in being accountable: free will and responsibility. We have argued that establishing ourselves as active agents in dilemmas, and actively pursuing choices and options, is not only crucial for ethical maturity but for managing effective implementation of decisions. Without it we can later be caught in regret or anger that we were 'pushed', and that will impede our ability to come to peace with the decision. This negative chain reaction can be avoided by taking more time in the beginning to centre ourselves within an effective frame of reflection and action.

Chapter 11

Component 2
Conscious ethical discernment and decision making

....

'The best approach to ethical decision making will always be one that fully integrates feelings, reason, and intuition.'

(Nash, 2002, p. 71)

'The time available for deciding does make a difference in the kind of decisions we make—a millisecond, an hour, a week, a forty day retreat provide different operating frameworks.'

(Callahan, 1991, p. 122)

This chapter will review some elements that go into making conscious ethical decisions. These are the moments when we deliberately set out to make a decision. We have reviewed some of the factors involved in ethical decision making in general: values and free will; relationships and context; moral character, habits and routines, the hesitation, attention and choices we make unconsciously and consciously. This chapter will explore other elements: the use of reason, emotion and intuition; how and at what levels we reflect; and, the contexts in which we find ourselves and the complexity of those circumstances.

The ethical deliberation involved in reaching ethical decisions, unlike ethical intuition, takes time and conscious effort—what neuroscientists call 'active, computational, expensive processes'. It will be somewhat, but not entirely, based on moral character, and will be influenced by the attitude with which we enter the process of decision making. Here we have time to examine, reflect and create an environment for ourselves in which a decision will be made with deliberation and thoughtfulness. What can help us here is:

- indifference and openness to the outcome. Am I open to possible outcomes and prepared to go with whatever emerges?

- having both courage and compassion—to be open and prepared to implement decisions that may be personally or professionally costly
- dealing with my fear
- allowing myself to reflect in deepening ways and beginning to think systemically, as well as individually
- staying with my feelings, even when painful
- being curious rather than evaluative
- knowing what I need to let go of
- keeping the context and its many challenges in mind.

It seems that we move into deliberative, reflective mode to make an ethical decision for four reasons. First, it is a situation we have not come across before and one where the unconscious decision does not come automatically. When we face new or complex situations that confuse our adaptive unconscious we become disoriented and we are not sure what to do. Our mental maps do not have directions for this decision. We pause and go into deliberation modality: we think, problem solve, reflect, discuss, review and evaluate options—and then we decide.

While it is a spontaneous ethical response to pick up a wallet dropped by a passer-by and return it to him, it takes some deliberation and thought to deal with a client who starts to bring her counsellor small presents. How do you handle the situation without hurting the client by appearing ungrateful for her small gifts, and how do you avoid being pulled into a new and different kind of relationship with her? It requires thinking through, reflecting, talking it over in supervision, and then deciding what needs to be done.

The second reason why more conscious deliberation needs to take over is that when a spontaneous decision emerges from the adapted unconscious (I know what to do), there is still a need for reflection and thoughtfulness to validate the decision. In this view, the conscious mode has been called the 'press secretary' of the unconscious, i.e., the ability to rationalise or give reasons for why the decision has been made. Haidt (2001) explains this: 'moral reasoning does not cause moral judgement: rather moral reasoning is usually a post hoc construction, generated after a judgment has been reached' (p. 814).

Several years ago one of us (Michael) made the decision to work with a man who had been jailed for accessing illegal pornography. Michael explained the process of making this decision. Having met him, I felt it was right and good to support him to rebuild his life and career. However,

I also had the need to bring this to supervision and get the reactions of my peer supervision group.

With deliberation, I looked at the basis upon which I might make this decision.

- When will authority (others, codes, principles, supervision) guide me?
- How will my past experience be of help?
- Can I involve my feelings in this particular decision?
- What part can reason play as I make up my mind?

The third reason is that deliberate and conscious ethical decision making can often involve language. Language helps us communicate with ourselves as well as others. Writing, creating a diary, sharing ideas—all use language that connects us to pools of wisdom and knowledge, and allow us to share that with others. Language is one of the foundations of our learning: not only can we learn, but we have the amazing ability of communicating that learning to others through language.

Fourth, conscious decision making has the ability to help us veto unconscious decision making. While we could make a decision intuitively, bringing that decision into consciousness allows us to review it and decide against it. There are times when our intuitions are not our best guides and need reason and deliberation to help them.

However, while we think we know why we do what we do, there is some evidence to suggest we are not always in touch with the real reasons why we make the decisions we do. 'This indicates that people are quite willing to tell a narrative to explain their actions even when this narrative cannot possibly be the causal locus of their behaviour' (Kurzban, 2008, p. 158). Perhaps even more disturbing is when we think our ability to talk consciously and deliberately about a problem in itself means we are attending to it ethically. Take the following example:

I (Elisabeth) was consulted by a clinician about his attraction to a client. This had already progressed to a significant degree: both had declared their feelings and were wrestling with whether this would advance their helping relationship or hinder it. As the story unfolded, I understood there had been some recent cuddling at the end of sessions, which signalled to him a slippery slope of behaviour. He said to me, 'I have given this a great deal of thought and I know you are going to tell me to stop this behaviour, that is why I have booked in to see you. However, I am at the end of the therapy with my client and I want to discuss whether there is any way I can progress my romantic relationship with her because I really want to.' Later I heard that, despite our discussion about all his own reasons (and his professional obligations) not to, he had gone ahead with a sexual relationship.

In this case, a conscious process seemed, on the surface, to satisfy a responsibility to deliberately challenge thinking, but ultimately other imperatives won out.

This corresponds to the 'theory-in-use' and 'theory-in-practice' distinction made by Argyris and Schon (1974) that what we do can differ from what we think we do. In this chapter on conscious discernment and deliberation, which sounds like the pinnacle of a well-reasoned process, what is our position about its place in the process? First, as suggested above, conscious deliberation will be required for certain types of decisions more than others. And second, when we are in ethical decision deliberation mode, it is worthwhile not just to make a decision deliberately, but to spend time looking at the process or processes that can be of best help in making this particular decision. We need a conscious process that has within in it checks and balances to ensure it does not become a 'tick the box' superficial process, and aims for the kind of ethical maturity we strive for. What will such a process look like and on what will we base our ulimate decisions?

Ethical complexity

Let us take a case scenario that is not unusual to help unlock some of the complications and uncertainty involved in an actual helping relationship, in this case a counselling arrangement. Ousep is working with a suicidal client who phones and leaves a succinct message on his answer-machine, 'That's it. I can't take any more. I am definitely going to end it tonight.' Ousep has been landed with an ethical dilemma. He is conscientious, cares deeply about his client, has great loyalty to the organisation that employs him to see this client, and wants to act to the highest professional standards. What does he do?

He has worked with Roland for two years now and this type of phone call is not new. Roland phones every few months and says something similar. Perhaps this is just his way of hearing Ousep's voice, being reassured there is someone there who wants him to live and, with this tiny morsel of hope, will struggle on until they meet again on Friday. Or did Ousep hear a slightly different note and tone in Roland's voice? Perhaps it is not the same kind of phone call as they have had before. The last few sessions have been deeply distressing and have hit new depths of despair and hopelessness for both of them. Is this a breakthrough or a breakdown? Ousep struggles with two possible outcomes. In the first, he decides to call the Ambulance Emergency Service and have Roland admitted to a psychiatric ward where there are people who already know Roland and will take Ousep seriously. To do or not to do? Ousep stares into the bleak decision making process which looks like it has a no-win ending. He thinks of his second option: he does nothing, he takes the chance that Roland will gain enough from the phone call to keep him going. But another image enters his consciousness. He imagines an early-morning phone call from Roland's only daughter, who visits him on her way to work each day, to say she has found him dead.

Using his scenario-planning method, Ousep plays a 'what if' game. What if he implements his first decision? Ousep imagines the results. He marshals the emergency forces that go straight to Roland's house, break down the door when he doesn't answer, section him and bundle him into a psychiatric ward where he spends three weeks before being released. 'Of course I wasn't going to commit suicide,' he tells Ousep angrily, 'how dare you betray me!' He is not sure he can trust Ousep again and a once strong, trusting relationship has been ruptured. Scenario two ends no better. Ousep imagines himself doing nothing and spending a sleepless night wondering what the morning will bring, accompanied by a series of possible beratings if Roland's daughter finds him dead. He imagines the question and already knows the answers: why didn't you call for help? You know how suicidal Roland is! He visualises the inquest, the look of betrayal from Roland's daughter, the tense and emotional meeting with his own manager who reminds him of the organisation's policy around suicidal clients and, finally, has to live with himself knowing he could have done something to help avoid Roland's death.

Ousep's decision making processes can work towards some kind of ethical conclusion in several ways. He can play it safe, for himself, his client and his organisation, and get the paramedics and emergency mental health team in and they can make the final decision. He has done what he should have done. Roland also might learn that he can only call wolf so often without being challenged. Ousep can back up this decision with a quick read of his ethical code that says without any ambiguity that where a client is a danger to himself, then the counsellor can break confidentiality and take whatever steps are needed to safeguard the client. Making this decision keeps him safe as a counsellor also—it would be unlikely, were there an ethical complaint against him, that he would be found guilty. He had done his duty well. On the other hand, he could decide to base his ethical decision on his relationship with Roland and let his knowledge, understanding and intuition speak to him. In this instance, it says, do nothing. Yes, he has heard Roland and has once again been touched deeply with the despair he hears. He connects, stays with Roland. He knows the risk he is taking. But he knows Roland too. His third stance is to put Roland at the centre of his decision. He does not want to ignore his responsibilities to look after himself personally and professionally, nor does he want to overlook his obligations to his organisation or the public at large, but he wants to put Roland solidly and clearly at the centre of his decision. What is the best thing to do for Roland? On what basis does he decide? His duty, safety and the law? His relationship with Roland? Or on what is best for Roland?

In the above short, but not uncommon, scenario, some of the complexities involved in making an ethical decision have been articulated. Ethical codes and how they might guide us to come to ethical conclusions have been touched on; the various stakeholders involved in this one ethical decision (Roland, his daughter, Ousep, Ousep's organisation, doctors, emergency teams, psychiatric wards, Ousep's profession and ethical complaints) have been mentioned; Ousep has struggled to anticipate further outcomes on the decision he will make in the present and the fallouts from different decisions in the future; the ambiguity of living with decisions when we will never know for sure what was the right/certain thing to do; the two different decisions that Ousep might make have been outlined, and some possible foundations that might lead Ousep to make one decision rather than the other have been traced.

We can be put off ethical reflection because of the real concern that it will not help, that there are too few definite parameters and it is far too complex. It could even feel more risky to open up the whole can of worms. The case brought by Ousep shows some of the difficulties involved, even though the surface has been touched only lightly. Other potentially complex demands facing Ousep have not been aired, e.g., the legal aspects of his decision making and what legal responsibilities he might have in this case. To limit options and resort to a rule-based decision alone could be adequate and would also stop all the discomfort and responsibility that weighs on Ousep's shoulders. However, let us hold the discomfort and persevere for the time being and see how we might give shape to some of the complexities involved.

The decision making cookbook

How are decisions made? What are the ingredients that go into making decisions and, in particular, ethical decisions? How can we be sure that any conscious approach truly attends to all of our drives and motivations, i.e., does not remain superficial and self-serving? We are going to outline five elements or factors here. Not that all five are needed or used in all decision making, but having access to all five provides the best basis for making mature ethical decisions. The five are:

Emotions

Reason

Complexity

Discerning the emerging future

Reflection

Figure 11.1: Ingredients in decision making

1. EMOTIONS AND DECISION MAKING

A number of authors have reinstalled emotion as a key factor in decision making. Lehrer (2009) draws on insights from contemporary neuroscience to state that: 'The simple truth of the matter is that making good decisions requires us to use both sides of the mind. For too long, we've treated human nature as an either/or situation. We are either rational or irrational. We either rely on statistics or trust our gut instincts. There's Apollonian logic versus Dionysian feeling; the id against the ego; the reptilian brain fighting the frontal lobes. Not only are these dichotomies false, they're destructive...there is no universal solution to the problem of decision making. The real world is just too complex... Sometimes we need to reason through our options and carefully analyze the possibilities. And sometimes we need to listen to our emotions. The secret is knowing when to use these different styles of thought. We always need to be thinking about how we think' (pp. 5–6). While recognising there is no single answer, Lehrer has reintroduced the role of emotion into decision making and warns us that we ignore our feelings in making decisions to our peril. Pizarro (2000) goes a step further and claims that 'affect can actually aid moral deliberations... when asked to make a judgement, individuals reference their mood and use it in aid for their subsequent judgement' (p. 360). He makes the point that emotions support reason by focusing our attention on a particular problem. He concentrates on the emotion of empathy as a key factor in ethical decision making.

An example of decision making using emotion took place when one of us (Michael) was running a two-day programme on ethical maturity. One of the exercises given to participants was: Think of a decision you have been trying to make or a decision where you have had trouble coming to a clear course of action. Now, try to make that decision on feelings and emotions alone. I had never asked a group to do an exercise like this before and was curious how it might work. In processing the exercise at feedback time, the group was intrigued by a woman who courageously shared her experience: 'I have been trying to make a decision for nine months. I have talked, reasoned, thought about it, and looked at it from every angle. I brought it here unresolved. Today I made the decision in 15 minutes with the help of the people in my small group who would not allow me to move away from my feelings. I had not been listening to my feelings. I now know what to do.'

I would not be so bold as to think that those 15 minutes were all that was needed for this woman to make a major decision she had struggled with for a considerable amount of time. No doubt the nine preceding months of thinking through and trying to resolve had paid some dividends. Perhaps the 15 minutes of allowing the feelings to communicate were the final icing on the cake. Damasio (1994) has argued that emotions can help speed up the decision making process and perhaps that is what happened. However, whatever the process was that resulted in a clear decision where none had been available previously, this was a clear realisation of the importance of allowing emotions a considerable say in ethical decision making. Perhaps, as Lehrer says above, she needed this 'style of thought' at this time to make this decision.

We have not discovered something new. Advertising has long known the important role of emotions in decision making. Rarely do ads try to convince us of the reasonable or rational thing to do—what they try to do is evoke an emotion within us that will influence our decision to buy. Psychographics is a branch of marketing that uses psychological insights into the minds of individuals and groups to target how they might be persuaded to buy certain products. One part of this approach is to define the feelings that might make a product appeal to a specific group, e.g., what feelings do I want to elicit in a 16-year-old girl to get her to buy this shampoo, or what emotions would entice this 40-year-old woman to buy this type of car, or what feelings would influence this 60-year-old man to come on this type of holiday? Advertisers know we make decisions emotionally, as well as rationally. Research on the brain has added weight to the recognition of the emotional bases of many of our decisions. Fine (2006) outlines its emerging influence: 'One of the hottest new topics in psychology is the clout our emotions wield over our choices' (p. 31). She presents her take on the role of emotions in decision making: 'Too much emotion and we wind up bawling over a ballpoint pen someone has taken from us...Too stingy with the emotions and the simplest decisions become irredeemably perplexing. Dampen down the emotions too much and we begin to lose grasp of our precious sense of self...better hope that your emotional brain is doing a reasonable job' (pp. 50–1). When do we make ethical decisions emotionally? When do we access our feelings as part of our decision making?

Marc Hauser (2006) has been more specific in his research on the role of emotions and moral life. He notes that the role of emotions is greater in situations where there are no clear adjudicating norms for what is right or wrong, and where the context is intensely emotional. Further, he found that decisions based more on an emotional response are harder to justify, even if there are clear feelings about the decision being right. In a famous example, Mark Twain tells the touching story of Huckleberry Finn, the 14-year-old white teenager and his journey with his friend Jim, the runaway slave. Huck has been taught that slavery is good and is very much against abolishing it. He knows he should turn Jim in to the authorities. The story relates his inner struggle: to obey the law, to follow his conscience, or to save Jim from the slave catchers? In the end, he follows his emotions and his love for Jim and refuses to give him up even though he cannot explain coherently why he comes to this decision. We could, perhaps now, tell Huck that his feelings and his intuitive moral decision was made on higher principles than the law.

Immanuel Kant, one of the most influential thinkers in moral philosophy, argued that emotions cannot be the basis of good moral decisions. He argued that they are fickle and lack reliability. This was due to his belief that emotion could not complement and be a resource to reason. Instead he saw emotion on the opposite side, along with irrationality and subjectivity. To Kant, emotions could only be a threat to, rather than an enhancement of, a person's autonomy (Hinman, 2008). It is not difficult to imagine circumstances where this could be the case, and people who seem emotive and irrational about their positions. TV evangelists, members of the gun lobby, military extremists, terrorists, even debates in our own houses of parliament, can look like reason- and fact-free zones depending on your own views and perspectives.

Our argument here is that our emotions are an important resource in conscious decision making, often being our first indicators of risk. Ongoing discomfort at an intuitive level drives us to seek consultation and clarity. What is important is how we reflect consciously on the nature of our emotional responses, and how they can be part of our ultimate description of the dilemma, and part of a defensible and deliverable action.

2. REASON AND DECISION MAKING

In the tradition of Aristotle, St Thomas Aquinas, Kant, Descartes and Kohlberg, we have assumed that human ethical decision making is a rational process. Kant, for example, believed that only reason could tell us what is good, and then would motivate us to act in accordance with what has been reasoned to be good (Hinman, 2008). This was the heritage of the period of Enlightenment, an understandable correlate of the incredible advances of modern science. The pursuit of fact and truth became paramount, and the pathway to these was reason. This tradition continues today (Steare, 2006; Kohlberg, 1982). Indeed, a number of existing models in making ethical decisions carry on this tradition (Carroll, 1996). Reason does seem to offer a straightforward and comparatively easy process. If you have to make a decision (e.g., buy a car or leave your partner, or decide to visit a client in hospital who is ill), then see it as a logical, reasonable set of sequential steps you go through to reach the right decision. In general, the stages of problem solving follow the outline in Figure 11.2.

> What is the problem? Clarify it; ensure you are clear about what the real problem is?
>
> Look at the options you have. Get them all out on the table.
>
> Evaluate these options one by one (you can look at the needs and responsibilities of various stakeholders if you want at this stage).
>
> Choose the best one for you?
>
> Implement it.
>
> Live with it.

Figure 11. 2: A rational approach to decision making

Duffy and Passmore (2010) critique this approach: 'A sequential linear series of steps greatly over simplifies the complex process of solving an ethical dilemma and has its own weaknesses. Such an approach is in danger of seeing dilemmas as simple decisions in contrast with complex or chaotic issues' (p. 142).

They offer a sequential, not linear, model that moves through six stages, called the ACTION model:

1. Awareness: ethical awareness.
2. Classify: identification of the issue as it emerges in practice and the ability to classify the issue as the dilemma.
3. Time for reflection, support and advice.
4. Initiate: articulate a number of solutions/options.
5. Option evaluation.
6. Novate: implement and incorporate the answer into one's ethical journey (see also Passmore and Mortimer, 2011).

Janis and Mann (1977) outline seven criteria for decision-making procedures (quoted in Sloan, 1986, p. 44) that fall within the reason/rational approach:

1. canvass a wide range of alternative courses of action.
2. survey the range of objectives to be fulfilled and the values implicated by the choice

3. weigh the costs and risks of negative consequences, as well as positive consequences, that could flow from each alternative
4. research new information relevant to further evaluation of the alternatives;
5. assimilate and take account of new information or expert judgement to which we are exposed, even when the information or advice does not support the action you initially prefer
6. re-examine the positives and negatives of all known alternatives, including those regarded originally as unacceptable
7. make detailed provisions to implement or execute the chosen course of action, with special attention to contingency plans that may be required if various known risks were to materialise.

(p. 11)

The use of reason alone as the basis of decision making has come under some recent scrutiny and criticism. From a background in South Africa, Breen (2011) suggests the use of reason alone can be at the root of some evils, 'Logic classifies, and within classes, everything must be the same. Logic encourages separateness, class war and apartheid. Logic lacks humanity. Logic gave Plato stability. Its abstractions offered a more satisfactory world altogether—a world of eternal truths, where there would be no change… the other functions of the psyche—feelings, sensation and intuition—were the dross. Without feeling, thinking is necessarily destructive' (p. 133).

There is no doubt that rational and problem solving approaches to ethical decision making are an essential component in ethical maturity. Rationality, consciousness and our ability to think through and imagine the future is what makes us human. While we do not see reason as the only or sufficient way to make ethical decisions, we do see it as necessary.

Some types of decisions are prone to rational decision making and, at times, are all that is needed. In fact, the use of reason, rules and universal principles can offer the most protection in situations where feelings run hot, for example in matters of human rights, boundary violations such as a counsellor sleeping with a client, or managing other moral temptations such as taking a bribe (assuming one is willing to accept and live with the rules set, as Kant would say, to do one's duty regardless of the feelings involved). Considering other factors, such as personal desire and individual circumstances, could lead to reason being thrown out the window. However, in many areas, reason and emotion are connected and it is not always reason that makes the decision. For example, in the field of marketing and image advertising Ragunathan (quoted in Wenger, 2010) suggests: 'The earlier you make the connection the better, because once consumers have decided they like a particular option (a decision based on emotional responses), the more difficult it is for them to backpedal. Their thinking falls in line with their emotions.'

3. COMPLEXITY AND ETHICS

Snowden and Boone (2007) warn us not to be simplistic in our approach to decision making. They alert us to the importance of careful assessment of the right relationship between cause and effect in how we see problems and in how we set out to resolve them. They refer to our tendency to leap to join the wrong dots via 'a fundamental assumption…that a certain level of predictability and order exists in the world' (p. 1). They say this is not so, and outline four contexts based on the relationship between cause and effect in making decisions:

1. *Simple contexts:* cause and effect are clear, and an answer is self-evident. I am asked by a manager to give her some specific information on a client I have been coaching for the company. The contract does not include giving information back to the company. The answer is clear. I tell the manager I cannot provide the information. I have worked out my decision using reason alone. A simple decision resolving a straightforward problem or issue. Simple problems can also involve emotional reactions that, in turn, lead to a clear-cut and immediate moral decision. Pizarro (2000) gives us an example: 'An individual may not give a second thought to decrying the actions of a young man who trips up an elderly woman, leaving the woman with clear, vivid signs of injury… in this case, the immediate empathic arousal (seeing an innocent victim in distress) leads to a judgement, and then prescribes an action' (p. 366).

2. *Complicated contexts:* cause and effect can be clear but not seen by everyone—there are a number of answers. More analysis is needed to come to a decision. I am asked by an HR director to provide information on the resilience of the individual I am coaching. He tells me that the person is going to be made redundant, but because of this person's history of depression he is prepared to postpone telling him if I, as his coach, feel the coachee is not strong enough to hear this news. While it seems a 'simple decision' to make, in fact it is more complicated and needs time to analyse, consider different perspectives, and evaluate what my role is and might be. I end up telling the HR director that, in my professional opinion, the coachee is strong enough to deal with being made redundant. I had, in this case, to use both reason and feeling, and the help of my supervision group to resolve a complicated issue.

3. *Complex contexts:* Right answers are not obvious and have to be worked towards. There is something about waiting for the way forward to appear. We don't know a priori what to do—it is not a given. Critchley (2010) captures this in the context of coaching: 'Thus the coach puts him or herself fully at risk 'on the high road' of coaching. The low road consists of a rather dry and instrumental coaching process that keeps both parties relatively safe and protected from the risk of fully embodied relational engagement. The high road requires the coach to be capable of self-awareness and reflexivity, to allow themselves to be subject to the process of relating rather than to be in control of it and hence to be open to being changed by the interaction' (p. 855). Implicit in this stance is the lack of knowledge in advance about what to predict, or indeed, what to do. This emerges from the relationship as, 'a series of gestures and responses, patterns of meaning emerge. This is a spontaneous dance of meaning making in which neither party can predict the other's response' (Critchley, 2010, p. 859). This makes a bit of a mockery of having an existing response outside the relationship. How can I possibly know what I will do, ethically or otherwise, if I am not in relationship with another? 'Do not touch your client' can be wise advice, but it must be seen, interpreted and made sense of in the light of a particular relationship, the individual client, and the context in which we are working. Critchley places this in the wider context of complexity theory (Snowden and Boone, 2007 do also): 'What we are learning from complexity science is that there appears to be a self organising principle in nature whereby order emerges from apparent disorder. The order cannot be predicted from the initial starting conditions but pattern emerges through interaction' (p. 861). If we are to stay with complexity theory as having some basis in reality, then we realise we cannot start with the ethical issue resolved, i.e., it is difficult to have the answer to what I would do before I am able to assess what has happened. The moment-to-moment relationship is a changing process about human interaction. 'I know what I will do in advance' is not really a human response, it is more robotic. It is treating human behaviour as if it were water in a bucket from a stream rather than a moving, fluid, changing process called a river. Can the ongoing, flowing, changing relationship with its moment-to-moment demands become the forum within which decisions are made? This seemed to be the case when Thorne (1987) presented a controversial ethical example where he worked with a client

named Sally, during which she sometimes removed her clothes. He talks about 'massaging with great gentleness her stomach, her shoulders and sometimes her buttocks'. How does he justify what in ordinary circumstances would be seen as a serious breach of ethical protocol? 'Intuitive promptings', he writes, 'enabled me to encourage Sally to undress, or on occasions to initiate a particular form of physical contact, whether it was simply holding hands or, as in the final stage, joining in a naked embrace'. More recently, he has backtracked somewhat and declared that such behaviour took place 'when an altogether different culture prevailed...the chapter describes work which was totally exceptional and remains unique. It was never intended to be a "model" for others' (Thorne, 2010).

Could we understand that this particular relationship and this particular intuitive response were what the client actually needed therapeutically, or do we, in advance, decide that such action should not be acceptable and even if of some benefit to the client, should not be viewed as within ethical boundaries? How far can we look to 'intuitive promptings' as a valid guide to action?

In another example I (Elisabeth) was consulting to a team of health professionals. If asked, I would say that I would never be party to any abusive or bullying behaviour. However, over the course of some years with this team there were infrequent, but significant, examples of bullying of a number of the female staff by the male manager. On each occasion the behaviour was debriefed in supervision and the worker decided not to lodge a grievance. This never felt right to me. I was resolved about the right of individuals not to complain, but I had to question my own position in consulting to a team where this occurred. For a time it seemed legitimate (on and off) to balance this with my duty to the collective group and the task of fostering worker resilience and safety through other means. Some years later, one worker did choose to complain. The investigation was not going to involve interviewing me as a matter of course. Her legal team were going to have to call me specifically. She asked me if I would stand up for her. This raised a number of issues. It was likely that I would have my contract terminated, which would affect my income. It also meant the team would lose their supervisor, whom they seemed to value. As the organisation had moved to restrict external consultants, there was a high chance I would not be replaced. Further, this worker would probably not return to her job, regardless of the outcome. This had to be balanced with my own, ongoing discomfort with the evident bullying and feeling my silence as an uncomfortable weight. I agreed to be interviewed, but also had to manage those other losses, which were not insignificant.

4. *Chaotic contexts:* here the relationship between cause and effect is impossible to determine because they shift constantly and no manageable patterns exist. Snowden and Boone (2007) suggest the way forward is to staunch the bleeding and be aware that 'A deep understanding of context, the ability to embrace complexity and paradox, and a willingness to flexibly change leadership style will be required for leaders who want to make things happen in a time of increasing uncertainty' (p. 8). A contemporary example of a chaotic context involved the London riots. From a great distance in Sydney, I (Elisabeth) was disturbed by one image on our news. One man had fallen in the street, seemingly dizzy and disoriented, perhaps ill. Another came to help him up. Within seconds two other men came upon him from behind and started going through his backpack. He was too weak to bat them away, and his helper stepped back a distance and watched. After his valuables had been taken, everyone moved away and the unwell man was again alone. There are many ways to think about this moment. There was the immediate context and the demonstration of care of a stranger by the initial helper. There was the loss of care, compassion and ethics with those who stole from him. But what was the bigger story? The structural inequity, political failures, poverty, class and racial tensions that seethed unresolved and were ripe to explode in the riots? How could people, who perhaps usually had some modicum of respect for others (in so far as they didn't pillage and steal with such enthusiasm and so openly) suddenly prey on any weakness? How do we help without intruding or imposing? Perhaps intruding and imposing is required. What is the best thing to do immediately, in the short term, and in the long term? In this case, if the two robbers had been arrested it would have solved that particular moment, but done nothing to correct the bigger social problem.

Knowing which kind of decision we are facing when we have an ethical problem or dilemma (simple, complicated, complex or chaotic) might help us in the process of deciding what to do.

4. DISCERNMENT, DECISION MAKING AND THE EMERGING FUTURE

Decision making involves the future. In the present, we draw on the past and its lessons, and decide what to do. When we make decisions we are preparing the future. St Ignatius struggled with this in the Middle Ages and was interested in what he called 'discernment'—how can I know what to do? In his context, his interest was 'doing the will of God' and to spend time discerning or trying to discover what that was became important in his life. He provided a few hints that can still help us today as we struggle with future decisions.

For St Ignatius, discernment was the ability to 'sense the new and its impact'; to be open to new signs that indicate what might be required from us. The head, the heart, intuitions and feelings all played a part in his process of discernment. Key to uncovering this discernment was what Ignatius called 'indifference': 'Are you open to what might be asked from you? Can you be indifferent to what it might be?' For him, indifference did not mean disinterest or being dispassionate—quite the opposite. How can I be passionate and fascinated by the future and yet, indifferent to whatever demands it makes? In other words, using all our faculties (emotion, reason, intuition) and creating an attitude of openness to the future (I am indifferent to what the demands of the decision will mean for me), I can begin to allow the future to speak to me.

Otto Scharmer (2007) uses the terms 'sitting at the feet of the emerging future' to describe a similar method of decision making. He is sceptical, and with good reason, about our ability to predict the future—which many of our decisions are based upon—and suggests we create environments, relationships and conversations that allow the future to emerge. His six stages are somewhat linear and sequential:

4.1 SUSPENDING—SEEING OUR SEEING

The first stage in discerning futures is the ability to suspend existing judgements and 'truths'. This involves two sub-stages. In the first, we allow ourselves to go into neutral stance and leave aside our judgments, evaluations and ways of making meaning. We sit and observe without forming conclusions— we stay with the pieces and don't try to relate to them (we 'camp out beside the problems').

In suspending our habitual way of thinking and judging, we automatically enter the second sub-stage—we notice the mental models and maps that make up our habitual ways of thinking and making sense of reality. We see our seeing. We notice our prejudices, our personal investments, our needs to control, our intentions, and where our motivation comes from within us. Suspension requires patience and a willingness not to impose pre-established frameworks or mental models on what we are seeing.

4.2   REDIRECTION—SEEING THE WHOLE

We now redirect attention to the sources and begin to think more systemically. In connecting the details and seeing the relationships involved, we allow the system to emerge. Now we develop a new relationship with the problems and the issues. We stay with our feelings, our intuitions and our reactions. But we go deeper. If Stage 1 helps us to see how we see, and enables us to suspend our seeing, then Stage 2 provides us with a new framework for perceiving. In redirecting our gaze we are concentrating, we become mindful and see from within the emerging whole.

We now talk of gut knowing, mind knowing and heart knowing. We are open to the new possibilities—what we could create, what might happen. We have larger intentions, we think bigger. We are no longer confined by our ethics of duty or obligation, but by a wider commitment of trust, concern and compassion. We reflect in ever-widening circles. We are in relationship with self, others, world—the relationship is one of co-creating and not alienation or separation. Perhaps we need silence. We slow down. We see from the bigger picture, from contexts. We think systemically.

4.3   LETTING GO

In Stage 3 we surrender, we wait with open heart, open mind and open will. We give up control, security, greed, publicity, compulsions, our competitiveness, our perfectionism, our drivers and our fear. We may have to leave aside our cherished loyalties to an approach, a value or an orientation. This links to Ignatius' sense of indifference: I am truly not invested in any one outcome, any one way of doing my work, any one theory or framework. We give up our 'pet' theories that have become prisons rather than freedoms. What we think we control, may be controlling us. The more we hold on to our compulsions, the less we are able to see, and the less we are able to see, the more blindly we stumble into the future.

4.4   LETTING COME

Having changed our way of seeing and making meaning, we now wait. We are attentive to the moment, to what is emerging. We watch, we notice, we observe and we listen. We don't clutch at it. We don't rush to define it. We allow it to speak. We wait patiently, creatively. We do not soothe our anxiety by finding a quick solution. When we try to control the future, we define it by what we fear. Out of mistrust, we push, we interfere and we grasp too quickly. The story of the helpful person who tries to help the caterpillar become a butterfly is well known. There is an old African saying that a baby takes nine months to develop no matter how many people are on the job. 'Letting come' means allowing the future to emerge as it chooses to come, which is often beyond our current conceptions. It means trusting that the future can be much, much bigger than we can envision.

4.5 CAPTURING THE VISION

As we begin to envision what seeks to emerge, we begin to attempt to focus it in a form of communication that has meaning for us. This is not an easy stage; often we wrestle with the words. And so it should be, because these will be the words that make a difference to us. These are the words that we will translate into actions.

4.6 IMPLEMENTING THE DECISION

Finally, we work out the emerging future in a commitment and a plan of implementation. We act to make it work, pragmatically from within and across, a deep knowledge of ourselves as individuals and as social systems. We act with the people we have learned to trust—through a journey we have trusted to unfold.

Both Ignatius and Scharmer present ways in which we create insights and awarenesses (discernment) about how we make decisions. How might we apply the above to ethical decision making?

5. REFLECTION

Reflection after a decision is a crucial part of integrating the action into our ongoing development in ethical maturity. In this phase we look at how the decision has played out, how it appears in hindsight, how others who are involved relate to it, how at peace we feel with the action taken. It may be that it is a good decision, but we still would choose not to repeat it for a whole host of reasons. Or, as Kant would demand, would our action be universalisable, that is, a recommended action for all to take in such circumstances? How have we grown and changed as a result of our deliberations? We believe that this is such an important (yet often neglected or underestimated) phase of ethical life that we have designated it Component 6 of our model.

What helps us make conscious ethical decisions?

We have argued that a number of skills, personal abilities and resources are crucial in order to make mature ethical decisions. We will apply them now to the task at the centre of this chapter: deliberate and conscious ethical decision making.

RESOURCES:

- knowledge of ethical theories, principles, codes, rules and applications
- a clear problem-solving model for ethical decisions; using supervision; using others to help make clear decisions, e.g., peers; wise elders

- dialogues and discussions with others (especially with those who might take a different ethical viewpoint).

SKILLS:

- systemic approach; holding together the needs of individuals, community, society and professions
- able to integrate emotion, intuition, reason and decision making;
- able to reflect deeply (reflection, self-reflection and critical self-reflection)
- able to be open, stand back from and keep bigger pictures in view (thinking individually, relationally and systemically); slowing down the pace, reflecting and keeping tabs on what is happening to me and others
- notice external pressures on me to make a decision one way or another.

SELF AWARENESS:

- access my feelings, hunches and intuitions to see if there is a clear and definitive answer without going to deliberation and conscious decision making
- aware of my own ethical stance (foundational beliefs)
- alert to the assumptions I bring to ethical discernment
- knowing me, my vulnerabilities, my biases
- awareness of how I tend to make decisions in general (can help me to know my strengths and my limitations in decision making, and to know when to harness the former and when to acknowledge the latter).

Conclusion

How can we make ethical decisions that are mature? The answer is, it *depends*. This seems to be the mature stance. There are times when we make decisions, including ethical decisions, one way and sometimes another. There is no one guaranteed method, sequential, linear or otherwise, that ought to be our guideline. There are times when emotion guides us, and other times reason. There are times when a combination of both is used where we 'think feelingly'. There are times when we allow authority to be the basis of our decision, and other times we allow our experience to determine our decision. There are times when we rely on the experience of others, and times when we go with our intuition. Sometimes the decision is immediate and needing no thought: sometimes the decision is made after short or long deliberation, reflection and attention. There are times when we make the decision in a flash; and some decisions take years to make. There are times when we have no time and must make an immediate decision; and times when we have no idea what to do and must wait patiently for an answer to emerge in its own time. Sometimes the decision is made unconsciously; sometimes a lot of conscious effort is needed. Sometimes ethical codes guide and support us; sometimes they are of little help. There are times when we play it safe, and times when we take risks. There are times when there are non-negotiables when we dig in and refuse to budge, and other times when there is lots of leeway and possibilities opening up a myriad of decisions. Sometimes there are universals and injunctions we cannot afford to ignore, and at other times there are rules we break because they are not in the best interest of our individual, team or organisational clients. There are times when we know and times when we haven't a clue. Sometimes we are scared and anxious, and sometimes brave and determined.

What is the point of writing on ethical maturity and ethical decision making if we end up with the conclusion that 'it all depends…sometimes we rely on one approach, and sometimes another'? Doesn't this end with a rather chaotic and unstructured approach to ethical navigation? While this position is unsatisfactory in not offering clear answers to specific questions, we believe this approach is more in keeping with modern life and contemporary living. Life and work are complex, complicated and, at times, chaotic. In that context we make decisions with more options in our decision making than we have ever had before. Not having one definitive way means our focus is not on the answers, but on how we make decisions, and challenges us to let go of certainty and immerse ourselves in 'real-time' ethics where often there are few 'givens'. However we make them, good ethical decisions are defensible by reason and need to be justifiable. Making ethical decisions is one step on the road towards ethical maturity.

Chapter 12

Component 2

The influence of the unconscious on ethical decision making

....

'Conscious decision making and unconscious decision making are seen as two distinguishable processes. Humans possess (at least) two different mental apparatuses that make decisions: one operates under conscious control, the other does not. This view does not exclude the possibility that both machineries interact, nor does it mean that either machinery has an exclusive domain, to which the other has no, or only rare, access.'

(Engel and Singer, 2008, p. 8)

'A wise person is one who knows what is good and spontaneously does it...this approach stands in stark contrast to the usual way of investigating ethical behaviour, which begins by analysing the intentional content of the act and ends by evaluating the rationality of particular moral judgements.'

(Varela, 1999, p. 4)

'The mind operates most efficiently by relegating a good deal of high-level, sophisticated thinking to the unconscious, just as a modern jumbo jetliner is able to fly on automatic pilot with little or no input from the human "conscious" pilot.'

(Wilson, 2002, p. 6)

'Even though we are defined by our decisions, we are often completely unaware of what's happening inside our heads during the decision-making process.'

(Lehrer, 2009, p. 16)

A number of recent authors have popularised the notion that most decisions are made unconsciously (e.g., Lehrer, 2009; Gladwell, 2005; Brooks, 2011). Brooks (2011) summarises how these writers see this process: 'We are living in the middle of a revolution in consciousness. Over the past few years geneticists, neuroscientists, psychologists, sociologists, economists, anthropologists, and others have made great strides in understanding the building blocks of human flourishing. And a core finding of their work is that we are not primarily the products of our conscious thinking. We are primarily the products of thinking that happens below the level of awareness' (p. x). They have backed up their assertions with reference to research in the field of neuroscience (Engel and Singer, 2008). The unconscious method, the fast way of making decisions, has also been suggested to be the best way of making decisions and the most accurate. This has raised questions about the role of conscious decision making, the slow route. Why has it evolved? The questions raised include the following:

- Is the conscious mind the rationalisation side of decision-making?
- Is the conscious mind the realm of reason, logic and analysis and the unconscious mind the realm of emotion and perception?
- Is the conscious mind the world of words and data, and the unconscious mind the domain of story, narrative, poetry, music, image, symbol and myth?
- How can we get the two minds working together in harmony?

Many, if not most, human decisions are made unconsciously. Kurzban (2008) uses the iceberg metaphor to suggest that the small visible tip of an iceberg is the conscious, deliberate process of decision making with the 'overwhelming majority of computation' left to the unconscious, being the part of the iceberg below water. Wilson (2002) uses the same metaphor to suggest that the role of conscious processes: 'may be more the size of a snowball on top of that iceberg' (p. 6). Modern insights into the brain and the realm of the unconscious have gone much further than Freud could ever have imagined to support his conclusions about the existence of the unconscious and its impact on the decisions we make. Gladwell (2005), in his bestselling book, *Blink*, points out that the unconscious is more of an 'adapted unconscious', which he compares to: 'a kind of giant computer that quickly and quietly processes a lot of the data we need in order to keep functioning as human beings...these are decisions that bubble up from the unconscious' (p. 11). This rapid form of human decision making implicitly processes information at the rate of millions of items per second (11,200,200 bits per second), while the conscious mode is roughly 40 pieces of information per second (Kurzban, 2008; Hardman, 2009). Gladwell subtitles his book, *The Power of Thinking without Thinking*. His stance on decisions made from the adaptive unconscious are threefold: a) that decisions made with the adaptive unconscious can be every bit as good as those made deliberately; b) that our intuitions and our adaptive unconscious can also betray us and let us down, and c) that we can train and educate ourselves to use our intuitive insights.

The adaptive unconscious

Wilson (2002) suggests we may have two selves: the conscious self and the adaptive unconscious self. Both are real and have their own personalities and their different ways of making decisions. They can be in sync or out of sync with each other. My conscious self may be both saying and experiencing my lack of fear in a situation (e.g., making a presentation) while my adaptive unconscious self might be experiencing terror at the prospect. If they are out of sync I will not understand why I slept in and did not make the presentation.

The adaptive unconscious, like all forms of the unconscious, develops from early infancy when we inherit our values, our culture and our social lives. From an early age we develop what Wilson calls a 'distinctive behavioural signature' (this is a life script, or an organising structure) that helps us fill in the 'If...then' sentence. If I am unwanted by my parents (and the adaptive unconscious will know this) then in a situation where my presentation is given negative feedback I may feel a deep sense of rejection and abandonment. I may interpret that I am no good rather than that my presentation is poor. The 'distinctive behaviour signature' has a 'scanning pattern' or template that selects pertinent information and data that supports my story.

At my (Elisabeth) children's school, one of the families comprises older children and two-year-old triplets. The triplets have been a source of wonder and excitement (and some sympathy for their parents) since their birth. As newborns, their mother would push a pram of three bassinets in long succession, like a row of sausages, to school. People would gather and peek in with delight. Those children expect people to smile and engage. As two-year-olds, they relate to the world as on their side, ready to assist and welcome them. Many hands reach out to help. I barely know them, but one ran up to me recently and asked me to hold her toy while she played, totally secure that I would say yes and wait for her to come back. At two, in an enclosed school yard, she had a good chance of being right about that. She based all her decisions on the security of being important, being responded to when needed, and that strangers (albeit in a safe environment) would be good to her and delighted with her.

The adaptive unconscious is that part of us that is inaccessible to ourselves (even through introspection or therapy), but which still learns (implicit learning) new behaviours, interprets them, stores them and sets goals for future behaviours. It is about the present and not the future.

How do we know it exists? By its effects. It is not accessible through our normal channels of self-awareness, but can be seen when we:

- examine our behaviour (rather than our private thoughts and intentions)
- consider what others think about us
- listen to and ask for feedback
- stay with intuitions and feelings
- consider how we construct the stories of our lives
- monitor and make sense of our distractions.

Wilson (2002) suggests that others may know us better than we know ourselves and, at times, notice our behavioural signature, which can be invisible to us. He suggests we will discover aspects of the adaptive unconscious by looking outwards rather than inwards.

Robert was always seen to be the life of the party: ready with a joke or a story that enthralled his audiences, always surrounded by people, laughing uproariously. Only his closest friends knew that humour kept people at bay more than drew them in, creating distraction and deflection whenever the conversation got too intimate. When asked a personal question he didn't want to answer, Robert's humour could be used in a pointed and sarcastic way, saying 'Back off!' Friends read Robert better than he read himself, and came to adapt their conversations with him, colluding with his defences, and picking their moment for a 'real' conversation. Robert was unaware how transparent he was, and how much he was 'managed' by others.

Conscious/unconscious divide

Engel and Singer (2008) describe the task of defining consciousness and the conscious/unconscious divide as 'unpleasant as nailing a pudding to a wall'. For Engel and Singer, a decision has been made consciously 'if a person is able to report the information taken into consideration as well as the way it was processed…if a person is aware of the mental process leading to it…When the prefrontal cortex has been engaged' (p. 3). They outline features of conscious and unconscious decision making in Table 12.1.

Conscious decisions (System 2)	Unconscious decisions (System 1)
Deliberate	Intuitive
Explicit	Implicit
Controlled	Automatic
Analytic	Holistic
Slow	Rapid
Ad hoc	Learned
Plastic	Patterned
Long view	Pre-packaged routines
Flexible	Procedural
Single system	Multiple systems

Table 12.1: Features of conscious and unconscious decision making

Experienced drivers drive their cars unconsciously—they go on automatic pilot until something happens that pulls them back into awareness. Naomi is driving on the motorway listening to her favourite radio station. She is thinking about the meeting she is driving to where she intends to pitch for a new piece of work with an organisation. Her mind is working with possible questions the panel might ask as she looks in her mirror, moves into the outside lane and passes some lorries. Without thinking again, she checks her mirrors and moves safely back into the slow lane. She continues to rehearse her forthcoming meeting while changing gears, adjusting her speed and keeping an eye on the road signs so that she does not miss Junction 22. The chances are that Naomi will not remember much of her drive. She has been driving intuitively or with automaticity where mindlessness has served her well. Not for a moment would we consider her driving dangerously or not driving at a high standard. Her mindlessness will immediately transform into mindfulness if something happens to make her think deliberately. She notices cars slowing in the distance and realises that a herd of cattle has wandered onto the motorway. Her attention moves from listening to the radio and thoughts for the forthcoming meeting to attending to the new driving challenge. She turns off the radio and focuses on how she can navigate the car through a herd of cattle without damaging car or cattle and, at the same time, warn other drivers behind her that there is a problem ahead. Safely through the hazard, she moves back into mindlessness and automatic driving. Naomi's brain is doing what it is supposed to do for all of us—hardwire us into habits so that we live unconsciously most of the time. She has 'learned pre-packaged routines' (Engle and Singer, 2008, p.10). Rock (2006) puts it well: 'So the way we talk, walk, interact, read emails, and manage our staff is, for the most part, deeply hardwired and therefore habitual. Our habits are literally unconscious to us; we don't "have in mind" what we are doing. You might take this further and say that once people have done a job for some time, they are unconscious much of their workday' (p. 13).

For the most part, this works well. On this basis, Engel and Singer (2008) ask 'If the consciously not controlled mental apparatus is so powerful, why did conscious, deliberate, serial control evolve at all?' (p. xiii). From an evolutionary point of view this is an important question, and from an ethics perspective it is vital in knowing when, and even how, we move from unconscious, intuitive decision making to conscious, deliberate decision making. While still unclear, Kurzban (2008) offers our best explanation to date. While unconscious decision making is helpful, it is not very social. He points out that while chimpanzees learn from each other how to use twigs to hunt for termites, it is not learned easily and 'imitation learning' in other animals is cumbersome. What conscious learning adds to this is that we humans not only teach and learn from each other implicitly and unconsciously, but we have the evolutionary advantage of language and communication to create social learning. What explicit and conscious decision making adds to our evolution as humans is simple: we learn and then we communicate our learning through language. We can create and share a pool of collective knowledge and wisdom that lasts over time, and we can develop a consciousness or self-awareness that 'knows' the person who is doing the knowing. When we pool our wisdom we can come up with common agreements such as 'We will all drive on the left-/right-hand side of the road', and we know the agent (me) who knows and follows this agreement—I know my intentions. Language has added a new dimension to decision making that other mammals do not have.

So if Naomi's personal, social or organisational relationships, and the decisions she has to make as part of her work are dealt with in the same way as her driving, i.e., mindlessly and automatically, then it will be no surprise if problems begin to emerge. Some issues, like the herd of cattle, need to be given conscious and deliberate consideration because they are 'new' and no assimilated learning is available from which to glean existing answers. One conclusion is that new situations, and new moral demands, require our attention and focus in ways that old situations do not—most of us do not have to think about whether or not we will torture someone, or drive over an old person walking across the street, or rob a bank, or blow ourselves and others up in a busy train station. These latter situations would only arise if they became possibilities for us because of the contexts in which we found ourselves, and then they would not be answered automatically—we would need a deliberate and focused attention on them to make up our minds about what we should do. Claxton (1981) puts it well, 'When all is flowing smoothly, no conscious product intervenes between perception and action. Only when no ready-made response exists—when the situation poses a problem—does conscious deliberation appear...once this happens, channels of conscious, verbal reason may become active, and we experience ourselves as 'thinking', 'deciding' or 'intending' (p. 166).

Unconscious decision making (what neuroscientists call 'fast, automatic, passive response') is both helpful and not helpful. Decisions we make without thinking, and that rely on established habits and automaticity, access our tacit knowing and save an amazing amount of energy for the energy-sapping brain (the brain uses about 20–25% of all our energy). Unconscious decision making is a necessary part of life. It would be difficult to get through each day if every decision made was subjected to reflection, consideration and attention before acting. It is no surprise that most of our decisions are made on an unconscious basis. Our brain works hard to help us create habits, routines and procedures that demand little thought or reflection. Habits not only save energy, but maintain us on a day-to-day basis when it is helpful to go into autopilot, access what we do well, and act on it. We also know, mostly from sports psychology and sports coaching, that conscious decision making and going into deliberate, thinking and reflective mode can have a negative effect on performance. When we do something well, it is best not to think about what we do, but to do it 'naturally', i.e., automatically. The time for thinking and reflecting is before or after the action or decision has taken place.

Langer (1989) is strong on how a lack of mindfulness builds up in life and results in poor learning—we move into routines that imprison us and blind us to new information. Socrates was the champion of waking people up and almost forcing them to think. He saw the danger in automaticity or routines, hence his famous remark that 'the unexamined life is not worth living'. Routines tend to lower our choices and offer us ways of life that become part and parcel of who we are without consideration of whether they still fit or suit us. It is easy to move towards fundamentalist positions regarding choice and to lead lives based on a series of unthought-through assumptions that impact and influence behaviour. Religions, cults and organisations often want us to adopt unconscious thinking and decision making processes. It leads us towards compliance and tends to reduce conflict.

Habits and unconscious behaviour can result in 'mindless' behaviour, where we do the same things over and over again without thinking about them. We can easily get 'into a rut' where ongoing and continual learning is avoided. 'But we have always done it this way' is the clarion call of the mindless approach—good in the sense of having been built on solid traditional foundations that have worked well in the past, poor in the sense that, if reflection were allowed into the equation, it might open us to new learning and more effective ways of 'doing it differently'. Doing an action habitually can dull us to its ethical implications: the first time someone lies, or robs or kills is often followed by guilt and remorse, but further down the line these feelings can disappear and the moral action is taken for granted. Furthermore, 'habit learning, which is very fast and durable, can be counterproductive for individuals and difficult to overcome, as for example in addiction' (The Royal Society, 2011b, p. 5).

Unconscious ethical decision making

Making decisions unconsciously means that we 'exploit the rich database of subconscious heuristics (problem solving) and therefore can process many more variables in parallel and cope better with unreliable and "noisy" variables' (Singer, 2011, p. 44). In brief, our brains fit incoming information into existing templates and make meaning of it. If the world is a depressing place for us (we have a depression template), then we will fit our experiences and events to that. This is the brain's fast way of making decisions. The result is that unconscious ethical decisions result in immediate action.

However, if a decision, said to be 'a commitment to a choice or course of action selected from more than one option' (Platt *et al.*, 2008, p. 126) is not accommodated easily by our existing knowledge or templates, then we are taken by surprise and need another mode of making decisions (Curran, 2008). We have to reconstruct our world not by way of assimilation, but by accommodation. Our knowing, the templates of our knowing, and our meaning-making perspectives move first to unconscious mode when we face an event or an experience (making a presentation, dressing in the morning, or swinging my golf club). For those who have done it many times with well-worn pathways in the brain, even when faced with a new presentation, new clothes and a different golf course, they will go automatically into intuitive/unconscious decision-making mode and 'get on with it' and will make good decisions.

However, we need a deliberate and conscious mode when faced with a new situation where we do not have the mental apparatus to help us assimilate. So when Naomi's sister goes for her first driving lesson, all systems will be on alert and in deliberate conscious awareness. When I open my mouth to speak, out comes English (in a reasonably well-organised and understandable fashion). I speak mostly without thinking (my brain goes into automatic English mode). However, when I land in France and try to make myself understood using French, there is no such automaticity. I have to pay attention to what I say, I have to stop and deliberate whether or not I have the right word, and I have to be humble enough to be corrected when I get it wrong. Working consciously and reflectively in Paris allows me to learn socially from others through language. Beginners in most areas of life do this. Varela (1999) calls this the moment of breakdown: 'It is at the moment of breakdown, that is, when we are not experts of our microworld *anymore*, that we deliberate and analyze, that we become like beginners seeking to feel at ease with the task at hand' (p. 18).

Intuitive ethical decisions (decisions from the adaptive unconscious)

Based on ethical character, many of our ethical decisions are made unconsciously—we do not need to think about them. They are instinctive, emotional and intuitive choices based on who we are. As Varela (1992) writes: 'When one *is* the action, no residue of self-consciousness remains to observe the action externally' (p. 34).

At times we find our moral characters leave something to be desired when we examine our first response, or even our intuitive response. This is illustrated in the following example. I (Michael) had to make an ethical decision about whether I should accept a referral for a client to coach. Due to his criminal background, I was anxious about possible repercussions, were it known I was coaching him. As I considered what to do, I realised I was putting myself and my professional safety at the centre of the ethical decision. As I began to shift the centre away from myself to others (the client, the profession, values), I became aware of how confined I had become in a position that most likely meant I would refuse to work with him. Embarrassed by my narrow self-centred approach, I managed to relocate the focus and decided to work with the client, acknowledging the professional risk. An awareness of how I had put my own safety as the foundation of the decision allowed me to shift and open up other possible decisions. This awareness also allowed me to look at my ethical decision-making processes, and review whether this was a characteristic ethical beginning point for me when faced with an ethical dilemma. I found it was. Now, I can be more conscious of that stance when making an ethical decision. I want it to be part of the ethical equation, but not the sole tenet on which I decide. Sartre's comment that we know our values from our choices was evident in this example.

This example is illustrative of how ethical decisions can be almost made before we have moved into a formal and conscious decision-making place. This is not necessarily bad or unjust, but if we recognise a lack of openness to other values we can also recognise predetermined stances that allow for little or no negotiation. I (Michael) supervised a counsellor whose own value set refused her permission to allow the young people she worked with to proceed to pregnancy termination. This option was not in her repertoire because of her strong commitment as a pro-life adherent. My job was to help her become aware of her non-negotiable ethical stance and to consider the implications of this for herself and for her clients. It was certainly not my job to change her values. I too have non-negotiable value sets in my personal and work life, and have refused to work with certain companies because of what they produce and sell. No doubt, it is worth re-evaluating those non-negotiables occasionally, to ensure that I do not get so set in my ways that I am not open to change. However, we do not come without values and principles, and there are no value-free relationships.

Intuitions and unconscious behaviours can indicate one's moral character—they give us a reading of the ethical stances and values held by the person. As we think of working with moral character and intuitive responses/habits of thought, good questions for trainers and supervisors are: How is moral character formed and what impacts on its formation over time? How can we support, help and coach individuals to develop their moral character as the basis for their ethical decision making? Do we believe moral character changes over time and can be made an active part of our learning dialogue, or do we think that core moral development is impossible and write people off as fixed and unworkable?

Entering the ethical arena

We have discussed that unconscious decision-making processes, influenced by our culture and traditions of thinking, core values and life influences, can result in habits reflected in our reactions and automatic decision making. We will look further at how our moral character forms at this foundational level, and how we might increase our ethical maturity through making our unconscious ethical decision-making processes more conscious.

There are grounds for thinking we are born with a moral intelligence, i.e., an innate sense of morality about what is good and bad. However, just as we are born with an innate ability to speak, we still have to learn to speak. As Paul Bloom (2010) notes in his research on the moral life of babies, we begin with a primitive and incomplete morality. 'To have a genuinely moral system...some things first have to matter, and what we see in babies is the development of mattering.' From there, we have to learn to be moral. Just as context impacts on the language we use and how we use that language, so context influences our moral stances. Lennick and Kiel (2005), in their book *Moral Intelligence*, distinguish between 'moral hardware'—the moral intelligence with which we are born and that is our internal moral compass—and 'moral software', which they see as moral competence—how we learn to act in accord with what is right and wrong.

The moral software is upgraded as we journey through life, still connected to the 'nurture' side of development as we enhance our inborn ability to know what is right and wrong. Context, relationships and experiences all contribute to that ability and, like language, can influence how proficient we become in making ethical decisions and being ethically mature. To take in this learning, and allow it to challenge and develop our usual gut response, requires conscious thought. We notice the new information when we feel uncomfortable or are in unfamiliar territory. However, to take that a step further by discussing it in some reflective way with a peer or supervisor can consolidate the learning into something more. Instead of leaving it as a 'one-off', we might consider what difference it has made to us to face this dilemma and what decisions we might make as a result in the future. For example, does it signal the need for further formal learning?

Making ethical decisions also makes us ethical. The more we make ethical decisions, and the more we deliberate on decisions made, the more we create an ethical attitude and an ethical stance that leads to a mature ethical character. Bell (2002) supports this proposition, 'ethical living is a process you go through so that as each new situation arises the inclination to choose ethically is stronger in you, even if the right path is less clear' (p. 36). In turn, ethical character results in ethical intuition where we just know what we need to do. Over Christmas, I (Michael) noticed an elderly lady leave her change on the counter where she was putting stamps on her cards. Without thinking, I picked it up, caught up with her, and gave her the money. It would not have crossed my mind to keep it. It is an intuitive part of my life to tell a cashier that he or she has given me the wrong change, as it is to return something I have found that is not mine. I wish I was as morally intuitive in other areas of my life. I am not, and therefore have to move into deliberation and conscious decision-making mode.

Some might object that this form of making decisions is far too subjective and open to all kinds of abuse. It is important to review your moral character and there are a few tests that might help substantiate your decision if you think your moral intuition leaves something to be desired. Bringing values to the fore and re-examining them helps. You can subject your decision to all those questions in the ethical conversation that justify or articulate why you did what you did.

- Would I recommend this course of action to others?
- Could I accept others doing what I have decided to do?
- If I were in front of a complaints committee how might I justify my course of action?
- What does my supervisor/mentor think about my decision?
- What advice would the wisest person I know give me?

One effective measure of a good ethical decision is the following guideline: If I am reluctant to talk about this or share it with others then I may need to review the decision I have made or the action I have taken.

Conclusion

In ethical decision making we can make decisions consciously and unconsciously. In this chapter we have considered the unconscious and intuitive method where ethical decisions emerge 'spontaneously'. We know what to do, what is wrong, what is good, and even what is better, in a way that seems instantaneous. Of course, these 'instant' decisions are the result of lifelong learning and fine tuning. Like an expert in wine, where a single taste can lead to a decision about its value, so with ethical decisions— our knowledge, expertise, former experiences, feelings all merge with the current situation and we sense, intuit and know something of what to do in the immediate circumstances. This is what Gladwell (2005) calls 'thin-slicing...the ability of our unconscious to find patterns in situations and behaviour based on very narrow slices of experience' (p. 23). It is clear that this would be the preferred option in making decisions—that they emerge spontaneously from our deepest selves. However, this happens best when we undertake regular conscious reflection, taking the time to revisit our habits and decide if they still work as an effective guide for our behaviour.

Chapter 13
Component 3
Implementing ethical decisions

....

'Five frogs sat on a log. Four decided to jump into the pond. How many frogs are left on the log? Answer: Five. Because in organisations the fact that you decide to do something doesn't mean you do it.'

(Old organisational saying)

'To know and not to act is not to know.'

(Chinese proverb)

'If not now, when?'

(Talmudic saying)

'Man is divided into a multiplicity of small I's. And each separate I is able to call itself by the name of the Whole, to act in the name of the Whole. To agree or disagree, to give promises, to make decisions, with which another I or the Whole will have to deal. This explains why people so often make decisions and so seldom carry them out... it is the tragedy of the human being that any small I has the right to sign cheques and promissory notes and the man, that is the Whole, has to meet them. People's whole lives often consist in paying off the promissory notes of small accidental I's'.

(Gurdjieff in Ouspensky, 1949, p. 60)

'The pathway to hell is paved with good intentions.'

(ancient saying)

'Just do it.'

(T-shirt slogan)

Were Aristotle writing this book it is likely he would not have a chapter on implementing ethical decisions, as it would not make sense for him to create a division between moral decision and moral implementation. Practical wisdom, what he called 'phronimos', is not just about knowledge and deciding what to do. It includes action, or as Aristotle put it, 'it gives orders' (Thiele, 2006, p. 21). This means that in practice, the ethical life is the enactment of being an ethical person. For Thiele, 'moral knowledge does not pre-exist its enactment…the phronimos is a knower of the good only insofar as he is a doer of the good' (p. 22). While there is no doubt this is the ideal, in reality, many of us need to build a bridge between our decisions and implementing them. Ask Darley and Batson (1973) who, in a now famous research project, placed divinity students in a difficult moral situation. Asked to present an impromptu talk, they were sent urgently to a hall where someone was waiting to record their presentation. Half of the students were told their presentation was on the parable of the Good Samaritan, the man who stopped to help another in need who would normally be seen as his enemy. On the way to their presentations, it was arranged that each of them would meet a person slumped against a wall who coughed twice as they passed by and groaned. The point of the research was to see if students who were studying theology, and acquainting themselves with the parable of the Good Samaritan, would stop and help. Those told they were running late almost all hurried by. The ones who stopped only did so because they felt they had some time to spare. Sobering thoughts. What a gap between what we know, what we think we would do, what we know we should do, and what we do.

Knowing what we want to do, even knowing what we should do, does not mean we do it. Knowledge and knowing can be good learning, but not necessarily embodied learning, i.e., learning that moves from head to action. Hawkins (2011) puts this well in the area of supervision and coaching:

'We noticed that a lot of coaching stopped at the level of awareness, insight and good intention. One of the biggest frustrations in coaches who come to supervision is that clients have an 'aha' moment in the session and do not follow through. We play that back to the coaches and say what needs to shift in the coaching to stop repeating that cycle? Then we came up with the notion that if the change doesn't happen in the room it's not going to happen outside the room so how do you help the coachee move from agreement to commitment, and from insight to action actually in the coaching session? How do you ensure you have embodied learning?' (p. 5).

Kohlberg (1984) points out that ethical judgement is necessary, but not sufficient, for ethical conduct. Knowing what to do does not mean we decide to follow through, and deciding to follow through does not mean we do follow through. In fact, sometimes feeling more clear about our position or definite in our reasoning, even our ability to explain it to others, feels like change, and as if something is now different. True enough, new thinking is different and that can feel empowering, but what difference does this really make in the scheme of things? Is knowledge enough, or is it sometimes another way we kid ourselves that something has happened, when everything is much the same? Is it ethical maturity or an ethical cop-out? Is ethical prevarication and ethical procrastination itself an ethical issue?

Most books on ethics provide guidance for decision making and action. Ethics is inherently practical in its outcomes (Koocher and Keith-Spiegel, 2008), and yet little is written on delivering on our ethical decisions. How does our reflection and exploration really change our decision? How is our increased wisdom going to change our life? To change us? The fact that we are looking at words that signify active processes: decision making, action, change, says that something is supposed to happen as a result of deliberation. In the final analysis of our ethical endeavours, it makes no positive difference if we do not act on that knowledge, and if we do not incorporate it into how we live our lives (Hinman, 2008). This is the signifier of ethical maturity. Yet, we find that good decisions, and even the will to do something different, need not lead to outward behavioural change. In this chapter, we issue a challenge to implement your ethical wisdom, and consider some of the elements that commonly lead to derailment.

The gap between knowing and doing

There can be quite a chasm between decisions to act and implementing that action, as those who have made New Year resolutions know all too well. Bernard and Jara (1986) discovered that a whopping 50 per cent of their clinical psychology graduate students would *not* do what they thought they *should* do in response to a peer's violation of an ethical code. In applying the same research to experienced clinical psychologists, would it surprise you to know similar results were found (Bernard, Murphy and Little, 1987)? It was not that either group did not know what to do, or even did not know what they should do—many felt they would not implement what they knew they should do. Similarly, Smith, McGuire, Abbott and Blau (1991) set out to investigate why clinicians say they would do less than they believe they should in ethical conflict situations. They too found 'that there is often a discrepancy between what clinicians know to be the ethically preferred course of action in dealing with professional-ethical dilemmas and their stated willingness to implement this ideal' (p. 238). A finding from this research is worth noting: in instances where clinicians said they would not do what they knew they should do (as outlined in codes or frameworks), the rationale or reason given was situational, e.g., there is something different about this instance, or personal reasons, e.g., the cost to me is too great, as this colleague is a friend. There seems to be a difference between professional consistency (where a person is consistent with their ethical code) and personal consistency (where their own values are what dictate the outcome).

One of us (Michael) was involved in an organisational setting where a much-loved psychiatrist was an alcoholic. His addiction had begun to have a serious impact on his work, and he would often be under the influence of alcohol during the working day. His professional colleagues and administrative staff, as well as his patients, all rallied round to protect him. He was so well liked and so generous with his skills and time, that they felt guilty in reporting him, despite the fact that many efforts to get him help had failed. 'Dr—is not well today' was a common phrase used to hide what everyone knew, but no one said. It was when he was hospitalised that the full extent of his illness was revealed. Only then did the reasons for *not* doing something emerge: 'I remember how supportive he was of me when I joined the team...how could I betray him?' 'He worked here for 15 years and there was no more dedicated member of staff...what a humiliation if I had reported him' 'He supervised my work and was always so insightful...I presumed he would deal with it in his own time and way.' And one of his patients remarked, 'He was vulnerable like the rest of us...that's what made him such a compassionate man...I loved him...I would never have told anyone that he was often drunk when he saw me.' This example confirms the research findings that personal issues (loyalty, admiration, friendship, not wanting to hurt) overcome professional stances (harm to others, disrepute to profession, incompetency, neglect) in keeping an ethical violation secret.

Even when an ethical decision moves into behaviour, there can be a gap between the decision made and the actual details of what is implemented. Damon (cited in Rest, 1986) asked children to distribute ten candy bars as rewards. In interviews, they discussed various methods for how a fair distribution ought to be made. However, when they were given the candy bars to distribute, their espoused scheme was different from what they actually did. They gave themselves more candy bars than their initial distribution scheme had suggested they ought to. What might this signal? A lack of commitment to the 'agreed' scheme? That self-interest wins out in the end? That the system was unjust? That it was too much to ask of children to give up candy? In a similar way, an ethical decision can be diluted when implemented by watering it down to make it more acceptable, or only implementing a part of the decision because of the price to be paid by the agent.

- Often a decision results in an action.
- Often a decision results in a delayed action.
- Often a decision results in no action.

The action or inaction taken can become another piece of information to consider. Does it suggest a further part of the ethical puzzle? Sometimes it is only when we are down to the wire that we realise we have missed a step in the process, or forgot to get a crucial detail sorted first. Sometimes it can be a good decision to put off action. For example, Debbie became aware that a fellow teacher was coaching children outside of school to earn extra money. This was not an unusual practice. However, Debbie became aware that one of her classroom students had sought out the teacher's coaching services, and that her colleague had agreed to see the child out of hours. This felt different. This could set up a sense of inequity and favouritism amongst students, and was a practice that would be frowned upon. Debbie wondered if she should speak up straightaway. However, she decided to wait another few weeks and find out if it was true. Debbie found out that it was true, but that it was a short-term arrangement for a specific purpose and not such a worrying precedent.

Sometimes waiting to see is useful, but we need to be able to tell the difference between waiting for a defined period and when that has slid into inaction.

For us, implementing ethical decisions we have made is part and parcel of the 'maturity' of being ethical. The movement from decision to implementation is an essential ingredient of ethical excellence and at times takes both resilience and courage. We want to look at how we can build bridges between what we know we should do and want to do, but occasionally do not do.

What stops us implementing ethical decisions?

There are a number of blocks or impasses as to why ethical decisions are not implemented. Figure 13.1 summaries some of these:

1. Personal cost.

2. Conflicting values.

3. Personal versus professional consistency.

4. Collusive stances.

5. Competing commitments.

6. Damage to the brain.

7. Sub-personalities (mini-selves) in conflict (zombie systems).

8. Willpower and procrastination.

Figure 13.1: What stops us implementing ethical decisions?

1. PERSONAL COST

It may seem like the action to be taken as a result of our ethical decision making will be too costly to ourselves, and might even put us in conflict with others or our own communities. Faye was treasurer of the parents' committee at her children's school. She became aware that the executive had been spending money on their own pet projects without consultation with the school community. A hefty contribution had been made to the school band coffers (the band having ten students) at the expense of new interactive whiteboards for the classrooms that all students could enjoy. Faye was not sure if there would be repercussions for her children if she took this to the school community. As Faye was new to the area her family had few friends and she did not want to burn any bridges with many years of schooling ahead.

Perhaps our ability to act is impeded by us being in survival mode ourselves, where the emphasis is on looking after the self and ensuring security and safety. This is a legitimate consideration. There is little point correcting an ethical quandary only to find you have thrown other parts of your life into intolerable difficulty, e.g., finances, employment, friendships. Even trying to implement such decisions can activate the amygdala, the threat mode of the brain that puts us into survival mode and tells us the stakes are too high to proceed. Whistle-blowers can find themselves in this situation. The cost of implementing an ethical decision, i.e., to go public with knowledge they have or to confront someone with their behaviour, outweighs the perceived and often real danger to themselves. ('I won't be believed. I will be seen as disloyal. I will lose my job.') It sometimes takes a lot of courage and bravery to stand up for what we believe in, to do something about it, and to bear the consequences.

Sometimes taking no action can be the only option we can see, and we might settle for this until more information comes to hand, or the balance is tipped in some way where proceeding seems a more viable option.

2. CONFLICTING VALUES

Making ethical decisions often puts us in a position of conflict with ourselves, our friends, our groups, our teams and our organisations. We can be torn as we stand in the middle of ethical awareness and ethical implementation. One of us dealt with a church situation where going public about abuse by a priest would have caused a lot of hurt and scandal in a particular parish. A church authority had even approached the individuals who had been abused and asked them to think of the negative implications for the church and the pastor involved. The poor individual who had to make this decision about publicising abuse that had happened was caught in an impossible dilemma. The right thing to do, and the decision made, was to make public what had happened, and yet loyalty to the organisation and the possibility of being blamed for what took place and ostracised (which is what actually happened) were in conflict. What a horrendous crossroad to stand at. Many groups face similar situations. As a Muslim who lives in a non-Muslim country who has knowledge of possible terrorist attacks, what is my ethical responsibility? Torn between loyalty to my Muslim community, family and friends, and responsibility for the welfare of the country where I live.

3. PERSONAL AND PROFESSIONAL CONSISTENCY

This can be the difference between espoused values and values in action, i.e., values we say we believe in and values that impact our behaviour and are worked out in actions. Making an ethical decision may involve what we would like to do, or think of as an action we would do, but in reality is not a value for us. A number of research projects on racism show that individuals who fight racism publicly may show an unconscious racism in their behaviour (see Wilson, 2002).

4. COLLUSIVE STANCES (THE BYSTANDER STANCE)

Another situation where the gap between decision and implementation widens is when we become seduced into colluding with what has happened and soft-peddle on our own position. Collusion is a moral stance where we rationalise ourselves out of doing something.

In one service I (Elisabeth) worked with, all the staff had a story to tell about the inadequate performance of the administrative assistant. In private, they were furious about how management tolerated this situation. However, no one was willing to speak up to the correct authority. One staff member said she felt sorry for the worker, another wondered if she had ever been trained properly and was doing the best she could, yet another said she was not willing to be to blamed for the sacking of the worker. In the end, the staff supported each other in their collusive position of no change, ultimately at the expense of everyone.

5. COMPETING COMMITMENTS

Kegan and Lahey (2009) offer competing commitments as one reason why we often do not implement what we want to. They talk about our 'immunity to change'. Just as our biological immune system exists to ward off threat, our mental immune system stands us in good stead most of the time. However, there are times when these systems mistake good change, or changes that might help us, as threats. Take the example of a manager who wants to delegate more, but never seems to achieve this. Kegan and

Lahey suggest that she looks at what she is afraid of if the commitment to delegate took place. In other words, the mental immune system has located a threat to the person. In this instance, the manager noticed she had a fear that if she delegated then things would not be done her way, and she would have to give up control over how work was managed. These latter fears were based on the assumption that if she delegated she would be held responsible for the outcomes she could not control and that she might fail.

For Kegan and Lahey, the competing commitment is always stronger than the commitment and based on a number of assumptions that have to be articulated, challenged and changed before the commitment can be realised.

For example, Bob knows his boss has taken short cuts in working with a tender for a job. Instead of going through the normal tender proposals and procedures, the boss decides unilaterally to give the project to one of his friends. Bob has an ethical dilemma. He is committed to fair and just procedures, and he is aware his boss has broken the rules. His commitment is to go higher and let his boss' boss know the situation. However, there is a competing commitment lurking close to the surface. He is afraid that if he goes higher there might be a negative rebound on him, and he could lose his job, be demoted and not get a good reference, which could impact on his future career. He decides to do nothing. The competing commitment (if I blow the whistle, my career might suffer) is stronger than his commitment to ethical practice within his company.

6. DAMAGE TO THE BRAIN

While not an everyday situation, damage to the brain can impede individuals moving from decision to action. Antonio Damasio and his team have studied patients whose 'ventromedial prefrontal cortex' has been damaged. This small part of the executive brain sorts out and sifts information, prioritises it and puts it in order of what needs immediate attention and what can be left for later. When it is damaged it does not affect the ability to rationalise and intellectualise, but it does cut the bridge between knowing and doing. Individuals whose ventromedial prefrotonal cortex has been damaged lack judgement—there is a disconnect between what you know and what you do. Knowing what to do, for them, does not result in implementing what they know.

The work of Damasio and his team is that patients with damage to the frontal lobes can problem-solve and argue for what is right and good, however 'it appears that these patients have normal moral competence, but abnormal moral performance' (Hauser, 2006, p. 229).

There is also some research that 'addiction weakens the learning mechanisms in the brain' (Brooks, 2011, p. 269). Knowing what to do is not the issue, knowing the harm that is taking place by not doing something different is also not the issue. An ability to translate this knowledge into actions seems to be the problem. Damage to the neural plasticity in the prefrontal cortex can mean the bridge between knowing what to do and making it happen has not been built, or if built, is uncrossable.

7. SUB-PERSONALITIES IN CONFLICT

Some authors have posited the idea of sub-personalities (Rowan, 1990; Towler, 2001) to explain why we do not implement the decisions we have made. Sub-selves and mini-selves can be used as ways to explain how different part of ourselves can be in conflict with one another. Gurdjieff (cited in Ouspensky, 1949), quoted at the beginning of this chapter, proposes a number of Is that at times talk on behalf of the whole person. He shows how each of the selves can hold the overall self to ransom to have its needs met and the whole self has to pay off the debt.

Think of the brain as having a pool of people at its disposal and then marshalling them into teams to do certain tasks. But the marshalling is not random—individuals are chosen because of their talents. They may work in different teams depending on what cluster of talents is needed to get the job done. Bachkirova (2011) calls these 'mini-selves' or 'mini-me's' and draws on Claxton's (1994) image of a discotheque of octopuses to illustrate what they do. Some are awake, some asleep; those awake tickle those asleep to get them involved.

In this frame, each of us have a series of mini-selves that are activated when action is needed. I can be courageous and brave (mini-self hero) when I need to make and implement an ethical decision. However, mini-self hero can come up against mini-self coward, who is afraid and anxious about implementing an ethical decision. An inner conflict or fight emerges. Who will win? It is worth returning to the story of the two wolves that the old Cherokee chief tells to teach his grandson about life on page 20 of the introduction.

While it is true that the sub-selves (sub personalities or mini-me's') collaborate, they often fight. Rowan (1976) writes: 'We can start to see how our sub-selves torture each other, how they play games with each other, how they play into each other's hands, and often how little they know each other. And once we know our sub-selves, and give them names, and find out what their nature is, what their motives are; they become powerless to harm us' (pp.151–2).

To recognise we are a series of sub-personalities each getting its own work done (the Hero, the Coward, the Crusader, the Rescuer, the Persecutor, the Victim, the Invincible One, the Child, the Needy One, the Parent, the Seducer, the Over Responsible, the 'Me-First',) helps us to realise why we do not do what we want to do at times. Sub-personalities fight, and from their conflict only one aspect of the personality may win. We can influence which aspects are likely to win more often by increasing their ethical 'musculature'. For example, by developing our ethical competence and wisdom, our moral courage can prevail. In addition, if we know the circumstances in which we are challenged most ethically, then we can be wary of falling into the habit of leading with our frailties. Eagleman (2011) continues this theme and sees the brain as a team of rivals comparable to an organisation, democracy or a family. It works because different parts of the brain perform different functions and this multi-party system allows it to solve problems in multiple ways. In fact, the brain continually finds new ways to solve problems. This 'team-of-rivals' approach means the brain sees, interprets and makes sense of information in different ways, and uses these to find what is hopefully the best way forward through our behaviour.

Christine is a new professional staff member in a drug and alcohol residential facility that otherwise employs ex-addicts as staff members. She believes in the empowerment model of offering this option to successful graduates of the programme, and values their ability to 'lead by example' in ways she can never do. However, there are constant compromises in observing colleagues with poor boundaries, becoming authoritarian, insisting that clients follow their lead because they 'know', and on some occasions she has been aware of one colleague meeting ex-residents outside work to score. In all cases to date, Christine has decided to say nothing. She was a whistle-blower in her last job and she lost all her work friends and, ultimately, her job. She started this job determined to 'get on better with colleagues' and to make it work at all costs. The trauma of her last job and the fear of that level of loss impacts on all her current decisions. It was going to be a long while, or a big ethical breach, before she would go to that much personal trouble for a job.

8. WILLPOWER AND PROCRASTINATION

'Tis easy to frame a bold resolution; But hard is the task that concerns execution' (Benjamin Franklin).

'Believe it, achieve it' (old proverb).

Baumeister and Tierney (2011) resurrect the old notion of 'willpower' to explain the bridge, sometimes the broken bridge, between making decisions and implementing those same decisions. Willpower, self control, self-regulation, agency and potency are terms used to explain the same process—how to ensure intention finds its way into behaviour, and that we have the energy, commitment and resilience to implement our decisions. How do we build up sufficient control, power and energy to bring the decisions we have made to fruition through action, performance or behaviour? In *Willpower: Rediscovering the Greatest Human Strength*, Baumeister and Tierney illustrate how lack of willpower or self-control results in many human problems, 'poor self-control correlates with just about every kind of trauma' (p. 2). We can see how unethical behaviour can occur as a result of lessening self-control in areas such as thinking, feeling, impulse, and performance. The perseverance of seeing things through, and the resilience to stay with decisions made to completion, are virtues needed if we are to be in control of and have sufficient willpower to implement our decisions. Today, more than ever before, there are good reasons for procrastination— getting distracted by the demands of emails, mobiles or laptops, or simply the increase in time demands in the modern day competing market.

The research of Baumeister and Tierney (2011) and others reach several conclusions:

- we have an infinite amount of willpower that becomes depleted as we use it
- we use the same stock of willpower for all manner of tasks
- each day we start off with a reasonable stockpile of willpower— especially if we sleep well and eat well
- throughout the day our stockpile is nibbled away at as we resist temptations and exercise self-control; giving in depletes willpower too
- when our willpower is depleted, impulses are much harder to resist, we make mistakes, and we give in more easily than we would normally.

The more self-control is exercised, the less is left for other tasks, especially ones that demand willpower and implementation of decisions. Having spent a day resisting temptation (not saying what I know will be hurtful, refusing to have that chocolate biscuit, agreeing to attend the meeting I know will be boring, holding back and not shouting at my children) and making decisions, suddenly there is nothing left in the willpower pot as evening creeps in. We give in where we have stood solid throughout the day. The evening is the graveyard of resolutions made and the lowest level of willpower energy simply because the willpower supply is at its lowest, used up on the many demands of life and work.

What does this mean for ethical implementation? The advice offered by Baumeister and Tierney (2011) is applicable here.

- Don't keep putting off implementing your decisions. Procrastination is the death-knell of actions we want to do, but keep getting distracted from doing. It seems there has been a large increase in 'dedicated ditherers—those who consider procrastination to be a defining personal characteristic' (p. 240). It isn't that procrastinators are not doing anything—their best strategy is to substitute one task for the one they most need to do. Positive procrastination can work if it is rewarding, as in delayed gratification or rewards that come later.

- Focus on one goal at a time because having many objectives often means that none get done well and some are never implemented.

- long-term goals produce more willpower than short-term goals, so fitting your decision into a bigger goal ensures there is more chance of it getting done.

- Keep track of how you are doing and do not try to do too much too quickly. Many plans, long-term and short-term, fail to materialise because individuals and groups are unrealistic about what they hope to achieve. Smaller, constantly monitored steps have the best chance of success.

- Keep rewarding success, even small incremental gains.

- Outsource control to others at times. Make them part of your contracts to implement important decisions. Try 'Ulysses contracts'—we agree with others to help us do what we know is difficult, e.g., the alcoholic who negotiates with his/her family that there will be no alcohol in the house, making public my resolutions, etc. Knowing our own weaknesses means we can involve others in helping us manage them.

- Make a specific plan about how to implement your decision. This mollifies your unconscious. Uncompleted decisions or tasks keep nagging away and deplete energy, but when completed the unconscious rests peacefully.

Bringing in the Chief Executive Officer to implement action

Eagleman compares the brain to the CEO of a company whose job is to keep the big picture in mind and ensure all subsystems run smoothly. The CEO does not normally get involved in the minutiae of the day-to-day running of small departments, but supports and encourages these departments to get on and do their bit for the overall welfare of the larger system. Eagleman (2011) calls these 'zombie systems', in that they work automatically, below consciousness and need little help from the CEO. When things go wrong, when departments (zombie systems) are not working, or in conflict with one another, then the CEO is called in to sort out the problems and get the zombie systems back on track. When new situations have to be tackled, i.e., there is no zombie system in place by which they work automatically, the CEO is alerted and springs into action. 'Consciousness is called in during the first phase of learning and is excluded from the game playing after it is deep in the system' (Eagleman, 2011, p. 142). The CEO, or consciousness, does what the zombie systems cannot do: deals with new situations, is creative and imaginative, and lays down new zombie systems so that extensions are added to the company. These new zombie systems have to get on with their brother and sister zombie systems, and again the CEO may have to act as mediator and preserve unity. The CEO strives to have the different systems work together for the service of the organisation, in this instance, the person.

Humphrey (2000) captures this well: 'I may indeed be made up of many separate sub-selves, but these selves have come to belong together as the one Self because they are engaged in one and the same enterprise: the enterprise of steering me, body and soul—through the physical and social world. Within this larger enterprise, each of my selves may indeed be doing its own thing: providing me with sensory information, with intelligence, with past knowledge, goals, judgements, initiative and so on. But the point—the wonderful point—is that each self doing its own thing shares a final common path with all the other selves doing their own things' (pp. 35–6).

Ethical choices are positions in which we are faced with the zombie systems agreeing or disagreeing. Jeremy, a shop assistant, is given $20 by a customer who thinks she is giving him $10. He gives her the change (from $10) and she walks away happy. Zombie system 1 (look after yourself and, if no one notices, then pocket the money) begins a dialogue or fight with Zombie system 2 (this is not your money and you should give it back to the person to whom it rightly belongs). Zombie system 3 weighs in (what will happen to your job if this is found out). The CEO notices the conflict and brings it into consciousness—his/her job is to mediate between the rival sections of the brain (in this case the three zombie systems). A decision is made: nobody noticed the transaction, there is no way you can be held responsible, it is a small amount of money—just pocket the change and get on with it.

It helps the CEO when a number of departments tackle the problem in different ways. While this sets up diversity, it harnesses the best of the departments and gives the CEO more possible choices and ways forward than if only one department made the decisions. From a decision point of view, Eagleman (2011) proposes that the best question is: 'Are there multiple, overlapping ways to solve this issue?' (p. 147).

Consciousness, or the CEO described by Eagleman (2011), is the director of the mini-selves, overseeing, reviewing, connecting, mediating and trying to make the best decision for the person. Our consciousness, or ego, has to be trained and developed to have the skills needed to resolve disputes and the maturity to realise that many of the mini-me's need to be heeded and given time. Some egos do not have that ability and only listen to one mini-me, e.g., the narcissistic person who only allows what is good for them into the equation, or the over-empathic mini-me that does not look after the needy (mini-me) self.

Educating the CEO to implement decisions

John Rowan (1976) offers a way to help the CEO take on the task of implementing decisions: 'Once we begin to think in these terms, many things become clearer—we can start to see how our sub-selves torture each other, how they play games with each other, how they play into each other's hands, and often how little they know about each other. And once we know our sub-selves, and give them names and find out what their nature is, what their motives are, they become powerless to harm us. A shadow is only strong when it is dark; once some light is shed on the scene, it changes colour and may disappear altogether' (pp.151–2).

Some questions we might ask ourselves: What mini-me's do I deny? Submerge? Repression of mini-me's does not annihilate them, but often makes them more needy (as Freud once said, we can become obsessed with what we repress). Can we work with this community of selves so they can best come to a decision?

Exercise

The following exercise outlines some questions to help begin the process of implementing ethical decisions. You might want to recall an ethical decision you made but never implemented in the way you had hoped. The process of answering these questions might give you insights into why that happened.

- What steps do I need to take to implement my ethical decision?
- What people are involved and who needs to be told?
- What restraints are there on me *not* to implement this ethical decision (politics, protection of someone or some organisation, rationalisation, my image, etc.)? How might I argue myself out of implementing it?
- What support is needed by me (or others) to implement this decision?
- What risks am I taking in implementing my ethical decision?

- What other ethical issues arise as a result of implementing this decision?
- What 'competing commitment' might mitigate against my implementing this decision to which I am committed (Kegan and Lahey, 2009)?
- What mini-selves are in conflict and can I name them?

Exercise: What helps and hinders you in implementing the ethical decisions you make?

Understanding how much our ethical values are connected to our identity can help us see how implementing decisions can be a natural process. As we have shown, where identity and ethics were integrated into who Socrates was, there was no inner conflict for him when he had to make an ethical decision as to whether to flee from the sentence passed on him. Where they combine (where I see my identity as integrating my values, e.g., as a husband, my identity is bound up with being faithful or not abandoning my children) there is every chance that what I decide to do, I will do. Where they are not combined (my identity is not connected to my faithfulness to one partner), there will be gaps in what I want to do, and even say I will do, and what happens.

Conclusion

Little is written on the bridge between making ethical decisions and implementing those decisions. Sometimes it is assumed they are one and the same process, and that making the decision is enough and implementation will follow automatically. We know this is not so. From an ethical maturity perspective we have argued that it is not sufficient. To have ethical wisdom is to have the courage, the resilience, and a way to build connections between deciding and doing. On this connecting pathway there are many obstacles that can waylay us and ensure our decisions never see fulfilment in action. Knowing what these obstacles might be, and how they affect us, helps to build our moral characters and stances and move us into unconscious implementation where we just act automatically without thought, deliberation and reflection. 'Just do it' is probably the most natural, spontaneous and mature way of ensuring that ethical thought, reflection, deliberation and decision results in action being taken.

Chapter 14
Component 4
Ethical accountability and moral defence

....

'Find the truth in what you oppose. Find the error in what you espouse.'

(Nash, 2002, p. 19)

'Every moral action must meet the test of publicity.'

(Rawls, 1971, p. 175)

'The narrator has a tendency not only to straighten the story line, but also to dramatise it, particularly if the story is planned for public consumption.'

(Bachkirova, 2011, p. 112)

'History is replete with atrocities that were justified by involving the highest principles and that were perpetrated upon victims who were equally convinced of their own moral principles. In the name of justice, of the common welfare, of universal ethics, and of God, millions of people have been killed and whole cultures destroyed. In recent history, concepts of universal right, equality, freedom, and social equality have been used to justify every variety of murder including genocide.'

(Mischel and Mischel cited in Rest, 1986, p. 134)

'I was always taught that a vital element of being a decent and moral human being was to be prepared to unequivocally take responsibility for one's failures and wrong doing, be they by commission or omission. That is, that I should have the moral courage, insight, maturity and enough compassion for myself and others to face the truth of my actions or inactions and take responsibility for their impact upon the lives of others… It allowed me to see that with courage, love, honesty and compassion there was little that could not be faced and that by facing that which I most feared I could grow as a human being and live a richer and more meaningful life.'

(O'Gorman, 2011)

'"Confabulation" is a term used to explain how people fabricate reasons to explain their behaviour.'

(Haidt, 2006)

'We make up explanations for what we do, and often are out of touch with why we do what we do: "…people's retrospective verbal accounts of their behaviour are actually theories about their behaviour constructed after the event. These theories may be correct, but sometimes they are not".'

(Nisbett and Wilson cited in Hardman, 2009, p. 180)

In telling our stories, if we listen carefully, we often hear ourselves embellish and edit the past as we capture it in words. 'Spin' is the modern word for retelling. How conveniently we tell and retell the stories of our pasts, adapting and weaving them to fit the present. Storytellers at heart, we know that memory is more than an historical account of what happened—it is a narrative that builds on the facts. In recounting, we deal with psychological truth, not necessarily objective truth. We construct, reconstruct and deconstruct the happenings in our lives. We tell stories as ways to give explanations for our behaviour. These stories can be based on a number of foundations: 'I must be stressed. I was beside myself. I was obsessed, or perhaps possessed. A vindictive God whispered in my ear. A mischievous gremlin led me astray. The ley lines were strong, the feng shui wrong, or the planets misaligned' (Claxton, 2005, p. 9). We are good at finding explanations for our behaviour; some concocted stories we do not believe ourselves; some far-fetched ones we do, and other explanations that are irrational, illogical and nonsensical. Defence mechanisms loom large in our lives and affect our explanations. We deny, project, transfer, dissociate and introject, as ways of explaining how we make sense of what we did.

We will do the same as we come to offer an account of our moral behaviour and our past moral decisions.

Bachkirova (2011) uses the image of the self as a narrator: 'the narrator is not a physical or mental substance—it is a linguistic function of the conscious mind that operates when the person attends to himself or herself' (p. 68). The job of the narrator is to explain in story format the behaviours and actions of a person. I see my behaviour from within myself. What were my intentions? How did I make sense of the experiences that were happening, and from outside myself? What were the reactions of others to my behaviour? What feedback did I receive? What were the consequences of what I did? Of course, much of what I perceive or see, either from within myself or from outside, can be selective and focused. I give attention to what I notice, and I notice from a background of expectation. So the story is influenced already by other stories of who I am, and where I come from, and the culture that has formed me. The story is organised and fashioned and created on a well-worn anvil of experience and prior learning. We have numerous 'filters' or spectacles through which events are seen and interpreted. The narrator is not an historian whose job it is to present the facts. Rather, the many filters interpret the facts and weave a narrative around it, filling in vague and unknown areas. The narrator is prejudiced in our favour and well able to select, even distort, the facts to fit with perceptions already well established. Fine (2007) puts it starkly: 'The brain biases, evades, twists, discounts, misinterprets, even makes up evidence—all so that we can retain that satisfying sense of being in the right. It is not only our long cherished beliefs that enjoy such devoted loyalty from our brains. Even the most hastily formed opinion receives undeserved protection from revision' (p. 104). The narrator is the PR system of the conscious brain, or the communications officer who takes what happens and justifies it to the world. Bachkirova (2011) presents how our wonderful narrator tells the story of the same behaviour from different perspectives:

- I am frank; you are outspoken; he is rude.
- I have a large frame; you are heavy; she is fat.
- I am appropriately cautious; you are fearful; he is paranoid.
- I am discriminating; you are prejudiced; she is bigoted.
- I merely assert my point of view; you push yourself on others; she walks all over people.
- I change my mind because I am flexible; you change yours because you are wishy-washy; she changes hers because she has no convictions (p. 114).

Where does this leave moral accountability? How will the moral (or immoral) narrator handle presenting what happened to the world? Will it involve spin, dissimulation, rejigging of events? Is it possible for the narrator to tell the truth, or just the truth that the narrator, in the service of the self, sees?

Blocks to accountability and responsibility

Mary Gergen (1999) writes that 'one can see life as composed of clots and conflicts and controversies, which are resolved by clarifying who is responsible for which misfortune. Whether it is the home, school, courtroom, highway or high seas, distributions of responsibility, blame, approbation and punishment persist' (p. 100). When we think of reflecting on decisions and being accountable for actions taken or not taken, perhaps what facilitates our rush to come up with a ready and pleasing justification is the fear of a spotlight of blame. Accountability sounds like something worthy of punishment, and tends to concentrate on assessing the ways we have fallen short and should do better next time. Unless we can work this through, this step toward ethical maturity is going to be uncomfortable and often avoided.

What are some of the differences between responsibility and accountability? Responsibility can be delegated and shared; you can be responsible 'up to a point' or you can have 'shared responsibility'. Responsibility can involve all elements up to the point of decision making, whereas accountability is about what comes *after* a decision is made. Accountability involves owning the decision or the action. Often employees are responsible for tasks, but the CEO is accountable for the final product or outcome. For professionals, accountability is inherent in all our service work. We are trained, and thus are ultimately responsible, i.e., accountable, for the service that follows. How does all this help us with our consideration of ethical accountability?

Judith Butler (2005), in exploring Foucault on the subject of accountability, writes that in assessing our own morality we should not be reduced to a 'self-berating psychic agency. From the outset, what relation the self will take to itself, how it will craft a response to an injunction, how it will form itself, and what labour it will form upon itself is a challenge, not an open question... It sets the stage for the subject's self-crafting, which always takes place in relation to an imposed set of norms...one invariably struggles with conditions of one's own life that one could not have chosen' (pp. 18–9). It is important we think about the decisions and actions we have taken with a full assessment of what we had to work with, as well as what we brought to the situation. The conditions of the decision do not become an excuse or a way to distance ourselves from the decisions. In the final analysis, the story has 'I' as its central character: 'I took this action, and I own my part in it.' This is not a denial of its limitations, but gives us an empowered spot in which to reside in making an analysis. Try to hold that position as we look at many of the ways we might be seduced into removing ourselves from central accountability in the story.

Talking to myself

Socrates' phrase 'the talk which the soul has with itself' illustrates a conversation where an individual confronts, challenges and dialogues with oneself as a way to uncover what has happened. In Socrates' words, it is a 'talk which has been held, not with someone else, nor aloud, but in silence itself' (Bruns, 1992, p. 37). This introspective stance begins the journey to articulate, justify, and confirm my ethical decision. Socrates' words, 'to thy own self be true', may be a solid foundation on which to consider how I make sense of my decision. Know yourself, spend time with yourself, talk to yourself. In the first instance, imagine the courtroom where you are judge, jury, prosecutor, defence lawyer and the jury. From the honest, no-fooling perspective of each, begin to uncover why you did what you did.

Self-deception

Knowing oneself is to know about how easy it is to fool ourselves. Two books of the same name, *Why We Lie*, one by Dorothy Rowe (2010) and one by David Livingstone Smith (2004), both review in some depth the psychological underpinnings of how easily we can fool ourselves. Smith (2004) looks at 'how evolutionary biology teaches us that the tendency to deceive has an ancient pedigree...nature is awash with deceit' (p. 1). The roots of self-deception and lying to oneself are, of course, in the unconscious mind. Rowe (2010) connects deception within the context of our storytelling ability. Just as we see the world as we are (not as it is), so we create stories to explain our subjective worlds and to suit ourselves. Our stories then become our realities, our truth, or even *the* truth.

Rationalisation

One form of self-deception in our explanations to self and others of why we did what we did is rationalisation. This is 'a justification of an action on grounds other than its primary motives. It is an intellectualising defence which maintains repression of an unacceptable wish' (Sloane, 1986, p. 21). In my earlier life, when asked why I (Michael) was motivated to become a counselling psychologist my typical answer was that I wanted to help others (make a difference in someone's life). This was a rationalisation. At that time, I was unaware of how being given power, respect, and even love, by clients was a more basic underlying motivation. It was, as the quotation above says, 'an intellectualised defence which maintained repression of an unacceptable wish'. I did not like to think that there were stronger, hidden, and less idealistic reasons why I chose to become a counselling psychologist. More honest with myself, I now see the reality of this. Rationalisation plays a large part in how we explain our ethical decisions.

Roger was hauled before an ethical committee for crossing a professional boundary. He had on numerous occasions held Debbie's hand during their counselling sessions, and had also hugged her when she had been very upset and distressed. She put in a complaint when he told her he was ending their sessions. His defence was that she needed a safe adult to be affectionate with, a man who could be trusted not to cross sexual boundaries as had happened in her past. Rationalisation provided this answer: his honesty (in another setting) revealed that he had enjoyed the physical contact that was missing from his own life.

Living out a script

Hass (1998) notes that all of us live with hurt, anger and disappointment, and that we excuse our behaviour too often by pointing to our injured past 'as if we are destined to live out a script that has been written by another and given to us to enact' (p. 171). This leaves us out of the assessment of accountability, and yet, it can be true enough that we were let down in some important ways. John Bowlby (1980) wrote on a similar theme: 'Every situation we meet with in life is construed in terms of the representational models we have of the world about us and of ourselves. Information reaching us through our sense organs is selected and interpreted in terms of those models, its significance for us and for those we care for is evaluated in terms of them, and plans of action conceived and executed with those models in mind' (p. 229). If we deal with psychological truth, rather than objective truth, it becomes important for us to know the representational models through which we filter information and that form our meaning-making perspectives. A knowledge of these will give insights into why we do what we do, and how we make sense of ourselves, our worlds and others.

Jill's two children have been removed from her care as a result of chronic neglect. Many services have been involved with her and her children, coaching, cajoling, assisting, and demonstrating. She is slowly working towards change. However, a core block for Jill is that, 'My parents didn't teach me any of this. I shouldn't be blamed. It's not my fault. Everyone is out to judge me.' Every so often she comes up against this felt injustice and stops and rails against it, before continuing on to achieve restitution with her children.

Hass (1998) suggests that the key counter to this is self-awareness. 'Know yourself. Look at your patterns of behaviour and do not accept superficial explanations for them ('I'm just making up for lost time'). Know where you have been in the past, and how those hurts may be manipulating you today' (p. 172).

Review

In Chapters 11 and 12 we looked at conscious and unconscious decision making. We noted that from an evolutionary viewpoint, conscious decision making emerged in humans as their executive brain allowed them to add to the value of unconscious decision making. What were the advantages of this evolved ability? First and foremost, the development of language permitted humans to communicate in ways other animals cannot. With this communication comes social learning (different from imitation learning alone), whereby we can share learning. Not only can we learn from each other, but we can learn about how we learn, and about the 'me' that is learning. As we consider this fourth component of ethical accountability, this human element comes into its own because now we move into the realm, not of what we do and what ethical decisions we make, but how we think about those decisions, how we look at our part (the 'me' bit) in making those decisions, and how through language and communication we can share with others why we did what we did. Ethical accountability clicks into higher-order brain functions of introspection, reflection, use of language, social communication and abstracting, which help us learn even more about how we make ethical decisions and how we justify them to ourselves.

Do we really know why?

To give reasons for and justify why we did what we did is surprisingly difficult. This is not because we cannot reasonably and rationally explain our intentions, but because often the reasons we give are not always the reason why we do things. Nash (2002) points out that the 'ultimate purpose of ethical analysis is to reach fully informed, grounded, defensible conclusions' (p. 165). Ethical accountability focuses on the defensible conclusions, which can be elusive when we are not in touch with many of the reasons why we act the way we do.

One of us (Michael) has trained supervisors in the prison service who manage the sex offenders treatment programme and provide support to tutors who run those programmes. In giving their accounts and reasons as to why they abuse children, it seems obvious that offenders are often completely out of touch with their real reasons. Teaching the child how to love, or quoting the Bible to justify their offending behaviour does not explain their own choices or acknowledge the obvious contrary effects of their behaviour. Do we know why we do what we do? Singer (2011) writes: 'We say, 'we have decided in this way because...' and then we give the reasons we are consciously aware of. However, much of the activity that actually prepared and determined the decision process escapes conscious recollection' (p. 43).

Singer (2011) points out that there are times when intention is consistent with action (we know why we are doing what we are doing) and suggests, 'there are also conditions where the real causes of an action dissociate from the reported intentions...the reported reasons for a particular action do not match the real reasons, but are experienced as if they had been at the origin of the performed action' (p. 44).

None of us can be sure we have mined out all the reasons why we have taken the decision/path we have. However, this does not mean we should not try to bring as much as we can into consciousness to understand ourselves and why we make and have made certain decisions.

PUTTING INTO WORDS WHY WE TOOK THE ETHICAL ACTIONS WE DID

The difference between intention and action: it is too easy to justify or tell moral narrative from the perspective of our intentions. Of course, our intentions are always 'good'. It is difficult for us to do deeds with bad intentions. Even when we intend bad actions, e.g., 'I will kill him, I will spread rumours about her and destroy her good name, I fully intend to embezzle money,' we have a neighbouring intention of doing them for good reasons, e.g., 'I will kill him because he deserves it for what he did to me, I will spread rumours because she needs to be brought down a peg or two, I will embezzle this money because money will give me access to the good life I am missing.' In narrating the story, it is easy to forget the bad intentions and the bad actions, and concentrate only on the good intentions as justification for why we did what we did. Haslam and Reicher (2008), in their review of the social psychology studies on tyranny, including Milgram, Zimbardo and Asch, point out that while they agree with the conclusion that ordinary people can do extremely harmful actions, they disagree with the reasons given for why they do them. Rather than simply a response to authority, or wanting to be part of a group, they claim, 'people do great harm, not because they are unaware of what they are doing, but because they consider it to be right' (p. 19). In other words, their intentions are good. The greatest evil can come from those with the highest ideals (intention versus action).

Depth of reflection: seeing the action from a number of perspectives

When we make decisions we often develop a justification to sustain that decision. When we come to evaluate our decision, that justification pops up first and may feel sufficient as an ongoing explanation.

Susan worked very long hours for a telecommunications company and was a valued employee. However, she often resented the hours she put in. She compensated herself for this through the use of her mobile phone for extensive personal use, and spent lunch times at her desk on Ebay, booking holidays and surfing the net. The company had a fairly flexible policy about these activities. However, it came to the attention of management that her usage of company resources was excessive and beyond the home/work balance policy they had in mind. When challenged, Susan was indignant and framed her 'rights' as related to the extra hours she was doing, her pay level and lack of work satisfaction. Initially, she was unable to see it from the management point of view, or even as an issue with regard to her own work boundaries and ineffective self-care.

Being aware of unconscious or subconscious reasons why I did what I did

Rhys had a huge reaction to the regular Friday morning staff meetings. He thought they were boring, poorly structured, a waste of time, and he *knew* others felt the same because they told him directly. He kept bringing this up with management, who acknowledged that things could be better. His boss also gave him feedback that Rhys appeared excessively critical, and while others were also unhappy, he appeared to really be eaten up by it. Rhys was outraged at this, and went into another round of complaints about the organisational process.

When there are structural, systemic or other individual contributions to the problem, it can be seductive to be drawn to these as an explanation, rather than as a symptom of the disturbance. It is *always* worth asking, 'But why else might I react this way?' This is not about self-blame or assuming personal work in place of correcting systemic problems. It is about being accountable for one's part so that other elements become more stark.

Rhys calmed down after work and talked this through with an old school friend whom he trusted. His school friend reminded him that groups of people had always caused him difficulty. He was often disappointed and angry in sport and school activities, and had always looked forward to events, but then was often let down. Rhys realised this was true. He longed for connections with others and yet felt disconnected in groups, and even marginalised. Once he realised he was reactive to poor group dynamics, he approached meetings differently and could even complain better—in a way others could hear. It did not take away from the group problem, but it did help him manage his part in the situation.

Listening to others and their 'take' on why I did what I did

As in the case of Rhys above, others can be a valuable resource if we listen to their take on things. Some are more comfortable with this role than others. In more formal peer arrangements, it can be valuable to ask others to listen for specific feedback: 'I am going to tell you what happened, and I want you to listen for what values I was trying to enact, the elements of what I was trying to do, and anything I missed.' This is only possible if you come from a position that it is acceptable to make mistakes and to learn from them. It also happens best in relationships of trust. If you fear judgement, or have already judged yourself harshly, then the opinions of others can feel very grating. It is possible to use others more incidentally. Rhys could have tried to notice—beyond the shared conversations where it appeared that he and his colleagues were on the same page—whether others were as affected as he was, and this could have started a journey of self-reflection. Wilson (2002) suggests that, at times, others know us better than we know ourselves. Uncomfortable as this is, it can also be a source of valuable information when looking at why we behave the way we do. Others see behaviour and action, and are not privy to the introspection, reflection and deliberation going on inside the head of the actor. They are in a good position, although a limited one, to give feedback on what they observe and notice. Some years ago a fellow trainer shared with one of us (Michael) that at times the humour I used could be a bit cruel and bordering on the sadistic. This came as a complete surprise, but on reflection I (Michael) saw its roots and understood why it was an unconscious part of my life. As a boy, I had developed the ability to verbally humiliate those who would bully me. As a result I was never bullied as a boy. My verbal skills enabled me to retaliate in a shaming manner that meant I was left alone. Unfortunately, I had forgotten to give up the skill when I grew up. My co-trainer had an insight into my behaviour that I did not have and, in sharing it with me, gave me a gift—an embarrassing one indeed—but one that helped me change my behaviour.

Knowing oneself

Knowing my 'defining principle' and how it affects my behaviour can provide valuable insights into why we do what we do. One of us (Michael) had a supervisee whose defining principle was one of 'rescuer'. Her life was built around finding and sorting out needy people. Unaware of this trait in her life, she defined what she was doing as 'supporting and helping my clients, and going the extra mile when needed'. In the case of one client, 'the extra mile' resulted in her being involved in the life of the client well beyond what her normal professional stance would suggest. When her client, a single woman who lived on her own, had a serious infection that confined her to bed, the counsellor brought her soup and meals for a few days until she was able to look after herself. Her accountability, i.e., her moral defence and rationale, for what she did was clear. The client had no one to look after her at this vulnerable time, the counsellor lived locally and could manage to drop in without too much difficulty. Since the counsellor was cooking for her own family it was little hardship to include one other in the meals. There was a lack of insight on the part of the counsellor of how her own 'defining principle' was impacting on her behaviour and pushing her into potentially unethical stances.

Being accountable

Component 4 in the model of the ethical journey towards maturity revolves around conversations that help us make sense of the ethical decisions we have made and, presumably, have implemented. The decision has been made, the follow up action is done, and now we look back and become 'retrospectively introspective'. We rationalise and articulate why we did what we did. If reflection-in-action was our support and help when we were making the decision, then reflection-on-action is our support as we draw on hindsight to review and evaluate how and why we made the decisions. Questions I could ask myself are in line with suggestions offered by Nash (2002) who posits a Moral Principle Framework as a method 'to justify, or defend an ethical decision based on a logical appeal to appropriate rules, principles and theories' (p. 115). He suggests some simple questions to help construct a rationale, or in more legal terms, a sound defence, for why we choose a particular course of ethical behaviour. What is your decision A? What is your decision B? (This is not a rank ordering.)

- What rules do you appeal to in order to justify and support each of the decisions?
- What principles do you appeal to in order to justify each of the decisions?
- What theories do you appeal to in order to justify each of the decisions?
- What conclusions do you reach regarding your final decision after you compare both justifications?
- What afterthoughts do you have now that you have made your final decision?

Nash (2002) then suggests we check our decision against the following questions for review.

- If my decision were to receive heavy media coverage, would I blush in shame or beam with pride?
- Could I explain my ethical decision with clarity and honour to those I love (my partner, my children, my closest friends)?
- Would my professional community support my decision with enthusiasm and without reservation?
- Would my personal integrity remain intact if my decision became known? If not, am I willing to compromise it for the sake of doing the expedient thing, or merely pleasing others?
- Could I defend my decision before the ethics committee of my professional organisation?

- Would I be happy and supportive if my colleagues, friends or family members made the same decision if they were in my shoes?
- Would I make the same decision again in similar circumstances?

Exercise: How do you defend the ethical decisions you make? Privately? Publicly?

Justifying and defending my decision

Nash (200) also suggests some rules that reflect Socratic principles to guide us as we meet and dialogue about ethical issues (p.26ff):

- Do not force premature closure—sometimes we do not have it neatly tied up at the end.
- Find the truth in what you oppose, and find the error in what you espouse.
- Read as you would be read, listen to as you would be listened to, question as you would be questioned, and pontificate as you would be pontificated to.
- If you don't stand for something, you will fall for anything.
- Stand up for what you believe, but don't stand over and don't stand on.
- Accept no opinion or idea uncritically—it might be false; and reject no text or opinion uncritically—it might be true.
- Find your own voice, but know when to lower it so that others can find theirs.
- Let us keep speaking, language is the medium through which we meet and learn.
- Don't worry if your ideas are not fully formed, or half-baked or not brilliant, we will help each other find the nuggets of gold hidden in the conversation.
- Remember Wittgenstein's saying that ethics and aesthetics are the same; stop to appreciate and admire the beauty of what it means to think morally.

And finally...

- Do not become defensive but be honest and notice where there are risks, lack of clarity, differences in viewpoints.
- Allow conflict and disagreement, and hold your own space.
- Move from a defensive position to one of openness, curiosity and honesty—this step can demand great courage if you feel that you did not make the right decision or factors influenced you to make a decision that was not the best one.

- Attend supervision and hear the thoughts and ideas of others.
- Gain insights into your own personality, your defining principle/s of life and how your behaviour can align to these.
- Be cautious of the obvious reasons for why you do what you do, and be open to other 'less charitable reasons' that might lurk beneath the surface.
- Challenge yourself with a moral audit, and suspect yourself, with kindness and brutal honesty, of other motivations for your actions.

Conclusion

In the end, we are not just responsible for our behaviour, we are responsible for our accountability and for putting into words why we did what we did for those who need those words. Accountability finds its expression in articulation. To justify or defend what we do, with honesty and insofar as we can, respectful and vulnerable explanations of ourselves are expressed through our actions. There has to be an 'I' in the explanation of our decisions and actions, and that requires us to not make or implement a decision without the tests of: 'What does this say about who I am?', and 'What matters to me?' By doing what I am about to do, am I meeting the main obligations and requirements in the decision-making process? Can I live with the decision? This puts another layer of importance on the thinking and decision-making process. If we are able to hold our own position in the face of all other demands in the moment, then this is an empowering and wise moment to cherish.

Chapter 15

Component 5
Ethical sustainability and peace

'Most of us when we are ill, or sad, or have been bad, like to think that there is something very special about ourselves. But when I looked, really looked, I saw that they, my colleagues too were very troubled souls at times. I realised yet again that they were no nicer to each other than are plumbers or union brothers, or priests or partly trained mud wrestlers. In spite of training, of personal therapy and of "working through", we were all a pretty rum bunch.'

(Martin, 2011, p. 14)

'Perhaps the history of the errors of mankind, all things considered, is more valuable and interesting than that of their discoveries. Truth is uniform and narrow; it constantly exists, and does not seem to require so much an active energy, as a passive aptitude of soul in order to encounter it. But error is endlessly diversified; it has no reality, but is the pure and simple creation of the mind that invents it. In this field, the soul has room enough to expand herself, to display all her boundless faculties, and all her beautiful and interesting extravagancies and absurdities.'

(Benjamin Franklin cited in Schultz, 2010)

'Every moral choice inevitably raises new doubts, new issues and new agendas.'

(Nash, 2002, p. 12)

'We shall not be surprised that at crucial moments of choice most of the business of choosing is already over. This does not imply that we are not free, certainly not. But it implies that the exercise of our freedom is a small piecemeal business which goes on all the time, and not a grandiose leaping about unimpeded at important moments. The moral life in this view is something that goes on continually.'

(Murdoch, 1985, p. 37)

'We can look back upon an earlier stage of moral development and see that all the components of good moral decision making were in an immature state of development.'

(Callahan, 1991, p. 144)

'Now what?'

(Sloan, 1986, p. 108)

Introduction

The decisions are made. Now, they have to be lived with. Not just now, but into the future when hindsight and new information may provide insight and knowledge that was not available at the time when the ethical decision was made and implemented. I (Michael) look back with regret to my early years of being a counselling psychologist and my work with one particular client. I worked with a young woman where I underestimated the importance of the counselling relationship to her. I told her I was moving away to another job (in another country) and would have to end our counselling relationship. However, I did point out that I had left sufficient time for us to end cleanly together. Her reaction was surprising to say the least. She felt let down, betrayed, rejected and abandoned, and walked out of the counselling room in anger and some despair, never to return. I handled the situation badly and insensitively with no awareness of how this news might impact on my client. While there were invaluable lessons to be learned from this example, the end result still has to be lived with. As you see, it has not been forgotten. But how has it been dealt with?

The achievement of ethical sustainability and peace (Component 5) plays a major part in ethical maturity. It demands us to have not only the resilience and abilities needed to deal with decisions made, but also requires us to learn from the past through critical reflection and critical self-reflection. This requires high-level skills and capability. This process, in itself, can seem like just another form of torment. The Greek philosopher, Pyrrho, noticed that even the most humble farm animals seem to achieve greater philosophical detachment than some of the wisest amongst us; our capacity to research and reason sometimes has us in knots of deliberation when perhaps acceptance would be a greater comfort. He came upon this insight when studying a pig who managed a storm at sea with equanimity when all (humans) around him were predicting the worst and openly afraid.

'Dare we conclude that the benefit of reason (which we praise so highly and on account of which we esteem ourselves to be lords and masters of all creation) was placed in us for our torment? What use is knowledge if, for its sake, we lose the calm and repose which we should enjoy without it, and if it makes our condition worse than that of Pyrrho's pig?' (de Botton, 2000, p. 120).

It is interesting to consider that the skills we needed in abundance earlier in our ethical journey could bite us at this point. Or we could use them

inadvertently in a way that makes us feel worse, not better. Examples include feelings of fear, regret and responsibility, all of which can arise when we look back at past actions and decisions, and can become a powerful cocktail of self-criticism rather than offering greater resolution.

What is the problem with being wrong?

In order to embark on this component of ethical maturity, we first need to clear the air about how we will cope with ourselves and others if we think we have made a mistake in our ethical decisions and actions. One option is to embrace mistakes as part of our very being: 'To learn that we have said or done a stupid thing is nothing, we must learn a more ample and important lesson: that we are but blockheads' (Montaigne cited in de Botton, 2000, p. 121).

However, even if in theory we give this passing acknowledgement, it does not always help when we explore the minutiae of our own circumstances.

Kathryn Schultz (2010), in her book, *Being Wrong: Adventures in the Margins of Error*, writes that 'like most pleasurable experiences, rightness is not ours to enjoy all the time, although our indiscriminate enjoyment of being right is matched by an almost equally indiscriminate feeling that we are right' (p. 4). She goes on to argue that being plagued with doubt and anxiety that we got something wrong is further evidence that we feel much better when we can be assured that we got things right in the first place.

Fortunately, we are often right in daily life. We have worked our lives out to the degree that most resolved decisions, from what to wear, how to get to work, how to make commonplace decisions, even what values we hold, can be argued to be right, at least for us in our particular contexts. 'Being right' is important because 'individually and collectively, our very existence depends on our ability to reach accurate conclusions about the world around us. In short, the experience of being right is imperative for our survival, gratifying for our ego, and, overall, one of life's cheapest and keenest satisfactions' (Schultz, 2010, p. 4).

This does not leave us well prepared for when we are wrong. Not only can it feel like scary and unfamiliar territory, it can leave us feeling foolish and ashamed, ignorant, lazy, perhaps crazy and, at times, morally degenerate. Schultz (2010) argues that paradoxically we live in a culture that both despises error and insists it is central to our lives: for learning, for imagination, as proof we are alive. 'Being wrong' may come upon us all of a sudden: realising mid-sentence that we are arguing something farcical, watching the value of carefully chosen shares plummet, watching your partner's face as they show they really hate the present you bought them. However, often the process of realisation is slow and comes upon us as

events unfold, as we grow and change, as new information comes to hand. 'If we want to isolate the wrongness implicit in our own gradual changes, we would need a kind of internal equivalent to (time-lapse photography)— which as it happens we have. Unfortunately it is called memory (and) it is notoriously unreliable' (p. 184). It can be difficult to remember exactly why we held the beliefs we did at some past point, why we voted in a particular way, what we were thinking when we bought that tie, said what we did to our mother, married that person, or thought hallucinogenics would be a fun thing to try. Schultz (2010) argues that gradual belief change protects us from the experience of error by attenuating it almost out of existence, whereas abrupt revelations that we were wrong can be a simultaneous revelation of a new truth, resulting in us 'vaulting over the experience of wrongness so quickly that the only evidence that we erred is that something inside us has changed' (p. 186).

So this is complicated. We need to accept our frailties and our capacity for error, while recognising 'being wrong' as a deeply uncomfortable, even dreaded experience. What we want you to consider is that if we can bear the reflection and investigation, and put ourselves at the centre of what happened, the 'I' in the narrative, there is much to learn and much that can be resolved on the way to being ethically mature. Some of the ways we get indicators that all is not well with our decisions and actions, such as ruminations, regret, self-criticism and defensiveness, are all signs that we suffer in the present for past actions. Reflection at this point is about resolving the lingering doubts and responsibilities that come with tough decisions, increasing preparedness for future decisions, and acceptance of learning being 'bumpy' and not always elegant along the way.

Getting ready to reflect

The kinds of issues that arise within this component on the journey to ethical maturity include the following:

- How can I let go of the situation and the dilemma and let myself make a decision?
- How can I deal with the anxiety around the final decision? Can I accept the limitations involved in the whole experience? (E.g., not having all the facts, living with hindsight.)
- What have I learned from the experience? What more is there to be learned from this/these experiences?
- What would I do differently the next time I have a similar ethical dilemma or problem?
- What personal and professional support do I need to live with the consequences of this decision?

- What help can I get if I find myself ruminating about or regretting the decision I made?
- How do I deal with feelings of guilt, shame or embarrassment about decisions I have made, especially where I feel it was a poor or a wrong decision?

Living with myself and my limitations

Reflection on past actions and ethical decisions inevitably faces us with our limitations, our wounds and our hypocrisies. This can be confronting and even lead to a crisis of confidence as we begin to know there are times we do not have the information we need and sometimes do not have the courage required of the situation. Few people have no regrets about the past and, even though we know it is over and finalised and we cannot change past events, we also know we have to live with the past and sometimes we have to engage actively in changing the meaning of the past.

- Can I accept that I too am wounded?
- Can I sustain my hope while doing this?
- How do I begin to accept my limitations and the impact these limitations have on my decision making?

Compassion and forgiveness

Treating ourselves with understanding and compassion is crucial at this point of reflection. There is some truth in the fact that we often treat ourselves more harshly than we do others. 'Research has shown that the way we relate to ourselves—whether we regard ourselves kindly or critically, in a friendly and affectionate way or with hostility—can have a major influence on our ability to get though life's difficulties and create within ourselves a sense of well-being' (Gilbert, 2010, p. xiv).

Compassion is not about being easy on ourselves, letting ourselves off the hook, or colluding with ourselves about what we have done. It is not about rationalisation or confabulation. Compassion is based on truth, but can only occur if we can hold at bay any associated activation of our harsh, critical and cruel self-critic. We are fragile human beings whether we like it or not, and we have to be able to accept our frailty and limitations. Our bodies let us down at times through illness, viruses and simply old age. So do our minds through memory or lack of it, selective perception, and our inability to hold many tasks together and to think systemically. Sometimes our options were limited by circumstances and timing, which later were found to be less of a hurdle than they appeared at the time. These are simply facts of life that for many people are difficult to accept, and being difficult to accept sometimes means people judge themselves harshly. Those who have drivers (compulsive stances that impel them) like 'be strong', be perfect', 'be right'—find it difficult not to evaluate themselves harshly when they fail or do not live up to their own expectations.

Part of self-compassion is self-forgiveness. When all is said and done, and we sit with the embers of our poor, failed or even wrong decisions, when nothing can be changed, there are times we forgive. We forgive ourselves for not being all we had hoped to be, for not living up to our own ideals and dreams, for colluding and standing by when we could have, and maybe should have, got involved and taken a stand. It can be easier to forgive others than to forgive ourselves.

- What would it mean to have more self-compassion?
- What do I need to forgive myself for?
- How do I go about the process of forgiving myself? (See Enright's (2001) four stages of forgiveness.)

Using reflection and supervision to facilitate learning from the past

Reflection-on-action is our retrospective method of learning from what we have done in the past. We stop, we put ourselves in an observer position, and we begin to mine out the learning/s from what has happened. We sit at the feet of our experience and ask that experience to teach us.

Reflection-on-action is our human way of making meaning in life (Mezirow, 2009). Reflection is the bridge between information and wisdom: more, it is the process that turns information and knowledge into wisdom. Through reflection, reflexiveness and critical thinking the events of our lives are made to make sense for us and give us choices about how to infuse these events with meanings we choose, rather than meanings chosen for us. We are meaning-making beings and it remains important for us to make sense of our lives by pondering on the events that shape and define us. Telling stories is one way to do that—we narrate our lives as methods of making sense of them for ourselves and to communicate the meaning we have made to others. However, our ways of making meaning can be narrow and rigid. Some individuals have only one way of making meaning, e.g., interpreting everything that happens to them through a victim stance. Others have diverse and multiple ways to make sense of events in their lives, e.g., yes, I was partially responsible for the heart attack because of my life style, it has been a wake-up call for me and is a message about changing some behaviours in my life. Some of our helping strategies involve us in supporting others to give different or new meaning to the events in their lives. Counselling, for example, is a way to change the meaning of events—clearly not the historical events themselves. What is previously given the meaning of being a tragedy, e.g., a divorce or an illness, can be re-interpreted and given new meaning, for example, as a new start or a new way to appreciate life. Coaching is often a way to help coachees make sense of their lives and their work, and at times it helps coachees adopt new perspectives on who they are and what they do.

One of the key tasks of supervision is in helping individuals and groups look at their work from new and different perspectives. It is a process that involves looking at what we do and how with super–vision, new eyes, new perceptions, new visions we can see things differently. Supervision is always about the quality of awareness, and in the dialogue, new, previously hidden aspects come into view. With reflection comes meaning at different levels. As I step outside my comfort zone and take an open stance, without judgement or shame, without blame or assumption and am open and indifferent to the outcome, what would I allow myself to think and reflect upon? Can I look beyond, beside, beneath, above, below, against, for... What would happen if I looked at myself, my client, our relationship, the organisation in another way?

Preparing for reflection-on-action involves letting go of our justifications and defensiveness, and managing the fear that arises in assessment. If the original decision felt costly and painful, reviewing it might seem excruciating. How might we get ourselves into the 'right frame of mind' so that we can truly learn from the past?

Moving from rumination and the curse of reflection

While we have the wonderful gift of reflection, too much reflection can become our enemy. Memory is a wonderful gift, and most of the time our problems revolve around being able to recall and access our memory. However, one of the drawbacks of memory is also not being able to forget or let go when we need to. At these times we start ruminating—becoming obsessed with thoughts and feelings that refuse to be banished or exorcised.

In his book, *The Curse of the Self*, Leary (2004) highlights the drawbacks of reflection. While a blessing and a highly human activity, there are times when reflection becomes our enemy, not our friend. It is more helpful to be mindless and unreflective when trying to get to sleep. Too much reflection, often called rumination, keeps many people awake at night or rouses them early in the morning when their reflective minds refuse to allow them to go back to sleep. Worry, which is a form of reflecting on the future, is equally troublesome at times when we get so caught up in our reflective concerns for the future that we miss what is happening in the present. It is good that we do not have to reflect on how we drive our cars, dress ourselves in the morning, manage our PCs or do the shopping. We do these tasks automatically. For actions and behaviours that do not demand creativity or imagination, going onto automatic pilot suits us well. Over-reflection has drawbacks in that it:

- interferes with memory
- puts us out of touch with what we already know
- disconnects us from cognitive processes (if you think too much about the presentation you are about to give it may well result in choking)
- can result in poorer performance
- can result in mental illnesses (compulsions, depressions, etc.)
- can result in unhelpful behaviour (there is some evidence that teenage girls smoke as a way of staying thin—the self-conscious pursuit of beauty at the expense of health).

The inner worlds of animals do not spin introspective webs of self-related thought. We, on the other hand, talk to ourselves. People live in their inner worlds when there is no need to, and even when it pulls them away from attending to life in the external world.

Living with knowing I made a poor decision

We all make decisions of which we we are not proud. We all make poor, immature and sometimes wrong decisions. We know they are wrong because we have to live with them, and as we live with them we see how they were wrong. Nicola is a good example. She was in a job that she enjoyed and that challenged her, with a supportive team, when she was head hunted by a competitor firm who offered to double her salary. Flattered and excited she accepted the offer without much thought. She knew she had traded what she had for money, but she hoped the other aspects of her current job (great team, challenging work) would come with the money. It didn't. Now she is unhappy, has little support in a cut-throat organisation, and does not find her work anywhere near as interesting as her previous position. On reflection, she made a poor decision.

Amy got married when she was 19 years old. Looking back, she didn't get married, as much as ran away from home. Now at 24 years old and with three children, she is depressed. Her husband has left and is living with another woman. She loves her children and would do anything for them. However, now she looks carefully at how she makes decisions, knowing how easy it is for a decision to also be an escape.

Poor decisions can also have positive consequences or outcomes. For example, I (Elisabeth) was in a job, many years ago, where I had a conflictual and unpleasant relationship with my direct boss. However, the organisation was good for my career, and offered me opportunities that I loved. I decided to apply for a promotional position which brought me in closer proximity to management, even though the dynamic remained poor and I didn't always feel good about myself within those relationships. Despite this, I talked myself into the interview and it was one of the worst experiences of my professional life. It went on for two hours, was not so much an interview as a grilling, a relentless accusation of my negative role in the workplace and relationship with him. I left in tears and was in shock for days, but it gets worse. I was offered the job, which was a big surprise, and, even more bizarre, I accepted it. I ignored that none of these events were OK, and I told myself that my love of the work and the career opportunity were worth it. In fact, I went on to do well in the job, it lived up to my expectations, and I worked on my relationship with my boss and we became a good team. I still look back on this as being one of the best career moves I made, but it has always rankled that I ignored all my own warning signs and bottom lines. If I had been true to myself, I should have left. I have to take the good from that decision, and accept my own lack of courage in resolving that phase of my career differently, but I still cringe at those events and would like to have done things differently.

Managing shame

Cavicchia (2010) outlines what shame means. Shame, and its milder form, embarrassment, are the feelings that alert us to when we might have transgressed an acceptable range of behaviour. Shame is an inner torment, a sickness of the soul. It is the most poignant experience of the self by the self. Shame is a wound felt from the inside, dividing us both from ourselves and from one another. It is sudden, unexpected exposure, coupled with blinding inner scrutiny. In shame, we find ourselves wanting as persons. Shame is not just about what I do, it is about who I am: I am bad, I am selfish, I am bigheaded. It combines the action with the person and will not allow a separation—instead of seeing myself engaging a bad action, I see myself as a bad person. Image and function become fused. Cavicchia also points out that we can develop a shame template: 'Early experiences contribute to each of us forming a unique, fingerprint-like susceptibility to shame...our unique individual shame templates remain with us in adult life. These templates are forged in relationship and are activated in relationships' (p. 881).

Integrating decisions into life ahead

Making decisions changes us in small, moderate and transformational ways. We are not the same person after some decisions. The transition from making, implementing, and even defending a decision to living peacefully with it is not automatic and does not happen seamlessly or comfortably. Some common reactions and experiences include:

- shock (disorientation)
- denial
- depression
- letting go (and learning)
- search for meaning (and learning)
- integration into my life and who I am.

Shock may or may not be experienced, especially if the justification stage has not gone well. With this can come some paralysis. Jack was the subject of a complaint from a client who claimed he did not provide sufficient support and help to her, and that he had crossed boundaries in their professional relationship. Jack felt he had gone the extra mile in supporting a vulnerable and isolated woman: writing some letters, sending a card from his holiday, visiting the client in her home. The ethics committee did not agree and required him to undertake extra supervision and training in boundary setting. He was shocked, hurt and disoriented. This lead to some denial on his part: denial of how he really felt, and about the true facts being seen and understood. He wondered if this profession was really for him. He felt misunderstood and betrayed, as if all his good work counted for nothing. Depression set in and he found his moods low and self-deprecating. In supervision and personal counselling, he began slowly to face up to what had happened. He had got it wrong. He had been hooked into rescuing a vulnerable client. He started looking at himself, his preconscious needs and slowly began to let go of some of his drive to rescue. He saw the meaning of what had happened and why it had happened. He had learned a lot. He knew the changes that had to take place and he began to refashion his personal and professional self. Two years later, Jack has integrated new learning into who he is and how he works professionally. He looks back with regret for what happened and willingly acknowledges his part. He also knows that this wake-up call was important for the next stage in his journey. He has come to terms with what happened.

Living with decisions made sometimes demands that we:

- live with lingering doubts and uncertainties, even while continuing to rehearse other scenarios and other possible endings and decisions
- continue to learn from what happened, even if it means opening up the case again and reviewing it in light of new experiences or new information
- be self-accepting and know that we are dealing with issues that often have no right answers
- avoid rumination and obsessive reflection through strategies like meditation, exercise, self-care and affirmation

- accept our limitations: we could only work with what we could know at the time (context, information, resources)
- are compassionate towards ourselves
- use writing and creating a diary to articulate our thoughts and feelings
- have places where we can speak about the issues and get the support we need to deal with whatever decisions were made
- use mistakes, poor decisions we have made already and hindsight to learn how to let go of perfectionism
- recognise if any apologies are needed or corrective action to be taken
- accept that we might make a different decision now if the issue was to arise again
- let go and forgive ourselves.

It might be worth asking yourself at this point: How do you take care of yourself when you have made an ethical decision? Especially one that contains a risk.

Conclusion

It is common to experience strong and uncomfortable emotion in relation to ethical decision making and past ethical events. However, little attention is paid to this in the ethics literature, and perhaps we are too quick to dismiss it and 'move on' ourselves. However, not only does negative rumination become wearing, it can shape future decisions by making us fearful of more discomfort, perhaps avoidant of difficult decisions and quandaries, rather than facing them with confidence that there is a way through. Thinking that once a decision is made it is 'finished' is often a fantasy, not a reality. Ethical decision-making models focus locally on getting the job done; however, reflection and reconsideration can commence at the tail end of decision making (when there is still time to modify or change the decision), as well as for a long time after. Even so, rarely is it recognised as an important factor in human decision making. We include it here because it fulfils three functions: it helps us come to terms with the decisions we have made; it helps us learn from the past and our previous decisions; and, it makes us more sensitive to ethical issues and dilemmas in the future.

Chapter 16

Component 6
Learning from experience and integrating new learning into moral character

....

'Learning from experience—making sense of what really happens in the business world (or in the world in general for that matter)—doesn't seem to be a priority for many management scholars.'

(Kets de Vries, 2009, p. x)

'The range of what we think and do is limited by what we fail to notice. And because we fail to notice that we fail to notice. There is little we can do to change until we notice how failing to notice shapes our thoughts and deeds.'

(Goleman, 1985, p. 24)

'Curiosity is an internal state occasioned when subjective uncertainty generates a tendency to engage in exploratory behaviour aimed at resolving or partially mitigating the uncertainty.'

(Berlyne, 1978, p. 98)

'Imagine asking people who they are and the only thing they can come up with is "I'm a Croat" or "I'm a Serb" or whatever. Imagine, these people were born that way and they haven't made any progress since.'

(Bosnian woman, cited in Oshry, 1995, p. 120)

Wilfred Bion thought that the most important of all human capacities is the ability to learn from experience (Bion, 1962). A recent survey would seem to back up his assertion: 'Senior executives believe the most effective learning and skills development comes through practical experience, whether the learning is on the job, project-based or experiential… Learning directly from the experience of others is also valued as important.'

(Voller, Blass and Culpin, 2011, p. 24)

The process of having made ethical decisions is itself fertile ground for learning from that experience, in terms of how to make future ethical decisions, and how to learn from those experiences in order to continue to build moral character. We revisit the ethical experience itself to set it up as a learning project. Learning from experience means that:

- data becomes information
- information becomes knowledge
- knowledge becomes wisdom
- wisdom becomes practical action
- practical knowledge becomes embedded in who we are.

Experience has to be shifted, examined, analysed, considered and interpreted in order to move it from information to knowledge, and from wisdom to action. How does this happen and how do we learn the skill of making meaning from experience itself? What process do we go through in order to learn from our own experience and how can we facilitate that process for ourselves and others?

As a student counsellor (Michael), my first client was a woman of about 50 years old called Maggie. I was 30 years old at the time. Maggie was lonely, found it difficult to make friends and lived alone, with few interests or hobbies. Her doctor had suggested counselling rather than start her on anti-depressants. Within a few sessions it was obvious Maggie saw counselling as a social event. She loved coming to the sessions, enjoyed having a place to chat and talk about herself, and was fascinated to discover she had an interested and supportive male counsellor who cared about her welfare. She adopted me and quickly began to make me the son she never had. Around the sixth session she brought me a small present—a pair of socks. I didn't want to seem ungrateful and refuse, and yet something warned me about crossing a boundary. I remember talking to my supervisor and he gently helped me to use what was happening between me and Maggie to think about the implications of some themes being played out in the counselling relationship, e.g., how I might be creating and encouraging dependency. Were there any connections to what was happening between now and the past, and was that working out in my roles as counsellor and a person? From my reflections in this accepting atmosphere, I learned some valuable lessons that have stayed with me throughout my professional life: about co-creating relationships, about how our own needs as helpers emerge within professional relationships, how to manage and hold boundaries without punishing, and how to deal with counselling relationships that were turning into other kinds of relationships. The experience of counselling Maggie and the ability to talk about that experience in a dialogic and accepting relationship made it a valuable learning experience.

Learning from experience

For Jim, the ordeal is over, even if his pain and suffering is not. The ethical complaint against him has been upheld by the complaints panel with a requirement that he submit to rigorous ongoing supervision and training in holding boundaries and being alert to conflicting values in counselling. What had happened? Jim worked as a counsellor in an organisational setting and was asked occasionally to provide services other than one-to-one counselling, e.g., training days on stress management and meditation. In this instance, he was asked to run a team development day for a dysfunctional small department team. Jim was seeing one of the team members for counselling and decided to run it past her so that she would know what was happening. She was surprised he had decided to take on this role knowing how difficult it would be for her (having shared some of the team dynamics during their sessions), and suggested he might ask someone else to take on this task. He reassured her he would be neutral, not take sides and be able to hold confidentiality. Despite her ongoing reservations, he went ahead and facilitated the team day. During the day his client was attacked (scapegoated) several times and, while he brought the process to the surface, he did not offer any other support to her during the day. He had not mentioned to the team that one of their members was in individual therapy with him, but a team member who knew made it public during the team event. The team development day ended rather disastrously and Jim's client took out an ethical complaint against him. The panel agreed with her that providing one-to-one counselling to her *and* facilitating the team of which she was a member was unacceptable. They found Jim guilty of crossing an ethical boundary.

In supervision, Jim reflects on what he has learned from the experience of going through an ethical hearing that has gone against him. While recognising his good intentions, he also realises he had not given enough understanding to his client and 'her right of way' in suggesting he might be setting up dual relationships. He wonders why and concludes that he convinced himself that he could hold it all together. He is aware also that he was flattered that the company had considered him fit for this role, and had allowed himself to be seduced by hopes that this new role might build up his credibility as a counsellor within the company. He forgot to don his empathy hat and put himself in the shoes of his individual client who was compromised by his acceptance of the role. He had not anticipated that another team member knew she was his counselling client and might make this public. At their last meeting his client, who had decided not to continue the counselling with him, had intimated that her trust in him had been dented, to say the least. In reflective dialogues with his supervisor, Jim was able to get in touch with his embarrassment and shame in having his reputation put on the line, and having to face colleagues who would know about the complaint and its outcome. However, he was open in asking the right questions: What does this event say about me? Can I be honest with myself about what happened? What have I learned about me? About clients? About boundaries? About working in an organisational setting as a counsellor? He is keen to use the experience as a learning platform to strengthen his practice.

Learning from experience is not automatic

Learning from experience is not always a given—it does not happen automatically. Many experiences in life teach us little or nothing. The price we pay for not learning from experience is that we tend to repeat what has happened, rather than be open to other choices. This is illustrated through the following example: 'Not long ago a medical study showed that if heart doctors tell their seriously at-risk patients they will literally die if they do not make changes to their personal lives—diet, exercise, smoking—still only one in seven is actually able to change. One in seven. And we can safely assume that the other six wanted to live, see more sunsets, watch their grandchildren grow up. They didn't lack a sense of urgency. The incentives for change could not be greater. The doctors made sure they knew just what they needed to do. Still, they couldn't do it' (Kegan and Lahey, 2009, p. 1). This is a good example of people not being able to learn from experience, e.g., a life-threatening heart attack, and not learning what is good for them *even when they face a life or death situation*. We can presume that one of the seven learned through allowing themselves to experience the impact of the event, reflect on it deeply, and to organise their lives to exclude what is unhealthy. The same principles apply with ethical decisions. Learning from them is not automatic. Moving into a strong defensive position often prohibits learning from taking place. Learning from experience is more than just a cognitive event about insights and awareness. It is learning that translates into action. For experiential learning to be true learning it must affect behaviour—it can be the greatest of all transformational learnings.

Learning from my experience or learning from the experience of others

One of us (Michael) was running a conference day in Dublin with about 150 people. One man, after the first experiential exercise, took the microphone and made a criticism of the environment—'I couldn't hear myself speak, the room was too noisy, there were too many people in the room. It ruined the exercise for me.' Michael asked, 'So why didn't you and your small group leave and find a quiet place?' His reply was, 'Could we have done that? I didn't know we had permission.' How interesting. This man had read his experience, knew what it was saying to him, but did not act on it because he had made a series of assumptions. If he had stopped, allowed himself to be disoriented, concluded this was not working for him and reflected on his options, he could have decided on another pathway. When experience speaks, even yells its message, we can be far from listening, trusting and allowing it to teach us and move us to action.

One man who arguably deserves the title the patron saint of learning from experience is Leonardo da Vinci, who referred to himself as 'unomo senza lettere' (man without letters) and 'discepolo della esperiencza' (disciple of experience) (Gelb, 1998). Da Vinci wrote, 'To me it seems that those sciences are vain and full of error which are not born of experience, mother of all certainty, firsthand experience which in its origins, or means, or end has passed through one of the five senses' (Gelb, 1998, p. 78). With a fierce commitment to firsthand knowledge, Da Vinci questioned authority, certainty and imitation, but he was not averse to accessing and integrating the experience of others. He read widely, consulted others and their works, and kept a large library. But these 'experiences by proxy', which is what he called the thoughts and ideas of others, were tested in the fire of his own experience. He raised experience to the greatest of learning heights: 'Experience never errs: it is only your judgment that errs in promising itself results as are not caused by your experience' (Gelb, 1998, p. 79). How you interpret, make sense of and give meaning to your experience is open to question, not the experience itself.

The process of learning from experience

In 1947, Raymond Queneau, a French author, published a fascinating book that makes the point of how events can be interpreted in many ways. In *Exercises in Style*, Queneau tells a simple half-page story and then retells it in 124 different ways, styles, and meanings. The point he makes is that any event, any happening, can be 'proliferated almost to infinity'—there are innumerable ways to interpret or tell the story. Knibb (2010) refers to this as a 'dynamic fluidity of lived experience' and Derrida (1981) describes an 'infinite possibility of meaning'. How an event is interpreted can depend on what you saw and heard, what you allowed yourself to see and hear, the background you come from, and how you make sense of this in the past, your culture, language and so on. Supervision and learning from experience is built on the premise that there are innumerable ways to interpret what happens to us in our work and the place to explore these is supervision.

In learning from experience we retell the stories and events of our practice and begin the journey of making sense of them. We tell our experience from within our own understanding, and then attempt to step outside that understanding to view how others have interpreted that event. I tell you the story, and then I listen as you tell me your story about my story from outside my story. We view the story through a series of narrow and wide lenses with which we zoom in and out as we tell and retell the story from other angles, perspectives, and styles. In the retelling we see, hear and understand more, and go back to our work with more wisdom, insight and better understanding. Though Queneau never uses the term, his book is about different ways to make meaning.

So back to the question of how we learn from our experience of the ethical decisions we have made. There are five steps in the learning from experience journey that can be applied to learning from the experience of making ethical decisions, implementing them, and living with that ethical journey:

1. Moving from evaluation to curiosity.

2. Paying attention to the context and the meaning given by the context.

3. Creating psychological and emotional safety to be open to learning from experience; tolerating the discomfort in learning.

4. Using reflection and empathy as the method of learning from experience.

5. Applying learning from experience to life and work and building it into moral character.

Figure. 16.1: Five steps in the learning experience

STEP 1: MOVING FROM EVALUATION TO CURIOSITY

In the process of learning from experience, we change from a mindset of evaluation to *curiosity*. When we evaluate we judge the action, and often ourselves or others, as to its outcome and effects. How stupid am I to have done that? I really got that wrong! Someone should have told me! Or, like Jim in the previous example, How could I have been so blind? When we invoke curiosity we more likely ask questions such as, Why did I do that?

What was happening in my life that distracted me? I wonder why those events/arguments seemed compelling at that time?

We argue that it is more valuable to embark on a process of curiosity *before* moving to evaluation. One way to discipline ourselves to do this, or to facilitate a process for others, is to consider the exercise of telling the story/circumstance again from a curious perspective, rather than an evaluative perspective.

One of us (Michael) was working with a supervisee who had been negative about her organisation for a while. Michael was beginning to feel irked by what felt like her constant 'helpless moaning'. He asked her to move from evaluating her organisation to being curious about what was going on. She looked puzzled for a moment, and then began to reframe her previous criticism:

'There is almost no communication in our department,' became, 'I wonder why individuals in our department do not communicate openly and honestly with one another?'

'She never delegates and then complains we don't take responsibility', became 'I am curious about why we have set up a subsystem in our department where the boss doesn't delegate and we don't take on responsibility?'

She ended up laughing, but felt that she had a lot more energy for the different issues confronting her (rather than just complaining).

Curiosity was the first step in learning for Leonardo Da Vinci. He would repeatedly send his students back to a scene he had asked them to paint with the suggestion that they 'look again'. For him, curiosity opened their eyes to what they had missed and there was always more to see. His notebooks, still extant, are full of questions such as: Why is the sky blue? Why do we have ripples in a pond when we throw a pebble into it? And so on.

The first step in learning from experience is to prepare myself for learning by creating an attitude of curiosity. I suspend where I am, my judgements and evaluations, and I look with an open gaze to what the experience may teach me. I will need courage as well, since learning from experience can uncover areas of my life and ways of thinking that are embarrassing, uncomfortable and that I keep outside my awareness.

STEP 2: NOTE THE CONTEXT IN WHICH THE BEHAVIOUR TOOK PLACE

Gregory Bateson (1972) encouraged us to consider how context can shape meaning. In learning from experience it can be useful to start your reflection by considering the context in which the experience has taken place. Often the meaning we attribute to an experience arises from the context through a form of 'inherited meaning'. For example, the context of

Michael growing up as a Catholic in Belfast meant inheriting a whole set of filters, assumptions, expectations, directives, loyalties, all of which provided pre-determined meanings to experience. The context of the organisation in which we work, the context of the culture in which we are embedded, and the relationships in which we exist, all contribute to how we make sense of our experiences in those settings. Meaning 'kicks in' before we are even aware of it, and always seems to fit, given it occurs habitually and always has a ring of familiarity. For example, if I have decided my boss is incompetent, it may be difficult to notice when she is not. If my family story is that 'we are universally unlucky', then winning a raffle does little to dent this ongoing story. Not only does the attributed meaning shape the interpretation of events, but it also shapes our choice of actions. If I have decided 'there is nothing to be done', then it is most likely I will keep talking myself out of taking any action at all.

One of our supervisees is an organisational consultant who is coaching an executive. She is telling me (Michael) about the strong reactions and feelings she has to him during her coaching session. I ask her if she has shared these with the coachee. She would normally, but she has not. As we unravel the issue we realise, like the coachee and many others in this company, she has been silenced. The context demands silence and the coach was 'infected' systemically with this culture of silence. Drawing on a curious mindset, we examined what had silenced her, and she realised she was conforming to the organisational norm of being compliant. This realisation freed her up to choose her own reaction to her coachee.

Noting the context in which experiences occur allow us to see if pre-packaged interpretation comes with the experience, and whether or not we can be open to new learning from old experience. If we do not accept the meaning the environment offers too readily, we can consider other possible meanings, and open doors to other possible learnings. It is worthwhile to question whether the meaning that comes with the context is one I want to accept and whether it is the only interpretation of events.

STEP 3: WHAT PSYCHOLOGICAL SAFETY IS NEEDED TO BE OPEN TO NEW LEARNING FROM EXPERIENCE?

Christine had been told through her childhood that she took up too much space and attention. She was seen to ask for too much and told that her judgement of things was poor. Despite this, she has achieved a high level of education, and has become successful in her chosen field. She is keen to bring about change in her organisation, as she believes some areas of operations are really sub-standard. However, when she raises her concerns, her colleagues dismiss them for a variety of reasons. Christine battles the feelings that arise. It would be unbearable for her to re-experience her

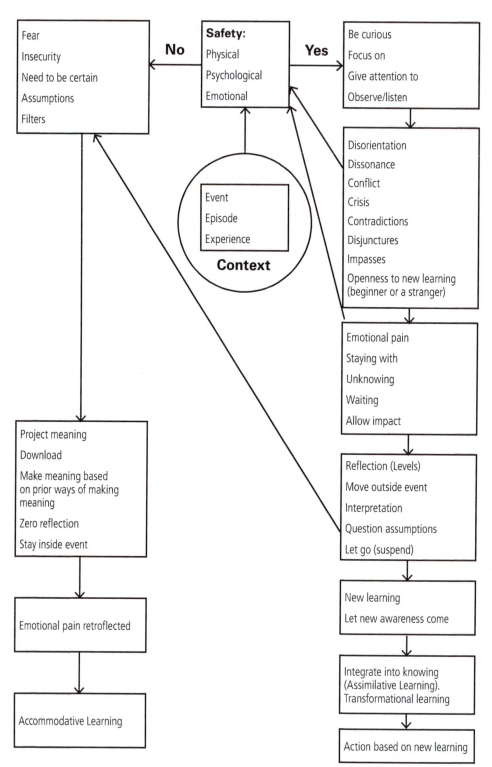

Figure 16:2 Process of learning from experience

judgement as 'poor' in her work environment, so she ends up gathering evidence for why everyone else is at fault. The possibilities that she is ahead of her time, or that her approach might need adjustment, or that her colleagues might have something valuable to add, are unavailable to her. She feels so triggered by the way she 'reads' the message that she becomes caught in a painful vortex of defensiveness and blame. She has started to think she needs to leave because the organisation is not good enough. This may be true, but it also may not.

If unsafe and insecure, we may head for accommodative learning to make sense of our experiences (see the left-hand column in Figure 16.2). With accommodative learning we project existing meaning onto the event from pre-existing knowledge, information or learnings. Nothing new is available to be learned knowledge is simply recycled or downloaded. At present, Christine cannot accept this is happening. She believes the organisation and her colleagues are at fault. Of course, at a deeper, darker level she fears she is at fault. At this time she does not feel safe enough to allow herself to be open to other possible interpretations, and she is certainly not open to learning how to see and do things differently.

This is where safety becomes so important. To be curious, we need to feel secure within ourselves. When there is a lack of emotional, psychological or physical safety generated by our own insecurities or the situation itself, we are not able to question or become curious, but remain stuck in an evaluative mode accompanied by judging, blaming and racing to conclusions.

When we are unsafe, even threatened, by any questioning of past events, we tend to retreat, defend and lose our ability to think rationally about what has occurred. Our fear of change and reflection keeps us where we are. Living with this kind of fear limits our choices in making meaning from experience (learning from experience). Instead, we grasp at the inherited or unconscious learning that comes by virtue of the established context or other habits of thinking. Fear is activated, which, in turn, connects us to the reptilian brain. Now we are dealing with a desperate quest for safety through the strategies of fight, flight, fragment or freeze, and have one way or limited ways to make sense of what is happening. As is the case with Christine, often we see ourselves as victims, which constructs the reflection in a way that leads us to avoid learning as it is simply too much of a threat.

Angela Brew (1993) uses her experience to illustrate active avoidance of learning:

'I did not want to know and I feared even facing the fact that I did not want to know. I have a whole repertoire of mechanisms and procedures to prevent me from finding out what I don't want to know. What is acceptable and unacceptable knowledge? The learning we do can be a way of avoiding what we need to know or should know. Our whole lives can be a defence against knowing those things we least want to acknowledge. We can build a whole edifice of knowledge in order to avoid facing what we do not want to know' (p. 87).

It can be difficult to stand 'outside' ourselves to become an observer of our own experiences, to become 'meta' to an issue. One of us was working as a coach with a man whose experience was 'shouting' at him to leave a toxic work environment. The man was too frightened and fearful to allow himself to consider that option. While the pain of this manifested inside him as depression, there were times when he would project this pain outside onto the terrible organisation that did not understand him, even though he never tried to explain his situation to them.

It is through critical reflection on our experiences that we can turn experiential learning into propositional learning, and expose the assumptions we take for granted. The process of socialisation constructs us, and the process of reflection deconstructs and reconstructs us.

One supervisee was anxious that the theory she had been taught did not seem to apply in practice with a particular client. Her experience was at odds with what she had been taught in her course, i.e., this theory works with all clients if you apply it the right way. She was fitting the client to the theory (accommodative learning), rather than adapting the theory to the client (assimilative learning). She expressed this by declaring, 'It's not working, it should work, the theory is there. Tell me what I am doing wrong?' When the reply was, 'Maybe it doesn't work here. Let's see if your experience can help you find another way', it placed the supervisee at a crossroads. 'Do I keep doing what I should be doing and have been told to do, or should I stop and think, trust my experience and learn another way?' Feeling safe in supervision, she opted to look at other possibilities.

While the context pulls us to make sense of experiences in our habitual ways, when we feel safe we can begin to allow ourselves to be curious. There are times when it is difficult to allow ourselves to question, notice, pay attention to, and observe the things that might disturb our previous ways of knowing, our knowledge and our loyalties. What would it be like if a Catholic in Northern Ireland allowed himself or herself to look at Protestant neighbours, be curious about who they were, why they think the way they do, and be open to new ways to make sense of their behaviour rather than the old ways they have inherited? Scharmer (2005, cited in Brown) puts it well: 'The first part of this process is to observe, observe, observe, which means stop the downloading and open up into a full immersion into the context. Then you retreat and reflect, allowing the inner knowing to emerge. You access your own source. So you go from the chaos of observation to the still, inner place where knowing comes to the surface… It requires a letting go of your old self in order to find your emerging authentic self.'

STAGE 4: REFLECTION AS THE MEDIUM OF LEARNING FROM EXPERIENCE
Rock (2009) suggests the four steps of ARIA as a method for making decisions: awareness, reflection, insight and action. With awareness we stay lightly with the issue or problem, keep it centre stage and allow it to impact us. We then reflect on the issue, and from reflection we wait for insight, which gives us the way ahead and the impetus to implement action. In Component 6 we focus on the reflection that leads to insight and the integration of new learning into our life.

In general, reflection is the ability to step back and pose hard questions such as: Why are things done this way? How could I do it differently? Reflection involves the ability to ask incisive questions and the persistence to find out the answers. Voller (2009) defines and describes reflection as, 'Purposeful focusing on thoughts, feelings, sensations and behaviour in order to make meaning from those fragments of experience. The outcome of this reflection is to create new understanding which in turn may lead to: increasing choices, making changes or reducing confusion' (p. 21).

The word 'reflection' comes from a Latin root meaning 'to bend back, to stand apart from and to stand outside of'. In reflection, we step back from an experience or event to gain a new perspective on what we, or others, have done: we explore our experiences to make sense of them, examine other ways to make sense of them, and even probe the methods we use to make sense of them.

Active and deliberate reflective processes can push the possibilities further than if we act alone. Such processes include counselling, coaching or supervision, or any means by which we might develop new eyes, new perceptions and new visions. One reason people choose such a service is to make a conscious move outside their context. Many state the benefit of an opportunity to talk to someone outside the organisation, or to someone with different experience or expertise, or even to travel across town in a new geographic direction to sit in a different space. Supervisees comment on the value of 'external' rather than 'internal' supervision for this reason— the sense that someone can help them see things from a different reference point than what can be found 'inside', whether this be themselves or their relational/work context. With new vision comes new perspectives and new meanings. We notice new things, and the quality of our awareness changes. With reflection comes meaning at different levels. As I step outside my comfort zone and take an open stance, without judgment or shame, without blame or assumption and am open and indifferent to the outcome, what would I allow myself to think and reflect upon? Can I look beyond, beside, beneath, above, below, against, for… What would happen if I looked at myself, my client, our relationship, the organisation in another way?

Rebecca wasn't sure what to do. The client she was working with, Ruth, had a horrendous history of abuse that ran throughout her family. Ruth's brother Jeremy had also been abused. Ruth had pulled her life together, had married and now had her own two-year-old son. Jeremy, who lived close by, was the only family member she kept in contact with. In the last counselling session Ruth said she was worried about Jeremy and wondered if he was giving too much attention to her son. He was around a lot, took lots of pictures (he was an avid amateur photographer), and loved to play with the little boy. Ruth was confused: was this an involved and doting uncle who enjoyed being part of a wider family, or were there hints here that Jeremy might cross a line?

Rebecca brought this issue to her small group supervision session. Together they reviewed what was happening and even played out a few scenarios of possible outcomes. In holding it up to the light, reflecting on it from various perspectives, Rebecca came away knowing she had to trust the instincts of Ruth who was highly attuned to abuse settings and had shown great accuracy in her own life in potential abuse situations.

Rebecca had engaged herself and her group in one of the elements of the higher brain functions that help us to make conscious decisions—the skill of reflection. Reflection is the process we use as humans to ponder on, think about, hold up to the light and question situations in a deliberate and conscious manner in order to make informed decisions. Reflection is the medium of learning from experience. Zero or low-level reflection can often lead to ethical immaturity, while the ability to reflect at ever deepening levels is a condition for ethical maturity.

In preparing for reflection-on-action an important questions to ask is: How do I get myself into the 'right frame of mind' so that I can truly learn from the past? From a non-defensive stance, I begin to ask some questions: What have I learned about me? What have I learned about how I make decisions? What have I learned?

The After Action Review (AAR) is a method devised by the US military in order to learn from experiences in the field. It comprises five steps and takes place after a military exercise. Five questions are asked in small groups where the ground rules are confidentiality and non-blaming.

1. What did we set out to do?
2. What happened?
3. What went well? What went badly?

4. What have we learned from this experience?
5. What will we do differently the next time we are faced with this situation?

When we are disoriented and confused, it is not easy to stay with what is happening. And yet, to learn we need to experience the impact of what is happening, and to stay with this impact for a while. If we move too quickly into evaluation or acceptance/rejection we can move too quickly away from the learning. In fact, sometimes *not* thinking too much about what happened is helpful. Allow the unspoken, the unsaid, even the inarticulate event to be in your awareness, as well as what is evoked or elicited by the event. During this 'plunging into reality' and immersion in experience, the challenge is to stay authentic and remain resilient. It is a time to be 'indifferent'—not unconcerned, but not making premature conclusions, being passionate about what is happening, but not already at the destination, and being prepared to go to the destination that emerges. Jarvis (2006) describes this world: 'In novel situations throughout life we have new sensations, so that we can rarely take the world for granted: we enter a state of disjuncture and implicitly we raise questions: What do I do now? What does this mean? What is that smell? The sound? And so on. There is a sense of unknowing' (p. 19). This place of ignorance and unknowing is often the point of transformation. We allow ourselves to be unsure, not to know, to stay with confusion in our sea of unknowing. We sharpen our attention.

Different resistances begin to emerge. In allowing the time, the painfulness of the experience, our defensiveness, strong feelings and blaming bubble to the surface and tempt us to retreat from new learning. Sometimes there is conflict with others, even our closest others, and honest reflection can put us in opposition to our own communities. We need an awareness of how we avoid and deny, and to know what the pitfalls might be that would stop us staying true to new learning. We resist having our world dismantled. It can be valuable at this stage to talk or write about what is happening—to get it out, to allow others to see and comment. Sometimes we have to face up to the negatives within such as our guilt and shame. When we enter the world of reflection, we see from where we are, from the position and stance we have taken in life. Can I take another viewpoint, enter another world and see the event from within that world? It is a different experience when you participate, rather than remain as an observer. We bring mindsets, beliefs, mental maps and assumptions to what we see, hear, touch, feel and smell. These are often insufficiently examined and tested.

Do not underestimate the pain and losses at this stage of learning. You may need moral support to help you move through these stages.

Step 5: Integrating new learning into moral character

The self-awareness and self-knowledge that can be achieved from reflecting on experience reaches its full potential when it is captured in language and is implemented in action. There is often a gap between insight and action, and this stage attempts to embed reflective awareness into our lives through changed thinking and behaviours.

To give attention to what we have learned is one way to help the brain focus and build new neural pathways. Rock (2009) suggests that, 'It is attention itself that changes the brain. By focusing on our new learning we are already helping the brain build new neural pathways to result in new behaviour' (p. 224). One way to achieve this is to create goals that focus our attention. Once goals are set, we are more alert to picking up information relevant to that goal. For example, couples who consider the scenario of what to do if their relationship doesn't work out are more attuned to information and events that may indicate their relationship is in trouble than couples who have never considered the possibility. For the latter, it comes as a surprise should they find themselves having relationship difficulties. Rock (2009) also writes about 'towards goals' and 'away goals'—what are you moving towards and what are you moving away from? Towards goals are usually more positive and have more connections to positive feelings and rewards. They move the focus from problems to solutions.

Paying attention to and creating new goals is a way to integrate new information into our lives. After a while these new behaviours become automatic, i.e., part of our moral make-up. For example, those who have gone through the process of giving up smoking go through these steps:

- I wonder what it would be like to not smoke (curiosity)?
- What does my context and environment appear to dictate, and what do I need to change from this imposed meaning to allow myself freedom to make a different choice (I may have started smoking because I thought it made me 'cool' or confident)?
- Am I safe enough to begin the journey of not smoking?
- What does reflection on smoking tell me?
- I make the change by giving my attention to something other than smoking, e.g., how good I feel, what I have saved financially from not smoking, how much longer I might live.
- After a while non-smoking is my new habit and it does not enter my mind to smoke.

- But I must be aware that I could relapse and ensure that I take precautions not to return to smoking.

Conclusion

One of the greatest gifts we have as humans is our ability to use our experience to learn. We give attention deliberately and intentionally to what has happened to us, or is happening to us, in order to learn from that experience. While other animals learn from experience, humans can make their experience an intentional focus of learning. This process can go either way—towards accommodative learning where experience relates to old ways of learning, or towards assimilative learning where the new experience transforms our ways of thinking and results in wisdom, maturity and new behaviour. In holding our ethical decisions up to reflective light, we learn from what we have done and create new habits of ethical excellence.

Chapter 17

Training in ethical maturity

··

'The best way to teach ethics is to live ethically: the best way to teach ethics is to teach ethically: the best way to write about ethics is to write ethically...I believe I am teaching ethics ethically when I enter into a faithful and trusting relationship with you.'

(adapted from Nash, 2002, p. 33)

'Educational programs should instil the view that ethical considerations should be an ongoing aspect of professional behaviour, rather than a concern that arises only in response to a problem.'

(Biaggio, Paget, and Chenoworth, 1997, p. 189)

'Teaching ethics can be conceptualised as progressing from a focus on conceptual issues and principles to an emphasis on practical issues and applications.'

(Corey, Schneider-Corey, and Callahan, 2005, p. 194)

'If ethics education is going to reach its goal of enhancing responsible professional practice, instructors must move beyond explanation of rules and laws and exhortations to do good... Education ought to be focused on ethics and ethical ideals, with instruction on legal issues and risk management as secondary concerns. All those involved need to keep in mind that ethics education is a necessary condition for ethical action, but action relies on more than knowledge and decision making skills: it demands a psychologist with an ethical professional identity.'

(Reynolds Welfel, 2011, p. 301)

'An applicant is being interviewed for a position in an organisation. "Do you lie, steal or cheat?", she is asked. "No," comes the reply, "but I am willing to learn."'

(Old organisational joke)

In commonplace conversations, it can be said you are ethical or not, of good moral character or not, just as in the same way people can be named as good or evil. The phrase 'leopards don't change their spots' is applied to individuals to indicate the intractable state of their character. We still think of moral character as a single, fixed unit, whereas in the lived world we know and experience its complexity. As soon as ethics was conceptualised as a *developmental* process, the possibility of formal training to enhance moral character, sensitivity and decision making could follow. There is now research that demonstrates ethical reasoning is improved by instruction during professional training (Bebeau, 2002, cited in Reynolds Welfel, 2011).

Until the last 15 years, many courses in the helping professions did not have specific ethics content. In my (Elisabeth's) undergraduate psychology training 25 years ago ethics was not mentioned. Nor has it been mentioned in masters degrees I have undertaken since (psychology, couple and family therapy, and management). As Pope and Vasquez (2007) suggest, we often learn about ethics, and what might constitute the rules of good practice, more implicitly than explicitly, e.g., chance conversations, and modelling by influential colleagues and organisations. The arena of supervision has been used as 'a fall back' place to take ethical issues and dilemmas. A common reply to the question, 'How would you deal with this ethical issue?', is 'I would take it to supervision.' A challenging question at this point would be to ask the practitioner what they would do if the supervisor was not available. While not deriding the importance of using supervision to manage ethical concerns, it can be used as an ethical 'cop-out' to make others responsible for our ethical choices.

While all these options can be 'good enough', they can be based on precarious learning. Even though we may have had no formal training, we can be measured directly on our ethical behaviour and it is simply assumed we know how to be ethical. There is more awareness in the community about professional misconduct (perhaps as a result of media and movie depictions of corrupt 'helping professionals'), and an increased emphasis on consumer rights, which means that industry groups must be seen to be able to police their own, and uphold professional standards for the good of the public. This begs the question about what it takes to be a 'good' and worthy professional (Reynolds Welfel, 2011).

In much of this book we have considered the relationship between the knowledge of values and duties, and the implementation of decisions and behaviour based on them. In this chapter, we will explore the role of training in reinforcing the relationship between values and practice, but we accept that training will never immunise people against poor decision making and corrupt practice. If there has been little input, and what input there has been is based on poor educational practices, then we have not even carried out a good attempt to get it right first time around.

Nowadays most courses make some effort to tackle ethics as part of the curriculum, although little is known about the actual content of such programmes and research suggests that there is significant disagreement about what is important to include (Walden, Herlihy Ashton, 2003; and Urofsky and Sowa, 2004). Some programmes do not offer formal courses in ethical decision making, but attempt to integrate ethics into existing programmes, e.g., view diversity, cross-cultural work and awareness, and dealing with difference as ethical issues in themselves. The drawback is there is often no consistent theory of ethical decision making that runs across the programme and each course fashions its own method. It is more common that there are one or two lectures on the topic in the duration of a helping profession course, often at the very end of the qualification.

In these instances, the question must be asked: what can be gained in covering the topic of ethical issues in such a short period of time? This approach may lead to trainers describing only universal principles, and running through the behaviours required to comply with the relevant professional code. This has been referred to as the 'pragmatic approach'. This approach has the advantage of introducing students to ethics in a way that is easy for them to see its relevance, given their desire to avoid professional censure in the future (Illingworth, 2004). However, even with this as the main educational focus, the teaching of ethics can be a more expansive exercise than simply reading through the code. Regardless of the approach, there does seem to be a 'learning from practice' attitude towards ethical sensitivity. In other words, it is only when we encounter and have to deal with ethical issues that we learn how to be ethical. Learning from experience is always valuable, however, structural foundations provide frameworks within which we can sift and interpret experience in order to make a more informed decision as to how to act in the most ethical way.

There are now a few courses that offer whole units on ethics, which provide more opportunity to explore the topic. For trainers who are in the habit of the 'brief mention', it may be quite a challenge to design a whole course in ethics. First, there has to be a shift from a sole focus on 'teaching-the-rules'. The term 'technical rationality' (Schon, 1983) applies to educational approaches that provide the theory and expect the application to take place automatically. Evidence-based practice is prone to this instrumental approach, i.e., once you have the 'evidence' your job is simply to follow procedures and apply fixed ways of working outlined in manuals that offer step-by-step processes to guide you on the right path. To make a move from theory to practice requires more of a process of discernment, of reflective application and an awareness of complexity. Schon (1983) coined the term 'the swampy lowlands' of practice to illustrate how the practitioner is, in fact, an artist who uses knowledge and theory as a skilled adaptor cutting their cloth to find solutions to particular situations rather than starting with the answers. Ethical training is much more of the latter.

Earlier we have noted research that demonstrates that, in general, it is not a lack of knowledge about rules that leads to ethical transgressions, but other personal failings or contextual influences. So what we need to be teaching is not, 'What are we going to do about dilemmas?', but 'How does one behave toward dilemmas?' It is not sufficient to look at 'What ought I do?', but to also look at 'Who ought I be?' in relation to the ethical dilemma (May, 1994). As Rest (1984) argued, for ethical action to occur we must be ethically sensitive, able to reason ethically, have the motivation to act ethically, and be ethically resolute. It makes sense that training must cover at least each of these dimensions. None of these steps state that in order to act ethically we have to 'do as we are told', and yet this has often been the focus of ethics education. For example, prison officers and forensic psychologists who work in prisons are often taught how to resist being manipulated by prisoners who are somewhat expert in this regard. However, all the understanding and teaching in the world has little effect if the individuals concerned have no insight into their own Achilles heel, i.e., where he or she tends to be vulnerable and needy. This personal knowledge, alongside an awareness of the strategies used by prisoners to manipulate, and some theory on how manipulation takes place, can together provide good armour against being gullible. In other words, knowledge on its own is insufficient.

We know there are many ways to learn how to be ethically sensitive, how to make ethical decisions, and how to live with the decisions we have made. You can read more about this in detail in Chapters 8 and 9. We can:

- learn from experience by trial and error, allowing our experience to teach us. Learning by doing is a powerful way of knowing
- use imitation learning, i.e., learning from the experience of others (called 'experience by proxy' by Leonardo da Vinci). This can occur through modelling, mentorship and even unconscious 'osmosis' as we drink in the example of others
- learn more formally in classroom or training room environments where explicit teaching takes place through lectures, input, reading materials, learning frameworks and models
- learn through the practice of skills and the development of capacities

- learn by considering ethical vignettes and playing with ethical dilemmas thought up by others
- learn from reflecting on our own ethical past and the ethical dilemmas and issues we have faced.

Training programmes on ethical maturity will be more effective if they include all these methods. This chapter explores the principles and teaching methods required to set up and run effective training programmes that will contribute to development in ethical maturity. We will provide some exercises and learning experiences that can help us to understand ethical concepts and develop some necessary skills for tricky ethical decision making. We also consider the process involved: contracting for the course, the ethical teacher and the ethical programme.

The training methods suggested are to occur within formal training events and aim to help participants learn how to make ethical decisions in their lives and in their work situation. We will not be delving into theories of learning or theories of teaching. Our approach is not one of risk management, popular in ethics education, but to assist trainees to build a solid ethical floor on which they can rely in their professional endeavours (Reynolds Welfel, 2011).

We will not cover the knowledge and skills needed to teach others (in this case, ethical maturity), nor will we spend time on the administrative side of teaching or training, i.e., setting up the learning environment, establishing learning relationships and partnerships, contracting with participants on the learning programmes, evaluating them and so on (although these are vital if real and transformational learning is to take place). All of these aspects contain ethical elements and may have ethical implications, but are outside what we will cover here.

Establishing an ethical frame for the programme

To begin any kind of programme in ethics, a number of important elements related to context and learning arrangements need to be organised. In all learning contexts there is an onus on the trainer to model the core skills, and never more so than in an ethics course. While students often have issues with aspects of their training experience, one thing that is at odds with an ethics course is the lack of potential for students to later say that some aspect of the course was unethical.

1. THE ETHICAL TEACHER

Before teaching a course on ethical maturity, it is worth considering what it takes to be an ethical teacher. More is taught through action than through words, and to exemplify what is being taught, in this case 'ethical maturity', is a significant challenge for any teacher. There is no doubt that relationships are at the heart of ethical maturity in training and teaching. How will the trainer relate ethically to the participants on the programme? And how does the trainer devise a programme that builds on values such as integrity and transparency, and, at the same time, avoids shame, humiliation, put-downs, bullying or toxic environments? A good question for trainers to ask themselves is, 'What do I need to attend to (physically, emotionally, psychologically and spiritually) in order to be the trainer or facilitator on this training programme in ethical maturity?'

Some sticky ethical moments that I (Elisabeth) have encountered include:

- Students approaching me after a lecture to ask if I am available to lecture in other projects they are involved with. While I may be a freelance contractor, in *that moment* I am contracted to an organisation and not free to market myself. However, sometimes it can be tempting.

- In teaching counselling skills, students ask if they could refer to my private practice. Again, this can be a conflict of interest, and not a wise referral if it involves their friends and family. What if the counselling is unsuccessful? Would it compromise an otherwise good experience of the training?

Some trainers in private courses market the course to their clients as a form of self-development. This sets up a dual relationship that can compromise both relationships and interrupt the course group dynamics. Issues such as fairness in assessments, allowing leeway for late assignments, and the combination of compassion on one hand with clear boundaries on the other can all lead to ethical uncertainty if not handled well. Knowing the difficult life situation of one student, Michael allowed special provision, which was then queried and demanded by another student who did not have similar background problems. The student making the complaint suggested that the tutors were being unjust and preferential in offering leeway to one student that was not available to all.

2. WHAT RELATIONSHIPS DO I ALREADY HAVE WITH THE STUDENT BODY?

In recognition of the potential for harm in dual relationships, trainers must concede they hold a position of power over students and their authority and conduct does have consequences. Early establishment of clear boundaries in the relationship is crucial. Creation and maintenance of boundaries, including providing students with information on what constitutes adequate boundaries and how to handle violations are essential (Sullivan and Ogloff, 1998). Consider for example a discussion of dual relationship guidelines in Week One of a course. The discussion could explore how public and private realms are managed in the course, and how everyone plays a part in the management of good boundaries. The trainers are the guardians of behaviour, but students need to be encouraged to step up to professional behaviour too. This is another learning and modelling moment.

Relationships between students can also erupt into ethical storms. Michael had a situation where the relationship between two students had disintegrated to such a degree that it was causing mayhem within the group, despite group and individual interventions to resolve it. Eventually one of the students resigned from the course. This lead to a lot of discussion around what ethical stances can be taken when relationships flounder. Should the tutors have done more to to provide mediation? Should one student be allowed to resign, while the other student remains on the course? Who should make the decisions in this instance, and how should the decisions be made? Sometimes the best boundaries and contracts leave gaps that have surprisingly few answers for situations like this.

3. Informed consent

Educators are recommended to ensure students are informed of the intricacies of ethics education and course requirements. This includes detail about the syllabus, methods of teaching and likely challenges that may arise. Potential effects and examples can illustrate likely challenges, and methods of support and resolution of difficulties explored. Careful attention needs to be given to issues of privacy, purpose and consent in teaching methods chosen. Too often, selected training exercises are 'old favourites', without sufficient reflection or review of changes in training standards. A 'socialisation period' should then follow where students are 'acclimatised' into learning strategies in practice (Morrissette and Gadbois, 2006). For example, if you want to stimulate robust debate in the exploration of ethical issues, how might you establish safety in the early weeks to ensure students develop the confidence to speak up and challenge each other without negative consequences?

The establishment of mutual and agreed ground rules for participation in the training is recommended. With shorter programmes, or where there is a large audience, it may be impossible to engage all participants in a negotiation process around ground rules. However, a programme on ethical maturity can begin by asking the participants in small groups to answer two questions:

- What do *I* need to attend to in order to be ethically mature on this training course?
- What do *we* need to attend to in order to be ethically mature on this training course?

As can be imagined, interesting lists emerge:

Personal	Collectively
Make sure I rest	Listen to and respect each other
Be on time	Respect diversity
Challenge assumptions	Clear contracts (clear psychological contracts)
Awareness of offensive ideas, values, behaviour	Use principles of adult learning
Be sincere	Build on autonomy
Respectful of difference	Privilege inquiry
Accept limitations	Be open to other ways of working
Take responsibility for self	Speak up

Table 17.1: List of Agreed Ground Rules for Training Participation.

The use of this process allows individuals, small groups and the large group to come to some agreed ethical ground rules about how to work together in ways that are ethically mature and might best support learning in the group by the group. Of course, working out ethical guidelines never covers everything and maybe this should be the case. Ethical dilemmas emerge from life relationships and in real time, and the best-laid plans are never quite sufficient. Dealing with the unforeseen is itself a way to be ethically flexible and understand that there are often no prior answers to deal with current situations. To find a way forward with integrity and maturity has to be worked through with much discussion, energy and sometimes a lot of hurt.

Participants need to be given the option to exclude themselves from training exercises they consider to be inappropriate or unsuitable for them. In effect, this demonstrates respect for autonomy. This is not the same as giving students permission to not participate in the training fully. It is about offering a range of learning opportunities so that students can work within any legitimate constraints, as well as have the chance to step out of their comfort zone. As an example of how this can be managed in practice, Proctor (2008) suggests that 'the working ground rules include participants' responsibility for saying when they do not want to be included in an exercise. Instead, we ask them to participate actively by taking an observer role and feeding back what they have noticed from a particular focus and position' (p. 195).

4.   THE INDUSTRY AND COMMUNITY CONTEXT

The training cannot occur in a vacuum. Professional imperatives and requirements such as a professional code provide a context for the training. What is important is that knowledge of the code is not equated with moral sensitivity or ethical action. At the same time, any training course needs to have a component on the rules to be learned and lived by. What makes this more alive within people and industries are the following:

- exploration of the dilemmas that exist in working by a professional code, by an organisational code, and by personal and professional values
- recognition that the code is a starting point, and not an end point for investigation
- acknowledgement that codes will always require interpretation, translation and supplementation from other people and resources. Trainees need to know how to do this effectively (Reynolds Welfel, 2011).

Training principles and practices

1. Starting with the student's ordinary moral sense

We know that trainees will come to us with a set of morals, experiences and views that inform their ongoing daily ethical decision making. Reynolds Welfel (2011) argues that trainers must not only meet students where they are 'but also view ethics education as an acculturation process not limited to a single course, activity or time period. The fundamental task is to help students develop an ethical professional identity (and in continuing ethics education, to assist them in updating that professional identity to keep it consistent with current professional values)' (p. 288). She suggests our task is to mesh ethics education with the student's pre-existing ethics culture while adopting the culture of the new profession. This is a substantial challenge and involves two aspects: being the professional, and doing (enacting) the tasks of the professional. Becoming/taking on the role of professional (e.g., psychologist, coach, pastoral minister, counsellor, etc.) means taking in the values and principles so that you might then embody them. From this place, it becomes more likely you can enact the behaviours of the professional. This means focusing on character and values in the first instance, before describing the behaviours required. Kant suggested that while it is possible to do one's duty without one's heart being in it, one is more likely to succeed in being ethical if the head and heart work together. Sartre was more demanding and saw 'bad faith' as the gap between what we did and what we really wanted to do. For him, acting in bad faith was never an ethically mature stance.

Reynolds Welfel (2011) suggests that if we are to get to know students ethics cultures, and for students to develop a conscious awareness of their own ethics cultures, it is important to understand their ethical 'sources'. While these can be drawn out through any class or written exercise, a specific tool might be for students to write an 'ethics autobiography', through which they reflect on their ethics histories, influences and current understandings about their emerging professional role. The following guiding questions are examples within such a task (Bashe et al., 2007 cited in Reynolds Welfel, 2011):

- What is your idea of right and wrong personal behaviour and where does this come from?
- What are three personal needs that you think might match well with the profession?
- What are three personal needs that you think might conflict with the profession? (p. 289).

Other exercises that Reynolds Welfel identifies to assist in self-understanding include these.

- Students identify their strengths and weaknesses, and consider how their greatest strengths can also lead to weakness, for example in holding a prized value (e.g., focusing on client autonomy) to the point of inhibiting practice (e.g., withholding an opinion that could be valuable and timely).
- An autobiography can be useful as an initial reflective tool, but also as a record of changes in ethical perspective.
- Ethical questionnaires can assist students to identify their ethical preferences and can be useful for reflection (see Forsyth, 1980; Hinman, 2008).
- The provocative statements exercise where students debate controversial statements about professional values and behaviours, with half taking the positive and half the negative view (Plante, 1995). This allows students permission to take on perspectives they would not otherwise hold, and to 'try them on for size'.

2. THE PRAGMATIC APPROACH

The 'pragmatic approach' in education has a focus on rules and procedures for the profession. At an undergraduate level, this could be important to prepare students to be clear about what they are signing up for as they enter the profession. It may also be important for training bodies seeking to meet compliance requirements at a minimum educational level. This does not have to be an approach that lacks creativity, nor does it need to exclude other learning goals. What is important is that students do not seek ethics as an end goal only in terms of external constraints, so that their task is to conform with requirements imposed by others. This is a 'surefire' way to excuse oneself from compliance when things get sticky, by assuming the main rules are for other people and other situations, and not me-in-this-situation. The aim is to acquire an understanding of the principles and values that give rise to the rules and to 'facilitate their internalisation of the values implicit in the rules' (Illingworth, 2004, p. 9). This involves both theoretical and applied approaches, and a clear understanding of why codes exist. After all, the rules are only useful if one knows how and when to apply them.

3. DEVELOPING METHODOLOGIES FOR TEACHING ETHICS

'The educational challenge is to develop people with insight who have the courage to ask difficult questions and who have the clarity of thinking to grasp what those questions are. We need to develop team players, as most ethical issues are in fact resolved as a result of good communication within teams...' (Vernon cited in Illingworth 2004, p. 25). What teaching methods and experiences might advance these goals?

Effective ethics training needs to embrace both training and educative opportunities (Longstaff, 1995). This distinction says that:

- ethics *training* involves processes and experiences designed to impart knowledge, understanding, and skills to people in order to ensure effective operation within their defined role
- ethics *education* involves processes and experiences designed to impart knowledge, understanding, and skills so that people operate with autonomy and authenticity in a way that is their own.

In practice, this involves the teaching of skills, standards, rules and techniques, as well as the provision of opportunities for individuals to apply them across diverse and unexpected circumstances that allow them to experience their individual interpretation. This tests their ability to hold standards 'under fire'. Longstaff (1995) argues that such opportunities for personal learning are not only respectful of individuals as independent thinkers and with personal agency, but also that 'individuals who have internalised the ethical principles that inform the conduct of their lives are more likely to be consistent and reliable in the application of these principles...autonomous moral agents will not only have settled convictions and dispositions, they will also be able to review the principles that they adhere to as circumstances change' (p. 6).

Rather than start by teaching ethical principles, it could be argued that without development of professional *virtues*, through which one achieves professional maturity and internalisation of professional virtues, one would be unable to effectively apply ethical principles (Jordan and Meara, 1990). Trainees need to understand what virtues and principles apply to the standards, especially where the code can seem to offer conflicting advice (Reynolds Welfel, 2011). Consider the example of mandatory reporting of child sexual abuse. The requirement and procedure of reporting can be determined, but how does the professional reconcile the competing duties of therapist and social control agent? How does reporting fit with the principle of client autonomy? What about the ethical questions of how and when the client might be told? Practices of reporting behind the client's back are common and result from a conflict between clinical notions of 'preserve engagement at all costs' and the requirement to 'tell the truth'. Helping professionals are expected to know the principles, and display dimensions of character not always articulated or explicitly developed in training. 'Professional character cannot be left to its own devises, particularly in the face of a pluralistic society and the contemporary pressures of the marketplace…professional ideals must include conscientious decision making, but they must also include virtuous deciders, who emphasise not so much what is permitted, but what is preferred' (Jordan and Meara, 1990, p. 112).

Strong arguments have been made for the use of cases in ethics training, as they can connect abstract concepts to real-life experience (Richardson, 1993; Falkenberg and Woiceshyn, 2008). However, finding cases that are effective teaching tools can be difficult—they can be too brief, too detailed, or insufficiently generalisable for robust learning. Well-constructed case examples demonstrate the variations in ethical violations/ situations that occur, the possible options for responding, and the ways in which minor infractions can lead to more significant misconduct over time. What is crucial is to discuss the subtleties in ethical challenges, rather than the most egregious violations that tend to make everyone sit up with prurient interest, but think 'that won't be me' (Reynolds Welfel, 2011). For example, it is easy to find case studies on the professionals who have sex with their clients, and far more difficult to come up with the 'non-sexy' examples around the nuances of informed consent.

Examples drawn from the trainee' own life/current work situation can be useful if the trainer adheres to the principles of thinking issues and options through, and not giving advice. Film, television and newspapers can provide a rich source of examples for debate, and students themselves may suggest options in this regard if encouraged to do so. Training sessions could begin with discussion of 'ethical news of the week' where trainees bring material that has crossed their ethical radar. This material may be used throughout the session to enhance learning in debates, role plays or illustration of theories.

Gibson (2008) provides specific mechanisms by which real-life ethical dilemmas of students may be analysed against a personal appreciation of their values to promote creative and enriching classroom dialogue. The most effective examples are true to life and have a complexity that is not reduced to a simple solution. Gibson starts with the simple question, 'What is the problem here?' and watches as individuals construct the ethical issue, i.e., their perception of the moral problem. This provides an opportunity for self-reflection around personal value systems. Students are then asked to consider 'subjective responsibility', i.e., internally imposed expectations, and 'objective responsibility', i.e., the concerns thrust upon us by external forces. This allows for discussion around relational values. Do we have more moral accountability as the relationship moves closer to us? Gibson's hope is that by the end of this process individuals will have articulated their 'personal value portrait' (p. 341).

The important provision of opportunities for constructive controversy, as opposed to individualistic learning, involves comparisons between incompatible ideas and opinions in order to synthesise novel solutions. In such processes, students can feel uncomfortable, destabilised and uncertain about their own views, and develop new insights based on the struggle and new information. Constructive controversy as a teaching method can result in greater achievement and higher quality decision making, higher-level cognitive reasoning and positive attitudes to other disputants. The art is to set an exercise where debate is constructive and not destructive (Tichy et al., 2010). Students should have the chance to argue different sides of any debate, which gives them permission to explore unfamiliar reasoning and positions different to their own.

This should occur with a number of goals in mind:

- to learn not to impose one's view on others
- to foster skills that enable the student to work out their own thinking, use independent judgement, and take responsibility for their ideas
- to establish a balance between self-effacement, which does little to stimulate the student's thinking, and the imposition of ideas that stifle the student's thinking
- to develop self-awareness so that one's own views can be distinguished from those of others
- to develop skills and practice in ethical decision making in a manner that involves the use of theory, but not always in an explicit way (adapted from Boele, 1995).

Beale (cited in Illingworth, 2004) has a teaching focus that enhances reflective practice, and argues that to be fit to practise in one's profession requires life-long, self-directed learning. This learning is crucial for self-care, to listen to intuition and uncertainty, to feel the anxiety of ethical disquiet, and to begin the process of analysis and problem solving. As a balance to this more individual strategy and skill, Beale suggests the use of drama, either through observation or participation in performance. This takes a debate further through enactment of roles and the experience of the fit of different opinions. The use of narrative (biography, visual arts, fiction, poetry, music, students' and others' stories) can be moving and imaginative ways to bring perspectives to life. In considering such teaching methods, the goal is for students to experience themselves and others at the level of values, morals and ethics. To become more self-aware, as well as more attuned to the diversity of views, some of which they may choose to entertain for themselves before the end of the training. They need to do this without seeking the 'right' view, but rather the view that is right for them, and to understand what it means to hold and manage different views to others.

We have noted that professionals can be attuned ethically, and even make good decisions, and then be unable to implement them. On this basis, it is important to foster skills around ethical resoluteness, but this is perhaps challenging for trainers to conceptualise. Reynolds Welfel (2011) suggests using role models, social justice examples, and even cases where people made decisions that had some negative consequences to bring the complexities of ethical action alive. To explore in detail how unethical action causes suffering, rather than minimise its consequences can also help trainees to picture the results of possible actions.

4. STUDENT LEARNING OUTCOMES

In the helping professions, it is a challenge to consider how we might encourage debate, extend students' views and develop the emotional resilience necessary for the work. Care needs to be taken in selection of teaching methods. It is not difficult to think of a provocative training exercise, but does it have an educational goal, or does it have more of an experimental goal about human nature? In a course about sexuality, a lecturer took students to nudist beaches, gay night clubs, swingers' bars and sex shops. While the activities did mirror the course content, students objected to off-campus activities, and argued that the educational goals could be met in other ways. The activities also had the potential to put students at emotional, and even legal, risk (Koocher and Keith-Spiegel, 2008). How many trainers have taken students to institutions of various kinds with an explicitly noble goal, e.g., to help at soup kitchens, but result in students having an ill-defined, gratuitous experience of watching those more disadvantaged than them? And what of the rights of the people being observed?

It is impossible to predict how students will react to the provocative material that accompanies an ethics course, either at the time or as a delayed reaction. Students need to know they can excuse themselves, how they can get support and debriefing, and to have these options enshrined in any course materials. Where possible, trainers should focus on evidence-based material, and should not encourage lengthy, involved or repetitive debriefings about material/exercises themselves. Student perceptions of the training, and monitoring of the emotional experience of students as a whole, can occur at regular debriefings where feedback can be sought and problems tackled early (Morrissette et al., 2006; Koocher and Keith-Spiegel, 2008). Students should not receive better grades for being more 'in touch with their emotions' or for higher levels of personal disclosure. We need an awareness of the many learning styles, and ways to involve ourselves in learning. A person who 'opens up' and makes training 'easy' for us should not be valued above another who is involved in the experience in a different way, nor should students be made to feel bad or inadequate if they are more reticent or private. Students want to be the 'best I can be'. This cannot be measured in grades, nor can it be universally defined. It behoves us to engage students in their definition of being 'the best I can be' so that we can establish a co-defined benchmark for individual progress (Lewis and Cheshire, 2007).

Modelling is our most effective teaching tool. Students will be more likely to follow what we *do* rather than what we *say* are the right things to do. This involves open discussion and debate, including potential disclosure by trainers of their own ethical positions and struggles. The aim is for a climate of openness within the frame so that conversation provides the opportunity for change and review. If students have an ethical position, such as 'right to life', but are entering a profession that purports a 'non-judgemental' stance, we need to be able to assist them into a position where conflict between these two positions can be managed. The only way to know that these conflicts occur is to foster a climate where they can be tabled (Corey et al., 2005; Charles et al., 2005).

Training as a mutual experience

We need to establish that ethical practice, like the educational endeavour itself, is a mutual process for the most part. A benchmark for behaviour and participation needs to be set, and all held to account on the achievement of this benchmark. Crocket, Kotze and Flintoff (2007) prepare counselling students for respectful, rigorous professional dialogue within the requirements of higher education by writing to students and talking in class about the following:

- that you will bring to your assessments competence in counselling practice, and that competence will be appropriate to this time in the programme

- that you will seek opportunities for reflection and learning and invite others to participate in that
- that learning involves stepping into new territories of being and thus perhaps includes experiences of discomfort
- that applause and reassurance can obscure opportunities for learning and are practices to be used sparingly
- that together we will originate practice beyond what we might individually
- that you will originate practice that I have not
- that, assuming competence in learning and practice appropriate for this stage in the program, we will both be robust and rigorous in our explorations of practice possibilities.

(pp. 3–4)

This information provides transparency in training philosophy, as well as informed consent. It also states something of the trainer's philosophy of teaching, and what values the students are encouraged to have/foster.

Working with diversity

It is now considered best ethical and educational practice to demonstrate responsiveness to the world around us and to be sensitive to different cultures and practices (Walden et al., 2003). The classroom environment itself needs to reflect diverse beliefs and perspectives, rather than a mono-cultural perspective and homogenous experience. Students should not be asked to speak for their culture, nor can the trainer be an expert on all aspects of diversity counselling (Boyer-Fier and Ramsey, 2005). Instead, it is a challenge to work with teaching approaches and experiences that reinforce an openness to difference by allowing for difference, fostering student questioning and experimentation, rather than instruction on how human relationships should be managed (Lewis and Cheshire, 2007).

Morals and ethics vary across cultures, e.g., in some cultures, the value of respect for elders/those in authority will mean that engagement in exercises of robust classroom debate will be impossible for some students. Training exercises need to allow students to explore their position, as well as different positions, without the reference point for success always being set by the dominant culture. Michael had a South African student on a counselling programme who explained that in his culture it was disrespectful to look an elder or a teacher in the eye. This behaviour had been interpreted on a previous training as deviousness and his avoidance of personal contact. He felt the need to explain this in advance in case a similar interpretation took place.

The limitations of ethics training

A generic course on ethics will not be sufficient for all specialised work. While foundational requirements of ethical practice apply in an introductory individual counselling programme, when students specialise later, e.g., couple and family therapy at a postgraduate level, they should have separate and distinct training on ethics within their special context and populations (Levitt, 2004). In some courses, a whole module on ethics would be appropriate and could include: foundational and advanced concepts; professional and personal management of self; values and the helping relationship; diversity issues; client rights and confidentiality; boundary issues and dual relationships and, special topics such as clinical specialisations, research issues, community or group work (Corey *et al.*, 2005). There is no shortage of possibilities. Courses need to be both industry standard and practice specific.

Where to from here?

Ideally, ethics training should be achieved at the level of curricular infusion, where all lectures are developed with ethics (and issues of diversity) in view, accompanied by regular review of ethical dilemmas. This method allows more opportunities to develop ethical virtues. Beale (cited in Illingworth, 2004) refers to 'embedded learning', where the words 'ethical' or 'moral' may never be mentioned. Instead, learning occurs when students consider an area of professional interest that has an ethical dimension, but is not confined to the subject of ethics alone. She argues that ethics learning and teaching can be embedded in terms of its objectives and/or its mode of delivery. This teaching and learning framework could mean the whole faculty of a course considering how they will include ethics (and diversity) in their subjects. For example, in any case study or role play the lecturers ask 'Could this be used to advance ethical issues? Could I add an ethical dimension to this learning experience?' In this way, students can continue to work through examples and issues right across the curriculum. If students have continual opportunities to approach ethics from a variety of angles, implicit and explicit, there is a greater chance they will internalise moral sensitivity, as well as develop the skills required to identify and approach ethical dilemmas in practice.

Conclusion

Ethics education improves ethical orientation, the ability to make a higher moral judgement in difficult situations, enhances moral reasoning and improves self-concept as a moral person (Lau, 2010). This is not a given, but is a developmental process—something to be worked towards and never quite achieved.

In the helping professions in particular, it is important that students experience their ethics education as an opportunity to learn through their own struggle and development, rather than being left to be blindsided by ethical dilemmas in practice and feeling clueless about how to proceed. Too often ethics training is viewed and experienced as a 'tick the box' exercise with a focus on regulations and 'shall nots' that students often believe they already have sorted out for themselves. The challenge for trainers is to take the training experience to a level that touches the trainee, to get to what matters, and to foster personal and professional growth as a result. This requires thought and creativity, but in the end means that both the trainees and trainer will be more engaged in the process of ethical maturity. This book provides a basis for training in ethical maturity. In taking the six components as foundational anchors in ethical maturity, our challenge and the challenge facing all trainers in ethical maturity is to provide the relationships, the environments, the contracts, the theory and the practice of helping students integrate these six into their existing personal and professional lives. We have no doubts about the challenge of that task.

Part Three
Applied ethical maturity in challenging contexts

Overview of Part Three

Throughout this book we have explored influential aspects of ethical decision making, from the internal (values, beliefs, personal history) to the external (context, authority, systems). In this section, we explore these themes in relation to three specific applications: organisational behaviour, gift giving and bribery in social and work relationships, and ethics in research. We have chosen these topics for the following reasons:

1. All of these contexts/issues are influential in the helping professions, the main focus of this book.

2. All of these contexts/issues allow us to illustrate the themes and topics of this book in an applied way.

3. As context and circumstance are said to influence whether individuals will make or implement their ethical decisions, we look at how these contexts in particular may affect ethical decision making.

Chapter 18

Organisations, contexts, ethics and maturity

'When we don't see systems, we see individual personalities. Our explanations are personal, and our solutions are personal. Fix the individual. When we see systems, quite another world opens up to us. What we have here is not a personal problem but a social disease—a disorder of the "we".'

(Oshry, 1995, p. 167)

'Research has found that a team that is made up of two emotionally unstable and two stable members performed as badly as a group of all unstable members…negative relationships have a greater impact on job satisfaction and organisational commitment than do neutral or even positive relationships.'

(Kusy and Holloway, 2009, p. 18)

'I once managed a portfolio company for a private equity firm. Its chairman didn't teach me many things but he made up for it by teaching me one big lesson. One day he told me that one of my executive directors had been rude to "an outsider". I apologised and said I would deal with it. 'You're not getting it,' he said. 'What I'm interested in is: what is it about your behaviour that makes him think he has permission to act in this way?' I've used that story in my coaching for over a decade—ending it with either of these two questions: "What is it about your behaviour that allows your people to behave in this way?", or "What is it about your organisation that gives permission to behave in this way?" My experience over the years is that creating space for certain kinds of behaviour can quickly pervade entire institutions. It may well be started, tolerated or even ignored by the leadership.'

(Stephen Barden, personal communication)

'Leaders get the behaviour they tolerate.'

(Charan, 2011, p. 62)

As I look back on my life, I (Michael) am amazed at what little awareness I had of the dramatic impact on my behaviour of the contexts in which I lived and worked. Not only did I not understand the dynamics of those systems and groups, but I had no insight into how they influenced (directed and determined might be better words) what I did. Growing up in a large family system of nine children and two parents made me into a systems-person, one who learned unconsciously how to read the family group dynamics, and who knew instinctively how to play the system to get what I wanted. I learned, without knowing I had learned, where power was in a system and how to manipulate it to get what I wanted. Then and later in life, I rarely got caught as I travelled, chameleon-like, throughout systems, changing colour as needed. I knew how to transgress without getting caught, how to play one person against another, and how to get what I wanted without appearing demanding. All that tacit knowing came from my experience of living and growing up in an organisation called the family.

My systems journey gives life to the idea that when you have no awareness of the systems you are part of, you are a prisoner of them — 'the fish is the last to know about the sea'. As I look back with more self-awareness and honesty, I see that my political self was less than ethically aware and often ethically inactive. In one organisation of which I was a part some horrible things happened. Individuals formed little cliques of best friends and became entrenched within these safe silos. No attention, awareness, empathy or consideration was given to those who, for whatever reason, were alone or isolated. They were left to fend for themselves. Scape-goating took place, but went unrecognised and unnoticed. There was a lot of hidden suffering but, content with my involvement in the system, I failed to recognise its downside. It suited me or I was able to arrange it to suit me. It has made me aware of how easily unethical behaviour can slip unnoticed into organisations and groups, and after a while becomes an accepted part of the overall work of the individuals, groups and teams that make up the collective. The 'good people' who make up this system would be shocked were someone to call them ethically immature or ethically negligent.

If Bateson (1972) is right when he says that contexts can shape meaning, then we need to look to the contexts in which human behaviour occurs in order to make sense of that behaviour. For most of us those contexts involve the families, groups, teams, partnerships and organisations, private, public and voluntary to which we belong. While individual ethics apply when men and women make ethical decisions on behalf of themselves, organisational ethics apply when someone, a couple, a group or a collective makes ethical decisions on behalf of an organisation to which they belong.

Egan and Cowan (1979) tell the story of upstream/downstream helping. A man walking along a river bank notices someone struggling in the water. He dives in and pulls the person to safety on the bank. As he is resuscitating the individual he hears another cry and sees another person in the river. He dives in again and hauls out another unfortunate individual. After pulling out two more drowning individuals from the river, he is seen to walk away. Someone shouts to him, 'Hey, there is another person in the river' to which he replies, 'I am going upstream to see who is pushing these people into the river'. Egan and Cowan use this example to look at where we put our efforts in helping individuals—do we sort out the immediate emergency or do we look further into the system to see systemic causes to individual problems? Most of us would see both types of intervention as necessary; however, it takes more effort to sort out the dysfunctional organisation than to deal with and support the individual who is a casualty of an organisation. Individuals adopt the characteristics of the unethical contexts in which they live and work. Dysfunctional organisations can produce dysfunctional individuals and teams, and unethical organisations can produce unethical individuals and teams.

Unethical organisations

The Cloyne Report (2011) was an independent inquiry into clerical sexual abuse of children in one of the Catholic diocese in Ireland. This and several other reports, the Ryan Report (2009), the Murphy Report (2009) and the Ferns Report (2005) came to similar conclusions: that there was a systemic problem in the Catholic Church that gave rise to the horrendous physical, psychological, emotional and sexual abuse of children, 'And in doing so, the Cloyne Report excavates the dysfunction, disconnection, elitism—the narcissism—that dominates the culture of the Vatican to this day. The rape and torture of children were downplayed or 'managed' to uphold instead the primacy of the institution, its power, standing and 'reputation'… This calculated, withering position being the polar opposite of the radicalism, humility and compassion upon which the Roman Church was founded (Kenny, 2011).

Kenny (2011) articulated what many had been saying for some time: a systemic and systematic culture of immorality had found its way into this worldwide organisation and ensured silence, collusion, immorality and hidden depths of abusiveness. How could an organisation, dedicated to spreading a message of love, care, compassion and concern descend to such depths of in-built unethical behaviour? How could monitors and guardians of ethical stances not notice when their own behaviours had moved far away from ethical excellence?

This is just one example of what could be considered an unethical organisation. Others abound. In 2001, the collapse of the giant company Enron unveiled an organisation built on unethical practices: profits were exaggerated, debts were concealed and immoral accountancy practices were used. Of interest, Enron had a detailed 64-page code of ethics and its corporate mission statement subscribed to values such as respect, integrity, communication and excellence. With the fall of Enron came the fall of Arthur Anderson, the accounting firm responsible for auditing the accounts of Enron, among others. Founded in 1913 by Arthur Anderson, the firm was built on a strong base of ethical accounting recounted in a story about Arthur Anderson himself. Asked to sign off on accounts that were flawed, Arthur Anderson is recorded as saying, 'not for all the money in America', even though this particular account involved a major client. 'Think straight, talk straight' was his motto (Mele, 2009, p. 3), and his stance and the integrity of his company resulted in their successful expansion into 84 countries. In 2001, many years later, this same firm was found guilty of security violations in waste management, and a year later found guilty of obstructing justice in the Enron saga. It heralded the end of Arthur Anderson. It seems these were not just one-off issues. A radical change had occurred within the culture of Arthur Anderson, from the early days where 'earnings were sacrificed for integrity' to a culture where greed pervaded all sections of the organisation. No one set out to change the culture of Anderson, Enron or the Catholic Church. However, over time, a climate like a mist enveloped the organisation and the members breathed in the toxic environments that changed their way of thinking and being. The mist obscured their perceptions and they either did not see, or refused to see, what was there. Organisational culture and group climates are infectious: members 'catch' the unconscious moods, norms and emotions of the organisation and live them out in their everyday lives without awareness.

Were lessons learned? The worldwide banking collapse approximately seven years later seems to indicate that practices within the banking communities were far from ethically sound and little learning had been transferred from previous experiences. The recent BP scandal in the Bay of Mexico highlighted further unethical practices — short cuts were taken to save money to the detriment of safety. There are many other organisations that have hit the headlines because of immoral, poor or unethical practices. Amongst these are British Airways and their 'dirty tricks' campaign against Virgin Atlantic, the 'expenses scandal' amongst MPs in the British Government, and the recent phone-hacking scandal at the *News of the World* (owned by News International).

We can step beyond a consideration of unethical organisations to the horrendous cruelty and behaviour by countries against their own citizens and against other countries. The rise of Nazism in Germany created concentration camps, the break-up of the former Yugoslavia saw scenes of ethnic cleansing, and the images of genocide in Rwanda stay with us. Less talked of, but just as poignant, was the situation in Turkey. Under the

Ottoman rule, Christian Armenians were seen as second-class citizens. In 1915, a law was passed to confiscate their property and Armenians were marched from Turkey to the Syrian town of Deir ez Zor. One and a half million Armenians were killed in concentration camps near Turkey's border with Syria (see Baron-Cohen, 2011, p. 9). This was another holocaust in the twentieth century alongside the Jewish holocaust during the Second World War.

These are a few examples, from many, of where organisations, groups, institutions and corporations were what we call 'systemically' unethical. This means there is not just one, or a few, or even many individuals who are unethical, but that a climate or culture of unethical practice pervades the organisation. If ethical behaviour emerges from ethical character, and ethical character is forged in our communities of practice, then the character (culture) of organisations can have a great impact on individual behaviour and, at times, skew it towards the harmful.

Individual or organisational?

There has been much debate about whether the same requirements can be made of organisations as for individuals. Can organisations be required to act 'ethically' when they are a structure, not a being? Former British Prime Minister, Margaret Thatcher, once famously remarked that '...there is no such thing as society. There are individual men and women, and there are families. And no government can do anything except through people, and people must look to themselves first' (Keay, 1987, p. 8). In an obvious sense, she was right. Should we think similarly that there is no such thing as an organisation, only individuals? An alternative view is that organisations have enough structural complexity to be considered agents who can be called to account for their actions. An organisation is, by definition, organised, which means it can make collective decisions and act on those decisions. They may not be held responsible in the same way as individuals, but can be held responsible in ways appropriate to organisations (Kitson and Campbell, 1996). 'Because organizations are not natural persons, formal rules are important in establishing their moral status. Although they have their own cultures, organizations do not possess emotions, a conscience, intellect or will. They are composed of individuals who have these things, but...private judgements can bring calamity on a society or organisation' (Grace and Cohen, 2009, p. 236).

While organisations cannot be held accountable in the same way as individuals, they can be held to account for policies and practices (e.g., Shell and pollution, Nike's practice of moving factories offshore to take advantage of cheaper wages). Although individuals may be charged with behaviours (e.g., in the News of the World phone-tapping scandal), this may reflect strongly on the leadership of the organisation. In such examples, one part of the organisational system cannot be seen as separate to all other parts. No doubt, there is such a thing as 'collective responsibility' where more than one person has to shoulder the blame or the responsibility for what happens in a large group of people. Beyond these examples, is it ever right to talk about the ethical or unethical organisation?

What happens in organisations that give rise to unethical behaviours? We suggest the following possibilities and influences:

Systemic view: This approach views organisations as systems where behaviour becomes part of the system itself. It is said the system is more than the sum of its parts, i.e., there is something beyond the assessment of one individual that is at play when a group of individuals come together in common enterprise. Werhane (2002) argues that systems are defined by the 'mental models or mindsets' that operate within any given system, and establish parameters through which experience, or a certain set of experiences, is organised or filtered. Through these mental models that operate on individual and system levels, aspects of experience are selected for attention, and those aspects that do not fit the 'filter' are bracketed and excluded. While filters can change, they can have a strong influence on, and even determine, our conscious and unconscious response to ethical situations.

Some of the more corrupt mindsets used to explain corporate misdeeds include 'moral amnesia' (Werhane, 1999) or 'moral silence, deafness and blindness' (Bird, 1996, cited in Seabright and Schminke, 2002). It has been argued that unethical workplace behaviour can take a great deal of active reasoning, planning, vengefulness, insensitivity and dehumanising of others, which flies in the face of the previous emphasis on immoral behaviour being an act of ignorance, thoughtlessness or omission (Seabright and Schminke 2002).

In Chapter 2 we summarised the famous Zimbardo and Milgram experiments. Both are relevant to the influence of context on ethical decision making. The Zimbardo experiment, which involved the construction of a fake prison and the allocation of volunteers into roles of either guards or prisoners, told us about the way in which bad contexts make people behave in ways otherwise alien to their nature. It explains why we can have 'collective madness' that 'creates closed moral universes in which the irrational suddenly becomes rational, the immoral becomes moral' (Overy, 2011, p. 663). A number of factors emerge in relation to systemic influences:

1. Ordinary people can behave in harmful and immoral ways if the context supports it.

2. Contexts can override individual characteristics at times.

3. Novel situations, in particular, are powerful in getting us to do what we would not normally do.

4. When people feel anonymous they can be induced to do what they would not usually do.

5. It is easy for the need to belong to become conformity, compliance and in-group behaviour.

6. Sometimes there are absolute ethical codes that allow no degrees of freedom, and no room for extenuating circumstances or individual (ethical) adaptation—these codes drive behaviour towards cruelty because of their inflexibility.

7. It is possible to take a stand against situational and contextual influences to act unethically.

Kusy and Holloway (2009), among others, have suggested ways in which organisations can create and support a climate that tolerates unethical behaviour and can even encourage it unconsciously:

The structure changes to accommodate the behaviour: imperceptibly, and even unconsciously, the organisation adapts to the behaviour. Examples in Nazi Germany (see Gigerenzer, 2008, p. 2) indicate how a story (or heuristic) of 'Don't break ranks' entered the military system, and even when this conformity meant violating the moral imperative of 'Don't kill innocent people', soldiers would conform to be seen as part of their group. Likewise in the Catholic Church, an ethos of clericalism (priests can do no wrong) led to a culture of collusive silence, even when those in authority knew about child sexual abuse. Over time, this pervasive silence can 'pull in' innocent people. Slowly, the organisation begins to tolerate unethical behaviour so that it becomes an accepted (or at least tolerated) practice.

Individuals in key positions in the organisation influence thinking and reactions: toxic leaders set up toxic practices that become part of the system. Often a centralised authority that demands obedience results in a culture of compliance and acceptance, even when behaviours are immoral. Religious cults often set out to do away with independence among members, thereby being able to operate without challenge. As Kusy and Holloway (2009) suggest, 'Toxic personalities are part of a complex system, which is the source of their power. Therefore, a solid grounding in systems dynamics is required to combat their hold on the organisation' (p. 10).

Gellerman (1986) presents four rationalisations to explain how managers justify unethical behaviour in organisations:

1. deny the activity is unethical, or even enters an ethical sphere

2. claim the activity is in the best interest of the organisation and employees would be expected to undertake this activity for this reason

3. maintain the activity will never be made public, or the person or organisation found out

4. suggest the organisation or company will back the person who undertakes the activity because the activity helps the company.

Even when 'good people' are in charge or around, often they are unaware of when unethical behaviour takes place, and even when they are aware, they may not realise its implications. In the Catholic Church, many leaders tolerated priest paedophiles and simply changed them from place to place to avoid having their deeds discovered. In that way, they contributed to the unethical behaviour and colluded with perpetrators. 'Ethical fading' is a term used to indicate situations where questions are not asked and moral discomfort is discounted.

Secrecy, silence and collusion: these often maintain the behaviour of the organisation. Harvey (1996) in *The Abilene Paradox and other Meditations on Management,* writes on this concept of collusion—how easy it is for us all to be passive, silent and comply with what is happening around us, even when we disagree with it privately. Two chapters of his book speak to this in particular: Eichmann in the Organisation and The Organisation as a Phrog Farm (he spells the word 'frog' as 'phrog' so as not to insult real frogs). Both chapters outline how easily a culture of 'I only did what I was told' can become endemic in groups and organisations. Denial enters into the organisation and unethical behaviour is rationalised, as is collusion.

'Power over' is used to keep individuals afraid and compliant. Machiavelli, in the Middle Ages, was asked to advise the king on how he could stay in power. Since this time, his famous book, *The Prince,* has been the 'bible' for those who want to wield power over others. He presents the strong leader as one who motivates through fear and separation. 'Fiefdoms' emerge in organisations where individuals enjoy a sense of power and separation from the rest of the organisation, and use this personal power effectively without accountability (Pilgrim, unpublished paper).

'Groupthink' is a term devised by Janis (1972) to describe a feature that can happen in groups of people. As group members try to minimise conflict and work toward harmony, compliance and intolerance of alternative views can become the order of the day. Groupthink is a psychological demand on members of an organisation to not rock the boat, but to join together. At its most positive, it can result in a strong, cohesive body moving in the same direction, a group that is often benign, productive and bonding. At its most negative, it can become a closed system where dissent or disagreement is

not tolerated, and those who do not align with the majority are excluded or punished. Groupthink often results in group blindness. Janis (1972) defined it as, 'A mode of thinking that people engage in when they are deeply involved in a cohesive in-group, when the members' strivings for unanimity override their motivation to realistically appraise alternative courses of action' (p. 9). Hart (1998) developed a concept of groupthink as 'collective optimism and collective avoidance'. Groupthink can result in cruelty and harm. Closed or corrupt systems can exclude important data simply because 'this is the way we do things around here'. In the exploration and resolution of ethical dilemmas, culture, norms and peer relationships all influence ethical development and understanding. Of course, this may be very limiting as a closed group can self-reference constantly and have no mechanism for internal critique. Even at our best, systems theory signals that we are not independent operatives. What does this mean for how we understand and assess ethical responsibility and accountability?

Image becomes more important than anything else: the reputation, image and public persona of the organisation can become the most important element and override other concerns, especially ethical ones. There are instances when those in power in organisations protect the image of the organisation at any cost. For example, some bishops in the Catholic church influenced individuals who had been abused *not* to reveal these facts publicly because of the negative image it would give to the organisation. When the image becomes the most important value, then it becomes easy to sacrifice ethical principles.

In the News of the World phone-tapping scandal, it has been argued that the corrupt behaviour arose from a skewed loyalty to the paper and the desire to make it number one with readers at any cost. If the only measure of success is the popularity of the paper, then ethics (as well as other costs) become hidden from view.

Staff become more important than the product or delivery: Martin (1984) referred to the 'corruption of care', which he defined as occurring when 'the primary aims of care—the cure of alleviation of suffering—have become subordinate to what are essentially secondary aims, such as the preservation of order, quiet and cleanliness'. He describes how in many caring organisations the care and welfare of the clients/patients can become subordinated to the needs of staff. This can be seen also in established institutions such as education where many excellent ideas to support the education of children never see the light of day because they don't suit the teaching staff. What has happened in such organisations (and companies) is that the purpose and aim of the organisation gets highjacked and the needs of the deliverers (the staff) become predominant. In the light of this, the customer is neglected and, in some instances, abused.

Task hatred and task corruption

Organisations are formed to not only undertake a primary task, such as producing particular products or services, but also need to attend to internal functions to ensure their survival. Beyond the common experience of letting the worst jobs slide to the bottom of the in-tray, task avoidance can be a sign of more significant and potentially sinister processes. For the task to become corrupt, Chapman (1999) argues that the change to the task needs to be motivated destructively, whether at a conscious or unconscious level. Changes to the task can involve:

- *substitution*, where people make a secondary task the primary task, e.g., Chapman (1999) gives an example where steelworkers became so captured by industrial action that it became their primary focus
- *amputation*, where parts of the task are 'lopped off' in favour of other parts of the task, e.g., Elisabeth worked with an organisation that provided welfare and housing services to people recently released from jail. Staff would interview people who were about to be released with regard to their needs upon re-entering society. The staff were treated very badly by prison staff when they went to visit, being seen as 'do-gooders' for people who 'aren't worth it'. As a result, staff actively and openly hated going. After a while, staff 'forgot' to go and visit, or were 'too busy'. On these occasions, released prisoners simply came straight to the organisation for their assessment and referral. Over time, this became the norm, until eventually there was no mention of ever going to the jail, and it was as if the practice never existed. Management seemed to never notice that anything had changed, even though a part of the service had been cut out altogether, and clearly the client group would have valued the reassurance of a pre-release visit to guarantee aspects of their future
- *simulation*, where there is the appearance of doing the task rather than genuine task engagement, e.g., in one organisation Elisabeth was involved with, a director of mission was appointed after many client complaints. As this role was largely excluded from any key decision-making processes, its importance was suggested at a symbolic, rather than a functional, level
- *mutation*, where the primary task of a system is twisted to such a degree that the doer of the task is damaged in some way, e.g., Chapman (1999) writes of her experience of marketing a charity

and realising that the charity was more interested in lining its own coffers than delivering services to clients.

Chapman (1999), notes the circumstances in which hatred of task is more likely to occur:

- *When the task itself is hated*, i.e., the work is, by any measure, deeply unpleasant.

- *Where a personality or personal history of individuals links to a characteristic of the task to produce hatred,* e.g., in the case of Bob, who became an accountant (when he had really wanted to become an actor) because all the sons in his family became accountants and joined the family business. He was given all the accounts of creative arts organisations to appease him, but it fostered his jealousy and resentment, and resulted in poor service delivery.

- *Where the task becomes corrupted to the point of impossibility*, e.g., Chapman (1999) gives the example of the Catholic church, which she argues has moved its task from 'standing for the people before God' to 'standing in for God with the people', which means the church has claimed an impossible organisational task, i.e., that of being God. She sees this as having occurred over nine centuries, which says a lot about the 'ethical fading' mentioned earlier, but also how the original task can get 'forgotten' when there is compelling new history to view.

- *System pathology and the power of yearning:* Chapman notes that every organisation has unpleasant, or even hated, tasks. The problem is not whether they exist, but how the hatred is processed, e.g., how do traffic wardens or employees of tobacco companies talk about the load they carry in fulfilling a work task that they perhaps have mixed feelings about? How is organisational yearning managed: the longing for something else (a conflict-free workplace); being deserving but unrecognised; identifying with the cause or client group, and experiencing a feeling of being 'ripped off'? How are such feelings talked about within the organisation?

Chapman concludes that these phenomena, if uncontained, unmanaged, or unnoticed, can result in corruption of the role, boundaries, values, and ultimately, the employees themselves. This process can be managed through conscious reflection and engagement of the issues—we will come back to this theme again.

Scapegoating individuals to mask organisational behaviour

Gigerenzer (2008) makes the point that many organisations 'force' staff to engage in activities that protect the business, but are not necessarily good or ethical practice in service delivery. He provides many medical examples of situations where there was a double standard (having to prescribe what in their professional opinion was not helpful) that squeezed the practitioner between the proverbial rock and hard place when facing their patient. In one example related to overservicing for breast cancer screening, 'Not a single female doctor in this group (of 60 physicians) participated in screening, and no male physician said he would do so if he were a woman. Nevertheless, almost all physicians in this group recommended screening to women' (p. 43). He gives a further example: 'The family doctor said that he now has no choice but to overtreat patients, even at the risk of doing unnecessary harm, in order to protect himself' (p. 43). Gigerenzer uses the term 'moral split brains' to describe how organisations put employees in situations of a double-bind, where they are supposed to do one thing (give the best treatment to their patient), but feel forced to do something else (to safeguard themselves).

It is easy for organisations to move towards a reductionism that uses 'the bad apple' explanation for unethical behaviour. This misses the cultural and systemic nature of organisations and what happens within them, and exonerates the organisation by blaming individuals for organisational problems.

Awareness of the shadow side of organisations

Egan (1994), in *Working the Shadow Side: A Guide to Positive Behind-the-Scenes Management*, identifies the shadow-side of an organisation as the 'unspoken, unacknowledged, behind-the-scenes stuff that stands in the way of getting things done' (p. xi). As we see it, unethical behaviour takes place in the shadow side of the organisation, which represents the opposite of our positive intentions and practices, the 'negative side', or the 'dysfunctional organisation'. The following are examples of when that shadow side has become corrupt:

- police who break the law
- educational systems that neglect the education of their own staff
- helping professionals who neglect their own self-care
- health-care staff such as nurses and doctors who may be required to work double shifts to look after others while their own health suffers

- religious institutions where religious people become self-centred and instead of loving, begin to abuse.

In one example, a group of senior, experienced psychologists worked in a group practice founded by Peter, the managing director. Peter's wife ran the office. Every week there was a compulsory group lunch offered as part of team building for the group. The office secretary became aware that Peter was having a sexual relationship with a client who had come to the practice through an employee assistance programme with one of their major organisational customers. The practice income largely depended on this contract. One by one, the secretary approached each of the practice members, looking for a solution (she didn't want to mention it herself as she was good friends with Peter's wife). No one else knew what to do. They all knew that they all knew, but no one broke the silence. Everyone felt worried about their livelihood, their relationships with Peter and his wife, the damage to the client and to the profession of psychology. The lunches became silent affairs where, in the end, no one could even continue social chatter in the face of the conversation that could not be had. Eventually, there was a client complaint and the affair was exposed, releasing everyone from the silence, but not solving the problem of their own collusion, and the responsibility each held to care for that client and uphold their professional obligations.

The shadow side emerges when:

- poor performance is not tackled
- conflict is not dealt with
- difficult personalities are not confronted
- rules are not enforced, or are done so unjustly
- we preach what we do not practice
- promotions are not based on merit.

Five areas of the shadow side of an organisation may be implicated.

1. *Organisational culture*: the difference between the published and espoused beliefs, values and norms, and the unpublished or covert assumptions, beliefs, values and norms.

2. *Personal styles*: e.g., aggressive style, arrogant style, shaming and humiliating style. Personal agendas can be in conflict with the organisational agenda: does an individual's personal style add value to the organisation or is it in opposition to it? Jeffrey Pfeffer (1994) studied the dynamics behind the success of companies that provided the greatest return to stockholders over a 20-year period (1972–92). The principal factor in the success of the five top companies, he discovered, was the way they managed people—knowing

when to intervene and confront, when to support and guide, when to coach, when to counsel, when to leave things alone, when to change direction.

3. *Social systems:* what kind of systems are there in our organisation — in-groups, out-groups, cliques, tribes, warring factions? Social systems in organisations are discussed rarely and can be very costly — it can seem impossible to get rid of a person because they belong to particular groups.

4. *Politics:* power issues, competition for scarce resources, turf protection, members and groups who want to prevail. The politics of self-interest where covert, self-interested deals are done can be included here. How do we negotiate?

5. *Hidden organisation:* what are the hidden organisational activities — getting around the rules, fudging the budget, renaming things, creative accountancy?

We can find ourselves in the shadows when we are unaware of what is going on, when things have been intentionally hidden, and when we have blind spots, naivety, or don't want to know. Much unethical behavior happens in the shadow side of organisations. When the meaning of this behaviour and the impact it has on individuals and teams goes unrecognised, we miss how and where unethical mindsets and practices enter an organisational setting.

How do you identify the shadow side of an organisation? Some useful questions to consider are:

- what is covert?
- what is not discussed around here?
- what do you *not* have permission to talk about?
- what is unspeakable?

Creating ethical organisations

How might the six components in ethical maturity help us create more enlightened and mature ethical decision making within organisational settings?

COMPONENT 1: BUILDING ETHICAL SENSITIVITY AND MINDFULNESS IN ORGANISATIONAL SETTINGS

For organisations to reach for and remain ethically mature, the abilities of conscious deliberation, vigilance and mindfulness seem to be the most essential. In the examples of unethical organisations given above, poor ethical standards entered organisations mostly by default. In not noticing what is happening, in not monitoring and taking 'moral pulses', poor standards emerge and become the norm. When they are noticed, it is often with some shock. The question 'How did we manage to get here?' is often asked after the event with sincere dismay that so few could see what was happening.

How do we take the moral pulse of an organisation? How can an organisation ensure its ethical values are incorporated into its cultural climate and infiltrate all working aspects of the organisation?

> 'An organisation which has thought through its ethical stance and developed a fuller, better managed approach to ethical issues is more likely to be producing ethical behaviour on a regular basis than one which has only a reactive approach. Congruence between espoused values and values in practice is crucial. How an organisation responds to unethical conduct by one of its members will also be a good indicator of the strength of its ethical pulse' (Kitson and Campbell, 1996, p. 120).

Good governance involves inclusive practices that bring all relevant parties into the process. To strive for above-average performance is important, but is only achievable if the culture is one in which the basic goodness of people can be fostered; usually, this involves a supportive social environment in which people can reflect consciously on their actions and operations. Such a culture privileges education over regulation, and allows opportunities to take responsibility for individual action (Longstaff, 1996b). The two enemies of such a culture are a general lack of integrity within people or the organisation, where people say one thing but do another, and through a lack of thought in which people do things because 'that's the way we do things around here' (Longstaff, 1996a). Organisations can develop checks and balances on their thinking through regular dialogue with their business and professional networks, and by including people from other professions/industries on management committees, and lay people in any review process. There is said to be a non-linear relationship between an individual's sense of moral propriety and the tacit expectations of their colleagues. 'This means that both affect, and are affected, by the other... colleagues may reciprocally influence one another's moral sensibilities in unexpected ways' (Painter-Morland, 2006, p. 92). We need to be around each other in a range of forums and discussions to allow important information to arise. Sometimes what needs to be known, or can engender change, comes about through an unconscious shift in sensibilities. At other times, such as in a written code, we can be explicit and clear with what we mean to say.

Some specific checks may include these.

- Does the organisation have a code of ethics or an ethical framework to which all subscribe, know about, believe in and practice? What happens when these practices are not adhered to?

- What about espoused values and values in practice?
- Can we look at the values, attitudes and beliefs of the organisation?
- Are goals, policies, structures and the strategies to achieve them articulated?
- What are the everyday, accepted, unchallenged, processes and procedures?

Kitson and Campbell (1996) suggest four ways to build ethical climates within organisations (corporate governance).

1. Conduct an ethics audit. This self-assessment exercise identifies how individuals and groups in the organisation see ethical issues. The audit can take place in different areas; policy, systems, standards and performance.
2. Create public and accessible codes/frameworks of ethics and conduct to which all staff are inducted and made aware.
3. Create structures that support ethical behaviour at all levels of the organisation, and involve accountability and responsibility. They can include ethics committees and methods by which key people will know if unethical practices are taking place, e.g., how to support whistleblowers. Ethical behaviour will be rewarded publicly (through promotions, salary, etc.) and unethical behaviour will be seen to be punished.
4. Unethical behaviour is dealt with promptly and clearly according to guidelines.

Given it is so difficult, when one is part of an organisation, to see and make sense of what is happening in that organisation, a helpful way to create some ethical vigilance is to have a 'guardian angel' or a 'critical friend' whose job is to monitor, notice, articulate and give feedback when shoddy practice or less-than-acceptable moral behaviours take place. Departments in some organisations act as critical supports to other departments on new and creative projects—their job is to critique and play 'devil's advocate' to new ideas, future plans and normal workings for each other. The idea is to have someone, or another team, take a different and objective position and perspective. It would be an interesting idea to have 'ethical maturity monitoring' become part of that role.

Component 2: Discerning and making ethical decisions in organisational settings

Two major questions for organisations are 'Who makes ethical decisions?' and 'How are they made on behalf of the group or groups involved?' Are individuals expected to make decisions on behalf of the company: on their own, with others, or as a result of consultation? How are these decisions arrived at, and what processes are in place to protect the rights of employees, customers, shareholders, the environment and other players in the ethical equation? Despite the fact that many organisations have codes of ethics, they often lack an individual or group whose task it is to align the decisions made with the values, mission statements and tasks of the organisation. Ethics committees can act as organisational monitors for what is ethically sustainable in today's world.

Many problem-solving models are presented for making ethical decisions. Nash (1981) offers one that is typical and can be used in organisational settings.

- Do you have an accurate definition of the problem?
- How would you define the problem if you stood on the other side of the fence?
- How did the situation occur in the first place?
- To whom and what do you give your loyalty as a person, and as a member of the corporation?
- What is your intention in making this decision?
- How does this intention compare with the probable result?
- Whom would your decision or action injure?
- Can you discuss the problem with the affected parties before you make your decision?
- Are you confident that your decision will be as valid over a long period of time?
- Could you discuss your decision with your boss, your CEO, the board of directors, your family, society as a whole?
- What is the symbolic potential of your action: if understood, if misunderstood?
- Under what circumstances would you allow exceptions to your stand?

In order to embrace such a challenging and self-reflective model, organisations need to:

- stay with emotions (organisations are not good at this)
- take time to reflect and review
- listen to feedback
- allow disagreement and discussion
- listen to those who are whistle-blowers
- problem solve and make deliberate choices
- establish ethical watchdogs.

Since ethical decisions fall within the overall organisational decision-making process, it can be valuable for organisations to review this process. Are decisions made top-down? In other words, do those in power and with the designated role of manager or director make the decisions that others implement? How much consultation takes place before decisions are made? How much difference, disagreement and taking of opposite sides is allowed or even encouraged? As Oshry (1995) points out, the clarion cry of the 'bottoms' — those who have to do the work — is that they have no power to influence what happens in their organisations and, therefore, no participation in decision making that matters. Even when they know things are going wrong, they do not share these with authorities for many reasons: because they don't see it as their job to do so; because they can rejoice in watching their managers fail; because they are afraid of the consequences if they are seen to disagree or be negative; or, because they don't want to be seen as bearers of bad news.

It is helpful to look at what factors influence decision making in a particular organisation. Is it the bottom-line 'profit' that is most important, or are other interests allowed to enter the decision-making process such as care of the environment, the welfare of employees, or the interests of customers?

Component 3: Implementing ethical decisions in organisational settings

We return to the organisational conundrum quoted earlier: 'Five frogs sat on a log. Four of them decided to dive into the pool. How many frogs were left on the log? The answer is: five. Why? Because in organisations the fact that you decide to do something doesn't mean it happens.' Organisations are notorious for making decisions that never see the light of day, and this includes ethical decisions. The most common reason is 'everyone is responsible and no one is responsible'. It is important to get down to details when ethical decisions have to be implemented, and questions such as the following tend to 'nail down' these details.

- Who is responsible for implementing the decision?
- When it will be implemented?
- What resources are needed to implement it, and does the person or group responsible have those resources?
- How will we know that the decision has been implemented?
- What criteria do we have for evaluating the implementation and the effectiveness of the decision once it has been implemented?
- What are the personal and professional costs?

One of us (Michael) worked as an external consultant for an organisation that repeatedly made the decision to devise a professional standards package, a code of ethics. The decision was handed from one director to another with each 'being too busy' to make it a priority or even allow it to come to the top ten of his/her 'to-do' list. Eventually, the decision was delegated to a committee, to devise and implement. I was asked to be part of this committee, which, from the beginning, was a quagmire of individuals from different departments of the company, fighting for their own territory and scoring points off other departments. Every department insisted on being represented, which resulted in a large, unwieldy group of over 30 people. You can visualise the proceedings as over 30 individuals came together to try to agree on what an ethical code might look like. At one meeting, I was so distracted from the task, and the chair person so incapable of managing the destructive process, that I did a calculation of how much it cost, in financial terms, for this body of people to have met for three occasions for approximately ten hours. My conservative estimate was that the company, to date, had spent in the region of $75,000 on this project. Of course it was not visible money—it came from salaries, expenses, etc., and therefore went unnoticed. I suggested that if they paid me for two days I would come back with an outline of a code of ethics and practice for them to consider. They agreed, it happened and, as far as I know, it is still the ethical framework that guides them. At times, organisations need outside help to create ethical structures and, in particular, to build bridges that help cross from intention to action.

COMPONENT 4: JUSTIFYING WHAT WE DO

One of the most powerful symbols of the ethical position of an organisation is the establishment and subsequent enactment of a code of ethics. Ultimately, 'the point of a code of ethics is to declare professional or organisational standards for all to see. It is an invitation for those outside the profession to judge it and its practitioners by the standards it declares. It announces to members of a profession that certain standards and values should be respected in practice. It sets a level playing field for all practitioners. It is an instrument for accountability and responsibility. And it is an affirmation of the identity of the organisation, profession or industry' (Grace and Cohen, 2009, p. 240).

Codes of ethics are usually written to enshrine minimum standards below which a professional will not operate. In reality, however, many practitioners operate well above the standard and, as a consequence, can then find the code of little use when confronted with an ethical dilemma. To call a code 'aspirational' does not mean that we hope to be ethical one day. Instead, we admit there will always be room for improvement in judgement and behaviour with respect to the values in the code, but that we aspire to get it exactly right every time. 'We realise that these things involve judgement calls and we aspire to always exhibit excellent judgement' (Grace and Cohen, 2009, p. 245). Codes do not provide an exhaustive list of rules, but rather provide guidance on some behaviours and protocols for how to approach problem solving. A professional will use their code, other research, peers and supervisors in decision making. Ultimately, both the accepted standard for professional practice and rigour in decision making will be important evidence in confident, justified, ethical outcomes.

Organisations can use this component in two ways. First, through open and transparent sharing of their codes of practice, ethical stances, values and ethical principles in advance with others. We do not know of many companies who, in doing business with their partners, share their ethical positions from the beginning, especially if there is something that might be seen as negative. I (Michael) was part of a small team pitching for an executive coaching contract with a large bank. At our presentation we were asked about outcomes and what we could guarantee in the way of transformational learning for individuals and for the organisation. One of our team shared that executive coaching sometimes resulted in individuals leaving the company and moving on, which had been our experience in a recent company. Sometimes, she also pointed out, executive coaching resulted in individuals being more assertive, more questioning, which was not always welcomed by management. Since we were the last to present (of five groups tendering for the job), it was fascinating that in the feedback we received we were told we were the only group that had taken the initiative to describe possible negative outcomes as a result of executive coaching. Ethical maturity behoves individuals and companies to be honest about all outcomes, not just the positive ones they want to highlight.

In addition to sharing their values beforehand, organisations can spend time after the event reviewing decisions they have made, not simply to justify them, but to open them up for discussion around the process and content of those decisions. Some examples of good retrospective questions are: Why did we make that decision? Why did we make it that way? What happened as a result of the decision we made? How might we make it differently and perhaps more maturely? To answer these questions without scapegoating or blaming can generate valuable insights that can be drawn upon for future decision making.

COMPONENT 5: LIVING WITH THE DECISIONS MADE

There are times when companies and organisations have to 'make good' the damage done when they are, or are seen to be, responsible for unethical behaviour. There are now numerous examples of apologies as part of righting wrongs, for example when the Australian Prime Minister issued a public apology on behalf of Australians to the Aboriginal people; when the Catholic Church at its highest level (the Pope), and at more local levels (bishops), have made public apologies for the unethical behaviour of some of its clergy. Apart from the apologies there is often restitution, e.g., as a result of the BP oil spillage in the Gulf of Mexico, BP set aside billions of dollars to 'make good' environments and recompense individuals and groups affected by the oil spill.

Living with ethical decisions, already made and implemented, can present a number of challenges to organisations. First, it may be confirming and affirming that the decision was a good decision and the best we could make in the circumstances. This process adds to our collective, organisational pool of wisdom and can be called upon in the future when similar decisions need to be made. Second, it may mean living with decisions we know to be less than mature and reflecting on what happened that might have lead to that conclusion. Sometimes we live with the fact that our decision was inadequate, made for dubious reasons, and not in the best interests of all involved. Third, we may have to live with decisions made we now know to be wrong, but did not know at the time. Michael worked with one of the emergency services during some of the London tragedies—the King's Cross tragedy and the *Marchioness* boat disaster on the Thames. Several of the helpers had been required to make difficult life-or-death decisions about what to do and who to save. Looking back, they saw how in some circumstances they might have done things differently, but in the chaos and immediacy of the situation had to make their best choices with the limited knowledge they had at the time. Our job (as psychologists) was to help them come to terms with the choices made and to help their organisations live with those choices. Fourth, organisations may have to live with choices they made that they knew were wrong at the time and that may have resulted in harm, hurt and even death to others. This is by far the most difficult choice to live with both individually and as an organisation, and mostly, in our view, needs external help to manage the delicate processes involved.

COMPONENT 6: LEARNING FROM WHAT WE DO AND INTEGRATING
IT INTO INDIVIDUAL AND ORGANISATIONAL LIFE LEARNING

The US Army has a centre called CALL (the Centre for Army Lessons Learned), a central agency that collects the learning from individuals and groups in the field and co-ordinates that learning. The learning is then sent back into the field so that all may be benefit. Organisations could do well to follow suit and set up CLL centres (Centres for Lessons Learned), where information could be collected and the whole organisation would benefit from the experience of others making and implementing ethical decisions. In turn, this process could create an organisational moral character, which in turn would influence all its members.

Learning from decisions made is one of the most important learnings for organisations: not to do so often results in repeating the same behaviours. Learning from the past, or from decisions made, is not an easy process and often demands an honesty and openness that can leave organisations vulnerable. It is here that organisations can say all the right words (and even make the right apologies) for past mistakes, but may have learned little or nothing from the experiences they have gone through. There is something about how open we are to using our organisational experiences to mine out ways of working in the future that are ethically mature. For some companies, learning from experience means finding out who is at fault and sacking them, often claiming that there was 'one bad apple' in the bag that caused the problems. Learning from decisions made means learning systemically about who and what we are as an organisation and trying to make systemic sense of why events happened as they did.

Learning from experience in organisational settings often needs facilitation.Organisations can be too blind or collusive to open up their experience as a learning forum. Skilled outsiders can lead them gently to look at what happened and 'mine out' the processes that will build a more ethical company where lived and real-time experience becomes a vehicle for learning.

Conclusion

Moral knowledge is acquired through an ongoing process of trial and error. Beliefs, perceptions and regulations together constitute the moral culture of an organisation, informing the moral sensibilities of individual members. 'Moral agency does not reside in an isolated individual agent. Instead, it is a thoroughly relational affair' (Painter-Morland, 2006, p. 90). We can expect that wherever our organisations are at developmentally, and wherever our documentation is up to, we have to think, rethink, discover, reflect and learn together, over and over again. This should not be a burden and is, instead, what makes dialogue about ethics so interesting.

Chapter 19
Bought and sold
The ethics of gifts

'Corruption means bribery, extortion, fraud, deception, collusion, cartels, abuse of power, embezzlement, trading in influence, money-laundering and other similar activities.'

(Private communication, anti-corruption policy, UK company)

Introduced to Parliament in 2010, the Bribery Act came into force in Britain in July 2011. Its aim was to impose 'zero tolerance of bribery and corruption in all areas of commercial activity, affecting the way any business with a UK presence deals with public officials and economic partners anywhere in the world' (Rose anad Slade, 2010, p. 1). This act, for the first time in British history, gathers all the past and current relevant provisions into 'one coherent legislative instrument on bribery, containing four concise criminal offences' (Rose and Slade, 2010, p. 2). It is not beyond its time.

In order to create business partnerships, many companies, especially in dealing with other countries, have been compelled to conform to how business is conducted in these countries. They had little choice, or so they told themselves. The practices of many business routines in other countries and other companies were corrupt and unethical, falling within the definition of corruption outlined above. Bribery, facilitation payments, grease payments, introduction money, bid rigging, price-fixing were, and still are, the order of the day in many business contexts. In fact, a league table of corrupt countries scores 178 countries on their perceived level of corruption. The 2010 Corruption Perceptions Index shows that nearly three-quarters of the 178 countries in the index score below 5, on a scale from 10 (highly clean) to 0 (highly corrupt). These results indicate a serious corruption problem (see www.transparency.com).

Denmark, New Zealand and Singapore are tied at the top of the list with a score of 9.3, followed by Finland and Sweden at 9.2. Bringing up the rear is Somalia with 1.1, slightly trailing Myanmar and Afghanistan at 1.4, and Iraq at 1.5.

Transparency International has noted that the recent financial crisis has had a negative impact on bribery and corruption, and make the point that all nations need to bolster their good governance mechanisms. Their message is clear, 'Across the globe, transparency and accountability are critical to restoring trust and turning back the tide of corruption. Without them, global policy solutions to many global crises are at risk.'

The World Bank has published a report entitled: *The Puppet Masters: How the corrupt use legal structures to hide stolen assets and what to do about it* (Van der Does de Willebois *et al.*, 2011). The report explains that when corruption is rife in a company it becomes acute and relies on corporate legal structures (such as companies, foundations, trusts, complex money trails, strings of shell companies, and other spurious legal structures) to conceal ownership—hence the 'Puppet Master' title. The report lists 150 cases of 'grand corruption' and estimates a concealed ownership of 50 billion US dollars. The *Economist* (October 29th, 2011) lists the ten main culprits where deceit and anonymity has been used or abused to make immense profits. Top of the list is the USA, followed by Switzerland, Britain and the Bahamas.

From an ethical perspective, the norm in many organisations seems to be, 'Let us find out and do what we can legally get away with, and let's see how we can find legal loopholes to help us make as much money as possible'. Some go well beyond any legal requirements. This is often filed under the category of 'good business'. For many companies, the best test of a successful enterprise is the financial bottom line; if your designated duty is to deliver profit to shareholders, then how do you argue restrictions of trade based on ethics if it interferes with profit? If you have the capacity and opportunity to bend the rules, and thus increase your company deliverables, how far should you go? How far can you go, with your bosses affirming your methods, rather than turning a blind eye to practices they will say later were your independent decisions?

In this chapter we begin with an exploration of gift giving in its broadest cultural and organisational contexts. We then turn our attention to the way this plays out locally, interpersonally, in small teams, in private practice, and in our social and service relationships.

Ethical relativism

Those who argue some basis for different rules in different countries and contexts often use 'ethical relativism' to support their argument, so it is crucial we explore this philosophical tradition and its role in ethical decision making.

Ethical relativism is the belief that moral values are relative to particular cultures and cannot be judged outside that culture (Hinman, 2008). In this frame, particular moral values are not universal and are not absolute (Grace and Cohen, 1998). For example, in communities where there is accepted polygamy, or different rules about dress, or the speed limit, or national service, it is considered respectful to accept the notion that 'when in Rome, do as the Romans do'. Even if we do not agree with national service, or capital punishment, or living in communes, for the most part it is not for us (i.e., people outside those countries and cultures) to judge or intervene. It is important to understand rules and their meaning, for example, not wearing shoes or going hatless when it would afford offence, not climbing Uluru when it offends Aboriginal people, accepting a lai when arriving in Hawaii or Fiji. This we might say, is part of understanding culture and community when we travel, and is often the source of many interesting and rich experiences we can cherish when comparing other societies with our own on our return home.

It can be attractive to support ethical relativism because of its apparent support for toleration and the notion that it means being 'non-judgemental' (Longstaff, 1997). It can be seen to be very much about the 'live and let live' ideal; about acceptance of moral diversity. However, at its most extreme, the position that 'everything is relative' can suggest that one value cannot be greater than another, or that one cannot have a judgement or opinion in deciding between one thing and another at all. If this were the case, it would have serious consequences for human rights and social responsibility. There would be no basis to intervene if others were suffering or disadvantaged by extreme governments' practices such as genital mutilation, fiscal mismanagement, or natural disasters such as drought and famine. Relativism provides a rationale to stand back, appreciate and accept differences, but can also mean standing so far back as to care less about (i.e., morally disengage from) others in our global environment. This is the difference between those who can feel for people in Somalia as fellow humans in need, and those who see that Somalia is in the hands of its own government and capacity, and it is not our business to intrude (and not our problem either).

From our home vantage point, we can have contradictory views about the customs of others, and use them when it suits us. For example, it is popular in Australia to travel to Bali for a cheap holiday. It is often said that the Balinese 'love to barter' and is a kind of sport to them. It is common to hear stories of travellers proud to have beaten down the price for some item in the market from $5 to $1. There is little thought that the Balinese may not think bartering is their sport, but the traveller's sport. Further, the

Australian tourist who could well afford $5 does not always stop to think that the Balinese may need that other $4 to feed their family for that whole week. In the bigger picture, Australians might love to travel there, but if their citizens are arrested for transgressing rules, such as drug charges, there is outrage at home for the injustice. Implicit is a suggestion that 'we find you quite endearing, but do not attempt to feel superior by imposing rules that disadvantage us'.

Grace and Cohen (1998) note that relativism in business usually involves the argument that in other countries you can't do business by your usual rules: 'You have to realise that they have different expectations, and that the only way to deal satisfactorily with them is to play by their rules. What this kind of justification often amounts to is not respect for the host culture, but excuses for inducements, secret commissions and bribes. If a person respects the religious and cultural conventions of a country…then excuses are not necessary. Genuine respect is almost always self explanatory. But the payment of inducements is anything but self explanatory; it requires excuses' (p. 21). Often the excuse is that it is the only way to get things done.

There are many well-known examples of companies taking advantage of the financial, social or educational position of other countries to make a profit, e.g., Nestlé selling excess stock of baby formula to the Third World, Nike setting up operations in Asia in order to pay cheap labour, telecommunications companies setting up call centres in India to reduce costs. On a more local level, there are many examples of older Australian men said to 'buy brides' in Indonesia, often young women looking for a fresh start in a richer nation, not realising that their older partners are expecting servitude, gratitude and dependence. Perhaps at the moment of meeting, all parties could argue that they are getting something of what they wanted, as could be said with that market bargain in Bali. However, in order to celebrate such moments you have to disengage from any contextual understanding, any real appreciation of culture and community, and instead simplify and distil that moment into 'what I want, and what I choose to think you want'. Grace and Cohen (1998) suggest that claiming the mantle of cultural difference to justify secret deals and special favours is not ethical relativism at all, but is more akin to racism.

It is important to note that while debate continues about whether anyone outside a community can ever hope to, let alone has the right to, judge the activities of another community, in practice ethical relativism does not mean that 'anything goes'. There has been a great deal of work on the establishment of universal principles that different cultures and communities might adhere to, but operationalise differently. Hence, the development of agreed human rights' charters with principles related to human worth and dignity, and care of children. Without holding on to some moral anchors—personal, company or universal—one is more at the whim of reading the local situation in ways that suit. We may be able to justify these stances at a personal level, and our parent companies might validate the improved bottom lines as a result. However, there are examples where companies later cast their employees adrift, saying they did not know what was happening in practice. Many companies employ local agents to negotiate on their behalf, in effect setting up structures to both distance themselves from efforts on the ground, but also, to justify to themselves that it is respectful to the culture to have locals negotiate for them.

Navigating a position

The United States, the United Kingdom and Australia all have legislation with regard to business operation in other countries. However, some things are morally wrong, even if they are not illegal (Grace and Cohen, 1998) and companies and individuals need to consider their own positions. Longstaff (1997) says that from the position of an ethical relativist the only test that might be applied is the degree to which people are consistent within their own system. 'Outsiders have no authority to criticise, let alone correct. Consistent with this, people need not abandon their own ethical framework just because someone else lives a different kind of life' (p. 154).

HOW MIGHT THIS OPERATE IN PRACTICE?

A corporate lawyer from a major UK company (private communication) shared how difficult it is to deal with countries where bribery is the 'cultural' norm. These 'business methods' have become so ingrained they are seen as culturally acceptable and viewed as 'the way we do business around here'. The reaction this UK company, which works in over 50 countries, has received in drawing up its anti-corruption policy is first of all one of non-acceptance. 'This is the way we do business in our culture', they are told, with the implication that if they do not follow the customary laws they will not be involved as business partners. However, when they have insisted in holding to their anti-bribery and anti-corruption policies, they have been met with some strong reactions around colonialism and the imposition of colonial methods on other countries—in this case from Asian and some African countries. These countries feel that Britain is imposing its Western ways of working on them (as it has done in its colonial past)—'cracking the colonial whip'. This company has now devised an over-riding anti-corruption policy, has built in training for all their managers, with a code of conduct for managers aligned to the policy, has taken steps to prevent corruption and bribery, and is prepared to give up business rather than compromise these values. The belief of this company is that they will lose business in the short term, but in the long term they will be able to set up new business structures with business partners who will recognise the value of their anti-corruption policies. These policies, in their view, are not just in place in order to make more money (they clearly want to do that too), but to establish their set of values as solid, predictable ways of relating to others and their environments that have the result of sustaining good human relationships.

Another reaction from other cultures to the building in of anti-corruption and anti-bribery strategies is that they accuse companies of doing the same things, but under more acceptable headings, e.g., gifts and hospitality have long been part of business communities in Britain and other Western cultures. It has been standard practice for pharmaceutical companies to use strategies such as providing doctors with journal subscriptions, sponsoring professional development and conference events, providing stationary for the office, and so on. Many companies find legitimate, legal methods of showing their appreciation to their clients, e.g., during the recent selection of the World Cup committee the British delegation made gifts of expensive handbags to the wives of visiting delegates. Many firms hire hospitality tents or boxes, at major football stadia or sporting events such as Wimbledon or golf tournaments, to entertain their best clients free of charge. Is this bribery and corruption under a different name?

Companies have tackled this too. The British company mentioned above has a gifts and hospitality policy that has gone through a number of editions. Initially, the policy was an attempt to define what was acceptable in respect to gifts up to a certain value. However, this approach was found to be unacceptable when local context was taken into account, e.g., a gift valued at £25 had a different meaning if the £25 was spent in London, where it was not seen as much money, or in Mumbai where it was seen as a considerable amount. It could be compared to the drink/driving law where you know the limit, but are never quite sure how it applies to the individual (e.g., gender and body mass affect alcohol readings). One size does not fit all. In conclusion, the company have moved to one standard around not accepting or giving gifts of any kind. They have encouraged whistleblowers to report any violations of their policy and there have been instances of senior people being dismissed when they have been found to break the anti-corruption policy rules. The SFO (Serious Fraud Office in Britain) has had some high-profile results in recent years that give hope to the fact that unethical behaviour in organisations is being taken seriously: in 2009, Mabey and Johnson were fined 3.5 million pounds for the payment of bribes; in 2008, Balfour Beatty was fined 2.25 million pounds for irregular payments to a subsidiary in Africa; and, in 2009, Aon was fined 2.5 million pounds for failing to maintain adequate systems to combat bribery and corruption. The corporate lawyer mentioned above shared that impressive steps were being taken by unlikely candidates (e.g., the arms trade) to set up policies and strategies to tackle corruption, bribery and unethical practices.

Some steps and questions

Grace and Cohen (1998) suggest some questions to evaluate situations that ring your ethical alarm bells.

- When a new situation presents itself, ask how you would normally do things at home. What might make you think this situation warrants a departure from that practice?
- Would the government and public of the host country countenance the kind of pressure you are under?
- Would our shareholders welcome disclosure of our conduct and approve us acceding to this pressure?
- Would we welcome disclosure to our government and public of secret commissions and favours?

In short, 'if you would not be ashamed to declare your actions to the world, you probably have not done anything which stands in need of an excuse' (p. 21). They state that cultural and moral relativity should not come into it at all. 'In fact, normal hospitality and gift-giving that is part of business needs no excuses or appeals to relativism' (p. 22). It is when gifts become more substantial that organisations need policies and procedures to guide employees into effective and ethical practice.

Rose and Slade (2010) have set out crucial steps to set up and maintain anti-bribery and corruption policies within organisations. They suggest:

1. Obtain commitment from the board: explicit endorsement from the highest authorities are vital to make policies work.
2. Undertake a full, global risk assessment:
   - identify projects and contracts in high-risk sectors and/or jurisdictions
   - analyse behaviour of representatives/agents
   - review relationships with public officials
   - consider business development tools (gifts/hospitality) used to win new business.
3. Develop an anti-bribery action plan:
   - start with the high-risk areas
   - devise resources for policy development and training.
4. Create a code of ethics covering:

- bribery and corruption
- anti-trust compliance
- environmental protection and Corporate Social Responsibility (CSR).

5. Create policies to guide compliance with the code which cover:
   - dealing with representatives/agents
   - gifts and hospitality
   - facilitation payments
   - contracts with competitors and third parties
   - donations and lobbying
   - handling cash and dealing with expenses.

6. Create a system of checks and controls within the financial management system to ensure implementation of policies.

7. Integrate the anti-bribery procedures into the company's structure through:
   - communication
   - training (e.g., knowing where there is an issue and how to react)
   - compliance support to staff (e.g., 'whistleblower' facilities)
   - relations with third parties (e.g., contractual provisions, advice and support)
   - HR (performance reviews should include implementation of the policies)
   - document retention (ensuring an 'audit trail' of compliance issues and how they were dealt with.)

(p. 8)

Everyday gifts

Those of us operating within a smaller network of relationships, or within smaller communities (such as a private practice in a city suburb) might think that issues of bribery and corruption only relate to big business and global markets. It is important to look at the ethical 'small print' in our own actions with respect to gifts. It is not uncommon to give and receive gifts as ways of showing appreciation, but also as ways of 'oiling the wheels' of ongoing everyday business. While none of us would baulk at the thought of giving a tip for services well received, as in a restaurant or to a tour guide (but even here the motivation could be to get preferential treatment, which sullies the ethical waters), perhaps we should think of our underlying motives when we give gifts. Why am I giving a gift at Christmas to the dustman or the postman? Is it a simple 'thank you' for your services throughout the year or might it be from a different intention, 'I am anxious that if I don't give you something for Christmas, which you expect, then you will get your own back on me in some way.' We all know the story of the disgruntled waiter who spits in the soup of a difficult customer.

What about gifts our clients give us? Is there a difference between a gift that represents 'I am thinking of you' in the middle of the working relationship, compared to a gift at the end of a contract? It has been argued that when we ask our clients to do something for us, such as change their appointment time so we can go home early, it can also have the meaning of a gift they have given us. If we 'value add' services, such as to suggest a client attend one of our other services, or that they seek the services of a recommended colleague, then is there some overt or covert kickback in that process? If a coach recommends a client takes up Amway (and is a distributor him/herself) is that being generous or intrusive with knowledge and suggestion?

It is worth asking: 'What is the meaning of this gift and why is it given or why is it received?' However, it is also important to check this out with the person involved. Our assumption that it is an appropriate gift of 'thanks' might be our desire to see it as such. Sartre's term 'bad faith' comes to mind here when something externally good (giving a gift, complimenting, doing something for someone) is done with bad or harmful intentions. It is disrespectful to the individual and to the relationship.

When is a gift more than a gift, and when does it become a bribe or a manipulation, or a hidden debt that needs repaying at some future date? We are very much victims of the 'law of reciprocation'—if I do something for you then you owe me something in return. Hence the saying, 'there are no free lunches'—they hide a request, a demand, a debt or something that needs to be done to pay off the free lunch.

It is important to tune in to your moral antennae on this issue. In one example with a trainee, I (Elisabeth) was given a gift of financial significance that felt deeply uncomfortable to accept. The gift also occurred in a context of power, where I had a strong say in graduation and work at the end of that relationship. I was clear that the person had no intention of 'buying me', but rather felt so grateful for the start the programme gave her that she wanted to show her gratitude. However, her gratitude was in proportion to her low self-esteem…she really had no need to be *that* grateful. Although I risked offending her, I had to give the gift back. It did cause a breach that was difficult to work through because of the context of power in which it was situated—exactly the problem with the gift in the first place. I am not sure we ever really got past this, but it still felt the right thing to do, compared to accepting the gift outright.

It is also important to be aware of cultural differences. For example, I (Elisabeth) do a lot of work with various culturally diverse groups, and the generosity with hospitality really stands out to me, coming from a restrained Anglo-Celtic background. Many a meeting is accompanied by fabulous food, and it is offered with a view to creating care and connection between participants. In another context, a team mentor refused to allow food at meetings as he believed it distracted from the work, although on special occasions he would send food away with the team when it was, for example, a team member's birthday. In one instance the food was part of the work and the relationship, in another it was seen to undermine the work and relationships. Further sources of ethical refelection are who gets to determine the meaning and to speak of what is allowed.

Conclusion

While much remains to be done, there seems to be greater awareness among many organisations, companies, and teams that to behave ethically is not just good business, but creates relationships and environments where connections are built on what is valuable between people and communities, rather than how one group profits at the expense of another. Ultimately, this has the direct result of company pride and staff retention. Policies, procedures, training and organisational strategies are devised so that organisations can become more ethically mature and 'care' for and guide their employees and their environments. However, the seduction to accept the overture, benefit from the circumstances or gifts is very human, and often validated openly by the effect on the financial bottom line. The mix of money, relationships and business presents complex ethical challenges. This complexity exists in equal measure for the sole practitioner as it does within company structures. It is compounded by the human desire to get something for free. What we raise here is whether we are ever really 'free' to enjoy something that has not come honestly or ethically. Even if there is not a direct sanction, there may be a blow to our moral self.

Chapter 20

The ethics of research
Enhancing knowledge and being ethically mature[1]

'A particularly striking example is the sea-water experiment...a thinking chemist could have solved it...within the space of a few hours by the use of nothing more gruesome than a piece of jelly, a semipermeable membrane and salt solution... But what happened instead? The vast armies of disenfranchised slaves were at the beck and call of this sinister assembly: and instead of thinking, they simply relied on their power over human beings...' [to put them in tanks of salt water at various temperatures to determine their limits of endurance and survival]. Opening statement for the prosecution by Brigadier General Telford Taylor at the Nuremburg military tribunals in the trial of Dr Karl Brandt and others, 1947. Brandt hanged 1948.

(Kennedy and Grubb, 2000, p. 1671)

'What was done cannot be undone. But we can end the silence. We can stop turning our heads away. We can look you in the eye and finally say on behalf of the American people what the United States government did was shameful, and I am sorry... To our African American citizens, I'm sorry that your federal government orchestrated a study so clearly racist.'

(President Bill Clinton apologising in 1997 for the Tuskegee syphilis experiment 1932–72 (Clinton, 1997))

A well-respected and internationally renowned researcher in the psychology of young people came to see me two years ago to discuss the ethics of a major project for which he had just received a large grant. He was eager to get to grips with the considerable logistical and intellectual challenges involved in the research. Towards the end of explaining the key challenges of the research, he concluded, 'Just tell me what I need to do ethically and let me concentrate on the research'. He had approached me as the faculty

---

1   This chapter is authored by Professor Tim Bond, Head of the Graduate School of Education, University of Bristol, UK.

research ethics officer for social sciences and law in a research-intensive UK university. It was clear he was disconcerted by the dismay on my face at his plea. It was one of those brief exchanges that opened a chasm of differences of view between us that might easily have ended in acrimonious dispute. As an experimental scientist working in social sciences, he had a view of ethics as a discrete and *lower* order of professional knowledge and practice, in comparison to the *higher* order of scientific knowledge derived from the rigorous application of reason to systematic observations and measurements. What was apparent immediately was the contrast between two deeply held values. He had an obvious commitment to the well-being of his research subjects. I had observed him in his earlier work with adolescents to be creative and compassionate in ways that met their needs. At the same time, he was attentive to maximising the quality of his research. He was able to demonstrate a high level of compatibility between potentially competing agendas to a level that suggested considerable ethical maturity. This explains why I was taken off guard by his request to be told what to do to satisfy ethical requirements. He seemed to communicate a view of ethics as merely a set of rules to be satisfied before the real work could begin. Another dimension to this brief exchange that struck me with even greater force was the contrast between his confidence and eminence as a scientist, and his willingness to become like a child dependent on parental guidance in matters of ethics. He was putting himself in a position of ethical immaturity. Our discussions continued long after the immediate and urgent issues at the beginning of his project had been resolved. Our dialogues provided the spark that motivated me to begin to examine the implications of research ethics as integral to research activity, and what this requires of the researcher in terms of ethical maturity.

Ethical maturity is invaluable when facing issues that arise during periods of change, or in situations where determination of the best ethical outcome is contested. The maturity to think through issues from primary principles, to determine the best available way to proceed, to implement the ethical decision, to be accountable for the actions taken, and to reflect systematically on the outcome in order to inform future ethical judgement are all characteristics associated with ethical maturity. In the changing field of practice, there are always alternative possibilities, so the idea that we can make a decision and live peacefully with the consequences may be questionable. In some ways, this chapter may make peace of mind more problematic because some of the ideas and analysis are intended to open up a possible reconsideration of some of the established norms of research ethics, especially for researchers in social sciences, but also to some degree in biomedical research. Ethical maturity is tested when we decide whether to follow an established norm, or to re-evaluate the norm and be accountable for the adoption of an alternative response.

In research ethics, it is commonplace to consider issues in the language of principles. Principles provide a convenient way to combine values with a commitment to action that is compatible with rational analysis. However, the language of principles becomes less useful when used to consider responses to large-scale shifts in ethical priorities prompted by significant historical or cultural events. It needs a conceptual language more adept at capturing broader trends, especially moments of change or disruption. I therefore introduce 'warrant' as a concept to help to identify distinctive ethical positions within research ethics. The warrant is the moral basis for an ethical stance that gives it a distinctive authority to take priority over any competing ethical claims. Warrants may gain their authority from an aversion to evil or serious wrongs, e.g., slavery, or a positive assertion of a moral or ethical vision, e.g., treating all people as equal. Research ethics has examples of how both types of warrants claim dominance in the ethical landscape for researchers. Ethical maturity requires sensitivity and watchfulness for shifting between warrants, each with their distinctive strengths and limitations, in order to inform ethical decision making within specific research projects.

The language of warrants alone can be rather impersonal, which can be useful in carefully considered and detached decision making. However, my experience is that most people become quite passionate and fully engaged in ethics discussions. To discuss ethics involves reason, emotion and intent to address what is most meaningful or sense-making about life. We often adopt a position or react against something that we represent to ourselves in stark personal terms, which draws together significant features of a more complex position or viewpoint. Do I want to be more like a person who holds *this* position, or *that* position? This process can be clarifying and merits inclusion in any representation of the lived experience of ethics. To this end, I introduce 'archetypes' as a way to communicate the moral energy within a particular warrant. Archetypes are representations of good or evil addressed by the warrant in human form. They are stereotypes that simplify complex choices into a single manageable point of reference or generalisation. They also carry all the dangers of stereotypes. They tend to oversimplify and need to be treated with scepticism as adequate representations of real people or situations in all their complexity and diversity. However, archetypes do play a role in the social consciousness of most people based on readily recalled personal experience, and are transmitted in cultural traditions as unconscious legacies and points of reference. For example, when I am unsure how best to respond to the emotional turbulence of an adolescent son or daughter, I sometimes have the presence of mind to step back and think what would the good parent do now? I find myself thinking of my own experiences of being well-parented in similar situations, or of previous times when we have found a successful way through the difficulties. If I dig a little deeper, I find myself confronting choices between regimented or child-centred parenting as the social archetypes of my generation in the UK. Conversations with researchers who are confronting ethical choices suggest they too have ethical archetypes of the 'good' and 'bad' researcher as points of reference that coexist with other resources they apply to assist in their ethical decision making. In this chapter, I use archetypes to represent an ethical warrant in personal terms in order to evoke its embodied form. I hope they add variety to a short, but purposeful, overview of the last 70 years of research ethics.

Warrants of atrocity and harm avoidance

The perennial issue in research ethics is to balance any benefits from the research against the potential harm to the people being researched. Typically, this judgement is taken in a particular moment of time. There is a strong association between generative times in the origins of research ethics with moments of extreme moral repugnance which thereafter influence the way research ethics are understood and regulated.

The origins of contemporary research ethics lie in the horrors of the Nazi concentration camps. The atrocities of genocide against non-Aryan races, particularly Jews and gypsies, the mass murder of moral minorities such as homosexuals and political dissidents, and the extermination of disabled people took place on an unprecedented scale due to a combination of a fundamentalist quest for racial purity as a moral and political goal, and the deployment of the mechanisation of an advanced industrial society. As the mass extermination of millions of people of all ages on an industrial scale in Nazi concentration camps became apparent in the final stages of the Second World War, it provoked widespread horror at the extent of suffering and genocide. This revulsion was compounded by the discovery of experiments that had taken humans to the extremes of pain and suffering to discover the limits of human survival following sudden decompression at high altitude in planes or submersion in sea water at various temperatures following shipwreck. Reading the transcripts from the Nuremberg trials of the doctors in charge of these experiments is a chilling experience (Katz, 1972, p. 292; Kennedy and Grubb, 2000, p. 1667). They are a powerful reminder of how a single-minded moral certainty in pursuit of a nationalist cause can expunge empathy and compassion for human suffering, especially when underpinned by the cruel logic of war. The medics in charge of the experiments had impressive professional and academic credentials, which were used in the tribunals to establish their professional credibility and respectability. Their moral and legal defence of doing 'what was necessary' to win the war, or to obey the orders of a superior military commander, were judged as inadequate justifications for their actions. These doctors faced a death sentence and hanging. Even more ethically troubling than the experiments concerned with the survival of combatants in the air or at sea were experimental operations on children, frequently twins, with no or limited anaesthetic for reasons that seem to have had more to do with unaccountable power over life and death, rather than medical experimentation in pursuit of a systematic line of inquiry, however dubiously conceived. The most infamous of these experimenters, Dr Mengele, escaped to South America, where it is reported he lived out his life as an unrepentant Nazi until he drowned accidentally or suffered a stroke while swimming in old age. In the popular imagination he represents the demonic researcher, 'the Angel of Death' as he was known in Auschwitz concentration camp, a man so driven in the quest for knowledge that all moral scruples were sacrificed. Closer examination of eye-witness accounts suggests bad science undertaken carelessly by a deeply abusive person who would delight in giving sweets to children and being called 'Uncle Mengele' in the knowledge that he would shortly send them to their death or inflict considerable suffering. These were not only war crimes and crimes against humanity, but the attempt to defend them as research was morally troubling and risked bringing all research into disrepute. These crimes focused attention on the ethics of humans as research subjects with unprecedented urgency and gravity of purpose. The moral basis for research that involved humans as subjects needed to be established.

Towards the conclusion of the trials of doctors responsible for many of the concentration camp experiments, the military tribunals at Nuremberg created a code of ten principles designed to protect human subjects in research known as the Nuremberg Code. This code formed the basis of the Helsinki Declaration adopted by the World Medical Association (WMA) in 1964 which, with periodic updating, remains the primary point of reference for the ethics of medical research. The Helsinki Declaration established what have come to be regarded as the seminal issues in research ethics:

- Research should be based on sound science that is undertaken competently.
- The conduct of the research should be reviewed by an independent committee.

- The responsibility for human subjects in biomedical research remains the responsibility of the medic, even when consent from the subjects has been obtained.
- The objective of the research should be proportionate to the inherent risk to the subject.
- Concern for the interests of the subject must always prevail over the interests of science and society.
- The right of research subjects to protect their integrity must be respected.
- The hazards in any research must be believed to be predictable;
- accuracy in reporting results is essential.
- A subject's involvement in research should be based on their informed consent and the right to withdraw consent at any time.
- Dependent relationships between the researcher and subject require particular care.
- Special provisions are required for people incompetent of giving consent.

(Periodic revisions have expanded these original 11 sections to 35 paragraphs in the World Medical Association 2008 edition.)

The primary warrant for these developments was atrocity avoidance. What followed is in many ways just as chilling ethically because researchers seemed to fail to make any connection between the widely publicised and discussed Nuremberg trials and their own studies.

In 1972, the *New York Times* exposed an experiment that involved poorly educated black rural workers in Tuskegee who had been prevented systematically from receiving treatment for syphilis in order to study the natural progression of the disease. Six hundred men had been recruited with the promise of medical treatment for 'bad blood' and free burial insurance (Jones, 1993) four hundred and one of these were known to be infected with syphilis. The collection of medical samples including spinal fluid was disguised as 'treatment'. The duplicity of pretending to offer treatment was compounded by strenuous efforts to prevent treatment for men conscripted into the armed services during the Second World War. This withholding of treatment was not confined to some toxic treatments of questionable effectiveness in use at the start of the study, but included withholding penicillin, the first validated effective cure, from the late 1940s onwards. As a consequence, approximately 130 men died of syphilis or related complications, 40 wives were infected, and about 20 children were born with congenital syphilis. In particular, what is chilling is the evidence of ethical debate between leading figures in the study. However, the quest for medical knowledge, and racism, were sufficient to overcome any doubts. At the time it was exposed, the study was funded by the US Public Health Service (PHS). In the controversy that followed, it is reported that the head of PHS stated, 'The longer the study, the better the ultimate information we would derive' (Jones, 1981, p. 179). This comment encapsulates another archetype that haunts research ethics—researchers so intent on the quest for knowledge, and to protect the scientific purpose and validity of their study, that they lost sight of the humanity of the people being studied. As Jones observed, 'The men's status did not warrant ethical debate. They were subjects, not patients; clinical material not sick people' (Jones, 1981, p. 179). It is as though the inherent scientific commitment to objectivity reached such a level that it erased the moral stimuli of compassion and empathy. The moral distancing of scientist from research subject was compounded further by racism. As President of the United States, Bill Clinton apologised for the racism that imbued this study. However, contemporary documents suggest that other cultural factors combined with and compounded the racism that dehumanised the Tuskegee research subjects: attitudes to rural subsistence farmers; poverty; the disregard of meritocracy for perceived social failure, and a moral judgementalism of sexual conduct.

What is surprising is that it seems the Tuskegee study continued unquestioned by highly educated researchers, who shared the same professional background as the medics on trial at the Nuremberg trials, with no ethical connection made between the comparable exploitation of research subjects and disregard for their suffering. Is it possible that the gulf between the 'bad science' in the horrors of the concentration camps and the determined 'scientific rigour' in a community-based study was sufficient to blind the Tuskegee researchers to similarities in the harm being inflicted?

The end result of Tuskegee, and many other questionable research experiments, was the publication of the Belmont Report (National Commission for the Protection of Human Subjects 1979) and the subsequent USA legal regulation of research ethics involving human subjects guided by the ethical principles of respect for persons, beneficence, and justice. The ethical counterbalance to the pursuit of research in the quest for new knowledge was to ensure an independent ethical review of the balance between expected benefits and any harm to patients, in conjunction with strict requirements about the free and informed consent of any participants. The archetype of the researcher who relentlessly pursues the research with no regard for the impact on the researched was to be replaced by a principled researcher. The warrant was protection of the interests of research subjects as a core ethical obligation for the researcher reinforced by the placement of subjects in a position to make informed decisions about the level of risk to which they were willing to expose themselves. As becomes apparent later, there are benefits in the possession of an ethic based on several principles, but it takes ethical maturity, not to say wisdom, to find the appropriate balance between them.

A further consequence of Tuskegee was the introduction in the USA of enforced ethical review of all research that involved human subjects by independent review boards (IRBs), which has proved problematic for some social scientists (Israel and Hay, 2006; Schrag, 2010; Speiglman and Spear, 2009).

These two case studies reveal that any serious commitment to ethical maturity in research requires a courageous independence of judgement and discernment to see beyond the cultural conventions of the day. Research funding is always intensely competitive, which makes it even harder to look beyond what is endorsed by respected academics, leaders in cognate professions and the government of the day, all of whom may be highly influential in the distribution of awards. These challenges in the competition to become a successful academic may distract from giving due weight to any suffering involved in the research. While the next case study has been much criticised ethically, its findings suggest how hard it may be to develop a commitment to ethical action that will resist authority.

Acquiring ethical maturity and agency in the face of authority

The recognition of the ethical significance of suffering and harm caused to research subjects and action to protect them may be considerably harder than the usual challenges to convert intent into action. In a controversial attempt to understand how so many people appeared willing to comply with orders to undertake morally distasteful and psychologically troubling acts, a psychologist Stanley Milgram (1974) devised a series of experiments in 1961 at Yale University about obedience to authority. These experiments are described and considered more fully in relationship to compliance in Chapter 2. Members of the public were invited to participate in an experiment to investigate the beneficial effects of punishment on learning. Each member of the public was invited to inflict increasingly severe electric shocks on someone they believed was also a member of the public, like themselves, but was really an accomplice of the researchers. As in Tuskegee, the experiment was only possible with a substantial level of deception. Milgram found most members of the public were willing to inflict seemingly increasingly painful and dangerous electric shocks, even though many demonstrated severe emotional stress and questioned whether they should continue to inflict electric shocks at levels indicated as dangerous and ultimately potentially lethal. About two-thirds of participants in many variations of the experiment continued to the point of administering a final electric shock of 450 volts. Milgram (1974) summarised his experiment with an observation that should trouble all ethicists about the difficulty of converting ethics into action:

> 'The legal and philosophic aspects of obedience are of enormous importance, but they say very little about how most people behave in concrete situations...Stark authority was pitted against the subjects' [participants'] strongest moral imperatives against hurting others, and, with the subjects' [participants'] ears ringing with the screams of the victims, authority won more often than not. The extreme willingness of adults to go to almost any lengths on the command of an authority constitutes the chief finding of the study...'

These findings appear to be remarkably stable across time and relatively indifferent to changes in variables such as the social context for the experiment, a prestigious university laboratory, or a city centre office. They also appear to apply across cultures with the majority willing to obey personally distasteful or troubling instructions. Periodic repetitions of the experiments for documentaries and reality television have yielded broadly similar results.

The results of a range of obedience studies, including the Stanford Prison experiment reviewed in Chapter 2, are of considerable relevance to ethics in general. They indicate a limit to how ethical problems can be resolved by rules or legislation. It appears that authority can extinguish the desire to follow the ethical prompts derived from empathy and compassion. Even well-designed rules may have unwanted consequences when applied inappropriately. To be successful, an ethical system needs to establish a framework of ethical goals, expressed typically as principles in scientific research with a few firm prohibitions to avert the worst atrocities or infliction of harm. However, this requires an inescapable reliance on the researchers' moral commitment and agency as fellow human beings with ethical responsibility for the well-being of their human subjects. There is a place for independent and even authoritative reviews in order to avoid the worst excesses of research as exposed in Nuremberg and Tuskegee. However, the best protection for the many finer judgements involved across the life of a research project will depend on the ethical judgements and sensitivity of those with a direct involvement in running the research. The six components of ethical maturity set out in Chapter 1 create a reiterative learning cycle for researchers that supports the development and refinement of ethical judgement that is characteristic of ethical maturity.

The following case studies are examples of situations where the balance between mandatory rules and reliance on the ethical judgement of researchers is questionable. In each case, the established norms of ethical behaviour are being challenged for ethical reasons. I have selected issues of particular relevance to the helping professions and the sorts of issues that arise when research is undertaken as part of professional training, or when professional helpers become involved in research to inform their work.

Therapy or research?

A recurrent issue in research ethics is the extent to which it is acceptable for a professional helper to research their own clients or patients. The basis of this concern is the difference in intended outcomes for the subject of the work and the potential for exploitation of vulnerable people unless a clear ethical distinction is made. The primary purpose of any helping role is to provide assistance and benefit to the person in receipt of the service. Research serves a different purpose, which is the development of new knowledge, and is primarily for the benefit of people other than the patient. Typically, the beneficiaries of research may be future recipients of improved services and the researchers who may gain income and professional advancement.

It is routine for most helping professionals to offer high levels of privacy and confidentiality. What happens in therapy is protected as private knowledge and great care is usually taken to place personally identifiable information on sensitive issues within the control of the patient or client. This is in marked contrast to research, which seeks to generate knowledge with the intention of making it available to the public.

During preparation of ethical guidelines for researching counselling and psychotherapy (Bond, 2004), I obtained a range of contentious responses to the question of whether therapists should be permitted to research their own clients. Some saw this scenario as too fraught with blurred boundaries and potential conflicts of interest to consider it as a possibility. One person responded, 'I would be exploiting a therapeutic relationship based on hard won trust for other purposes. How could I know whether this person would have willingly disclosed this information for my research if I had not been their therapist? I find it much more straightforward to restrict my research to members of the public or other therapists' clients.' Another therapist doubted whether any consent to participate in research with their therapist could be freely given. 'I doubt my clients truly believe it when I say whether or not they take part in the research will make no difference to the therapy they receive. Some will be looking for advantages. Others will not want to displease or alienate me. I am not sure I really believe it about myself. It's hard not to be more attentive to someone who is making a sacrifice of time and effort to help in my research.' This stood in marked contrast to someone who saw little difference between a sensitively conducted research interview and a therapeutic conversation. 'I find little difference in people's positive evaluations of the benefits of being well facilitated in counselling or a research interview. Both value the opportunity for facilitated reflection and being carefully listened to. I face more of a challenge when reporting the results of my interviews for publication in ensuring that I am protecting my interviewees' interests while accurately reporting my research. That [sense of divided loyalties] simply doesn't arise in my therapeutic work.' The more I listened to the diversity of opinions, I began to appreciate how the many differences of opinion reflected the range of services offered, and the extent to which the research complemented the aims and methods of those services, or whether the research involved a significant change in activity with little immediate benefit to the client. Core values in the therapeutic theory that informed the helping relationship also appeared to influence views on combining research with helping relationships. This was not likely to be an issue where consensus based on reasoned judgements would be reached in favour of or against the practice of helping professionals researching their own clients. Instead, the ethically mature responses seemed to be based on an evaluation of a number of factors:

- evaluation of the extent to which the research would be compatible with the service provided—research that would disrupt therapy or undermine the benefits of therapy from therapists' perspectives would be evaluated as ethically undesirable
- evaluation of the impact of the research from a client's perspective, often based on some discussion with clients, was considered helpful in identifying any potential benefits and disadvantages to clients and the kinds of safeguards they would require
- evaluation of the wider social context to ensure that particular groups of people were not being over-researched in response to a current academic fashion or media interest, i.e., that the research would be likely to benefit clients in comparable social circumstances to those being researched, and that research on the socially disadvantaged would not only lead to improvements in treatment for the socially advantaged
- creation of distance from the operational ethical details of the research in order to evaluate how the potential benefits of the research weighed against the potential risks to research subjects as service users

- participation of clients in the research is based on their informed consent of any benefits and risk to themselves, and the purpose of the research
- clients have the right to consent or refuse participation in the research without suffering any reduction in availability of the primary service, and be able to withdraw at any time on the same basis
- dependent on the type of research, clients can be invited to comment on data, interpretation of data, or the draft report, and might be offered a summary of the outcomes of the research.

There was a strong expectation that the ethical basis of the research would be compatible with the relevant professional ethics and that any discrepancy, i.e., the management of confidentiality, would be drawn to the client's attention as an issue for consent. Whenever I have attempted to explore this topic, a recurrent issue seems to be the ethical desirability for the relationship between the therapy and the research to be transparent. It would be ethically inconceivable to combine therapy based on trust with research that requires deception.

Broadly speaking, I have been impressed by the care with which therapists approach the ethical issues involved in research in ways that are highly compatible with the recommendations of the Nuremberg Code and the Belmont Report. This often appears without any awareness of the extreme circumstances that prompted such public concern over research ethics. The ethical reasoning of therapists was often shaped around their understanding of the professional requirements of their role and a more nuanced appreciation of the ethical subtleties of judging benefits and risks in less extreme situations. Ethical maturity is reflected in the care with which they engage with their assessments, rather than following an imposed set of guidelines.

Waiting room study

The research warrants based on Nuremberg, Tuskegee and other attempts to avert extreme ethical abuses were to a large extent established and refined before the proliferation of research designs and methodologies that extended social sciences well beyond the typical scope of biomedical ethics. This has resulted in a recurrent concern in social sciences about how appropriate it is to transfer the ethical norms of the clinic and laboratory to other social contexts and research undertaken for other purposes. For example, let us imagine that a researcher is proposing to observe the behaviour of patients in a doctors' waiting room by sitting there to observe how patients move between the semi-public space of the waiting area to the privacy of the consulting room. What would be the appropriate ethical expectations for such a study? How would the ethical requirements be affected if the researcher maintains the role of being a discrete observer resembling a patient who is waiting for a much-delayed appointment. Would these ethical expectations change if the researcher actively interacted with other clients, patients or staff by asking questions and engaging people in conversation? Would it be different if the researcher sat outside the premises and observed behaviour as people entered and exited? How do our expectations of researchers change between public and private spaces, or between active engagement with research subjects or, by contrast, little or no direct engagement other than observation?

Such issues have taxed social historians, anthropologists and any researchers who use variations of ethnographic research based on systematic observation, interviews and evidence gathered from artefacts and documents. What is the appropriate warrant for this type of research? How far should it depend on the informed consent of the people being observed, or at what point does this become impractical or counterproductive? How far should the risks of social harm be treated as equivalent to physical harm in biomedical research, e.g., in a drug trial? At what point is it legitimate to pursue research in politics or the arts that may cause distress to individuals or whole classes of people?

These issues tax the ethical judgement of practitioners and researchers alike. From an English perspective, the authoritative independent reviews undertaken by IRBs in the USA following the Belmont Report appear to have been too entrenched in biomedical ethics to make a successful transition to the variability of social research. Canadian and Australian approaches appear to have benefited from their development after the regulation of research in the USA, and thus are more responsive to social research that serves a variety of human interests and uses a variety of methodologies. The situation in Britain is more fluid and still evolving. The risk of ethical imperialism, in which biomedical ethics unduly constrain social sciences and ethical engagement in the challenges of social sciences is a recurrent issue across the literature that has yet to be resolved satisfactorily in any jurisdiction. It reminds all researchers of the tensions between law and ethics. What is ethical may be unlawful. What is lawful may not be ethical. While these are substantial issues, it can be argued that they are applicable to a potential study of waiting-room behaviour.

How should a researcher approach the ethics of an observational study of waiting-room behaviour? I notice already that I have to approach this research with a series of Socratic questions because there are so many potential variables that might need to be taken into consideration.

Are the risks to the people being observed any greater than if they were not observed? Clearly, observations that are independent of the services provided and that can be reported in a thoroughly anonymised form represent a lower level of risk. What level of information should be provided to people who are being observed? Would knowledge they are being observed frustrate the purpose of the research, or is this an ethically inescapable prior condition that underpins the research and has to be taken into account in any findings? Should formal consent be sought from people before entering the waiting area, and how should the researcher respond to people who have not consented? Should they be provided with an alternative waiting area? Are there any characteristics of the people being observed that might make them especially sensitive to being observed, such as social vulnerability or paranoia? How will the potential benefits of the research weigh against the potential disruption caused by the study? This last question may involve weighing incommensurate benefits. How would you evaluate a study intended to improve the design of waiting areas against a development in sociological theory? Do you determine the potential disruption or risk of harm against the worst possible case or what is reasonably likely? To whom should the researcher be accountable?

Perhaps not surprisingly, waiting-room research is relatively rare but to contemplate such a project can help to pass the time as you wait for your own appointments. Its significance here is that it is just one of many situations that test the ethical maturity required to take into account the novel features of research in different contexts and undertaken for different purposes.

Meaningful and safe consent

The emphasis on consent is one of the ethical assay marks of research ethics. Both Nuremberg and Belmont emphasised consent as the essential protection of research subjects from abuse and exploitation. In many ways, they imposed a higher standard of respect for the autonomy and agency of research subjects than was characteristic of professional cultures that supported paternalistic decision-making on behalf of patients. Fifty years later, Western culture has become more egalitarian and the protection of the right to consent of an adult patient or client is both an ethical and legal entitlement in all areas of life. There is a a universal acceptance that meaningful consent should be both informed and freely given. Indeed, consent has become established so securely as a norm that it is now more meaningful to ask if reliance on consent has become excessive and counterproductive as an ethical practice in research.

It is clear that consent is a highly appropriate protection for anyone who participates in research that exposes them to risk of harm, involves the gathering and storage of personally identifiable information of a sensitive nature, or where the outcome of the research may affect the delivery of services to that person. However, it is possible to over-rely on consent that has been given too far in advance of the situation it relates to, or where the consent is to a hypothetical situation that may be experienced differently in reality (O'Neill, 2002, pp. 42–4). Perhaps the most significant way consent can be overstretched arises when a researcher relies on a subject's consent as protection against blame for some avoidable harm occurring to the research subject. The responsibility of the researcher for the well-being of experimental research participants is not erased by the subject's consent.

As part of my professional development as a research ethics officer I have wanted to experience research from the point of view of the research subject. I reasoned that if the core objective of research ethics is the protection of human subjects, then there could be no better experience than to be a subject in a variety of research projects. I was reassured to find how attentive researchers were to issues of consent across a wide variety of biomedical and social research. What I had not expected was to feel disconcerted by an over-reliance on written consent. For example, following a fractured right wrist, I joined the trial of a dietary supplement that carried a biomedically relatively low risk, and completed the appropriate consent form by ticking a box at the end of five or six statements and then signing once. On a return visit I was asked to write my initials next to each tick. As I awkwardly and painfully added the required initials, I wondered whose interests were being protected. In another project, I was asked to sign a consent form in advance of being interviewed on an audio recorder about aspects of my work for which I am publicly accountable. I thought this was disproportionate when my consent could have been recorded on tape. On another occasion I was interviewed on a personally sensitive topic in the USA, again on a tape recorder. Written consent forms are a legal requirement in the USA, so while they can sometimes feel like an imposition, on this occasion they provided ethical reassurance that the sensitivity of what was to be discussed was being treated with appropriate ethical seriousness. These incidents made me more appreciative of the significance of the way consent is gathered.

On another occasion, I was consulted in my role as a research ethics officer about difficulties encountered by researchers who were investigating the use of water-testing kits in rural areas of India. They encountered considerable anxiety from participants about signing consent forms. This anxiety seemed much greater for participants in the project than any concerns about being interviewed and demonstrating their use of the test kit. It became clear that in the local social structure there was a common experience that written documents could be used by people higher up the social ladder against people lower down in the social structure. The water attendants felt they were being asked to do something that was culturally inappropriate and that potentially added to the risks for them. It was an interesting example of how the method used to obtain and record the consent could undermine the ethical respect for someone's autonomy. Oral consent, even if it was tape-recorded, was experienced as more respectful. This consultation extended my ethical maturity to take greater account of the ethical context to ensure that the positive ethical intent is communicated in a manner that is culturally and contextually appropriate.

Research that involves vulnerable people, especially those with learning difficulties, requires considerable thought about whether or not the consent of a responsible carer or adult may be required in addition to the person concerned. Again, I learned a great deal from someone who was familiar with people with learning difficulties and the time needed to build the trust required for meaningful communications. In his research design for a study of friendship, he took great care to develop and pilot a series of line drawings that participants with learning difficulties could point to or talk about in order to communicate their feelings about involvement in the study and could be used as the basis of their consent.

Researching on the boundaries of knowledge

The use of new technologies poses particular ethical challenges for researchers. All research is a journey into the unknown. However, the use of new technology can make this a more substantial challenge of life-changing proportions for research participants, even though the research may be relatively innocuous for the subjects taking part. For example, Magnetic Resonance Image (MRI) scanners have opened up whole new areas of research on the functioning of the brain and the potential for observing brain activity while someone performs routine therapeutic and educational activities. The technology is so new that often researchers can see irregularities of unknown significance in the images that may become significant as the volume of observations accumulate over time. Researchers are faced with a choice between alerting someone to an observation of unknown significance that has the potential to worry them unnecessarily, or withholding information that has the potential to be beneficial at some future date. How to find the most ethical way to respond to this dilemma has been a subject of much debate between researchers (Howard-Jones, 2010, p. 124). As experience accumulates, the ethically mature response appears to swing more in favour of informing research subjects of any image irregularities or anomalies, while striving to ensure they understand the unknown significance of the observation at the current state of knowledge.

What would be the most ethical response if you could see in advance that the person was unlikely to be able to contain their anxiety and their quality of life would be diminished by such information?

Encounters with the unexpected

The ethical maturity of researchers is tested by the ethical concerns that arise from the margins or strictly outside the scope of the research. A researcher who visits homes to investigate the relationship between school and home life becomes aware of criminal activity or domestic violence. A teenager, at the end of an interview about mentoring, confides she is worried she might be pregnant and asks the researcher's advice. A researcher is stalked by a research participant either in person or electronically through social networks sites and email. Even in the best planned research, it is not practical to account for all eventualities. Often all that can be factored into the research plan are any predictable complications that would be reasonable to foresee within the main focus of the research. While interviews with people about traumatic events may be comforting for some, they may be distressing for others, and it might be reasonable to anticipate that some form of debriefing or emotional support would be an ethical requirement. The vulnerability of certain research subjects makes it unwise to not anticipate how the researcher should respond to some of the more likely difficulties encountered by those subjects. It would reveal a lack of ethical judgement and maturity to not develop a child protection strategy for researchers who work with young people in case a young person is discovered, during the research, to be the victim of physical or sexual abuse. Parallel strategies may be required for working with vulnerable adults.

Encounters with the unexpected are disconcerting, but it takes ethical maturity to not panic. In research teams, it is not unusual for the least experienced researcher to encounter the most challenging of the unexpected ethical dilemmas. These are the times when a lack of familiarity with the components of ethical maturity can show. The support of a more experienced researcher may be required to encourage the person to pause, review the situation, and to seek appropriate information and advice before evaluating the options. It is usually only medical emergencies and the prevention of serious crime, e.g., stopping a serious assault, that require rapid reactions without much opportunity for reflection and consultation, e.g., calling the emergency services.

Honouring the contribution of participants

The standard approach in clinical and laboratory-based research is to offer participants and subjects total anonymity in reporting the research. The value of the research is to produce generalised rules about processes or behaviours that are independent of any particular person. The emphasis on anonymity enables the dissemination of new knowledge without compromising the general expectations of professional confidentiality.

Research undertaken in the community can generate more complicated expectations. As a relatively immature ethical researcher, I remember acting on the familiar practices of biomedical research and being challenged when I offered anonymity. The response was, 'Is my contribution not good enough to be acknowledged? Am I too insignificant to share your limelight?' Variations on this response include a concern that the researcher should not appear to take over or colonise the experience and knowledge held by a community or cultural group. When I have researched self-help community groups, individuals or whole groups have sometimes wanted to be acknowledged in order to increase the visibility and awareness of their services, or to help with fund-raising. In my experience, it has been more difficult to manage situations where there is a mixture of requirements over anonymity and acknowledgement. The challenge is not to create a situation where the acknowledgments imply the identities of the anonymous contributors.

Some research designs treat the research participants as full collaborators in one or more aspects of the research process from the design through to data interpretation and validation. Such contributions usually would be evident in the report of the methodology, and would merit a note of thanks on an anonymous or a named basis.

Ethics beyond the boundaries of the research—sustained contact?

New ethical responsibilities have emerged as qualitative and narrative research methods have sought increasingly to study people's intimate relationships with others in detail or to investigate personal identities. A close link can be traced between an increased awareness of these responsibilities, and feminist philosophy and gendered approaches to relating and knowing. A re-thinking of the relationship between researcher and their research participants supported the development of relationships of sufficient quality to reveal insights into housework, childbirth and the role and position of women in society which would not have been possible under the old research paradigms. A new warrant of research ethics was created around caring as an ethically desirable virtue or disposition. It challenged notions of the interchangeability of researchers. In biomedical research it is considered a positive sign of the reliability of the research if anyone could repeat the experiment and get the same results. Anne Oakley (2005) pioneered some of the first major feminist research projects in the UK and challenged notions of objective detachment and strictly time-limited contact with research subjects. She captured her approach to the in-depth study of the lives of other people with the memorable phrase, 'No intimacy without reciprocity' (p. 226). She wrote about how she sustained friendships with the research participants long after the formal research had finished. The archetypes for this approach to research ethics is a caring mother figure who balances divergences in dependency and affiliation within a family (Noddings, 1986), or the emotional openness and mutual care of close friendships between women (Oakley, 2005).

Relationally-sensitive approaches to professional ethics are no longer regarded as exclusive to women, but highlight ethically desirable virtues to which men can aspire (Gatens, 1995).

A warrant of trust

Trust and being trustworthy has been a longstanding ethical concern of qualitative researchers. Egon Guba and Yvonna Lincoln, both researchers in education and qualitative research methodologies in the USA, were among the first to propose 'trustworthiness' as a quality criterion for qualitative research and a possible alternative to the quality criteria for empirical research based on 'validity' and 'reliability' (Lincoln and Guba, 1985; Guba and Lincoln, 1994). This could not be further from the position described at the beginning of this chapter, where the psychologist viewed the ethics of research as distinct from the research project itself. With a focus on trustworthiness as the ethical warrant, ethics have become integral to research both as an ethical imperative, and an indication of the quality of the research process and outcome. As I was reflecting on the ethical experiences of research into counselling and psychotherapy, I began to perceive a way to identify some of the key components of trust and trustworthiness as relational virtues that support a sustained relationship in the face of relational and existential challenges. The full warrant for trust is defined as 'a relationship of sufficient quality and resilience to withstand the challenges arising from difference, inequality, risk and uncertainty' (Bond, 2004, 2007). This approach is discussed in relation to ethical maturity in Chapter 7. The archetype for this approach is someone who has sufficient ethical awareness to be sensitive to the ethical diversity and challenges in others, while retaining sufficient relational skills and integrity to construct relationships across cultural differences. When a Maori leader challenged me with the 'haka' style of greeting, 'They tell me you are big in ethics: tell me what is the big thing in ethics that really matters.' I replied, somewhat timidly and hesitantly, 'Trust'. She wisely replied, 'We will see'. What followed was a mutual attempt to honour trust with the inevitable struggles across such wide cultural differences and a history of colonial relationships between 'pakaha' (pale skin) and Maori.

Trust is also being revived in less relational terms as a potential platform on which some of the rigidity and unwanted consequences of the earlier warrants around atrocity and harm avoidance may be redressed. There is a deliberate attempt to be more inclusive of the diverse research developed since the ethical crises that prompted the first attempts at research ethics. This is particularly evident in Canada, Australia and the UK. The willingness of the public to participate in research is of increasing concern as recruitment to research has become more problematic in the developed world, especially for biomedical research. The promotion of the benefits of research as a collective social responsibility is returning to the agenda as we are all beneficiaries of the improved healthcare and technologies that have transformed lives in the developed world. 'A Universal Ethical Code for Scientists' (Government Office for Science), to which social scientists contributed, opens with a statement by Sir David King (2007), the UK Government's Chief Scientific Adviser, 'Our social licence to operate as scientists needs to be founded on a continually renewed relationship of trust between scientists and society' (p. 1). The social sciences are not unique in experiencing difficulty with current approaches to ethical review and governance. The recent Rawlins Report (Academy of Medical Sciences, 2011) on streamlining ethics and governance for health research echoes this warrant for ethical review by balancing the 'need to promote high-quality research but also to maintain public and professional trust in an area that relates directly to individual safety and dignity' (p. 19). Trust seems to have been rediscovered as a focus for social cohesion, an increasing concern of economists and policy makers. The archetype is not focused solely on the researcher, but on the mutual interests and benefit that hold both researcher and subjects together.

The changing face of ethical maturity in research ethics

In this chapter I have attempted to chart how research ethics have adapted and widened their scope across the still expanding variety of activities that count as research. The development of ethical maturity, and acquiring the wisdom to respond to this diversity, is a lifelong challenge for the individual researcher and for the research community as a whole. When I first encountered the approach of Michael Carroll and Elisabeth Shaw to ethical maturity, I was struck by its relevance to individual researchers in learning how to be ethical. What impresses me is how relevant the ideas are to researchers as a learning community. We are all embedded in the micro-communities of our academic and professional associations. The concept of ethical maturity invites us to step back from the particular concerns and interests that drive these affiliations to find a shared sense of what it means to be ethical as researchers in the diversity of the academic community and the plurality of contemporary society. This is unlikely to be a stable state, if it ever were to be achieved. Rather, it will require continual renewal through reiterative learning that underpins both individual and collective ethical maturity.

Professor Tim Bond

Chapter 21

And finally...

'I try to point out to them—not always successfully—that all the answers they need are to be found inside them; they only have to be quiet enough to hear them...deep listening does not come easy... We're to stand still and pay close attention to what is really going on...it takes courage to stand still and find out who we really are.'

(Kets de Vries, 2009, p. xv)

'After all is said and done, there is more said than done.'

(Aesop)

'The spontaneous search for an intuitive solution sometimes fails—neither an expert solution nor a heuristic answer comes to mind. In such cases we often find ourselves switching to a slower, more deliberate and effortful form of thinking.'

(Kahneman, 2012, p. 12)

We have come to the end of our shared ethical maturity journey. We started out standing at ethical crossroads wondering what to do. Has writing the book crystallised our thinking, or illuminated ethical pathways, or made making ethical decisions any easier? It certainly has been a journey where an appreciation of the complexity of ethical decision making has come to the forefront. We recognise that ethical maturity is an ideal to be pursued, rather than an end-point to be achieved. What looks, and can be, incredibly simple can also be incredibly complex. We make ethical decisions all the time, easily, effortlessly and intuitively, and at other times we spend days, months and years wandering, searching and wondering what to do. We come to the end of this book in awe at the wonder of human beings and their abilities to deal with complex situations, many of which are unconscious. Making sense of the processes involved has been our task.

We are pleased to make a small contribution to the ethics literature. We have outlined a model of ethical maturity in keeping with our aim to challenge ourselves and others to strive for our ethical best. As human beings, at our best we are amazing—generous, co-operative, sacrificing, dedicated, loving and committed to the highest ideals. At our worst, we are horrible—cruel, destroying, selfish and destructive. We have tried to concentrate on who we are at our best, while trying to understand what makes us descend the steps to who we are at our lowest. Both are worth understanding because human beings are all these things—light and darkness, brightness and shadow, good and evil.

So what do we conclude as we come to the end of the book?

One conclusion is how incredibly simple and, at times, tempting it is to remain ethically unaware. We believe there are times when we unconsciously keep ourselves blind to ethical issues, and morally asleep, because it maintains simplicity and unaccountability. There is a saying that 'Most people don't know that there are angels whose only job is to make sure you don't get too comfortable and fall asleep and miss your life' (quoted in Zachary, 2000, p. xii). One of those angels should be appointed to ensure we don't fall asleep ethically and wander through life in blissful ethical ignorance. In writing a book about ethics, we became aware of how much ethical activity is missed, ignored, not noticed, and even denied. The process of writing has consciously, and no doubt unconsciously, fine-tuned our ethical antenna. It is so much harder now to deny the ethical undertones of life, work and relationships. It is difficult to say, 'I don't care, I am not responsible, and it has nothing to do with me', and it is difficult to ignore the challenge about what might be the best action to take—not the minimum I can get away with, or how generous I can be, but to ask 'What is the best human response to this situation that looks at me and beyond me?' In retrospect, it might have been wise to have included a psychological health warning at the beginning of this book about what might happen to readers when they pick up a book on ethical maturity! The transformational learning literature often refers to 'seeing in new ways', uses images such as 'scales falling from the eyes', noticing what had not been noticed before, and making sense and meaning of life events in different categories. Ethical maturity is a form of transformational learning where ethical arenas not seen before now become visible, and where ethical responsibilities not recognised before become accepted. We do not believe this book will propel its readers into elevated levels of ethical maturity, but we do believe it will be hard to read and not feel more attuned to the best of human nature. It has made us ask how we move from the minimum to the maximum, from what is necessary to what is good.

Writing this book has disturbed us. It has made us aware of how ethical fatigue, as with compassion fatigue, can enter lives surreptitiously and embed itself in everyday reactions. Of course, we need buffers to soak up the impact that can result if we allow ourselves to be sensitive to the many horrors that are happening in our world. It is easy to lay guilt trips on ourselves and others for not reacting as ethically or as humanely as we should. It is just as easy to raise barriers that make us immune to our responsibilities and cocoon us in our narrow selfish worlds. Neither extreme helps. To become more ethically aware demands more from us, and pushes us against the limits of our humanness. While this process causes discomfort, there is no harm in being more disturbed than we were.

Writing this book has made us more aware that we are social animals and, in the end, morality and ethics are based on our ability to be with one another. Churchland (2011) writes 'Within the mammalian family there about 5,700 known species—all species are at least minimally social' (p. 14). Empathy and compassion are the two qualities or virtues that keep us connected to others and to our world, and remain with us as the foundational arms of ethical maturity. When we are out of relationship and unconnected to others we are capable of great harm. The tradition of moral philosophy that says we must divorce ourselves from relationship, context and emotion has been challenged irrevocably by our current understanding of the brain and social influence. We are convinced that we need to use all of our responses, and that our reactions provide useful information. The task is to work our way through these reactions to action that makes sense to us, and fits with our values and the circumstances.

In telling friends and colleagues about the book in progress, there have been more conversations about ethics, and more people commenting, 'You can't do that and be writing a book on ethics!' While this is said in jest (although Freud once said there is no such thing as a joke) it seems to indicate that if you declare an interest in ethical development and reflection, others will become more alert and get involved. Unlike a passing craze with selling Avon or taking up exercise, you can't really say 'I don't care about ethics any more'. In all kinds of forums, talk about ethics seems to lead to more talk about ethics. It is worth it to declare your interest to others, and see what happens to support and extend you in your work.

The building of moral character through the choices we make, and the learning we glean from our actions, is a key element to being an ethically mature person. Ethics that come from within us, and are chosen by us, are more vibrant, real and lasting than the ethics that come from external sources, e.g., authority, or the constraints of rules and laws. Human choice is an essential component of human ethical maturity. To seek to maximise our choices is crucial to broaden our sense of the possibilities and to get the decision right.

Most ethical decisions are made on a realistic moment-by-moment basis without a lot of thought, reflection and deliberation, and this is how it should be. As Churchland (2011) points out, 'What gets us around the world is mainly not logical deduction' (p. 6). Our day-to-day decision making is a balancing and harmonising of constraints and satisfactions where we move intuitively to what is good for us. Most of the time we just know what to do and, in general, that is good and sufficient enough for us to remain ethical. We simply add up the pros and cons of a number of possible decisions and decide, by and large unconsciously, on the right one. If we jump into a stream to save a child, we don't usually work this out through logic or deduction—we just do it. This is what happens when we make many of our minor, and sometimes major, ethical decisions. Kahneman (2012) calls this 'System 1 Thinking', a fast and intuitive process that can also be wrong and gullible. System 1 needs backup and this is where 'System 2 Thinking' comes in, a process which encourages doubt and builds on questioning and deliberation.

There are times when we need to engage our rational brains (alongside other insights from emotions, intuitions, relationships, etc.), and begin a deliberate process of decision making. This is Kahneman's System 2 Thinking where we begin to pay attention and work our way towards ethical conclusions. Psychological processes involved can include reflection, discussion, waiting, consultation, reading, writing, using imagination to project ourselves into the future, as well as numerous other learning methods to support us to find what we should do, and what we want to do, as our best human response—for now. There are dangers and traps along the way in our thinking, perceptions, mental maps, our past and our present. We know how easy it is to seek out information that supports us in doing what we really want to do, but pretend we don't; we are aware of collusion or denial entering the scene and taking over; we realise that the way we frame the question and the ethical dilemma can lead to the conclusions we had already started with. Understanding ourselves and the way we work is a valuable asset on the ethical journey.

Sometimes it is best to get in touch with what is happening in ourselves before we begin to consult with others. We have internal ethical barometers that can guide us, but often we don't stop to register our responses and thoughts before we rush in a panic to seek outside guidance. On the other hand, we too often trust the judgements of others before we trust our own. Our first reaction, a gut feeling or intuition, is valuable and worth noting. Hold this reaction and articulate it for yourself. Watch what influences you as your reactions emerge (your safety, your biases, your values—just note and do not evaluate or dismiss too quickly). Be honest about your intentions and motives. There comes a time when the voices of others enter the dialogue and weave their influence. If these voices enter too early, we are swayed easily, if they enter too late, our subjectivity may win the day. Different perspectives can provide wider vision and help us to make mature choices. Of course, this depends on our ability to choose wise and experienced people to help us make decisions, and our confidence and humility to accept views that make sense to us, even when different to our own.

We know that despite our best intentions and well-established moral characters, contexts can overwhelm us and propel us towards actions that are anything but ethically mature. Sommers (2011) spends a whole book convincing his readers that 'we put all our eggs in the basket of personality, overlooking context' (p. 39). His aim is to relocate context at the centre of ethical decision making—it is not character *or* context, it is character *and* context. Having said this, there are times when context is overruled by character and we will not deviate from what we believe to be the best behaviour possible. In all the major research that reviews the impact of context on behaviour (e.g., Milgram, Zimbardo, Asch), there is always a small percentage of individuals who stand firm and resist contextual influences, e.g., experts in white coats or adopting the behaviour of others as their moral guides. At other times our moral character disappears and the impact of the context takes over and becomes our moral authority.

This is a helpful reminder to not become complacent or stand arrogantly on 'moral high ground'. Mysteries to ourselves, we wonder how on earth we do what we know to be wrong, unhelpful, and unethical when our beliefs and values are so well established. The realisation that we are moral contradictions in action is often the beginning of moral maturity.

Whether an ethical decision is made through System 1 or System 2 Thinking, it is worth testing in the fire of retrospection and justification. When we look back and learn from our past ethical decisions we are better prepared for the future. This demands us to tolerate the anxiety that comes with learning. Without this emotional competence we can flee into defensiveness and justification, which impacts our development.

Ken Wilber (2000), in setting out to discover why there are so many theories, philosophies, religions, political systems and points of view, concludes that all positions do indeed capture an element of truth—*partially*. We reach something of a similar conclusion in respect to ethical positions. Each is true—partially and in its own way. As always, the skill is to know which partial truth is relevant to this particular situation. As we point out in Chapter 9 when we consider how ethical decisions are made—it depends. There is no right answer. There are innumerable stances when faced with ethical dilemmas. Some believe we are born with a moral intelligence (Hauser, 2006; Haidt, 2001), and others contradict this view

(Prinz, 2012). While there is widespread diversity in moral beliefs, we seem to have universal ethical stances across cultures, races and countries. Ethical studies show there are few definites to which we all subscribe. Ethical maturity involves the ability to live with diversity and difference, and maintains the creative tension that comes from making ethical decisions when there is little certainty we are right.

Conclusion

You have picked up this book because ethics is on your radar in some way, as it is for us. You are drawn to think about and explore this territory. We hope this book has illuminated many useful ideas, exercises and thoughts, and has prompted you to have many more of your own. Our reference list is not exhaustive, but we hope it will provide more for you to draw from as you advance in this work.

References

Academy of Medical Sciences (2011). *A new pathway for the regulation and governance of health research.* London, UK: The Academy of Medical Sciences. Retrieved from www.acmedsci.ac.uk

Ainsworth, M., & Bowlby, J. (1965). *Child care and the growth of love.* London: Penguin Books.

Allan, J. (2010). The ethics column. *The Coaching Psychologist, 6*(2), 125–126.

Allan, J., Passmore, J., & Mortimer, L. (2011). Coaching ethics: Developing a model to enhance coaching practice. In J. Passmore (Ed.), *Supervision, ethics and continuous professional development* (pp. 161–172). London, UK: Kogan Page Limited.

Appiah, K. A. (2008). *Experiments in ethics.* Cambridge, MA: Harvard University Press.

Arendt, H. (1963). *Eichmann and the holocaust.* London: Penguin Books

Arendt, H. 1994 (1963), *Eichmann in Jerusalem: A report on the banality of evil.* London: Penguin Books.

Argyris, C., & Schon, D. A. (1974). *Theory in practice: Increasing professional effectiveness.* San Francisco: Jossey-Bass.

Armstrong, K. (2011). *Twelve steps to a compassionate life.* London: The Bodley Head.

Babiak, P., & Hare, R. D. (2005). *Snakes in suits: When psychopaths go to work.* New York: Regan Books.

Bachkirova, T. (2011). *Developmental coaching: Working with the self.* Maidenhead: Open University Press.

BACP (2010). *Ethical framework for good practice in counselling and psychotherapy.* Leicestershire: British Association for Counselling and Psychotherapy.

Baron-Cohen, S. (2011). *Zero degrees of empathy.* London: Penguin Books.

Baron-Cohen, S. (2011). *The science of evil: On empathy and the origins of human cruelty.* New York: Basic Books.

Bashe, A., Anderson, S. K., Handelsman, M. M., & Klevansky, R. (2007). An acculturation model for ethics training: The ethics autobiography and beyond. *Professional Psychology: Research and Practice, 38*(1), 60–67.

Bateson, G. (1972). *Steps to an ecology of mind: Collected essays in anthropology, psychiatry, evolution, and epistemology.* San Francisco: Chandler Publishing.

Bauman, Z. (1993). *Postmodern ethics.* Oxford: Blackwell Publishing.

Baumeister, R. F. (1997). *Evil: Inside human violence and cruelty.* New York: W. H. Freeman.

Baumeister, R. F. (1999). *The self in social psychology.* Philadelphia, PA: Psychology Press.

Baumeister, R., & Tierney, J. (2011). *Willpower: Rediscovering our greatest human strength.* London, UK: Penguin Press.

Baxter-Magolda, M. (1992). *Knowing and reasoning in college: Gender-related patterns in students' intellectual development.* San Francisco, CA: Jossey-Bass.

Belenky, M., Clinchy, B., Goldberger, N., & Tarule, J. (1996). *Women's ways of knowing.* New York, NY: Basic Books.

Bell, D. (2002). *Ethical ambition: Living a life of meaning and worth.* London, UK: Bloomsbury.

Berlyne, D. (1978). Curiosity and learning. *Motivation and Emotion, 2*(2), 97–175.

Bernard, J. L., & Jara, C. S. (1986). The failure of clinical psychology graduate students to apply understood ethical principles. *Professional Psychology: Research and Practice, 17*, 313–315.

Bernard, J. L., Murphy, M., & Little, M. (1987). The failure of clinical psychologists to apply understood ethical principles. *Professional Psychology: Research and Practice, 18*, 489–491.

Biaggio, M., Paget, T., & Chenoworth, M. S. (1997). A model for ethical management of faculty-student relationships. *Professional Psychology, Research and Practice, 28*(2), 184–189.

Bion, W. (1962). *Learning from experience.* London: Heinemann.

Bloom, P. (2010, May 5). The moral life of babies. *The New York Times.* Retrieved from http://www.nytimes.com

Boele, D. (1995). The training of a philosophical counsellor. In R. Lahav, & M. da Venza, Tillmanns (Eds.), *Essays on philosophical counselling* (pp.35–47). Lanham, MD: University Press of America.

Bond, T. (2004). *Ethical guidelines for researching counselling and psychotherapy.* Rugby: British Association for Counselling and Psychotherapy (BACP).

Bond, T. (2005). Developing and monitoring professional ethics and good practice guidelines. In R. Tribe & J. Morrissey (Eds.), *Handbook of professional and ethical practice.* Hove, East Sussex: Brunner-Routledge.

Bond, T. (2006). Intimacy, risk, and reciprocity in psychotherapy: Intricate ethical challenges. *Transactional Analysis Journal, 36*(2), 77–89.

Bond, T. (2007). Ethics and psychotherapy: An issue of trust. In R. E. Ashcroft, A. Dawson, H. Draper & J. R. McMillan (Eds.), *Principles of health care ethics* (2nd ed., pp. 435–442). Chichester: John Wiley and Sons.

Boszormenyi-Nagy, I., & Spark, G. M. (1984). *Invisible loyalties: Reciprocity in intergenerational family therapy.* New York, NY: Brunner/Mazel.

Boszormenyi-Nagy, I., & Krasner, B. R. (1986). *Between give and take: A clinical guide to contextual therapy.* New York, NY: Brunner/Mazel.

Bowlby, J. (1969/1982). *Attachment and loss: Vol. 1. Attachment* (2nd ed.). New York: Basic Books.

Bowlby, J. (1973). *Attachment and loss: Vol. 2. Separation: Anxiety and anger.* New York: Basic Books.

Bowlby, J. (1980). *Attachment and loss: Vol. 3. Sadness and depression.* New York: Basic Books.

Bowles, W., Collingridge, M., Curry, S., & Valentine, B. (2006). *Ethical practice in Social Work.* Sydney, Australia: Allen & Unwin.

Boyer-Fier, E., & Ramsey, M. (2005). Ethical challenges in the teaching of multicultural course work. *Journal of Multicultural Counselling and Development, 33*(2), 94–107.

Brandt, A. (1981, August). What it means to say no. *Psychology Today,* 70–77.

Breen, C. (2011). Re-cognising learning and teaching: Opening the space of possibility. In. S. Voller, E. Blass & V. Culpin (Eds.), *The future of learning: Insights and innovations from executive development* (pp. 131–149). Basingstoke, Hampshire: Palgrave McMillan.

Brew, A. (1993). Unlearning through experience. In D. Boud, R. Cohen, & D. Walker (Eds.), *Using experience for learning* (pp. 87–98). Buckingham, UK: Open University Press.

Brookfield, S. (2005). *The power of critical theory for adult learning and teaching.* Maidenhead: Open University Press.

Brooks, D. (2011). *The social animal.* London: Short Books

Brown, E. (2005, July). Otto Scharmer: Theory-U: Presencing emerging futures. *MIT Sloan School of Management News Briefs.* Retrieved from http://mitsloan.mit.edu/newsroom/newsbriefs-0605-scharmer.php

Bruns, G. L. (1992). *Hermeneutics ancient and modern.* New Haven, CT: Yale University Press.

Burger, J. (2011). Alive and well after all these years. *The Psychologist, 24*(9), 654–657.

Butler, J. (2005). *Giving an account of oneself.* New York, NY: Fordham University Press.

Butler, S. (2008). *The way of all flesh.* Forgotten Books: www.forgottenbooks.org (Original work published 1903).

Callahan, S. (1991). *In good conscience: Reason and emotion in moral decision making.* San Francisco, CA: HarperCollins.

Carroll, M. (1996). *Counselling supervision: Theory, skills and practice.* London: Cassell.

Carroll, M. (2009). From mindless to mindful practice: On learning reflection in supervision. *Psychotherapy in Australia, 15*(4), 40–51.

Carroll, M. (2010). Levels of reflection: On learning reflection. *Psychotherapy in Australia, 16*(2), 28–35.

Carroll, M. (2011). Ethical maturity: Compasses for life and work decisions—Part I. *Psychotherapy in Australia, 17*(3), 34–44.

Caspary, W. R. (2006). Dewey and Satre on ethical decisions: Dramatic rehearsal versus radical choice. *Transactions of the Charles S. Peirce Society, 42*(3), 367–393.

Cavicchia, S. (2010). Shame in the coaching relationship: Reflections on organisational vulnerability. *Journal of Management Development, 29*(10), 877–890.

Chapman, J. (1999). Hatred and corruption of task. *Socio-Analysis 1*(2), 127–150.

Charan, R. (2001, April). Conquering a culture of indecision. *Harvard Business Review, 79,* 74–82.

Charles, L. L., Thomas, D., & Thornton, M. L. (2005). Overcoming bias toward same-sex couples: A case study from inside an MFT ethics classroom. *Journal of Marital and Family Therapy, 31*(3), 239–249.

Chesler, P. (2001). *Woman's inhumanity to woman.* New York: Thunder's Mouth Press/Nation Books.

Churchland, P. (2011). *Braintrust: What neuroscience tells us about morality.* Princeton: Princeton University Press.

Cialdini, R. (2001). *Influence: Science and practice.* New York, NY: Allyn and Bacon/Pearson.

Clarkson, P. (1997). *The Bystander: An end to innocence in human relationships.* London: Whurr Publications.

Claxton, G. (1981). *Wholly human: Western and Eastern visions of the self and its perfections.* London: Routledge and Kegan Paul.

Claxton, G. (1994). *Noises from the darkroom: The science and mystery of the mind.* London, UK: Aquarian.

Claxton, G. (2005). *The wayward mind: An intimate history of the unconscious.* London: Little Brown.

Claxton, G., & Lucas, B. (2007). *The creative thinking plan.* London: BBC Books.

Clinton, W. (1997). *Remarks by the President in apology for study done in Tuskegee.* Washington DC: The White House, Office of the Press Secretary. Retrieved from http://www.cdc.gov/tuskegee/clintonp.htm

Cloyne Report (2010). *Commission of Investigation: Report into the Catholic Diocese of Cloyne.* Ministry of Justice: Ireland Dail.

Cohen, S. (2001). *States of denial: Knowing about atrocities and suffering.* Cambridge: Polity Press.

Corey, G., Schneider-Corey, M., & Callahan, P. (2005). An approach to teaching ethics courses in human services and counselling. *Counselling and Values, 49*(3), 193–207.

Corruption: Grand schemes: A World Bank report blasts the abuse of company registration for corrupt ends (2011, October 29). *The Economist, p. 70.* Retrieved from http://www.economist.com/node/21534761

Cozolino, L. (2008). *The healthy aging brain: Sustaining attachment, attaining wisdom.* New York, NY: W. W. Norton.

Critchley, B. (2010). Relational coaching: Taking the coaching high road. *Journal of Management Development, 29*(10), 851–863.

Crocket, K., Kotze, E., & Flintoff, V. (2007). Reflections on shaping the ethics of our teaching practices. *Journal of Systemic Therapies, 26*(3) 29–42.

Curran, A. (2008). *The little book of big stuff about the brain: The true story of your amazing brain.* Carmathen, Wales: Crown House Publishing.

Cyrulnik, B. (2007). *Talking of love on the edge of a precipice.* London: Allen Lane.

Dalai Lama, H. H., & Chan, V. (2004). *The wisdom of forgiveness: Intimate journeys and conversations.* New York: Riverhead Books.

Damasio, A. (1994). *Descartes' error: Emotion, reason and the human brain.* New York: HarperCollins.

Darley, J. M., & Batson, C. D. (1973). From Jerusalem to Jericho: A study in situational and dispositional variable in helping behaviours. *Journal of Personality and Social Psychology, 27*(1), 100–108.

Dawkins, R. (1976). *The selfish gene.* London: Oxford University Press.

Dean, J. W. (1976). *Blind ambition: The White House years.* New York: Simon & Schuster.

de Botton, A. (2000). *The consolations of philosophy.* London, UK: Hamish Hamilton.

Denis, L. (Ed.) (1964). *Groundwork for the metaphysics of morals: Immanuel Kant.* Ontario, Canada: Broadview Press Limited.

Derrida, J. (1978). *Writing and difference* (A. Bass, Trans.). London: Routledge & Kegan Paul.

Derrida, J. (1981). *Positions* (A. Bass, Trans.). London: Athlone Press.

de Waal, F. (2009). *The age of empathy: Nature's lessons for a kinder society.* London: Souvenir Press.

Donald, M. (2008). How culture and brain mechanisms interact in decision making. In, C. Engel & W. Singer (Eds.), *Better than conscious? Decision making, the human mind and implications for institutions.* Cambridge, MA: MIT Press.

Dudley, V. (1994). Feminist perspectives on the ethic of care. *Wisconsin Bibliographies in Women's Studies, 69.*

Duffy, M., & Passmore, J. (2010). Ethics in coaching: An ethical decision making framework for coaching psychologists. *International Coaching Psychology Review, 5*(2), 140–151.

Eagleman, D. (2011). *Incognito: The secret lives of the brain.* Edinburgh: Canongate Books.

Egan, G., & Cowan, M. (1979). *People in systems: A model for development in the human-services professions and education.* Pacific Grove, CA: Brooks Cole.

Egan, G. (1994). *Working the shadow side: A guide to positive behind-the-scenes management.* San Francisco, CA: Jossey-Bass.

Ekman, P. (2003). *Emotions revealed: Understanding faces and feelings.* London: Weidenfeld & Nicolson.

Engel, C., & Singer, W. (2008). Better than conscious?: The brain, the psyche, behaviour and institutions. In C. Engel & W. Singer (Eds.), *Better than conscious?: Decision making, the human mind and implications for institutions* (pp. 1-20). Cambridge, MA: MIT Press.

Enright, R. (2001). *Forgiveness is a choice: A step by step process for resolving anger and restoring hope.* Washington, DC. American Psychological Association.

Erikson, E. (1994). *Identity and the life cycle.* New York: W. W. Norton.

Evatt, C. (2010). *The myth of free will.* Sausalito, DA: Café Essays.

Falkenberg, L., & Woiceshyn, J. (2008). Enhancing business ethics: Using cases to teach moral reasoning. *Journal of Business Ethics, 29,* 213–217.

Ferns Report (2005). *Report presented to the Minister for Health and Children.* Dublin: Government Publications.

Fesmire, S. (2003). *John Dewey and moral imagination, pragmatism in ethics.* Bloomington, IN: Indiana University Press.

Fine, C. (2006). *A mind of its own: How your brain distorts and deceives.* Cambridge, UK: Icon Books.

Firestone, R. W., & Catlett, J. (2009). *The ethics of interpersonal relationships.* London, UK: Karnac Books.

Flaskas, C. (2009). The therapist's imagination of self in relation to clients: Beginning ideas on the flexibility of empathic imagination. *Australian and New Zealand Journal of Family Therapy, 30*(3) 147-159.

Fowler, J. (1981). *Stages in faith development.* San Francisco: Harper and Row.

French, R., & Simpson, P. (1999). Our best work happens when we don't know what we are doing. *Socio-Analysis, 1*(2), 216–230.

Fromm, E. (1964). *The heart of man: It's genius for good and evil.* New York: Harper and Row.

Frost, P. (1999). Why compassion counts. *Journal of Management Inquiry, 8*(2), 127–133.

Gatens, M. (1995). Between the sexes: Care or justice? In B. Almond (Ed.), *Introducing applied ethics* (pp. 42-57). Oxford: Blackwell.

Gelb, M. J. (1998). *How to think like Leonardo da Vinci.* New York: Random Books.

Gellerman, S. W. (1986, July/August). Why good managers make bad ethical decisions? *Harvard Business Review,* 85–90.

Gergen, K. (2009). *Relational being: Beyond self and community.* New York, NY: Oxford University Press.

Gergen, M. (1999). Relational responsibility: Destructive possibilities. In S. McNamee, K. J. Gergen & Associates (Eds.), *Relational responsibility: Resources for sustainable dialogue.* Thousand Oaks, CA: Sage Publications.

Gerhardt, S. (2004). *Why love matters: How affection shapes a baby's brain.* Hove, East Sussex: Routledge.

Gibbs, J. C. (2010). *Moral development and reality: Beyond the theories of Kohlberg and Hoffman.* Boston, MA: Allyn and Bacon.

Gibson, P. A. (2008). Teaching ethical decision making: Designing a personal value portrait to ignite creativity and promote personal engagement in case method analysis. *Ethics and Behaviour, 18*(4), 340–352.

Gigerenzer, G. (2008). Moral intuition: Fast and frugal heuristics? In Walter Simmott-Armstrong (Ed.), *Moral Psychology: The cognitive science of morality—Intuition and diversity* (Vol, 2, pp. 1–26). Cambridge, MA: MIT Press.

Gilbert, D. (2006). *Stumbling on happiness.* New York, NY: Knopf Publishing.

Gilbert, P. (2010). *The compassionate mind.* London: Constable..

Gilligan, C. (1982). *In a different voice: Psychological theory and women's development.* Cambridge, MA: Harvard University Press.

Gladwell, M. (2005). *Blink: The power of thinking without thinking.* London, UK: Allen Lane.

Goleman, D. (1995). *Emotional intelligence.* New York, NY: Bantam Books.

Goleman, D. (1985). *Vital lies, simple truths: The psychology of self-deception.* New York, NY: Simon Schuster.

Grace, D., & Cohen, S. (1998). *Business ethics: Australian problems and cases* (2nd ed.). South Melbourne, VIC: Oxford University Press.

Grace, D., & Cohen, S. (2009). *Business ethics* (4th ed.). South Melbourne, VIC: Oxford University Press.

Grayling, A. C. (2003). *What is good? The search for the best way to live.* London, UK: Weidenfield & Nicolson.

Greene, J., & Cohen, J. (2011). For the law, neuroscience changes nothing and everything. In J. Illes & B. J. Sahakian (Eds.), *The Oxford handbook of neuroethics.* New York, NY: Oxford University Press.

Greenson, R. (1960). Empathy and its vicissitudes. *International Journal of Psycho-Analysis, 41,* 418–424.

Guba, E. G., & Lincoln, Y. S. (1994). Competing paradigms in qualitative research. In N. K. Denzin & Y. S. Lincoln (Eds.), *Handbook of qualitative research* (pp. 105–117). Thousand Oaks, CA: Sage Publications.

Gurdjieff, C. (1949). In P. Ouspensky, *In search of the miraculous.* New York, NY: Harcourt Brace and World.

Haidt, J. (2001). The emotional dog and its rational tail: A social intuitionist approach to moral judgement. *Psychological Review, 108,* 814–834.

Haidt, J. (2006). *Happiness hypothesis: Putting ancient wisdom to the test of modern science.* London, UK: William Heinemann.

Hamlin, J. K., Wynn, K., & Bloom, P. (2010). Three month olds show a negativity bias in their social evaluations. *Developmental Science, 13*(6), 923–929.

Hardman, D. (2009). *Judgment and decision making: Psychological perspectives.* Oxford, UK: BPS Blackwell.

Hare, R. D. (1993). *Without conscience: The disturbing world of the psychopaths amongst us.* London, UK: The Guilford Press.

Harris, S. (2010). *The moral landscape.* London, UK: Bantam Press.

Hart, P. (1998). Preventing groupthink revisited: Evaluating and reforming groups in government. *Organizational Behavior & Human Decision Processes, 73*(2), 142–162.

Harvey, J. B. (1996). *The Abilene paradox and other meditations on management.* San Francisco, CA: Jossey-Bass.

Haslam, S. A., & Reicher, S. D. (2008). Questioning the banality of evil. *The Psychologist, 21*(1), 16–19.

Hass, A. (1998). *Doing the right thing: Cultivating your moral intelligence.* New York, NY: Pocket Books.

Hauser, M. D. (2006). *Moral minds: How nature designed our universal sense of right and wrong.* London, UK: Little Brown.

Hauser, M. (2006). The liver and the moral organ. *Social, Cognitive and Affective Neuroscience, 1,* 214–220.

Heidegger, M. (1978). *Being and time.* Oxford, UK: Blackwell Publishing.

Hinman, L. M. (2008). *Ethics: A pluralistic approach to moral theory* (4th ed.). Boston, MA: Thomson Wadsworth.

Hollis, J. (2003). *On the journey we call our life.* Toronto: Inner City Books.

Howard-Jones, P. (2010). *Introducing neuroeducational research: Neuroscience, education and the brain from contexts to practice.* London: Routledge.

Hugman, R. (2005). *New approaches to ethics in the caring professions.* New York, NY: Palgrave Macmillan.

Hume, D. (1996). *The philosophical works of David Hume.* Bristol, UK: Thoemmes Press.

Humphrey, N. (2000) One self: A meditation on the unity of consciousness. *Social Research, 67*(4), 32–39.

ICAP (Undated). *Code of ethics and practice for counsellors and psychotherapists.* County Wicklow, Ireland: Irish Association for Counselling and Psychotherapy.

Illingworth, S. (2004). *Approaches to ethics in higher education: Learning and teaching in ethics across the curriculum.* Leeds: University of Leeds, Philosophical and Religious Studies Subject Centre.

Inger, I., & Inger, J. (1994). *Creating an ethical position in family therapy.* London: Karnac Books.

Israel, M., & Hay, I. (2006). *Research ethics for social scientists.* London, UK: Sage Publications.

Janis, I. L. (1972). *Groupthink.* Boston, MA: Houghton Mifflin.

Janis, I. J., & Mann, L. (1977). *Decision-making: A psychological analysis of conflict, choice and commitment.* New York, NY: Free Press.

Jarvis, P. (2006). *Towards a comprehensive theory of human learning.* Oxford, UK: Routledge.

Johnson, C. E. (2007). *Ethics in the workplace.* Thousand Oaks, CA: Sage Publications.

Johnson, C. E. (2012). *Meeting the ethical challenges of leadership.* Thousand Oaks, CA: Sage Publications.

Jones, J. H. (1981/1993). *Bad blood: The Tuskegee syphilis experiment.* New York, NY: Free Press.

Jordan, A. E., & Meara, N. M. (1990). Ethics and the professional practice of psychologists: The role of virtues and principles. *Professional Psychology: Research and Practice, 21*(2), 107–114.

Kafka, F. (1914). *I am a memory come alive: Autobiographical writings.* New York, NY: Schocken Books.

Kahneman, D. (2011). *Thinking fast and slow.* London: Allen Lane

Kant, I. (1995). *Ethical philosophy: Grounding for the metaphysics of morals and metaphysical principles of virtue.* Indianapolis: Hackett Publishing.

Karen, R. (1994). *Becoming attached: First relationships and how they shape our capacity to love.* New York, NY: Oxford University Press.

Kassimeris, G. (2006). *Warrior's dishonour: Barbarity, morality and torture in modern warfare.* Hampshire: Ashgate Publishing.

Katz, J. (1972). *Experimentation with human beings.* New York, NY: Russell Sage Foundation.

Keating, T. (1997). *Invitation to love: Way of Christian contemplation.* London, UK: Continuum.

Keay, D. (1987, October 31). Interview with Margaret Thatcher: 'Aids, education and the year 2000'. *Woman's Own,* 8–10.

Kegan, R. (1994). *In over our heads: The mental demands of modern life.* Cambridge, MA: Harvard University Press.

Kegan, R., & Lahey, L. (2009). *Immunity to change.* Boston, MA: Harvard Business Press.

Kennedy, I., & Grubb, A. (2000). *Medical law* (3rd ed.). UK: Butterworths.

Kenny, E. (2011, July 20). Taoiseach's speech on Cloyne motion. *The Irish Times.* Retrieved from www.irishtimes.com

Kets de Vries, M. (2009). *Sex, money, happiness and death.* Hampshire: Palgrave Macmillan.

Khele, S., Symons, C., & Wheeler, S. (2008). An analysis of complaints to the British Association for Counselling and Psychotherapy, 1996–2006. *Counselling and Psychotherapy Research, 8*(2), 124–132.

King, D. (2007). *Rigour, response and responsibility: A universal ethical code for scientists.* London, UK: Government Office for Science, Department for Innovation, Universities & Skills. Retrieved from www.dius.gov.uk

King, P. M., & Kitchener, K. S. (1994). *Developing reflective judgment.* San Francisco, CA: Jossey-Bass.

Kitson, A., & Campbell, R. (1996). *The ethical organization: Ethical theory and corporate behaviour.* London, UK: MacMillan.

Knibb, J. (2010). *Special children/Mothering matters: A narrative inquiry into the lived experience of mothers of children with special needs.* (Unpublished doctoral dissertation). Graduate School of Education, University of Bristol, UK.

Special Children/Mothering Matters: A Narrative Inquiry into the Lived Experience of Mothers of Children with Special Needs. Doctor of Education Dissertation: Graduate School of Education: University of Bristol, UK.

Kohlberg, L. (1969). Stage and sequence: The cognitive-developmental approach to socialization. In D. A. Goslin (Ed.), *Handbook of socialization theory and research.* Chicago, IL: Rand McNally.

Kohlberg, L. (1982). *The philosophy of moral development.* San Francisco, CA: Harper and Row.

Kohlberg, L. (1984). *The psychology of moral development: Moral stages and the life cycle.* San Francisco, CA: Harper & Row.

Kohlberg, L., & Candee, D. (1984). The relationship of moral judgement to moral action. In W. M. Kurtines & J. Gewirtz (Eds.), *Morality, moral behavior, and moral development* (pp. 52-73). New York: John Wiley & Sons.

Koocher, G. P., & Keith-Spiegel, P. (2008). *Ethics in psychology and the mental health professions*. New York, NY: Open University Press.

Kuhse, H., Singer, P., & Rickard, M. (1998). Reconciling impartial morality and a feminist ethic of care. *The Journal of Value Enquiry, 32*, 451–463.

Kurzban, R. (2008). The evolution of implicit and explicit decision making. In C. Engel and W. Singer (Eds.), *Better than conscious? Decision making, the human mind and implications for institutions*. Cambridge, MA. MIT Press.

Kusy, M., & Holloway, E. (2009). *Toxic workplace: Managing toxic personalities and their systems of power*. San Francisco, CA: Jossey-Bass.

LaFollette, H. (1995). *Personal relationships: Love, identity and morality*. Oxford, UK: Blackwell Publishing.

Langer, E. (1989). *Mindfulness*. Cambridge, MA: Perseus Books.

Lau, C. L. L. (2010). A step forward: Ethics education matters! *Journal of Business Ethics, 92*, 565–584.

Leary, M. R. (2004). *The curse of the self: Self-Awareness, egotism, and the quality of human life*. New York: Oxford University Press.

Lehrer, J. (2009). *The decisive moment: How the brain makes up its mind*. Edinburgh: Cannongate Books.

Lennick, D., & Kiel, F. (2005). *Moral intelligence: Enhancing business performance and leadership success*. New Jersey: Wharton School Publishing.

Levitt, D. H. (2004). Ethical responsibilities in training marriage and family counsellors. *The Family Journal: Counselling and Therapy for Couples and Families, 12*(1), 43–46.

Lewis, D., & Cheshire, A. (2007). Te Whakaakona: Teaching and learning as one. *Journal of Systemic Therapies, 26*(3), 43–56.

Lewis, H. (2000). *A question of values: Six ways we make the personal choices that shape our lives*. Crozet, VA: Axios Press.

Lewis, T., Amini, F., & Lannon, R. (2003). *A general theory of love*. New York, NY: Vintage Books.

Lincoln, Y. S., & Guba, E. G. (1985). *Naturalistic inquiry*. Beverly Hills, CA: Sage Publications.

Livingstone Smith, D. (2004). *Why we lie: The evolutionary roots of deception and the unconscious mind*. New York, NY: St. Martin's Press.

Loevinger, J. (1976). *Ego development*. San Francisco, CA: Jossey-Bass.

Longstaff, S. (1994). Why codes fail and some thoughts about how to make them work. In N. Preston (Ed.), *Ethics for the public sector*. Sydney, NSW: The Federation Press.

Longstaff, S. (1995). *What is ethics education/training?* Sydney, NSW: St James Ethics Centre Publications.

Longstaff, S. (1996a). Foundations for corporate governance: Three rival versions of human nature. *Business Ethics: A European Review, 5*(2), 118–125.

Longstaff, S. (1996b, Autumn). What if people are basically good? *Living Ethics, 23*. Retrieved from http://www.ethics.org.au/living-ethics/what-if-people-are-basically-good

Longstaff, S. (1997). *Hard cases, tough choices: Exploring the ethical landscape of business*. South Melbourne, VIC: MacMillan.

Luxmoore, N. (2011). *Young people and the curse of ordinariness*. London, UK: Jessica Kingsley.

Mahon, B. J. (2002). *Forgetting oneself on purpose: Vocation and the ethics of ambition.* San Francisco, CA: Jossey-Bass.

Marquardt, N. (2010). Implicit mental health processes in ethical management behaviour. *Ethics and Behaviour, 20*(2), 128–148.

Marshall, S. L. A. (2000). *Men against fire: The problem of battle command.* Tulsa: University of Oklahoma Press.

Martin, P. (2011). Celebrating the wounded healer. *The Counselling Psychologist, 26*(1), 10–19

Martin, J. P. (1984). *Hospitals in trouble.* Oxford, UK: Blackwell Publishing.

Maslow, A. (1998). *Towards a psychology of being.* New York, NY: Wiley and Sons.

May, W. F. (1994). The virtues in a professional setting. In W. M. Fulford, G. R. Gillet, & J. Martin-Soskice (Eds.), *Medicine and moral reasoning.* New York, NY: Cambridge University Press.

Mele, D. (2009). *Business ethics in action.* Hampshire: Palgrave Macmillan.

Mezirow, J., Taylor, E. W., & Associates (2009). *Transformative learning in practice: Insights from community, workplace and higher education.* San Francisco, CA: Jossey-Bass.

Milgram, S. (1963). Behaviour study of obedience. *Journal of Abnormal and Social Psychology, 67,* 371–378.

Milgram, S. (1973). The perils of obedience. *Harpers Magazine,* December, pp. 62–77.

Milgram, S. (1974). *Obedience to authority: An experimental view.* New York, NY: Harper and Row.

Mitchell, S. A. (2000). *Relationality: From attachment to intersubjectivity.* Hillsdale, NJ: Analytic Press

Moon, J. (2004). *A handbook of reflective and experiential learning.* London, UK: Routledge Falmer.

Moon, J. (2008). *Critical thinking: An exploration of theory and practice.* Oxford, UK: Routledge.

Morrissette, P. J., & Gadbois, S. (2006). Ethical consideration of counsellor education teaching strategies. *Counselling and Values, 50,* 131–141.

Murdoch, I. (1985). *The sovereignty of good.* London, UK: Ark Paperbacks.

Nash, L. (1981, November/December). Ethics without the sermon. *Harvard Business Review, 59,* 79–90.

Nash, R. J. (2002). *Real world ethics: Frameworks for educators and human service professionals* (2nd ed.). New York, NY: Teachers College Press.

National Commission for the Protection of Human Subjects of Biomedical Behavioral Research (1979). *The Belmont Report.* Department of Health, Education and Welfare Publication Nos (OS) 78-0013 and (OS) 78-0014. Washington DC: Government Printing Office.

Nietzsche, F. W. (1974). *Thus spoke Zarathustra: A book for everyone and noone.* London: Penguin Classics.

Noddings, N. (1986). *Caring: A feminine approach to ethics and moral education.* Berkeley, CA: University of California Press.

Nucci, L. (1997). Moral development and character formation. In H. J. Wahlberg, & G. D. Haertel (Eds.), *Psychology and Educational Practice.* Berkeley: MacCarchan.

Oakley, A. (2005). *The Ann Oakley reader: Gender, women and social science.* Bristol, UK: Policy Press.

O'Gorman, C. (2011, September 3). *Initial thoughts on the response of the Holy See to the Cloyne report.* [Web log comment]. Retrieved from http://colmogorman. com/?p=730

O'Neill, O. (2002). *Autonomy and trust in bioethics: The Gifford lectures.* Cambridge: Cambridge University Press.

Oshry, B. (1995). *Seeing systems: Unlocking the mysteries of organisational life.* San Francisco, CA: Berrett-Koehler.

Overy, R. (2011). Milgram and the historians. *The Psychologist, 24*(9), 662–663.

PACFA (2011). *Code of ethics.* Melbourne, VIC: Psychotherapy & Counselling Federation of Australia (PACFA).

Painter-Morland, M. (2006). Redefining accountability as relational responsiveness. *Journal of Business Ethics, 66,* 89–98.

Passmore, J., & Mortimer, L. (2011). Ethics: A balancing act. In L. Boyce & G. Hernez-Broome (Eds.), *Advancing executive coaching: Setting the course for successful leadership coaching.* San Francisco, CA: Jossey-Bass.

Passmore, J., Allan, J., & Mortimer, L. (2011). Coaching ethics: The ACTION model. In J. Passmore (Ed.), *Supervision in coaching.* London, UK: Kogan Page.

Peck, S. (1983). *People of the lie: The hope for healing human evil.* New York, NY: Simon & Shuster.

Peterson, C., & Seligman, M. (2004). *Character strengths and virtues: A handbook and clarification.* New York, NY: Open University Press.

Pfeffer, J. (1994). *Competitive advantage through people.* Boston, MA: Harvard Business School.

Pilgrim, D. (unpublished paper). *Child abuse in Catholic settings.* University of Central Lancashire.

Pizarro, D. (2000). Nothing more than feelings? The role of emotions in moral judgement. *Journal for the Theory of Social Behaviour, 30*(4), 355–374.

Platt, M., Dayan, P., Dehaene, S., McCabe, K., Menzel, R., Phelps, E., Plassmann, H., Ratcliff, R., Shadlen, M., & Singer, W. (2008). In C. Engel & W. Singer (Eds.), *Better than conscious: Decision making, the human mind and implications for institutions.* Cambridge, MA: MIT Press.

Pope, K. S., & Vasquez, M. J. T. (2007). *Ethics in psychotherapy and counselling: A practical guide* (3rd ed.). San Francisco, CA: Jossey-Bass.

Porges, S. W. (2004). Social engagement and attachment. In C. S. Carter & L. Ahnerr (Eds.), *Attachment and bonding: A new synthesis—Dahlem Workshop Report 92.* Cambridge, MA: MIT Press.

Prinz, J. J. (2012). *Beyond human nature: How culture and experience shape our lives.* London: Allen Lane.

Pruyne, E., & Bond, D. (2011). Learning to lead in uncertain times through storytelling and improvisation. In S. Voller, E. Blass, & V. Culpin (Eds.), *The future of learning.* London, UK: Palgrave.

Queneau, R. (1998). *Exercises in style.* London, UK: John Calder.

Ramachandran, V. S. (2000, May 29). Mirror Neurons and imitation learning as the driving force behind 'the great leap forward' in human evolution. *Edge, 69.* Retrieved from http://www.edge.org

Rawlins, M. (2011). *The Rawlins Report: A new pathway for the regulation and governance of health research*. London, UK: The Academy of Medical Sciences. Retrieved from www.acmedsci.ac.uk

Rawls, J. (1971). *A theory of justice*. Cambridge, MA: Harvard University Press.

Rest, J. R. (1984). Research on moral development: Implications for training counselling psychologists. *The Counselling Psychologist, 12*(3), 19–29.

Rest, J. (1986). *Moral development: Advances in research and theory*. New York, NY: Praeger.

Reynolds, S. (2006). A neurocognitive model of the ethical decision making process: Implications for study and practice. *Journal of Applied Psychology, 91*, 727–748.

Reynolds Welfel, E. (2011). Teaching ethics: Models, methods and challenges. In S. J. Knapp (Ed.), *APA handbook of ethics in psychology (Vol. 2): Practice, teaching and research*. Washington, DC: American Psychological Association.

Reynolds Welfel, E. (2012). *Ethics in counseling and psychotherapy: Standards, research, and emerging issues* (5th ed.). Belmont, CA: Brooks/Cole.

Richardson, B. (1993). Why we need to teach crisis management and to use case studies to do it. *Management Learning, 24*, 138–148.

Rilke, R. M. (1993). *Letters to a young poet*. New York, NY: Norton.

Roberts, M. (1996). *The man who listens to horses*. London, UK: Arrow Books.

Robertson, I. (1999). *Mind sculpture: Unleashing your brain's potential*. London, UK: Bantam Books.

Rock, D. (2009). *Your brain at work: Strategies for overcoming distraction, regaining focus, and working smarter all day long*. New York, NY: HarperCollins.

Rose, I., & Slade, A. (2010). *Anti-bribery and corruption: The UK propels itself to the forefront of global enforcement* [Client Alert]. London, UK: Salans LLP. Retrieved from www.salans.com

Rowan, J. (1976). *Ordinary ecstasy: Humanistic psychology in action*. London, UK: Routledge.

Rowan, J. (1990). *Sub-personalities: The people inside us*. London, UK: Routledge.

Rowe, D. (2010). *Why we lie: The source of our disasters*. London, UK: Fourth Estate.

Royal Society (2013). *Brain Waves Model 2: Neuroscience: Implications for Education and Learning*. Available at www.royalsociety.org, accessed on 12 November 2012.

Sapolsky, S. (1994). *Why zebras don't get ulcers*. New York, NY: W. H. Freeman.

Scharmer, C. O. (2007). *Theory U: Leading from the future as it emerges*. Cambridge, MA: The Society of Organizational Learning (SoL).

Schon, D. (1983). *The reflective practitioner: How professionals think in action*. New York, NY: Basic Books.

Schrag, Z. M. (2010). *Ethical imperialism: Institutional Review Boards and the social sciences, 1965–2009*. Baltimore, Maryland: The John Hopkins University Press.

Schultz, K. (2010). *Being wrong: Adventures in the margin of error*. London, UK: Portobello Books.

Seabright, M. A., & Schminke, M. (2002). Immoral imagination and revenge in organisations. *Journal of Business Ethics, 38*, 19–31.

Sharansky, N. (1988). *Fear no evil: The classic memoir of one man's triumph over a police state*. New York, NY: Random House.

Shaw, E. (2011). Relational ethics and moral imagination in contemporary systemic practice. *Australian and New Zealand Journal of Family Therapy, 32*(1), 1–14.

Shoemaker, D. (2007). Moral address, moral responsibility and the boundaries of the moral community. *Ethics, 118,* 70–108.

Siegel, D. J. (2007). *The mindful brain: Reflection and attunement in the cultivation of well-being.* New York, NY: W. W. Norton.

Singer, W. (2011). A determinist view of brain, mind and consciousness. In The Royal Society, *Brain waves module 1: Neuroscience, society and policy (pp. 41–47).* London: The Royal Society.

Sloan, T. S. (1986). *Deciding: Self deception in life choices.* New York, NY: Metheun.

Smith, D. L. (2004). *Why we lie: The evolutionary roots of deception and the unconscious mind.* New York, NY: St. Martin's Press.

Smith, T. S., McGuire, J. M., Abbott, D. W., & Blau, B. I. (1991). Clinical ethical decision making: An investigation of the rationales used to justify doing less than one believes one should. *Professional Psychology: Research and Practice, 22*(3), 235–239.

Snowden, D. J., & Boone, M. E. (2007, November). A leader's framework for decision making. *Harvard Business Review, 85,* 68–76.

Soderberg, H. (2002). *Doctor Glas* (P. B. Austin, Trans.). UK, The Harvill Press (Original work published 1905).

Sommers, S. (2011). *Situations matter: Understanding how context transforms your world.* London: Riverhead Books.

Speiglman, R., & Spear, P. (2009). The role of Institutional Review Boards: Ethics: now you see them, now you don't. In D. Mertens & P. Ginsberg, *The handbook of social research ethics* (pp. 121–134). Thousand Oaks, CA: Sage Publications.

Stacey, R. (2010). *Complexity and organisational reality.* Oxford, UK: Routledge.

Steare, R. (2006). *Ethicability: How to decide what's right and find the courage to do it.* London: Roger Steare Consulting Limited.

Sullivan, L. E., & Ogloff, J. R. P. (1998). Appropriate supervisor-graduate student relationships. *Ethics and Behaviour, 8*(3), 229–248.

The Royal Society, Science Policy Centre (2011a, January). *Brain waves module 1: Neuroscience, society and policy.* London: The Royal Society.

The Royal Society, Science Policy Centre (2011b, February). *Brain waves module 2: Neuroscience–implications for education and life long learning.* London: The Royal Society.

Thich Nhat Hanh (1993). *Please call me by my true name.* Berkeley, CA: Parallax.

Thorne, B. (1987). Beyond the core conditions. In W. Dryden (Ed.), *Key cases in psychotherapy* (pp. 48–77). London, UK: Sage Publications.

Thorne, B. (2010, January 28). Stark facts exposed about anti regulation therapist. *Times Higher Education Supplement.* Retrieved from http://www.timeshighereducation.co.uk

Tichy, M., Johnson, D. W., Johnson, R. T., & Roseth, C. J. (2010). The impact of constructive controversy on moral development. *Journal of Applied Social Psychology, 40*(4), 765–787.

Towler, J. (2001). Which sub-personality is supervising today. In M. Carroll & M. Tholstrup (Eds.), *Integrative approaches to supervision* (pp. 174–182). London, UK: Jessica Kingsley.

Tuskegee University. (2012). *Impact on health care.* Retrieved from http://www.tuskegee.edu/about_us/centers_of_excellence/bioethics_center/impact_on_health_care.aspx

Urofsky, R., & Sowa, C. (2004). Ethics education in CACREP-accredited counselor education programs. *Counseling and Values, 49*(1), 37–47.

van der Does de Willebois, E., Sharman, J. C., Harrison, R., J. W. Park, & Halter, E. (2011). *The puppet masters: How the corrupt use legal structures to hide stolen assets and what to do about it.* Washington DC: The World Bank.

Varela, F. J. (1992). *Ethical know-how: Action, wisdom and cognition.* Stanford, CA: Stanford University Press.

Voller, H. (2010). *Developing reflective practice in counselling and psychotherapy.* D. Prof. University of Middlesex.

Voller, S., Blass, E., & Culpin, V. (2011). *The future of learning.* Hampshire: Palgrave Macmillan.

Walton, M. (2007) Leadership toxicity: An inevitable affliction of organisations? *Organisations and People, 14*(1), 19–27.

Walden, S. L., Herlihy, B., & Ashton, L. (2003). The evolution of ethics: Personal perspectives of ACA ethics committee chairs. *Journal of Counselling and Development, 81,* 106–110.

Wenger, D. (2010, April 21). Do you make buying decisions based on logic or emotion? A tale of two chickens. *McCombs Today.* Retrieved from http://blogs. mccombs .utexas.edu/mccombs-today

Werhane, P. H. (1999). *Moral imagination and management decision making.* New York, NY: Oxford University Press.

Werhane, P. H. (2002). Moral imagination and systems thinking. *Journal of Business Ethics, 38,* 33–42.

Whyte, D. (1994). *The heart aroused: Poetry and the preservation of the soul.* New York, NY: Bantam Books.

Wilbur, K. (2000). *A theory of everything.* Boston: Shambhala Publications.

Wilson, T. D. (2002). *Strangers to ourselves: Discovering the adaptive unconscious.* Cambridge, MA: Harvard University Press.

World Bank (2011). *The puppet masters: How the corrupt use legal structures to hide stolen assets and what to do about it.* New York, NY: World Bank.

World Medical Association (2008). *Ethical principles for medical research involving human subjects.* Adopted at Seoul, Korea: 59th World Medical Association General Assembly. Ferney-Voltaire France: World Medical Association. Retrieved from http://www.wma.net/en/30publications/10policies/b3/index.html

World Medical Association (1964). *Declaration of Helsinki: Ethical principles for medical research involving human subjects* (1st edition). Ferney-Voltaire France: World Medical Association.

Zachary, L. (2000). *The mentor's guide: Facilitating effective learning relationships.* San Francisco, CA: Jossey-Bass.

Zimbardo, (2007). *The lucifer effect: How good people turn evil.* St. Ives, NSW: Random Books.

Subject Index

Author Index